Mastering TCP/IP
for NT Server

Mastering™ TCP/IP for NT® Server

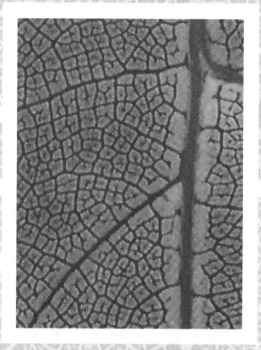

Mark Minasi
Todd Lammle
with Monica Lammle

NETWORK PRESS®
SYBEX

San Francisco • Paris • Düsseldorf • Soest

Associate Publisher: Gary Masters
Acquisitions Manager: Kristine Plachy
Acquisitions & Developmental Editor: Neil Edde
Editor: Anamary Ehlen
Project Editor: Kim Wimpsett
Technical Editor: Matthew Fiedler
Book Designers: Patrick Dintino, Catalin Dulfu
Graphic Illustrator: Steve Brooks
Electronic Publishing Specialist: Bob Bihlmayer
Production Coordinator: Theresa Gonzalez
Proofreaders: Charles Mathews, Duncan Watson, Eryn Osterhaus
Indexer: Ted Laux
Cover Design: Archer Design
Cover Photograph: The Image Bank

Screen reproductions produced with Collage Plus.

Collage Plus is a trademark of Inner Media Inc.

SYBEX is a registered trademark of SYBEX Inc.

Mastering is a trademark of SYBEX Inc.

TRADEMARKS: SYBEX has attempted throughout this book to distinguish proprietary trademarks from descriptive terms by following the capitalization style used by the manufacturer.

The author and publisher have made their best efforts to prepare this book, and the content is based upon final release software whenever possible. Portions of the manuscript may be based upon pre-release versions supplied by software manufacturer(s). The author and the publisher make no representation or warranties of any kind with regard to the completeness or accuracy of the contents herein and accept no liability of any kind including but not limited to performance, merchantability, fitness for any particular purpose, or any losses or damages of any kind caused or alleged to be caused directly or indirectly from this book.

Library of Congress Card Number: 97-68480
ISBN: 0-7821-2123-3

Manufactured in the United States of America

10 9 8 7 6 5 4 3

To my brothers Steve, Dave, and Matthew, all far away in meat miles but thankfully close thanks to the Internet, and to the siblings that they've brought me, my sisters-in-law Eloisa and Debbie.

Acknowledgments

Thanks to Sybex's Gary Masters and Neil Edde, who took my nascent idea and made it possible by introducing me to Todd and Monica, offering suggestions on the project's direction, and most of all believing in the idea. It's a terrible shame that most books these days will only be purchased by a publisher if they're a "me-too" clone of another, already successful book. That's not the case with Sybex books—but it also means that Gary is willing to take chances, even though they don't all work out.

We would like to recognize with much appreciation our friend and colleague Phil Yee, whose brilliant technical contribution and network lab have served to ensure this book's quality and integrity. Phil is an experienced networking professional who is a network manager at OnTrak Systems, Inc. in San Jose, California. This project owes a great debt to Phil's exacting mind and technical expertise.

Todd also would like to acknowledge Jan Merbach, a long-time friend, who always believed in him, more than he ever did!

Many thanks are due, again, to our developmental editor, Neil Edde, and copyeditor, Anamary Ehlen. Neil's sharp intellect, wry wit, and positive attitude, combined with his limitless patience, guided the development and evolution of this project. Without Anamary's profound ability to direct, organize, and problem-solve, this book would not have been possible. Also, our technical editor, Matthew Fiedler, was one of the best we ever worked with. Many thanks, Matthew! Thanks also to Sybex's Theresa Gonzalez, production coordinator; Bob Bihlmayer, electronic publishing specialist; and Kim Wimpsett, project editor; for all their work to make this book a reality.

Contents at a Glance

Table of Contents

Introduction

For years, networking at corporations and even homes or small offices was largely the province of NetBEUI and IPX networks. NetBEUI, a Microsoft and IBM protocol, was pretty good for small networks, and, as IBM and Microsoft used them as their protocol, it was only logical that you would too. The part of the world that didn't use IBM or Microsoft networks—in fact, the majority of the PC networking world—used IPX, the protocol that came with Novell NetWare. As Novell had the largest market share, IPX was the network protocol of choice for most corporations. We all knew that there was a protocol out there used by government and educational networks called TCP/IP, but most of us didn't know much about it, as the main TCP/IP-using network—the Internet—was something of a private club, one that you could only be a part of if you were in the university, government, or military realms. In the early 1990s, however, that began to change.

By 1992, it became clear that (1) the Internet was becoming important, and (2) TCP/IP was a high-quality, vendor-independent platform for networking. Between 1994 and 1995, IP eclipsed IPX as corporate America's foremost network protocol. All of a sudden, everyone in the technical profession had to know TCP/IP.

Naturally, as a forward-thinking type of guy, I figured in 1992 that I'd better sit down and learn TCP/IP. So I looked around for a good book on the subject. There were a number on how to use the Internet, some quite good, but they tended to be UNIX-centric—not the end of the world, but a bit of a barrier for someone using OS/2, and later NT. There were also a few decent books on actually administering a TCP/IP network, but again within a world completely UNIX-centric.

Now, I was able to use those books to learn TCP/IP, but it was an uphill battle. And it's odd but true that most TCP/IP books are UNIX books, because I now and then hear statistics to the effect that there are more WWW servers running NT than UNIX at this point. There must be a lot of Web administrators out there reading UNIX material and trying to translate it to NT.

Hence this book.

Ever since its first appearance, it has been hard to find high-quality documentation and educational materials about NT. That's why I wrote *Mastering Windows NT Server*, another book from Sybex that you may know. While much of that book covers elements of TCP/IP, it isn't the book's central focus.

But I've always wanted to write a guide on TCP/IP network administration using just NT: a soup-to-nuts, A-to-Z guide to running an intranet without any UNIX. As my other book went into its fourth edition, I met another Sybex author, Todd Lammle. Todd is the author of a terrific MCSE review guide on TCP/IP (*MCSE: TCP/IP Study Guide*), so I asked him if he'd be willing to take the TCP/IP material from my NT book and expand it into a complete TCP/IP network administration guide. He agreed, and the result is the book you hold in your hand. Todd is actually half of a great writing team, and his wife Monica is the other half. Todd's the techie, Monica's the word-smith, and together they turn out a mean product; they did quite a job. My original vision for this book was basically to take the TCP/IP chapter in the NT book and augment it a bit—Todd's job was only to edit and expand. What he and Monica have actually done is to add tons of new material and take this farther than I ever planned.

What It's All About

The book starts off with TCP/IP basics: IP addresses, dotted quad format, and network types. Then it progresses into the "plumbing" parts of TCP/IP, the parts that you don't see too many books cover in much detail—there are tons of books on how to build a Web server, but not too many about how to solve routing problems. You'll learn about subnet masks and subnetting, and progress from there to a good knowledge of IP routing and network design. We've included coverage of the newest NT IP routing software, the software called "Steelhead" while in beta. This new free software from Microsoft allows you to turn your NT Server into a powerful IP router. Now, we're not suggesting that you should throw away your Cisco routers, but if you find it necessary to press your PC into service as an IP router, NT can do the job—and we show you how in this book. Another "plumbing" area that more and more of us face is the concept of proxy servers, machines that act as both gate-ways to the Internet and, in a small way, guardians of our network. Again, Microsoft has a product that can assist here, their Proxy Server—and you'll read about it here.

Once you have your network in place, you'll need to solve a lot of adminis-tration issues. The first such issue is distributing IP addresses to all of your sys-tems. This is done with the Dynamic Host Configuration Protocol, covered in Chapter 7. Then, your machines must be able to find each other, and they do that with two systems: The first is the Windows Internet Naming System, or WINS. The second is the Domain Naming System, or DNS. You'll learn to set up and maintain servers on both of these systems in Chapters 8 and 9. Beyond the housekeeping, you'll want your network to offer something useful. Probably the most basic Internet function is mail, and you'll see how to create an electronic mail server in Chapter 14. Closely following mail is the World Wide Web, covered in Chapter 13. An older but still important system is FTP, the File Transfer Protocol, covered in Chapter 11. And, finally anyone connecting their network to the Internet must be concerned with security, so we'd be remiss if we hadn't included Chapter 15 on Internet security.

We intended for you to use this book in two ways: First, and mainly, this should provide you with the information you need to build an intranet from scratch. Second, if you're pursuing an MCSE certification, you'll find that this can be a useful background review tool.

On behalf of all of us, thank you for buying this book and we wish you the best of luck in building your Internet connection or intranet!

CHAPTER

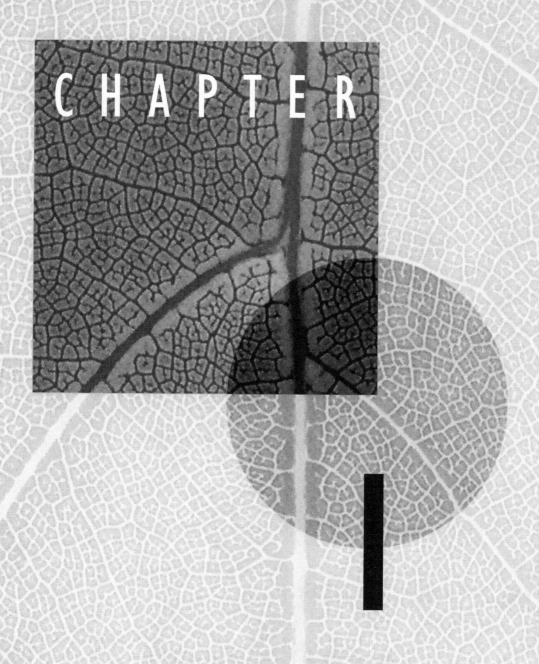

1

TCP/IP: Its Basis and Background

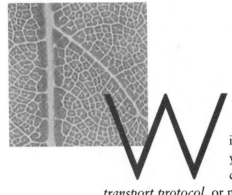

With the runaway growth of the Internet in the last few years, the term *TCP/IP* has rocketed from obscurity to celebrity. It's become a "must-know" concept. This *transport protocol*, or network language, bears some similarities to NetBEUI, SNA, IPX/SPX, or X.25, with one very important difference: Most of these transport protocols are designed to work well in either a LAN environment *or* a WAN environment—*not in both*. By contrast, TCP/IP is highly effective in either one. As you'll see in this chapter, it's this *multi-platform* versatility that's one of its greatest strengths.

Here's what to expect from this chapter. In it, we'll accomplish several things:

- Explain TCP/IP and the Internet

- Introduce you to some important tools for locating information on the Internet

- Clarify the Internet's development through RFCs

- Explore the design goals of TCP/IP and discover its purpose

When you're done, you'll have at minimum a *dangerous* knowledge of TCP/IP. Reading through the rest of this book should solve that, and elevate your status to that of a true "wizard."

A Brief History of TCP/IP

Let's start off by asking, "What *is* TCP/IP?" Transmission Control Protocol/Internet Protocol is a collection of software created over the years, much of its development subsidized by large infusions of government research money. Originally, TCP/IP was intended for the Department of Defense (DoD). Putting our tax dollars to good use, the DoD tends to buy a *lot* of equipment, and much of that equipment is incompatible with other equipment. For example, back in the late '70s when the work that conceived TCP/IP began, it was nearly impossible to get an IBM mainframe to talk to a Burroughs mainframe. That was because the two computers were designed with entirely different *protocols*—something like Figure 1.1.

FIGURE 1.1

Compatible hardware, incompatible protocols

To get some idea of what the DoD was facing, imagine picking up the phone in the U.S. and calling someone in Spain. You have a perfectly good hardware connection, as the Spanish phone system is compatible with the American phone system. But despite the *hardware* compatibility, you face a *software* incompatibility. The person on the other end of the phone is expecting a different protocol for communication; that is, they likely speak Spanish. It's not that one language is better or worse than the other—they're simply different, and so, fluent understanding between the English and Spanish speakers just isn't going to happen. Rather than force the Spanish speaker to learn English or the English speaker to learn Spanish, we could teach them both a new language like Esperanto, the "universal language" designed in 1888. If Esperanto were used in our telephone example, it's likely that neither speaker would use it at home, but they would when communicating with each other.

That was how TCP/IP began—as a simple, *alternative* communications language. As time went on, TCP/IP evolved into a mature, well-understood, robust set of protocols, with many sites adopting it as their *main* communication language.

ARPANET and the Birth of the Internet

Although it was an important goal of the first defense intranetwork, the original DoD network wasn't intended to just link military sites. Much of the basic research in the U.S. was funded by an arm of the Defense Department called the Advanced Research Projects Agency, or ARPA. ARPA gave, and still gives, a lot of money to university researchers to study all kinds of things. ARPA thought it would be useful for these researchers to be able to communicate with one another, as well as with the Pentagon. Figures 1.2 and 1.3 illustrate networking both before and after ARPANET implementation.

FIGURE 1.2

Researchers before ARPANET

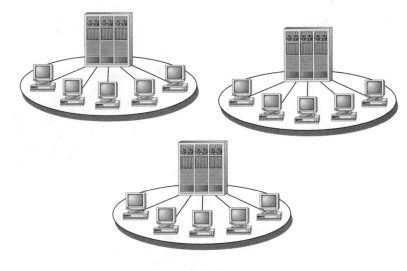

FIGURE 1.3

Researchers after ARPANET

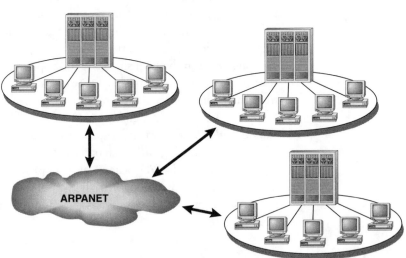

The new network, dubbed ARPANET, was designed and put in place by a private contractor called Bolt, Barenek and Newman. For the first time, it linked university professors both to themselves and to their military and civilian project leaders around the country. Because ARPANET was a network that linked separate, private university networks with distant military networks, it was a "network of networks."

ARPANET ran atop a protocol called the Network Control Protocol (NCP). NCP was later refined into two components, the Internet Protocol (IP) and the Transmission Control Protocol (TCP). The change from NCP to TCP/IP is the technical difference between ARPANET and the Internet. On January 1, 1983, ARPANET packet-switching devices stopped accepting NCP packets and only passed TCP/IP packets, so, in a sense, that date can be thought of as the "official" birthday of the Internet.

The primordial Internet goo known as ARPANET became the Internet after a few evolutionary steps. Probably the first major development occurred in 1974, when Vinton Cerf and Robert Kahn proposed the protocols that would become TCP and IP. (We say "probably" because the Internet didn't grow through a centralized effort, but rather through the largely disconnected efforts of several researchers, university professors, and graduate students, most of whom are still alive—and almost *all* of whom have a different perspective on what the "defining" aspects of Internet development were.) Over its more than 20-year history, the Internet and its predecessors have gone through several stages of growth and adjustment. Ten years ago, the Internet could only claim a few thousand users. At last count, five *million* computers and 100 million users were on the Internet. The Internet appears to double in size about every year. It can't do that indefinitely, so it's certainly a time of change for this huge network of networks. As with life forms, adaptability facilitates both change and survival, so it's easy to appreciate why TCP/IP's versatility is so important.

Internet growth is fueled not by an esoteric interest in seeing how large a network the world can build, but rather by just a few applications that require the Internet to run. One of the most important is Internet e-mail, followed closely by the World Wide Web, with File Transfer Protocol (FTP) bringing up the rear. We'll discuss these more thoroughly later in this chapter.

Originally, Internet protocols were intended to support connections between mainframe-based networks—basically the only type that existed through most of the 1970s. Then came the 1980s which saw the growth of UNIX workstations, microcomputers, and minicomputers. Since the development of the Berkeley version of UNIX was funded mostly with government money, the government said, "Put the TCP/IP protocol suite in that thing." There was some resistance at first, but adding IP as a built-in part of Berkeley UNIX has helped both UNIX and intranetworking grow. The IP protocol was used on many of the UNIX-based Ethernet networks that appeared in the 1980s and still exist to this day. As a matter of fact, you probably have to learn at least a smidgen of UNIX to really fly around the Internet. Don't let that put you off! In the next few chapters, we'll teach you all the UNIX you'll still need, plus show you just how much of the old UNIX stuff can now be fulfilled by NT.

NSF's Contribution and the Internet of Today

In the mid-1980s, the National Science Foundation created five supercomputing centers and put them on the Internet. This served two purposes: It made supercomputers available to NSF grantees around the country, and provided a major "backbone" for the Internet. The National Science Foundation portion of the network, called NSFNET, was the largest part of the Internet for a long time. It's now being superseded by the National Research and Education Network (NREN). For many years, commercial users were pretty much kept off the Internet. As most of the funding was governmental, you had to be invited to join the Net. Now, those restrictions have been relaxed, and as more commercial providers link up, more traffic goes over commercial routes than via government channels—at least in the continental United States. Since the Internet is *already* privatized for the most part, the onetime concern about the Internet's death due to a lack of government funds is now passé.

The Internet is often referred to as the "Information Superhighway." It's easy to see why people say that; after all, it is sort of a high volume, long-haul trucking service for data. The Internet is growing so rapidly because it has so much to offer. Businesses use it as a medium through which to get things done, advertise, locate a customer base, find information, and sell their wares. It's a virtual treasure trove for researchers, students, and educators. Internet use has even added words to our language and changed our customs—some employees now "telecommute" to work through it. A good example is this very book, which was sent back and forth between the authors, editors, and publisher via the Internet as it was being written.

If your company isn't on the Internet now, it will be, should be... and soon! Remember when fax machines became popular in the early 1980s? Overnight people stopped saying, "Do you have a fax?" and just started saying, "What's your fax number?" It's getting so that if you don't have an Internet address, your existence may be questioned. For any doubting us out there, Mark's Internet mail address is `mark@mmco.com`. Todd and Monica's is `globalnetsys@earthlink.net`. See. We're real!

Goals of TCP/IP's Design

Okay, it's time to get our hands a little dirty! Let's delve into some of the techie aspects of the Internet's main protocols. When the DoD started building this suite of network protocols, they had some definite objectives in mind. Understanding those design goals helps understand why it's worth making the effort to use TCP/IP in the first place. Anyway, here's a list of those DoD objectives:

- Good failure recovery, i.e., fault tolerance

- Ability to connect new networks without disrupting existing services

- Ability to handle high error rates

- Independence from a particular vendor or type of network

- Very little data overhead

It's likely that no one had any idea how pivotal those design goals would be to the amazing success of TCP/IP both in private intranets and in the Internet. Let's take a more detailed look at each one of those objectives now.

Good Failure Recovery

Remember, this was to be a *defense* network, so it had to work even if portions of the network framework suddenly and without warning went offline. In other words, think about San Francisco getting absolutely blown off the map. With good fault tolerance in our network, I could still get the needed info online to L.A. from N.Y. via another route, without missing a beat.

So with San Francisco gone, just how are those packets going to get to L.A. in time to get the information we need? Packet switching, that's how. Check out the Network layer in Chapter 2 for more information on packet switching.

Ability to Add New Subnetworks "on the Fly"

This second goal is related to the first one. It proposes that it should be possible to add entire new networks into an intranet, no matter the size, or to the Internet itself, without interrupting existing network service.

In some networks we have built, our clients can easily plug a new *hub* into a existing router port and, *poof,* they have a new subnet fully up and running. By designing the network for growth and predefining the router, the customer can add new subnets "on the fly." Adding a router into the existing network, and hooking up an ISDN or T1 line to an Internet service provider (ISP), enables an instant presence on the Internet, and is also an excellent growth-oriented tactic. Only the TCP/IP protocol suite allows for this kind of flexibility.

Ability to Handle High Error Rates

The next goal was that an intranet should be able to tolerate high, perhaps unpredictable, error rates, and yet still provide a 100-percent reliable end-to-end service. TCP/IP is able to handle switching lines if congestion or an outage occurs. It's also able to retransmit missing or damaged packets. When data needs to be sent from New York to California, the big possibility of missing or damaged data looms ominously. TCP/IP ensures that all data gets delivered, regardless of line problems along the way.

Host Independence

As mentioned before, the new network architecture should work with any kind of network, and not be dedicated or tied to any one vendor. It must be nonproprietary. This is essential in the '90s. The days of "We're just an IBM shop" or "We only buy Novell stuff" are gone for many, and going fast for others.

Very Little Data Overhead

The last goal was for the network protocols to have as little overhead as possible. To understand this, let's compare TCP/IP to other protocols. While no one knows what protocol will end up being *the* world's standard protocol or suite of protocols 20 years from now, one of TCP/IP's rivals is a set of protocols built by the International Organization for Standardization (ISO). ISO has some standards that are very similar to TCP/IP's—standards named X.25 and TP4. But every protocol packages its data with an extra set of bytes, kind of like an envelope. The vast majority of data packets using the IP protocol have a simple, fixed-size 20-byte header. (We promise to explain *soon* how it is that TCP and

IP are actually two very different protocols, and what it is those protocols do!) If all possible options are enabled, the maximum size that the header can be is 60 bytes. The fixed, 20-byte portion always appears as the first 20 bytes of the packet. In contrast, X.25 uses dozens of possible headers, with no appreciable fixed portion to it. But why should *you* be concerned about overhead bytes? Really, for one reason only: *performance*! Simpler protocols mean faster transmission and packet switching.

RFCs: Refining TCP/IP

In life, if it's there long enough, politics will find it. Sometimes, this is even good. Sometimes it is absolutely necessary, as is the case when the goal is setting *standards* for TCP/IP. These standards are published in a series of documents called *Request for Comments*, or *RFCs*, and they describe the internal workings of the Internet.

RFCs and standards are not one and the same. Though many are actual standards, some RFCs are there for informational purposes or to describe a work in progress. Still others exist as a sort of forum providing a place for industry input relevant to the process of updating IP standards.

The Internet's standardization process resembles that of a bill becoming a law. Similarities include the fact that there exists more than one governing body and interested parties watching closely and making decisions about it. Another resemblance is that an RFC document goes through several stages, each subjecting it to examination, analysis, debate, critique, and testing on its way to becoming a standard.

RFC Status Types and Development

First, an individual, company, or organization proposing a new protocol, an improvement to an existing protocol, or even simply making comments on the state of the Internet creates an RFC. If it deems it worthy, after at least a six-month wait, the IESG (Internet Engineering Steering Group) promotes the RFC to the status of *draft standard*, where it re-enters the arena of review before finally becoming a bona fide Internet standard. It is then published and assigned a permanent RFC number.

If the standard is changed or updated in any way, it gets a whole new number, so, rest assured—you've got the latest model. Also handy to note: If what you're looking at *is* a revised edition, the dated version or versions are referenced on its title page. Also noteworthy, a letter that follows an RFC's number indicates the status of that RFC. Following is a list of status designations for Internet protocols:

- **Historic:** These are protocols that have either been outmoded or are no longer undergoing consideration for standardization.

- **Experimental:** Protocols being experimented with.

- **Informational:** Exactly what you might think.

- **Proposed Standard:** Being analyzed for future standardization.

- **Draft Standard:** In home stretch—the final review period prior to becoming a standard.

- **Standard:** An Internet protocol which has arrived, and is fully official.

There are also instructions for the treatment of Internet Protocols. They are:

- **Limited:** Of possible use to some computer systems. Highly specialized or experimental protocols are sometimes given this designation. Historic protocols can be given this status as well.

- **Elective:** These protocols may possibly be implemented.

- **Recommended:** These should be implemented.

- **Required:** Protocols considered a "must." They are required to be implemented on the Internet.

Important to note is the fact that not every protocol enjoying wide usage on the Net is an Internet standard. TCP/IP's NFS (Network File System) is a stellar example. Developed by Sun Microsystems, the NFS is a critical TCP/IP protocol, and is therefore inextricably entwined with the Internet. This protocol, though indispensable, has not received approval from the Internet Activities Board (discussed in the next section), and so cannot be given the status of standard.

Internet Activities Board (IAB)

The IAB is a committee responsible for setting Internet standards and for managing the process of publishing RFCs. The IAB is in charge of two task forces: the Internet Research Task Force (IRTF) and the Internet Engineering Task force (IETF). The IRTF is responsible for coordinating all TCP/IP-related research projects. The IETF focuses on problems on the Internet.

For more information on the Internet, try (you guessed it) the Internet. There's a memo called Internet Official Protocol Standards, and the last time we checked, its publishing number was RFC 1800. It describes the above process much more thoroughly than space allows us here.

Researching RFCs on InterNIC

The InterNIC Directory and Database, provided by AT&T, is a service that furnishes us with sources of information about the Internet, including RFCs. A WHOIS server provides a white page directory of Internet users and a Gopher database provides access to Internet documents. InterNIC is a primary depository that offers many options for retrieval. Have fun!

Previously, the best way to check out RFCs, and to get up-to-date information about their sources, was to send an e-mail to: rfc-info@isi.edu, including the message: **help: ways_to_get_rfcs**. If you weren't looking for a specific RFC, you downloaded a file named rfc—inde.txt, which offers the complete banquet of all the RFCs in the whole wide world. Today, the easiest way to go RFC hunting is to point a Web browser at www.internic.net, which will lavish you with a nice searchable interface. Still, RFCs may be obtained via FTP from these servers:

- ds.internic.net (InterNIC Directory and Database Services)

- nis.nsf.net

- nisc.jvnc.net

- ftp.isi.edu

- wuarchive.wustl.edu

- src.doc.ic.ac.uk

- ftp.ncren.net

- ftp.sesqui.net

- nis.garr.it

Locating Information on the Internet

Indeed the Internet has become a popular "place" to hang out. Other than its obvious commercial potential, whether you dine to Debussy, or sky surf to S.T.P., there's something for you there. However, the way to go about tapping into that enormous expanse of information can be, well, less than clear and simple. You're not alone if you and Alice in Wonderland have had a little too much in common on this one. You know what you're after—you know it's out there...but *where*? And what's the fastest, easiest way to get to it? Fortunately, TCP/IP has application protocols that address these issues. We'll look at four methods of finding information on the Internet, known as *information retrieval services*:

- WAIS

- Archie

- Gopher

- World Wide Web (WWW)

WAIS

Wide Area Information Servers allow you to search for a specific document inside a database. WAIS is a distributed information service that offers natural language input as well as indexed searching that lets the results of initial searches influence future searches. You can Telnet to `ds.internic.net` to access a WAIS client. Log in as **wais**, without a password. WAIS searches may also be done in the WWW.

Archie

A program called Archie was created to help users find files. Archie works by indexing a large number of files. Periodically, participating Internet host computers will download a listing of their files to a few specified computers called Archie servers. The Archie server then indexes all these files.

When you are looking for a specific file, you can run the Archie client software and *query* (search through) the Archie server. The Archie server will examine its indexes and send back a description and location of the files that match your query. You can then use FTP to transfer the file or files. Archie is essentially an indexing and search tool.

Gopher

Another great Internet tool is Gopher. Created at the University of Minnesota, where the school mascot *is* a gopher, it organizes topics into a menu system and allows you to access the information on each topic listed. Through its menu system, you can see at a glance what information is available there. There are many levels of submenus, allowing you to burrow down to the exact type of information you're looking for. When you choose an item, Gopher transparently transfers you to another system on the Internet where your choice resides.

Gopher actually uses the Telnet protocol to log you into the other system. This action is hidden from users, who just see the Gopher menu interface. This means that Gopher doesn't merely tell you where your information is located, as Archie does, but also transparently takes you to it. Gopher could be characterized as a menuing tool, a search tool, and a navigation tool that sends you places.

World Wide Web

The World Wide Web (WWW) is a type of data service running on many computers on the Internet. These computers utilize a type of software that allows for text and graphics to have cross-links to other information. You can access a WWW server, and a particular Web page, to see a terrific (depending on its creator's talent) graphic display of text, pictures, icons, colors, and other elements.

To access the Web server, you use client software called a *browser program*. Through a browser, you can choose an element on the Web page, which can then cross-link you to a computer animation, or play sounds, or display another Web page. Browsers can even contact another Web server located across the world. All the Web servers on the Internet are collectively referred to as the World Wide Web and can be thought of as Jungian consciousness for computers.

The most popular World Wide Web browsers are Netscape's Navigator and Microsoft's Internet Explorer. For how much longer in this order, well, only the Shadow knows.

But enough about the Internet for now. Let's go unto the next chapter and define some things that we've been talking about—namely, just what *are* TCP and IP? By this point, we're sure our discussion has raised more than one question about this complex networking engine and what's all involved in it. The next chapter will not only serve to clarify the TCP/IP picture, but will also illustrate how it operates and why.

CHAPTER

2

TCP/IP Communication
Layers and Their Protocols

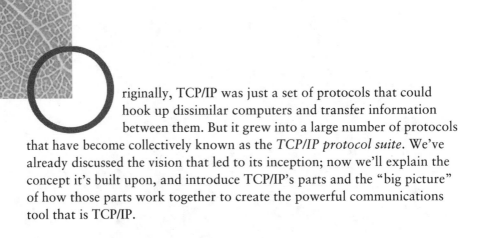

riginally, TCP/IP was just a set of protocols that could hook up dissimilar computers and transfer information between them. But it grew into a large number of protocols that have become collectively known as the *TCP/IP protocol suite*. We've already discussed the vision that led to its inception; now we'll explain the concept it's built upon, and introduce TCP/IP's parts and the "big picture" of how those parts work together to create the powerful communications tool that is TCP/IP.

The OSI Reference Model

The International Organization for Standardization is the Emily Post of the protocol world. Just like Ms. Post, who wrote the book setting the standards—or protocols—for human social interaction, the ISO developed the OSI (Open Systems Interconnection) reference model as the guide and precedent for an open protocol set. Defining the etiquette of communication models, it remains today the most popular means of comparison for protocol suites. Why should you learn the OSI reference model? Well, to help you troubleshoot problems, of course! It makes you sound smart in meetings, too.

The OSI reference model has seven layers:

- Application

- Presentation

- Session

- Transport

- Network

- Data Link

- Physical

Figure 2.1 shows the way these "macro-layers" fit together.

FIGURE 2.1

The macro-layers of the
OSI reference model

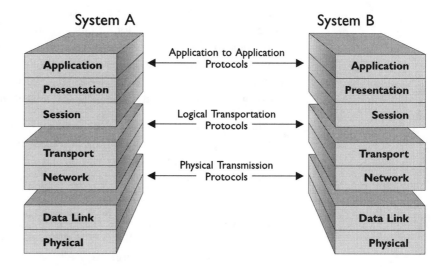

The OSI model's top three layers—Application, Presentation, and Session—deal with functions that aid applications in communicating with other applications. They specifically deal with tasks like filename formats, code sets, user interfaces, compression, encryption, and other functions relating to the exchange occurring between applications.

The Transport and Network layers deal with the logical transmission of data. They take care of the sizing of packets sent and received from each application, and then handle the routing of them. They also set the degree of reliability for packets reaching their destination, and the logical addressing of each machine.

The bottom layers—Data Link and Physical—handle the physical transmission of data. They take what is passed down to them and put it into a format that can be sent over a variety of physical transmission media like cable, fiber optics, microwave, and radio. They encode data into different media signals to match the specific media over which they'll be transmitted.

Application Layer

The Application layer of the OSI model supports the components that deal with the communicating aspects of an application. Although computer applications sometimes require only desktop resources, applications may unite communicating components from more than one network application (for example, things like file transfers, e-mail, remote access, network management activities, client/server processes, and information location). Many network applications provide services for communication over enterprise networks, but for present and future internetworking, the need is fast developing to reach beyond their limits. For the '90s and beyond, transactions and information exchanges between organizations are broadening to require internetworking applications like the following:

- **The World Wide Web (WWW):** Connects countless servers (the number seems to grow with each passing day) presenting diverse formats. Most are multimedia, and include some or all of the following: graphics, text, video, even sound. Netscape Navigator, Internet Explorer, and other browsers like Mosaic simplify both accessing and viewing Web sites.

- **E-Mail Gateways:** Again versatile, e-mail gateways can use Simple Mail Transfer Protocol (SMTP) or the X.400 standard to deliver messages among differing e-mail applications.

- **Electronic Data Interchange (EDI):** This is a composite of specialized standards and processes that facilitates the flow of tasks like accounting, shipping/receiving, and order and inventory tracking between businesses.

- **Special Interest Bulletin Boards:** These include the many chat rooms on the Internet where people can connect and communicate with each other either by posting messages or simply typing a conversation live, in real-time. They can also share public domain software.

- **Internet Navigation Utilities:** Applications like Gopher and WAIS, as well as search engines like Yahoo, Excite, and Alta Vista, help users locate the resources and information they need on the Internet.

- **Financial Transaction Services:** These are services that target the financial community. They gather and sell information pertaining to investments, market trading, commodities, currency exchange rates, and credit data to their subscribers.

Application Program Interfaces

An important thing to mention here is something called an *application program interface (API)*. Used jointly with Application layer services, it is often included by developers of protocols and programs in the package with their products. They are important because they make it possible for programmers to customize applications and reap the benefits of their wares. An API is essentially a set of guidelines for user-written applications to follow when accessing the services of a software system. It's a channel into the harbor. Remember BSD UNIX? It has an API called Berkeley Sockets. Microsoft changed it slightly and renamed it Windows Sockets. Indeed, things from Berkeley *do* get around!

Presentation Layer

The Presentation layer gets its name from its purpose: presenting data to the Application layer. It's essentially a translator. A successful data transfer technique is to adapt the data into a standard format before transmission. Computers are configured to receive this generically formatted data, then convert it back into their native format for reading. The OSI has protocol standards that define how standard data should be formatted. Tasks like data compression, decompression, encryption, and decryption are associated with this layer.

The Abstract Syntax Representation, Revision #1 (ASN.1), is the standard data syntax used by the Presentation layer. This kind of standardization is necessary when transmitting numerical data that is represented very differently by various computer systems' architectures.

Some Presentation layer standards are involved in multimedia operations. The following serve to direct graphic and visual image presentation:

- **PICT:** A picture format used by Macintosh or PowerPC programs for transferring QuickDraw graphics.

- **TIFF:** The Tagged Image File Format is a standard graphics format for high-resolution, bitmapped images.

- **JPEG:** These standards are brought to us by the Joint Photographic Experts Group.

Others guide movies and sound:

■ **MIDI:** The Musical Instrument Digital Interface is used for digitized music.

■ **MPEG:** The Motion Picture Experts Group's standard for the compression and coding of motion video for CDs is increasingly popular. It provides digital storage, and bit rates up to 1.5Mbps.

■ **QuickTime:** Again for use with Macintosh or PowerPC programs, it manages these computer's audio and video applications.

Session Layer

The Session layer's job can be likened to that of a mediator or referee. Its central concern is dialog control between devices, or nodes. It serves to organize their communication by offering three different modes—simplex, half-duplex, and full-duplex—and by splitting up a communication session into three different phases. These phases are connection establishment, data transfer, and connection release.

Simplex Mode

In simplex mode, communication is actually a monologue with one device transmitting and another receiving. To get a picture of this, think of the telegraph machine's form of communication: .....--..----...---

Half-Duplex Mode

When in half-duplex mode, nodes take turns transmitting and receiving—the computer equivalent of talking on a speaker-phone. Some of us have experienced proper conversation etiquette being forced upon us by the unique speaker-phone phenomenon of forbidden interruption—the speaker-phone's mechanism dictates that you may indeed speak your mind, but you'll have to wait until the other end stops first. This is how nodes communicate when in half-duplex mode.

Full-Duplex Mode

Full-duplex's only conversational proviso is *flow control*. This mitigates the problem of possible differences in the operating speed of two nodes, where one may be transmitting faster than the other can receive. Other than that, communication between the two flows unregulated, with both sides transmitting and receiving simultaneously.

Formal Communication Session Phases

Formal communication sessions occur in three phases:

- In the first, the connection-establishment phase, contact is secured and devices agree upon communication parameters and the protocols they will use.

- Next, in the data transfer phase, these nodes engage in conversation, or dialog, and exchange information.

- Finally, when they're through communicating, nodes participate in a systematic release of their session.

A formal communications session is connection oriented. In a situation where a large quantity of information is to be transmitted, rules are agreed upon by the involved nodes for the creation of checkpoints along their transfer process. These are highly necessary in the case of an error occurring along the way. Among other things, they afford us humans the luxury of preserving our dignity in the face of our closely watching computers. Let us explain... On the 44th minute of a 45-minute download, a loathsome error occurs... again! This is the third try, and the file-to-be-had is needed more than sunshine. Without your trusty checkpoints in place, you'd have to start all over again. Potentially, this could cause the coolest of cucumbers to tantrum like a two-year-old. Instead, to preserve our dignity, we have checkpoints secured (something we call *activity management)*, ensuring that the transmitting node only has to retransmit the data sent since the last checkpoint. Very cool.

It's important to note that in networking situations, devices send out simple, one-frame status reports that aren't sent in a formal session format. If they were, it would unnecessarily burden the network and result in lost economy. Instead, in these events, a *connectionless* approach is used, where the transmitting node simply sends off its data without establishing availability, and without acknowledgment from its intended receiver. To clarify this concept, picture a message in a bottle, floating wherever the current takes it. There's no guarantee where it will come ashore, or if it even will. Similar to this are messages appropriate for *connectionless communication*—these messages are short, sweet, they go where the current takes them, and arrive at an unsecured destination.

Following are some examples of Session-layer protocols and interfaces:

- **Network File System (NFS):** Developed by Sun Microsystems and used with TCP/IP and UNIX workstations for allowing transparent access to remote resources.

- **SQL:** The Structured Query Language developed by IBM provides users with a simpler way to define their information requirements on both local and remote systems.

- **RPC:** The Remote Procedure Call is a broad client/server redirection tool used for disparate service environments. Its procedures are created on clients and performed on servers.

- **X Window:** Widely used by intelligent terminals for communicating with remote UNIX computers. It allows them to operate as though they were locally attached monitors.

- **ASP:** Another client/server mechanism, the AppleTalk Session Protocol both establishes and maintains sessions amid AppleTalk client and server machines.

- **DNA SCP:** The Digital Network Architecture Session Control Protocol is a DECnet Session-layer protocol.

Transport Layer

Services located here both segment and reassemble data from upper-layer applications and unite it onto the same data stream. They provide end-to-end data transport services and establish a logical connection between the sending host and destination host on an internetwork. Data integrity is ensured at this layer by maintaining flow control, and also by allowing users the option of requesting reliable data transport between systems. Flow control prevents the problem of a sending host on one side of the connection overflowing the buffers in the receiving host—an event which can result in lost data. Reliable data transport employs a connection-oriented communications session between systems, and the protocols involved ensure and achieve the following:

- The segments delivered will be acknowledged back to the sender upon their reception.

- Any segments not acknowledged will be retransmitted.

- Segments are sequenced back into their proper order upon arrival at their destination.

- A manageable data flow is maintained in order to avoid congestion, overloading, and loss of any data.

An important reason for different layers coexisting within the OSI reference model is to allow for the sharing of a transport connection by more than one application. This is because the Transport layer's functioning happens segment by segment, and each segment is independent of the others. This allows different applications to send consecutive segments, processed on a first-come, first-served basis, that can either be intended for the same destination host, or multiple hosts.

Figure 2.2 shows how the Transport layer sends the data of several applications originating from a source host to communicate with parallel applications on one or many destination hosts. The specific port number for each software application is set by software within the source machine before transmission. When it transmits a message, the source computer includes extra bits that encode the type of message, the program it was created with, and which protocols were used. Each software application transmitting a data stream segment uses the same preordained port number. When it receives the data stream, the destination computer or computers are empowered to sort and reunite each application's segments, providing the Transport layer with all it needs to pass the data on up to its upper-layer peer application.

FIGURE 2.2

Transport layer data segments sharing a traffic stream

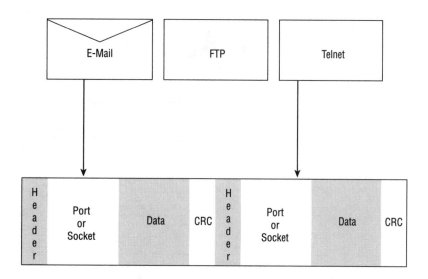

In reliable transport operation, one user first establishes a connection-oriented session with its peer system. Figure 2.3 portrays a typical connection-oriented session taking place between sending and receiving systems. In it, both hosts' application programs begin by notifying their individual operating systems that a connection is about to be initiated. The two operating systems communicate by sending messages over the network confirming that the transfer is approved, and that both sides are ready for it to take place. Once the required synchronization is complete, a connection is fully established, and the data transfer begins. While the information is being transferred between hosts, the two machines periodically check in with each other, communicating through their protocol software, to ensure that all is going well and the data is being received properly. The following bullet points summarize the steps in the connection-oriented session pictured in Figure 2.3:

- The first "connection agreement" segment is a request for synchronization.

- The second and third segments acknowledge the request, and establish connection parameters between hosts.

- The final segment is also an acknowledgment. It notifies the destination host that the connection agreement is accepted and that the actual connection has been established. Data transfer can now begin.

FIGURE 2.3

Establishing a connection-oriented session

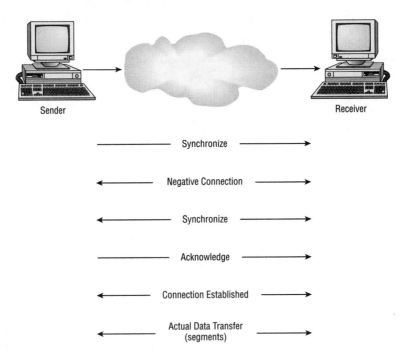

Sender   Receiver

———————— Synchronize ————————▶

◀———————— Negative Connection ————————▶

◀———————— Synchronize ————————▶

———————— Acknowledge ————————▶

◀———————— Connection Established ————————▶

◀———————— Actual Data Transfer
(segments) ————————▶

During a transfer, congestion can occur because either a chatty, high-speed computer is generating data traffic faster than the network can transfer it, or because many computers are simultaneously sending datagrams through a single gateway or destination. In the latter case, a gateway or destination can become congested even though no single source caused the problem. In either case, the problem is basically akin to a freeway bottleneck—too much traffic for too small a capacity. Usually, no one car is the problem, it's that there are simply too many cars on that freeway—all attempting to go in the same direction at the same time.

When a machine receives a flood of datagrams too quickly for it to process, it stores them in memory in much the same manner a reservoir exists to buffer the torrent of water rushing into it from a flooding river. This buffering action solves the problem only if the datagrams are part of a small burst—a fleeting event like a flash flood. However, if the datagram deluge continues, a device's memory will eventually be exhausted. Its flood capacity will be exceeded, and it will discard any additional datagrams that arrive, as a reservoir would open its gates to keep from overflowing. But, no worries—because of transport function, network flood control systems work a whole lot better than those that exist in the real world. Instead of dumping resources and allowing data to be lost, the transport can issue a "not ready" indicator, as shown in Figure 2.4, to the overzealous sender. This mechanism works kind of like a stoplight, signaling the hyper sending device to stop transmitting segment traffic to its overwhelmed peer. When the peer receiver has processed the segments already in its memory reservoir, it sends out a "ready" transport indicator. When the machine waiting to transmit the rest of its datagrams receives this "go" indicator, it can then resume its transmission.

FIGURE 2.4

Transmitting segments with flow control

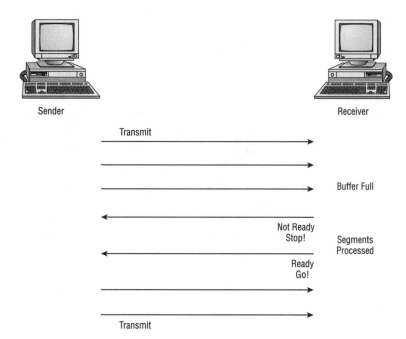

In fundamental, reliable, connection-oriented data transfer, datagrams are delivered to the receiving host in exactly the same sequence they're transmitted, and the transmission fails if this order is breached. Other things that will cause a failure to transmit are any data segments being lost, duplicated, or damaged along the way. The answer to the problem is to have the receiving host acknowledge receiving each and every data segment. Data throughput would be low if the transmitting machine had to wait for an acknowledgment after sending each segment; so because there's time available after the sender transmits the data segment, and before it finishes processing acknowledgments from the receiving machine, the sender uses the break to transmit more data. How many data segments the transmitting machine is allowed to send without receiving an acknowledgment for them is called a *window*.

Windowing controls how much information is transferred from one end to the other. While some protocols quantify information by observing the number of packets, TCP/IP measures it by the number of bytes. In Figure 2.5, we show a window size of one and a window size of three. When a window size of one is configured, the sending machine waits for an acknowledgment for each and every data segment it transmits before transmitting more. Configured to a window size of three, it's allowed to transmit three data segments before an acknowledgment is received. In our simplified example, both the sending and receiving machines are workstations. Reality is rarely that simple, and most often both acknowledgments and packets will commingle as they travel over the network and pass through routers. Routing complicates things, but not to worry, we'll be covering applied routing later in the book.

Reliable data delivery ensures the integrity of a stream of data sent from one machine to the other through a fully functional data link. It guarantees the data won't be duplicated or lost. The method that achieves this is known as *positive acknowledgment with retransmission*. This technique requires a receiving machine to communicate with the transmitting source by sending an acknowledgment message back to the sender when it receives data. The sender documents each segment it sends, and waits for this acknowledgment before sending the next one. When it sends a segment, the transmitting machine starts a timer, and retransmits if it expires before an acknowledgment for the segment is returned from the receiving end.

In Figure 2.6, the sending machine transmits segments 1, 2, and 3. The receiving node acknowledges it has received them by requesting segment 4.

FIGURE 2.5

Windowing

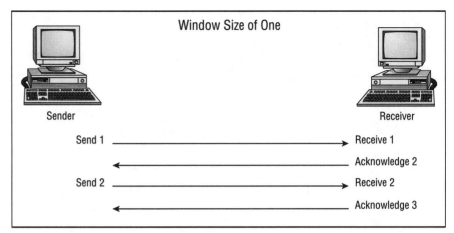

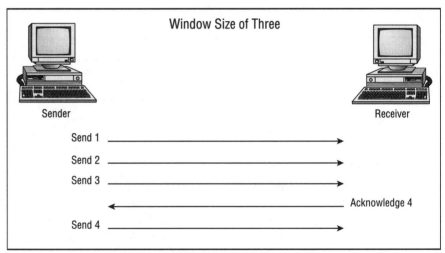

When it receives the acknowledgment, the sender then moves on to transmit segments 4, 5, and 6. If segment number 5 doesn't make it through to the destination, the receiving node acknowledges that event with a request to resend it. The sending machine will then resend the lost segment and wait for an acknowledgment, which it must receive to resume the transmission by sending segment 7.

FIGURE 2.6

Transport layer
reliable delivery

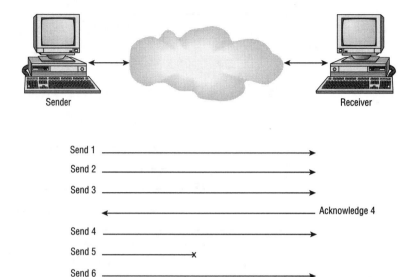

Network Layer

In life, there are lots of roads leading to Rome. The same holds true with the complicated cloud of networks, and the proper path through them is determined by protocols residing in layer number three—the Network layer. Path determination makes it possible for a router to appraise all available paths to a given destination, and decide on the best one. Just as mountain climbers use topographical maps to orient themselves to the lay of the land and determine the best route to the top, routers use network topology information when orienting themselves to the network, and evaluating the different possible paths through it. These network "maps" can either be configured by the network's administrator or obtained through dynamic processes running on the network. The Network layer's interface is to networks, and it's employed by the Transport layer to provide the best end-to-end packet delivery services for it. The job of sending packets from the source network to the destination network is the Network layer's primary function. After the router decides on the best path from point A to point B, it proceeds with switching the packet onto it—something known as *packet switching*. This is essentially forwarding the packet the router has received on one network interface, or *port*, onto the port that connects to the best path through the network cloud to that particular packet's destination. We'll cover packet switching more thoroughly later on.

An internetwork must continually designate all paths of its media connections. Figure 2.7 illustrates that each line connecting routers is numbered, and those numbers are used by routers as network addresses. These addresses possess and convey important information about the path of media connections. They're used by routing protocols to pass packets from a source onward to its destination. The Network layer creates a composite "network map"—a communication strategy system—by combining information about the sets of links into an internetwork with path determination, path switching, and route processing functions. It can also use these addresses to provide relay capability and interconnect independent networks. Consistent across the entire internetwork, layer three addresses also streamline the network's performance by preventing unnecessary broadcasts that gobble up precious bandwidth. Unnecessary broadcasts increase the network's overhead and waste capacity on any links and machines that don't need to receive them. Using consistent end-to-end addressing that accurately describes the path of media connections enables the Network layer to determine the best path to a destination, without encumbering the device or links on the internetwork with unnecessary broadcasts.

FIGURE 2.7

Communicating through an internetwork

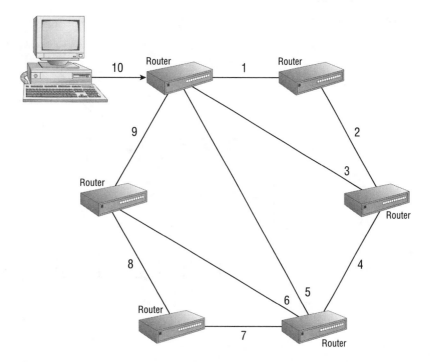

When an application on a host wants to send a packet to a destination device located on a different network, a data-link frame is received on one of the router's network interfaces. The router proceeds to decapsulate, then examine, the frame to establish what kind of Network-layer data is in tow. After this is determined, the data is sent on to the appropriate Network-layer process, but the frame's mission is fulfilled, and it's simply discarded.

Detailed in Figure 2.8 is the Network-layer process examining the packet's header to discover which network it's destined for. It then refers to the routing table to find the connections the current network has to foreign network interfaces. After one is selected, the packet is re-encapsulated in its data-link frame with the selected interface's information, and queued for delivery off to the next hop in the path toward its destination. This process is repeated every time the packet switches through another router. When it finally reaches the router connected to the network on which the destination host is located, the packet is encapsulated in the destination LAN's data-link frame type. It is now properly packaged and ready for delivery to the protocol stack on the actual destination host.

FIGURE 2.8

Network-layer process

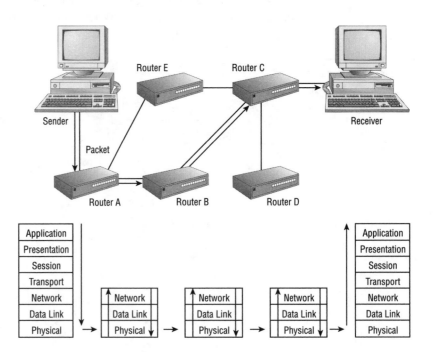

Data Link Layer

The Data Link layer provides the service of ensuring that messages are delivered to the proper device, and translates messages from up above into bits for the Physical layer to transmit. It formats the message into *data frames* and adds to it a customized header containing the hardware destination and source address. All of this added information surrounding the original message forms a sort of capsule around it much like the way various engines, navigational devices, and other necessary tools were attached to the lunar modules of the Apollo project. These various pieces of equipment were only useful during certain stages of space flight, and were stripped off the module and discarded when their designated stage was complete. Data traveling through networks is much the same. A data frame that's all packaged up and ready to go follows the format outlined in Figure 2.9.

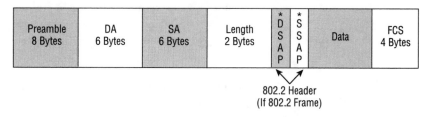

- The preamble, or *start indicator*, is made up of a special bit pattern that alerts devices to the beginning of a data frame.

- The destination address (DA) is there for obvious reasons. The Data Link layers of every device on the network examine this to see if it matches its own address.

- The source address (SA) is the address of the sending device and exists to facilitate replies to the messages.

- In Ethernet_II frames, the two-byte field following the source address is a type field. This field specifies the upper-layer protocol to receive the data after data-link processing is complete.

- In 802.3 frames, the two-byte field following the source address is a length field, which indicates the number of bytes of data that follows this field and precedes the frame check sequence (FCS) field. Following the length field could be an 802.2 header for Logical Link Control (LLC) information. This information is needed to specify the upper-layer process since 802.3 does not have a type field.

- The *data* is the actual message, plus all the information sent down to the sending device's Data Link layer from the layers above it.

- Finally, there's the frame check sequence (FCS) field. Its purpose corresponds to its name, and it houses the CRC—the Cyclic Redundancy Checksum. An IP packet contains a bit of data called a checksum header, which checks whether the header information was damaged on the way from sender to receiver. CRCs work like this: The device sending the data determines a value summary for it and stashes it within the frame. The device on the receiving end performs the same procedure, then checks to see if its value matches the total, or sum, of the sending node. Hence the term *checksum*.

Checksum works a bit like counting all of the jellybeans in your bag, then passing the bag to someone else to give to your friend. To make sure none of the jellybeans get pilfered along the way, you send along a message stating the total number of jellybeans in the bag and asking your friend to recount them. If your friend arrives at the same total, you both can safely assume none were snagged en route—that your jellybeans were successfully transmitted without error.

WAN Protocols at the Data Link Layer

The typical encapsulations for synchronous serial lines at the Data Link layer are:

- **High Level Data Link Control (HDLC):** The ISO created the HDLC standard to support both point-to-point and multipoint configurations. Unfortunately, most vendors implement HDLC in different manners, so HDLC is often not compatible between vendors.

- **Synchronous Data Link Control (SDLC):** A protocol created by IBM for use with their mainframes to connect remote offices which uses polling media access. Created for use in WANs, it became extremely popular in the 1980s, as many companies were installing 327x controllers in their remote offices to communicate with the mainframe in the corporate office. SDLC defines and uses a polling media access, which means the primary (front-end) asks or polls the secondaries (327x controllers) to find out if they need to communicate with it. Secondaries cannot speak unless spoken to, nor can two secondaries speak to each other. (Master/slave terminology was used until it was deemed distasteful and not politically correct.)

- **Link Access Procedure, Balanced (LAPB):** Created for use with X.25, it defines and is capable of detecting out-of-sequence or missing frames, and retransmitting, exchanging, and acknowledging frames.

- **X.25:** The first packet-switching network. This defines the specifications between a DTE and a DCE.

- **Serial Line IP (SLIP):** An industry standard developed in 1984 to support TCP/IP networking over low-speed serial interfaces in Berkeley UNIX. With the Windows NT RAS service, Windows NT computers can use TCP/IP and SLIP to communicate to remote hosts.

- **Point-to-Point Protocol (PPP):** SLIP's big brother. It takes the specifications of SLIP and adds login, password, and error correction. See RFC 1661, if you're bored on a rainy day, for more information as described by the IETF.

- **Integrated Services Digital Network (ISDN):** Analog phone lines converted to use digital signaling. They can transmit both voice and data.

- **Frame Relay:** Upgrade from X.25 where LAPB is no longer used. It's the fastest of the WAN protocols listed because of its simplified framing, with no error correction. It must use the high-quality digital facilities of the phone company, and is therefore not available everywhere.

High Speed Ethernet at the Data Link Layer

Bottom line—users need bandwidth, and 10Mbps isn't good enough; they need 100Mbps—switched! 100Mbps Ethernet rises to this call well. Some of the new technologies are:

- **100BaseFX:** Ethernet over fiber at 100Mbps using 802.3 specs.

- **100Base4**: Again using 802.3 specs, 100Mbps over category 3, 4, or 5 cabling.

- **100BaseTX**: Fast Ethernet over category 5 cabling. It's compatible to the 802.3 specifications.

- **100BaseVG AnyLan:** IEEE movement into fast Ethernet and Token Ring which seems to be going nowhere fast, mostly because it is *not* compatible with the 802.3 standards.

Physical Layer

The Physical layer focuses on two responsibilities: It sends bits and receives bits. Bits only come in values of 1 or 0—a Morse code with numerical value. The Physical layer communicates directly with the various types of actual communication media. Different kinds of media represent these bit values of 1 and 0 in different ways. Some use audio tones, while others employ *state transitions*—changes in voltage from high to low and low to high. Specific protocols are needed for each type of media that describe the proper bit patterns to be used, how data is encoded into media signals, and the various qualities of the physical media's attachment interface.

At the Physical layer, the interface between the data terminal equipment (DTE), and the data circuit-terminating equipment (DCE) is identified. The DCE is usually the service provider, and the DTE is the attached device. The services available to the DTE are most often accessed via a modem or channel service unit/data service unit (CSU/DSU).

The following Physical layer standards define this interface:

- EIA/TAI-232

- EIA/TIA-449

- V.24

- V.35

- X.21

- G.703

- EIA-530

- High-Speed Serial Interface (HSSI)

The DoD Reference Model

The DoD model is a condensed version of the OSI model. It comprises four instead of seven layers:

- Process/Application

- Host-to-Host

- Internet

- Network Access

Figure 2.10 shows a comparison of the four-layer DoD model and the seven-layer OSI reference model. As you can see, the two are similar in concept, but have a different number of layers with different names.

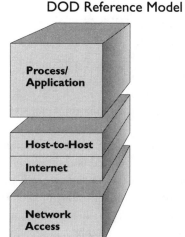
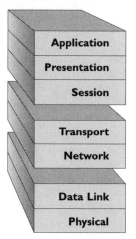

While the DoD model and the OSI model are truly alike in design and concept, with similar things happening in similar places, the specifications on *how* those things happen are different. This leads to a much different suite of protocols for the DoD model than those existing for the OSI model. Figure 2.11 shows the TCP/IP protocol suite, and how its protocols relate to the DoD model layers.

FIGURE 2.11

The TCP/IP protocol suite

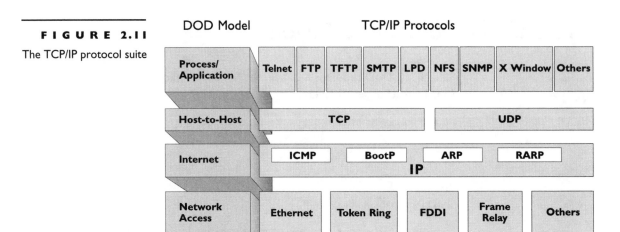

Process/Application Layer

The DoD model's corresponding layer to the OSI's top three is known as the Process/Application layer. A whole lot of work gets done at this layer, and in it is found a vast array of protocols that combine to integrate the various activities and duties spanning the focus of the OSI's Session, Presentation, and Application layers. We'll be zooming in for a closer examination of these protocols shortly. The Process/Application layer defines protocols for host-to-host application communication. It also controls user interface specifications.

As we explored earlier, one of the original design goals for the Internet was to have applications that could run on different computer platforms and yet, somehow, still communicate. The cavalry arrived in the form of Process/Application layer protocols, which address the ability of one application to communicate with another, regardless of hardware platform, operating system, and other features of the two hosts.

The Process/Application Layer Protocols

Most applications written with TCP/IP protocols can be characterized as *client/server* applications. This means that there are two major parts to the software involved, and that it's probably running on two different machines.

The server part of this software duo usually runs on the machine where the data is actually residing. This machine is the Big Dog. It tends to be powerful because much of the data processing, as well as storage, is done on it. It works like this: The client software sends requests to the server software for it to fulfill.

Some typical requests include searches for information, printing, e-mail stuff, application services, and file transfers.

In addition to communicating with the server, another function of client software is to provide an interface for the user. It also allows you to mess around with the data you've managed to coax from the server.

These matters in hand, we'll move along and investigate just what sort of protocols populate the DoD model's Process/Application layer.

Telnet   The chameleon of protocols, Telnet's specialty is *terminal emulation*. It allows a user on a remote client machine, called the Telnet client, to access the resources of another machine, the Telnet server. Telnet achieves this by pulling a fast one on the Telnet server, dressing up the client machine to appear like it's a terminal directly attached to the local network. This projection is actually a software image, a virtual terminal that can interact with the chosen remote host. These emulated terminals are of the text-mode type and can execute refined procedures like displaying menus that give users the opportunity to choose options from them, accessing the applications on the duped server. Users begin a Telnet session first by running the Telnet client software, then logging onto the Telnet server.

Telnet's capabilities are limited to peeking into what's on the server. It's a "just looking" protocol. It can't be used for file sharing functions like downloading stuff. For the actual snatching of goodies, one must employ the next protocol on the list: FTP.

FTP (File Transfer Protocol)   This is the "grab it—give it" protocol that affords us the luxury of transferring files. FTP can facilitate this between any two machines that are using it. But FTP is not just a protocol—it's also a program. Operating as a protocol, FTP is used by applications. As a program, it's employed by users to perform file tasks by hand. FTP also allows for access to both directories and files, and can accomplish certain types of directory operations, like relocating into different ones. FTP teams up with Telnet to transparently log you into the FTP server, and then provides for the transfer of files.

Wow! Obviously, a tool this powerful would need to be secure—and FTP is! Accessing a host through FTP is only the first step. Users must then be subjected to an authentication login that's probably secured with passwords and usernames placed there by system administrators to restrict access. (And you thought this was going to be easy!) Not to fear, you can still get in by adopting the username "anonymous," but what you'll gain access to once in there will be limited.

Even when being employed by users manually as a program, FTP's functions are limited to listing and manipulating directories, typing file contents, and copying files between hosts. It can't execute remote files as programs.

TFTP (Trivial File Transfer Protocol)   TFTP is the stripped-down, stock version of FTP, though it's the protocol of choice if you know exactly what you want and where it is to be found. It doesn't spoil you with the luxury of functions that FTP does. TFTP has no directory browsing abilities; it can do nothing but give and receive files. This austere little protocol also skimps in the data department, sending much smaller blocks of data than FTP. Also noteworthy is that TFTP will only open boring, public files, thereby depriving you of both the rush of having gotten away with something *and* the feeling of being special and privileged. There's no authentication as there is with FTP, so it's insecure, and few sites actually support it due to the inherent security risks.

NFS (Network File System)   Introducing...NFS! This is a jewel of a protocol specializing in file sharing. It allows two different types of file systems to interoperate. It's like this... Suppose the NFS server software is running on a NetWare server, and the NFS client software is running on a UNIX host. NFS allows for a portion of the RAM on the NetWare server to transparently store UNIX files, which can, in turn, be used by UNIX users. Even though the NetWare file system and the UNIX file system are not alike—they have different case sensitivity, file name lengths, security, and so on—both the UNIX users and the NetWare users can access that same file with their normal file systems, in their normal way.

Imagine yourself as an African from Kenya back at the airport in Bavaria, heading toward the baggage claim area. With NFS in tow, you're equipped to actually retrieve your luggage, in a non-annihilated state, and get it through customs—all whilst chatting glibly in Swahili as you normally would! Additionally, the good news doesn't end there. Where Telnet, FTP, and TFTP are limited, NFS goes the extra mile. Remember that FTP cannot execute remote files as programs? NFS can! It can open a graphics application on your computer at work, and update the work you did on the one at home last night on the same program. NFS has the ability to import and export material—to manipulate applications remotely.

SMTP (Simple Mail Transfer Protocol)   Out of baggage claim, and into the mail room... SMTP, answering our ubiquitous call to e-mail, uses a spooled, or queued, method of mail delivery. Once a message has been sent to a destination, the message is spooled to a device—usually a disk. The server software at the destination posts a vigil, regularly checking this spool for messages, which, upon finding, proceeds to deliver to their destination.

LPD (Line Printer Daemon) This protocol is designed for printer sharing. LPD daemon along with the LPR (Line Printer) program allows print jobs to be spooled and sent to the network's printers.

X Window Designed for client/server operations, X Window defines a protocol for writing client/server applications based on graphical user interface. The idea was to allow a program, called a client, to run on one computer and allow it to display on another computer that was running a special program called a window server.

SNMP (Simple Network Management Protocol) Just as doctors are better equipped to maintain the health of their patients when they have the patient's medical history in hand, network managers are at an advantage if they possess performance histories of the network in their care. These case histories contain valuable information that enables the manager to anticipate future needs and analyze trends. By comparing the network's present condition to its past functioning patterns, managers can more easily isolate and troubleshoot problems.

SNMP is the protocol that provides for the collection and manipulation of this valuable network information. It gathers data by polling the devices on the network from a management station at fixed intervals, requiring them to disclose certain information. When all is well, SNMP receives something called a baseline, a report delimiting the operational traits of a healthy network. This handy protocol can also stand as a watchman over the network, quickly notifying managers of any sudden turn of events. These network watchmen are called agents, and when aberrations occur, agents send an alert called a trap to the management station.

The sensitivity of the agent, or threshold, can be increased or decreased by the network manager. An agent's threshold is like a pain threshold; the more sensitive it is set to be, the sooner it screams an alert. Managers use baseline reports to aid them in deciding on agent threshold settings for their networks. The more sophisticated the management station's equipment is, the clearer the picture it can provide of the network's functioning. More powerful consoles have better record-keeping ability, as well as the added benefit of being able to provide enhanced graphic interfaces that can form logical portraits of network structure.

The Host-to-Host Layer

This layer parallels the functions of OSI's Transport layer, defining protocols for setting up the level of transmission service for applications. It tackles issues like creating reliable end-to-end communication and ensuring the error-free delivery of data. It handles packet sequencing and maintains data integrity.

The Host-to-Host Layer Protocols

The broad goal of Host-to-Host layer protocols is to shield the upper layer applications from the complexities of the network. These protocols say to the upper layer, "Just give me your data, with any instructions, and we'll begin the process of getting your information ready for sending." The following sections describe the two main protocols at this layer in detail.

TCP (Transmission Control Protocol)   TCP has been around since networking's early years when WANs weren't very reliable. It was created to mitigate that problem, and reliability is TCP's strong point. It tests for errors, resends data if necessary, and reports the occurrence of errors to the upper layers if it can't manage to solve the problem itself.

This protocol takes large blocks of information from an application and breaks them down into segments. It numbers and sequences each segment so that the destination's TCP protocol can put the segments back into the large block the application intended. After these segments have been sent, TCP waits for acknowledgment for each one from the receiving end's TCP, retransmitting the ones not acknowledged.

Before it starts to send segments down the model, the sender's TCP protocol contacts the destination's TCP protocol in order to establish a connection. What is created is known as a virtual circuit. This type of communication is called connection-oriented. During this initial handshake, the two TCP layers also agree on the amount of information to be sent before the recipient TCP sends back an acknowledgment. With everything agreed upon in advance, the stage is set for reliable Application layer communication to take place.

TCP is a full-duplex connection, reliable, accurate, jellybean-counting protocol, and establishing all these terms and conditions, in addition to following through on them to check for errors, is no small task. It's very complicated, and very costly in terms of network overhead. Using TCP should be reserved for use only in situations when reliability is of utmost importance. For one thing, today's networks are much more reliable than those of yore, and therefore the added security is often a wasted effort. We'll discuss an alternative to TCP's high overhead method of transmission next: UDP.

UDP (User Datagram Protocol)   This protocol is used in place of TCP. UDP is the scaled-down economy model, and is considered a *thin* protocol. Like a thin person on a park bench, it doesn't take up a lot of room—in this case, on a network. It also doesn't offer all the bells and whistles of TCP, but it does do a fabulous job of transporting stuff that doesn't require reliable delivery—and it does it using far less connection information.

There are some situations where it would definitely be wise to opt for UDP instead of TCP. Remember that watchdog SNMP up there at the Process/Application layer? SNMP monitors the network, sending intermittent messages and a fairly steady flow of status updates and alerts, especially when running on a large network. The cost in overhead necessary to establish, maintain, and close a TCP connection for each one of those little messages would reduce a normally healthy, efficient network to a sticky, sluggish bog in no time. Another circumstance calling for the deployment of UDP over TCP is when the matter of reliability is seen to at the Process/Application layer. NFS handles its own reliability issues, making the use of TCP both impractical and redundant.

UDP receives upper-layer blocks of information instead of streams of data like its big brother, TCP, and breaks them into segments. Also like TCP, each segment is given a number for reassembly into the intended block at the destination. However, UDP does *not* sequence the segments, and does not care in what order the segments arrive at the destination. At least it numbers them. But after that, UDP sends them off and forgets about them. It doesn't follow through, check up on, or even allow for an acknowledgment of safe arrival—complete abandonment. Because of this, its referred to as an *unreliable* protocol. This does not mean that UDP is ineffective—only that it doesn't handle issues of reliability.

There are more things UDP doesn't do. It doesn't create a virtual circuit, and it doesn't contact the destination before delivering stuff to it. It is therefore considered a *connectionless* protocol.

Key Concepts of Host-to-Host Protocols

The following list highlights some important characteristics to keep in mind regarding these two protocols.

TCP	UDP
Sequenced	Unsequenced
Reliable	Unreliable
Connection-oriented	Connectionless
Acknowledgments	Low overhead
Virtual circuit	

Instructors commonly use a telephone analogy to help people understand how TCP works. Most of us understand that before you talk with someone on a phone, you must first establish a connection with that other person—wherever they may be. This is like a virtual circuit with the TCP protocol. If you were giving someone important information during your conversation, you might say, "Did you get that?" A query like that is like a TCP acknowledgment. From time to time, for various reasons, people also say, "Are you still there?" They end their conversations with a "good-bye" of some sort, putting closure on the phone call. These types of functions are achieved through TCP.

Alternately, using UDP is like sending a postcard. To do that, you don't need to contact the other party first. You simply write your message, address it, and mail it. This is analogous to UDP's connectionless orientation. Since the message on the postcard is probably not a matter of life or death, you don't need an acknowledgment of its receipt. Similarly, UDP does not involve acknowledgments.

The Internet Layer

This layer corresponds to the Network layer, designating the protocols relating to the logical transmission of packets over the entire network. It takes care of the addressing of hosts by giving them an IP address, and handles the routing of packets among multiple networks. It also controls the communication flow between two applications.

There are two main reasons for the Internet layer: routing, and providing a single network interface to the upper layers. None of the upper-layer protocols, and none of the ones on the lower layer, have any functions relating to routing. Routing is complex and important, and it's the job of the Internet layer to carry it out. The protocol IP is so integral to this layer, the very name of it is the name of the layer itself. So far, in discussing the upper layers, we've begun with a brief introduction, and left any specific treatise on their resident protocols to supporting sections. Here, however, IP, though only a protocol, *is* essentially the Internet layer. We've therefore included it in our introductory talk on the layer. The other protocols found here merely exist to support it. IP contains the Big Picture, and could be said to "see all," in that it is aware of all the interconnected networks. It can do this because all the machines on the network have a software address called an IP address, which we promise to cover later much more thoroughly.

The second main reason for the Internet layer is to provide a single network interface to the upper-layer protocols. Without this layer, application programmers would need to write "hooks" into every one of their applications for each different network access protocol. This would not only be a pain in the neck, it would lead to different versions of each application—one for Ethernet, another one for Token Ring, and so on. To prevent this, IP, lord of the Internet layer, provides one single network interface for the upper-layer protocols. That accomplished, it's then the job of IP and the various Network Access layer protocols to get along and work together.

The Internet Layer Protocols

All network roads don't lead to Rome—they lead to IP, and all the other protocols at this layer, as well as all the upper-layer protocols, use it. Never forget that. All paths through the model go through IP. The following sections describe the protocols at the Internet layer.

IP (Internet Protocol)   IP looks at each packet's IP address. Then, using a routing protocol, it decides where this packet is to be sent next, choosing the best path. The Network Access layer protocols at the bottom of the model don't possess IP's enlightened scope of the entire network; they deal with only point-to-point physical links.

Identifying devices on networks requires having the answers to these two questions: Which network is it on, and what's its ID on that network? The first is the *software address* (the right street); the second, the *hardware address* (the right mailbox). All hosts on a network have a logical ID called an IP address. This is the software address, and it contains valuable encoded information, greatly simplifying the complex task of routing.

IP takes segments from the Host-to-Host layer and fragments them into *datagrams* (packets). IP also reassembles datagrams back into segments on the receiving side. Each datagram is assigned the IP address of the sender and the IP address of the recipient. Each machine that receives a datagram makes routing decisions based upon the packet's destination IP address.

ARP (Address Resolution Protocol)   When IP has a datagram to send, it has already been informed by upper-layer protocols of the destination's IP address. However, IP must also inform a Network Access protocol, such as Ethernet, of the destination's hardware address. If IP does not know the hardware address, it uses the ARP protocol to find this information. As IP's detective, ARP interrogates the network by sending out a broadcast asking the machine with the specified IP address to reply with its hardware address. ARP is able to translate a software address, the IP address, into a hardware address—for example, the destination machine's Ethernet board address—thereby deducing its whereabouts. This hardware address is technically referred to as the media access control (MAC) address.

RARP (Reverse Address Resolution Protocol)   When an IP machine happens to be a diskless machine, it has no way of initially knowing its IP address. But it does know its MAC address. The RARP protocol is the psychoanalyst for these lost souls. It sends out a packet that includes its MAC address, and a request to be informed of what IP address is assigned to its MAC address. A designated machine, called a RARP server, responds with the answer, and the identity crisis is over. Like a good analyst, RARP uses the information it does know about (the machine's MAC address) to learn its IP address and complete the machine's ID portrait.

BootP   BootP stands for Boot Program. When a diskless workstation is powered on, it broadcasts a BootP request on the network. A BootP server hears the request, and looks up the client's MAC address in its BootP file. If it finds an appropriate entry, it responds by telling the machine its IP address, and the file—usually via the TFTP protocol—from which it should boot.
BootP is used by a diskless machine to learn the following:

- Its IP address

- The IP address of a server machine

- The name of a file that is to be loaded into memory and executed at boot up

ICMP (Internet Control Message Protocol)   ICMP is a management protocol and messaging service provider for IP. Its messages are carried as IP datagrams. RFC 1256, ICMP Router Discovery Messages, is an annex to ICMP, affording hosts extended capability in discovering routes to gateways. Periodically, router advertisements are announced over the network reporting IP addresses for its network interfaces. Hosts listen for these network infomercials to acquire route information. A *router solicitation* is a request for immediate advertisements, and may be sent by a host when it starts up. The following are some common events and messages that ICMP relates to:

- **Destination unreachable**: If a router cannot send an IP datagram any further, it uses ICMP to send a message back to the sender advising it of the situation.

- **Buffer full**: If a router's memory buffer for receiving incoming datagrams is full, it will use ICMP to send out this message.

- **Hops**: Each IP datagram is allotted a certain number of routers that it may go through, called hops. If it reaches its limit of hops before arriving at its destination, the last router to receive that datagram throws it away. The executioner router then uses ICMP to send an obituary message informing the sending machine of the demise of its datagram. This is network population control.

The Network Access Layer

The bottom layer of the DoD model monitors the data exchange between the host and the network. The equivalent of the Data Link and Physical layers of the OSI model, it oversees hardware addressing and defines protocols for the physical transmission of data.

Network Access Layer Protocols

Programmers for the DoD model didn't define protocols for this layer; instead, their focus began at the Internet layer. In fact, this is exactly the quality that makes this model able to be implemented on almost any hardware platform. Obviously, this is one of the reasons why the Internet Protocol suite is so popular. Every protocol listed here relates to the physical transmission of data. The following are the Network Access layer's main duties:

- Receiving an IP datagram and *framing* it into a stream of bits—ones and zeros—for physical transmission. (The information at this layer is called a frame.) An example of a protocol that works at this level is CSMA/CD, or Carrier Sense, Multiple Access with Collision Detect. Again, purpose equals name. It checks the cable to see if there's already another PC transmitting (Carrier Sense), allows all computers to share the same bandwidth (Multiple Access), and detects and retransmits collisions. Essentially, it's the Network Access layer's highway patrol.

- Specifying the MAC address. Even though the Internet layer determines the destination MAC address (the hardware address), the Network Access protocols actually place that MAC address in the MAC frame.

- Ensuring that the stream of bits making up the frame have been accurately received by calculating a CRC (Cyclic Redundancy Checksum) jellybean count.

- Specifying the access methods to the physical network, such as Contention-based for Ethernet (first come, first served), Token-passing (wait for token before transmitting) for Token Ring , FDDI, and Polling (wait to be asked) for IBM mainframes.

- Specifying the physical media, the connectors, electrical signaling, and timing rules.

Some of the technologies used to implement the Network Access layer are:

LAN-oriented protocols:

- Ethernet (thick coaxial cable, thin coaxial cable, twisted-pair cable)

- Token Ring

- FDDI

- ARCnet

WAN-oriented protocols:

- Point-to-Point Protocol (PPP)

- X.25

- Frame Relay

WAN physical layer protocols provide the same information and services the physical layer does for LANs: electrical, mechanical, operational, and functional connection services, only for wide-area networking services. One other difference is how these services are obtained. For a LAN, you would call

Cisco, 3Com, Bay, Cabletron, or other such vendors. For WAN services, you would typically call a WAN service provider like Pac-Bell, AT&T, or other alternate carriers known as Regional Bell Operating companies (RBOCs), and Post, Telephone, and Telegraph (PTT) agencies.

WAN protocols are defined by:

- International Telecommunication Union-Telecommunication Standardization Sector (ITU-T), which used to be the Consultative Committee for International Telegraph and Telephone (CCITT)

- International Organization for Standardization (ISO)

- Electronic Industries Association (EIA)

- Internet Engineering Task Force (IETF)

WAN standards usually describe and use both the Data Link and Physical layer specifications.

Now that we understand where TCP/IP came from and the different protocols related to it, we'll move on to Chapter 3 and take a look at IP addressing and subnetting a TCP/IP address.

CHAPTER

3

IP Addressing and Subnetting

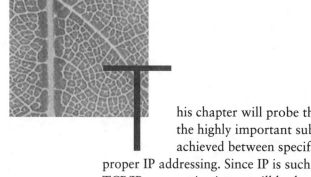

his chapter will probe the basics of TCP/IP further to explore the highly important subject of how accurate communication is achieved between specific networks and host systems through proper IP addressing. Since IP is such an integral part of the Internet and TCP/IP communications, we'll look at it again in greater detail to make sure its function is absolutely clear to you. You'll find bundles of information on how and why communication between devices happens, why it doesn't when it fails, and how to configure machines on both LANs and WANs to ensure solid performance for your network.

What Is IP Addressing?

An IP address is a numeric identifier assigned to each machine on an IP network that designates the location of the device it's assigned to on the network. As mentioned earlier, this type of address is a software address, not a hardware address, which is hard-coded in the machine or network interface card.

Ethernet (Hardware) Addresses

Each Ethernet board's Ethernet address is a unique 48-bit identification code. If it sounds unlikely that every Ethernet board in the world has a unique address, then consider that 48 bits offers 280,000,000,000,000 possibilities. Ethernet itself only uses about one-quarter of those possibilities (two bits are set aside for administrative functions), but hey, that's still a lot of possible addresses. In any case, the important thing to get here is that a board's Ethernet address is predetermined and hard-coded into it. Ethernet addresses, which are also called Media Access Control (MAC) addresses, are synonymous with Token Ring addresses or Ethernet addresses, and are expressed in 12 hex digits. (They have nothing to do with Macintoshes!) For example, the Ethernet card on the computer we're writing this book on has MAC (Ethernet) address 0020AFF8E771 or, as it's sometimes written, 00-20-AF-F8-E7-71. The addresses are centrally administered, and Ethernet chip vendors must purchase blocks of addresses. In the example of our workstation, we know that it's got a 3Com Ethernet card because the Ethernet (MAC) address begins 00-20-AF—the prefix owned by 3Com.

You can see an NT machine's MAC address in a number of ways. You can type **ipconfig /all** at a DOS prompt, check the listing under hardware address, or run Windows NT Diagnostics and click on Network/Transports.

The Hierarchical IP Addressing Scheme

In contrast to the 48 bits in a MAC address, an IP address is a 32-bit value. Another difference is that IP addresses are numbers set at a workstation (or server) by a network administrator—they're not a hard-coded hardware kind of address, unlike the Ethernet address. That means that there are four billion distinct Internet addresses.

It's nice that there's room for lots of machines, but having to remember—or having to tell someone else—a 32-bit address is not fun. Imagine having to say to a network support person, "Just set up the machines on the subnet to use a default router address of 10101110100101010010101100010111." Hmmm... not much of a ring to that! We humans just don't think that way. To avoid confusion and a whole bunch of mistakes, we definitely needed a more brain-friendly way to express 32-bit numbers. It's out of that need that *dotted quad* notation was created.

To clarify this, IP addresses can be represented as $w.x.y.z$, where w, x, y, and z are all sets with decimal values between 0 and 255. An example IP address is 199.34.57.53. Each of the four numbers are called *quads*, and each of these quads would be equivalent to one of our letters: 199 for w, 34 for x, 57 for y and 53 for z. It's called dotted quad notation because the quads are connected by dots.

Each of the numbers in the dotted quad corresponds to eight bits of an Internet address. As the value for eight bits can range from 0 to 255, each value in a dotted quad can be from 0 to 255. For example, to convert an IP address of 11001010000011111010101000000001 into dotted quad format, it would first be broken up into eight-bit sets:

11001010 00001111 10101010 00000001

If you're not comfortable with binary-to-decimal conversion, don't worry about it: Just load the NT calculator, click on View, then Scientific, and then press the F8 key to put the calculator in binary mode. Enter the binary number, press F6, and the number will be converted to decimal for you.

Each of those eight-bit numbers would be converted to their decimal equivalent. Our number converts as follows:

11001010	00001111	10101010	00000001
202	15	170	1

Which results in a dotted quad address of 202.15.170.1.

The whole idea behind 32-bit IP addresses is to make it relatively simple to segment the task of managing the Internet or, for that matter, *any* intranet. The 32-bit IP address is a structured, or hierarchical, address, as opposed to a flat, or nonhierarchical one. Although either type of addressing scheme could have been used, the hierarchical variety was chosen, and for a very good reason.

Because it seemed, in the early days of the Internet, that four billion addresses left plenty of space for growth, the original designers were a bit sloppy. They defined three classes of networks of the Internet: large networks, medium networks, and small networks. The creators of the Internet used 8-bit sections of the 32-bit addresses to delineate the difference between different classes of networks.

A good example of a flat addressing scheme is a social security number. There's no partitioning to it, meaning that each segment isn't allocated to numerically represent a certain area or characteristic of the individual it's assigned to. If this method had been used for IP addressing, every machine on the Internet would have needed a totally unique address, just as each social security number is unique. The good news about this scheme is that it can handle a large number of addresses, namely 4.3 billion (a 32-bit address space with two possible values for each position—either zero or one—giving you 2^{32}, which equals 4.3 billion). The bad news, and the reason for it being passed over, relates to routing. With every address totally unique, all routers on the Internet would need to store the address of each and every machine on the Internet. This would make efficient routing impossible even if a fraction of the possible addresses were used.

The solution to this dilemma is to use a two-level, hierarchical addressing scheme that's structured by class, rank, grade, and so on. An example of this type is a telephone number. The first section of a telephone number, the area code, designates a very large area, followed by the prefix, narrowing the scope to a local calling area. The final segment, the customer number, zooms in on the specific connection. It's similar with IP addresses. Rather than the entire 32 bits being treated as a unique identifier as in flat addressing, a part of the address is designated as the *network address*, and the other part as a *node address*, giving it a layered, hierarchical structure.

The network address uniquely identifies each network. Every machine on the same network shares that network address as part of its IP address. In the IP address 131.59.30.56, for example, the 131.59 is the network address.

The node address is assigned to, and uniquely identifies, each machine on a network. This part of the address must be unique because it identifies a particular machine—an individual, as opposed to a network, which is a group. This number can also be referred to as a *host address*. In the sample IP address 131.59.30.56, the 30.56 is the node address.

Class A, B, and C Networks

The NIC (Network Information Center) assigns to a company a block of IP addresses according to that company's size. Big companies get Class A networks (there are none left; they've all been given out), medium-sized companies get Class B networks (we're out of those, too), and others get Class C networks (still some left). Although there are three network classes, there are five kinds of IP addresses, as you'll see in Figure 3.1.

How one would subdivide an IP address into a network and node address is determined by the class designation of one's network. Table 3.1 provides a summary on the three classes of networks, which will be described in more detail in the following sections.

TABLE 3.1

Summary of the three classes of networks

Class	Format	Leading Bit Pattern	Decimal Range of First Byte of Network Address	Maximum Networks	Maximum Nodes per Network
A	Net.Node.Node.Node	0	1–127	127	16,777,216
B	Net.Net.Node.Node	10	128–191	16,384	65,534
C	Net.Net.Net.Node	110	192–223	2,097,152	254

F I G U R E 3.1

Internet network classes
and reserved addresses

0XXXXXXX AAAAAAAA	LLLLLLLL	LLLLLLLL	LLLLLLLL

Class A addresses: Values 0-126

01111111			

Reserved loopback address: Value 127

10XXXXXX AAAAAAAA	AAAAAAAA	LLLLLLLL	LLLLLLLL

Class B addresses: Values 128-191

110XXXXX AAAAAAAA	AAAAAAAA	AAAAAAAA	LLLLLLLL

Class C addresses: Values 192-223

1110XXXX			

Reserved multicast addresses: Values 224-239

11110XXXX			

Reserved experimental addresses: Values 240-255

A = Assigned by NIC
L = Locally administered

To ensure efficient routing, Internet designers defined a mandate for the leading bits section of the address for each different network class. For example, since a router knows that a Class A network address always starts with a zero, it might be able to speed a packet on its way after reading only the first bit of its address. Figure 3.2 illustrates how the leading bits of a network address are defined.

Class A Networks

A large network would have its first eight bits set by the NIC. The network's administrators have the remaining 24 bits to configure. The left-most eight bits could have values between 0 and 126, allowing for 127 Class A networks. Really big companies like IBM get these, and there are only 127 of these addresses. As only eight bits have been taken, 24 remain; that means that Class A networks can contain up to 2 to the 24th power, or 16 million hosts. Examples of Class A nets are BBN (1.0.0.0), General Electric (3.0.0.0),

FIGURE 3.2

Leading bits of
a network address

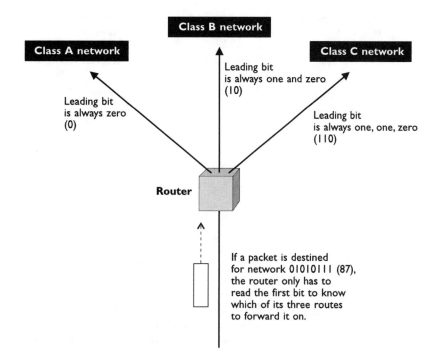

Hewlett-Packard (16.0.0.0), Apple (17), Columbia University (15), Xerox (13), IBM (9), DEC (16), and M.I.T. (18).

The Class A format is:

Network.Node.Node.Node

For example, in the IP address 49.22.102.70, 49 is the network address, and 22.102.70 is the node address. Every machine on this particular network would have the distinctive network address of 49.

With the length of a Class A network address being a byte, and with the first bit of that byte reserved, seven remain for manipulation. That means that the maximum number of Class A networks that could be created would be 128. Why? Because each of the seven bit positions can either be a zero or a one, thus 2^7 or 128. To complicate things further, it was also decided that the network address of all zeros (0000 0000) would be reserved (see Table 3.2). This means the actual number of usable Class A network addresses is 128 minus 1, or 127.

	Address	Function
T A B L E 3.2 Reserved IP addresses	Network address of all zeros	Interpreted to mean "this network"
	Network address of all ones	Interpreted to mean "all networks"
	Network 127	Reserved for loopback tests. Designates the local node and allows that node to send a test packet to itself without generating network traffic
	Node address of all zeros	Interpreted to mean "this node"
	Node address of all ones	Interpreted to mean "all nodes" on the specified network; for example, 128.2.255.255 means "all nodes" on network 128.2 (Class B address)
	Entire IP address set to all zeros	Used by the RIP protocol to designate the default route
	Entire IP address set to all ones (same as 255.255.255.255)	Broadcast to all nodes on the current network; sometimes called an "all ones broadcast"

Take a peek and see this for yourself in the decimal-to-binary chart (Table 3.3.) Start at binary 0 and view the first bit (the left-most bit). Continue down through the chart until the first bit turns into the digit one (1). See that? Sure enough, the decimal range of a Class A network is 0 through 127. Since the Much Ado About Nothing Address (all zeros) is one of those special, reserved-club members, the range of network addresses for a Class A network is 1 through 127. Eventually, we'll see that another Class A number is in that club—number 127. This little revelation technically brings the total down to 126.

	Decimal	Binary	Decimal	Binary	Decimal	Binary
T A B L E 3.3 Decimal-to-binary chart	0	0000 0000	5	0000 0101	10	0000 1010
	1	0000 0001	6	0000 0110	11	0000 1011
	2	0000 0010	7	0000 0111	12	0000 1100
	3	0000 0011	8	0000 1000	13	0000 1101
	4	0000 0100	9	0000 1001	14	0000 1110

	Decimal	Binary	Decimal	Binary	Decimal	Binary
TABLE 3.3 *(cont.)* Decimal-to-binary chart	15	0000 1111	36	0010 0100	57	0011 1001
	16	0001 0000	37	0010 0101	58	0011 1010
	17	0001 0001	38	0010 0110	59	0011 1011
	18	0001 0010	39	0010 0111	60	0011 1100
	19	0001 0011	40	0010 1000	61	0011 1101
	20	0001 0100	41	0010 1001	62	0011 1110
	21	0001 0101	42	0010 1010	63	0011 1111
	22	0001 0110	43	0010 1011	64	0100 0000
	23	0001 0111	44	0010 1100	65	0100 0001
	24	0001 1000	45	0010 1101	66	0100 0010
	25	0001 1001	46	0010 1110	67	0100 0011
	26	0001 1010	47	0010 1111	68	0100 0100
	27	0001 1011	48	0011 0000	69	0100 0101
	28	0001 1100	49	0011 0001	70	0100 0110
	29	0001 1101	50	0011 0010	71	0100 0111
	30	0001 1110	51	0011 0011	72	0100 1000
	31	0001 1111	52	0011 0100	73	0100 1001
	32	0010 0000	53	0011 0101	74	0100 1010
	33	0010 0001	54	0011 0110	75	0100 1011
	34	0010 0010	55	0011 0111	76	0100 1100
	35	0010 0011	56	0011 1000	77	0100 1101

	Decimal	Binary	Decimal	Binary	Decimal	Binary
T A B L E 3.3 (cont.) Decimal-to-binary chart	78	0100 1110	99	0110 0011	120	0111 1000
	79	0100 1111	100	0110 0100	121	0111 1001
	80	0101 0000	101	0110 0101	122	0111 1010
	81	0101 0001	102	0110 0110	123	0111 1011
	82	0101 0010	103	0110 0111	124	0111 1100
	83	0101 0011	104	0110 1000	125	0111 1101
	84	0101 0100	105	0110 1001	126	0111 1110
	85	0101 0101	106	0110 1010	127	0111 1111
	86	0101 0110	107	0110 1011	128	1000 0000
	87	0101 0111	108	0110 1100	129	1000 0001
	88	0101 1000	109	0110 1101	130	1000 0010
	89	0101 1001	110	0110 1110	131	1000 0011
	90	0101 1010	111	0110 1111	132	1000 0100
	91	0101 1011	112	0111 0000	133	1000 0101
	92	0101 1100	113	0111 0001	134	1000 0110
	93	0101 1101	114	0111 0010	135	1000 0111
	94	0101 1110	115	0111 0011	136	1000 1000
	95	0101 1111	116	0111 0100	137	1000 1001
	96	0110 0000	117	0111 0101	138	1000 1010
	97	0110 0001	118	0111 0110	139	1000 1011
	98	0110 0010	119	0111 0111	140	1000 1100

	Decimal	Binary	Decimal	Binary	Decimal	Binary
TABLE 3.3 *(cont.)* Decimal-to-binary chart	141	1000 1101	162	1010 0010	183	1011 0111
	142	1000 1110	163	1010 0011	184	1011 1000
	143	1000 1111	164	1010 0100	185	1011 1001
	144	1001 0000	165	1010 0101	186	1011 1010
	145	1001 0001	166	1010 0110	187	1011 1011
	146	1001 0010	167	1010 0111	188	1011 1100
	147	1001 0011	168	1010 1000	189	1011 1101
	148	1001 0100	169	1010 1001	190	1011 1110
	149	1001 0101	170	1010 1010	191	1011 1111
	150	1001 0110	171	1010 1011	192	1100 0000
	151	1001 0111	172	1010 1100	193	1100 0001
	152	1001 1000	173	1010 1101	194	1100 0010
	153	1001 1001	174	1010 1110	195	1100 0011
	154	1001 1010	175	1010 1111	196	1100 0100
	155	1001 1011	176	1011 0000	197	1100 0101
	156	1001 1100	177	1011 0001	198	1100 0110
	157	1001 1101	178	1011 0010	199	1100 0111
	158	1001 1110	179	1011 0011	200	1100 1000
	159	1001 1111	180	1011 0100	201	1100 1001
	160	1010 0000	181	1011 0101	202	1100 1010
	161	1010 0001	182	1011 0110	203	1100 1011

	Decimal	Binary	Decimal	Binary	Decimal	Binary
T A B L E 3.3 *(cont.)* Decimal-to-binary chart	204	1100 1100	222	1101 1110	240	1111 0000
	205	1100 1101	223	1101 1111	241	1111 0001
	206	1100 1110	224	1110 0000	242	1111 0010
	207	1100 1111	225	1110 0001	243	1111 0011
	208	1101 0000	226	1110 0010	244	1111 0100
	209	1101 0001	227	1110 0011	245	1111 0101
	210	1101 0010	228	1110 0100	246	1111 0110
	211	1101 0011	229	1110 0101	247	1111 0111
	212	1101 0100	230	1110 0110	248	1111 1000
	213	1101 0101	231	1110 0111	249	1111 1001
	214	1101 0110	232	1110 1000	250	1111 1010
	215	1101 0111	233	1110 1001	251	1111 1011
	216	1101 1000	234	1110 1010	252	1111 1100
	217	1101 1001	235	1110 1011	253	1111 1101
	218	1101 1010	236	1110 1100	254	1111 1110
	219	1101 1011	237	1110 1101	255	1111 1111
	220	1101 1100	238	1110 1110		
	221	1101 1101	239	1110 1111		

As said, each Class A network has three bytes (24 bit positions) for the node address of a machine. That means there are 2^{24}, or 16,777,216, unique combinations, and therefore precisely that many unique node addresses possible for each Class A network. If math just isn't your thing, we'll explain—again, using the multifarious jellybean. Say you packed 24 of those tasty little critters in your briefcase for a snack. Considering you only have 24, and therefore no intention of sharing, you divide your beans (bits), into three equal mouthfuls (bytes), readying them for lightning-quick consumption. While divvying them up, you notice how pretty they are, and get totally side-tracked—now absorbed in arranging them in various patterns and recording each grouping until you exhaust all possible unique combinations. Counting all your sequence entries, you make an important discovery: When one possesses 24 jellybeans, there are 16,777,216 possible unique combinations in which one can arrange them—or, 2^{24}. Try this next time you're bedridden, or just unspeakably bored.

Because addresses with the two patterns of all zeros and all ones are reserved, the actual maximum usable number of nodes per a Class A network is 2^{24} minus 2, which equals 16,777,214.

Class B Networks

Medium-sized networks have the left-most 16 bits preassigned to them, in theory, leaving 16 bits for local use to be set by the administrator. Class B addresses always have the values 128 through 191 in their first quad, then a value between 0 and 255 in their second quad.

In a Class B network the format is:

Network.Network.Node.Node

For example, in the IP address 131.59.30.56, the network address is 131.59, and the node address is 30.56.

With the network address being two bytes, there would be 2^{16} unique combinations. But the Internet designers decided that all Class B networks should start with the numbers 1 and 0. So, in reality, this leaves only 14 bit positions to manipulate, and therefore 2^{14} or 16,384 unique Class B networks. Consult jellybeans if confused.

If you take another peek at the decimal-to-binary chart (Table 3.3), you will see that the first two bits of the first byte are 10 from decimal 128 up to 191. Therefore, if you're still confused, even after a jellybean session, remember that you can always easily recognize a Class B network by looking at its first byte—even though there are 16,384 different Class B networks! All you have to do is look at that address. If the first byte is in the range of decimal 128 to 191, it is a Class B network.

A Class B network has two bytes to use for node addresses. This is 2^{16}, minus the two patterns in the reserved-exclusive club (all zeros and all ones), for a total of 65,534 possible node addresses for each Class B network. Microsoft and Exxon are examples of companies with Class B networks.

Class C Networks

Small networks have the left-most 24 bits preassigned to them, with only one measly byte remaining for the node address. This means that Class C networks can't have more than 254 hosts, but, as the NIC has 24 bits to work with, it has a large supply of Class C network addresses to dish out.

The first three bytes of a Class C network are dedicated to the network portion of the address, The format is:

Network.Network.Network.Node

In the example IP address 198.21.74.102, the network address is 198.21.74, and the node address is 102.

In a Class C network, the first *three* bit positions are always the binary 110. The calculation is such: Three bytes, or 24 bits, minus three reserved positions, leaves 21 positions. There are therefore 2^{21} or 2,097,152 possible Class C networks.

Referring again to that decimal-to-binary chart in Table 3.3, you will see that the lead bit pattern of 110 starts at decimal 192 and runs through 223. Remembering our handy, non-calculatory, easy-recognition method, this means that although there is a total of 2,097,152 Class C networks possible, you can always spot a Class C address if the first byte is between 192 and 223.

Each unique Class C network has one byte to use for node addresses. This leads to 2^8 or 256, minus the two special club patterns of all zeros and all ones, for a total of 254 node addresses for each Class C network. The last C network, when it's assigned, will be 223.255.255.*x*. Remember, the owner of that network will be able to control only *x*.

Additional Classes of Networks

Another class of network is Class D. This range of addresses is used for multicast packets. The range of numbers is from 224.0.0.0 to 239.255.255.255.

A multicast transmission is used when a host wants to broadcast to multiple destinations. Hosts do this when attempting to learn of all the routers on its network. Using the ICMP protocol, it sends out a router discovery packet. This packet is addressed to 224.0.0.2, fingering it as a multicast packet to all the routers on its network.

There is also a Class E range of numbers starting at 240.0.0.0 and running to 255.255.255.255. These numbers are reserved for future use.

Unless you revel in chaos, and desire to add stress to your life, neither Class D nor Class E addresses should be assigned to nodes on your network.

Reserved Addresses: You Can't Use *All* of the Numbers

As alluded to earlier and shown in Table 3.2, there's a whole bunch of numbers you simply cannot give to a machine. They're called the loopback address, the network number, the broadcast address, and the default router address.

The Loopback Address

The address 127.0.0.1 is reserved as a loopback. This means if you send a message to 127.0.0.1, then it should be returned to you, and will be unless there's something wrong with your connection on the network. And so, no network has an address 127.*xxxxxxxx.xxxxxxxx.xxxxxxxx*, (an unfortunate waste of 24 million addresses!)

The Network Number

Sometimes you need to refer to an entire subnet with a single number. It's therefore necessary to have an official way to refer to a range of addresses. For example, to tell a router, "To get this message to the subnet that ranges from 100.100.100.0 through 100.100.100.255, first route to the router at 99.98.97.103," you've got to have some way to designate the range of addresses 100.100.100.0 through 100.100.100.255. We could have just used two addresses with a hyphen between them, but that's a bit cumbersome. Instead, the address that ends in all binary zeros is reserved as the network number, the TCP/IP name for the range of addresses in a subnet. In our 100.100.100.*x* example, the shorthand way to refer to 100.100.100.0 through 100.100.100.255 is "100.100.100.0".

Notice that this means you would never use the address 100.100.100.0— you *never* give that IP address to a machine under TCP/IP.

For example, to tell that router, "To get this message to the subnet that ranges from 100.100.100.0 through 100.100.100.255, first route to the router at 99.98.97.103," you would type something like route add 100.100.100.0 99.98.97.103. (Actually, you'd type a bit more information, and we'll get to that in an upcoming section on using your NT machine as a router, but this example gives you the idea.)

IP Broadcast Address

There's another reserved address, as well—the TCP/IP broadcast address. It looks like the address of one machine, but it's actually the address you'd use to broadcast to each machine on a subnet. That address is all binary ones.

For example, on a simple Class C subnet, the broadcast address would be *x.y.z*.255. When would you need to know this? Some IP software needs this when you configure it; most routers require the broadcast address as well as the network number. So if we just use our Class C network 199.34.57.0 (see how convenient that .0 thing is?) as a single subnet, then the broadcast address for our network would be 199.34.57.255.

Default Router Address

Every subnet has at least one router; after all, if it didn't have a router, then the subnet couldn't talk to any other networks, and we wouldn't have an intranet.

By convention, the first address after the network number is the *subnet mask*. For example, on a simple Class C network, the address of the router should be x.y.z.1. This is not, by the way, a hard-and-fast rule like the network number and the IP broadcast address—it is, instead, a convention.

Suppose you have just been made the proud owner of a Class C net, 222 .210.34.0. You can put 253 computers on your network, because you can't use the following addresses:

- 222.210.34.0, which describes the entire network

- 222.210.34.255, your broadcast address

- and 222.210.34.1, which will be used either by you or your Internet service provider for a router address between your network and the rest of the Internet

Now, once you get a range of addresses from the NIC, then you are said to have an *IP domain*. (Domain in Internet lingo has nothing to do with domain in the NT security sense.) For example, Mark's IP domain (which is named mmco.com, but we'll cover names in Chapter 5) uses addresses in the 199.34 .57.0 network, and Mark can have as many NT domains in there as he likes. However, from the point of view of the outside Internet, all of his NT domains are included in just one Internet domain, mmco.com.

Who Assigns Network Addresses?

If your network will be connected to the Internet, you must be proper and petition the official Internet authorities for the assignment of a network address. An official Internet organization called the Network Information Center (NIC) can assist you in this process. For further information, contact:

Network Solutions
InterNIC Registration Services
505 Huntmar Park Drive
Herndon, VA 22070

You may also obtain help by sending e-mail to:

`hostmaster@internic.net`

If you're just going to build your own intranet and you don't want to connect to the Internet, then you don't have to call up the NIC to get addresses. If you ever want to connect to the outside world, however, then you should get an NIC-approved address before moving very far forward with TCP/IP. You can always get an address and use it internally until you're ready to "go public."

For the most part, you are now able to obtain valid IP addresses from your Internet service provider (ISP). The NIC would prefer for you to do it that way, as it cuts down on work they need to do. See `ftp://rs.internic.net/ internet-number-template.txt` for rules regarding obtaining numbers.

Subnetting a Network

If you had a tiny intranet, one with just one subnet, then all the devices in your network can simply transmit directly to each other, and no routing is required. If you actually had a network like this, then TCP/IP is overkill, and you probably should use NetBEUI instead. If an organization is large and has a whole bunch of computers, or if its computers are geographically dispersed, it makes good clean sense to divide its colossal network into smaller ones connected together by routers. The benefits to doings things this way include:

- **Reduced network traffic.** We all appreciate less traffic of any kind! So do networks. Without trusty routers, packet traffic could grind the entire network down to a near standstill. With them, most traffic will stay on the local network—only packets destined for other networks will pass through the router.

- **Optimized network performance,** a bonus of reduced network traffic.

- **Simplified management.** It's easier to identify and isolate network problems in a group of smaller networks connected together than within one gigantic one.

- **Ability to assist.** Essentially different than being "able" to span large geographical distances. Because WAN links are considerably slower and more expensive than LAN links, having a single large network spanning long distances can create problems in every arena listed above. Connecting multiple smaller networks makes the system more efficient.

All this is well and good, but if an organization with multiple networks has been assigned only one network address by the NIC, that organization has a problem. As the saying goes, "Where there is no vision, the people perish." The original designers of the IP protocol envisioned a teensy Internet with only mere tens of networks and hundreds of hosts. Their addressing scheme used a network address for each physical network.

As you can imagine, this scheme and the unforeseen growth of the Internet created a few problems. To name one, a single network address can be used to refer to multiple physical networks. An organization can request individual network addresses for each one of its physical networks. If these were granted, there wouldn't be enough to go around for everyone. Another problem relates to routers. If each router on the Internet needed to know about each existing physical network, routing tables would be impossibly huge. There would be an overwhelming amount of administrative overhead to maintain those tables, and the resulting physical overhead on the routers would be massive (CPU cycles, memory, disk space, and so on).

An additional consequence is that since routers exchange routing information with each other, a terrific overabundance of network traffic would result. Figure 3.3 illustrates some of these problems.

Although there's more than one way to approach this tangle, the principal solution is the one that we'll be covering in this book...subnetting.

Subnetting is a dandy TCP/IP software feature that allows for dividing a single IP network into smaller, logical subnetworks. This trick is achieved by using the host portion of an IP address to create something called a subnet address.

Subnetting is network procreation. It's the act of creating little subnetworks from a single, large parent network. An organization with a single network address can have a subnet address for each individual physical network. Each subnet is still part of the shared network address, but it also has an additional identifier denoting its individual subnetwork number. This identifier is called a subnet address. Take a parent who has two kids. The children inherit the same last name as their parent. People make further distinctions when referring to someone's individual children like, "Kelly, the Jones's oldest, who moved into their guest house, and Jamie, the Jones's youngest, who now has Kelly's old room." Those further distinctions are like subnet addresses for people.

This practice solves several addressing problems. First, if an organization has several physical networks but only one IP network address, it can handle the situation by creating subnets. Next, because subnetting allows many physical networks to be grouped together, fewer entries in a routing table are

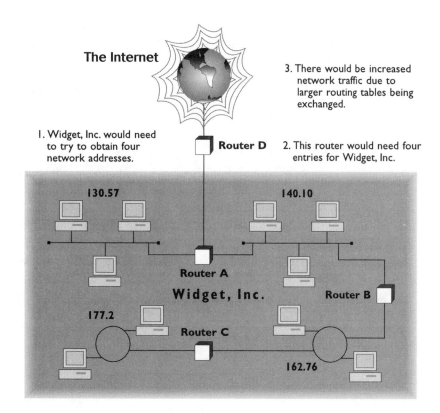

The Internet

3. There would be increased
network traffic due to
larger routing tables being
exchanged.

1. Widget, Inc. would need
to try to obtain four
network addresses.

Router D   2. This router would need four
entries for Widget, Inc.

130.57   140.10

Router A

Widget, Inc.   Router B

177.2

Router C

162.76

required, notably reducing network overhead. Finally, these things combine
to greatly enhance network efficiency.

Information Hiding

As an example, suppose that the Internet refers to Widget, Inc. only by its single
network address, 130.57. Suppose as well that Widget Inc. has several divi-
sions, each dealing with something different. Since Widget's network administrators have implemented subnetting, when packets come into its network, the
Widget routers use the subnet addresses to route the packets to the correct
internal subnet. Thus, the complexity of Widget, Inc.'s network can be hidden
from the rest of the Internet. This is called *information hiding*.

Information hiding also benefits the routers inside the Widget network. Without subnets, each Widget router would need to know the address of each machine
on the entire Widget network—a bleak situation creating additional overhead and

poor routing performance. But alas because of the subnet scheme, which alleviates the need for each router to know about every machine on the entire Widget network, their routers need only two types of information:

- The addresses of each machine on subnets to which it is attached

- The other subnet addresses

How to Implement Subnetting

Subnetting is implemented by assigning a subnet address to each machine on a given physical network. For example, in Figure 3.4, each machine on subnet 1 has a subnet address of 1. Next, we'll take a look at how a subnet address is incorporated into the rest of the IP address.

FIGURE 3.4

The use of subnets

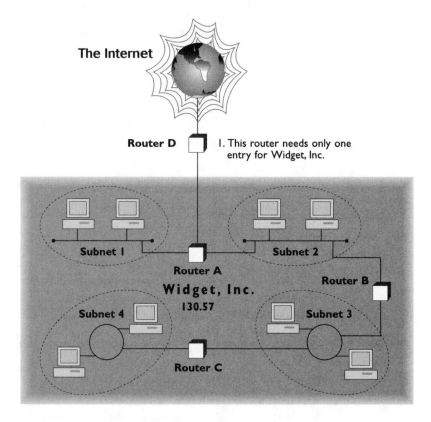

The network portion of an IP address can't be altered. Every machine on a particular network must share the same network address. In Figure 3.5, you can see that all of Widget, Inc.'s machines have a network address of 130.57. That principle is constant. In subnetting, it's the host address that's manipulated. The subnet address scheme takes a part of the host address and redesignates it as a subnet address. Bit positions are stolen from the host address to be used for the subnet identifier. Figure 3.5 shows how an IP address can be given a subnet address.

FIGURE 3.5

An IP address can be given a subnet address by manipulating the host address.

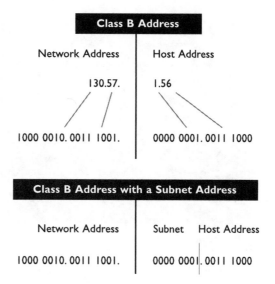

Subnetting a Class B Network

Since the Widget, Inc. network is the Class B variety, the first two bytes refer to the network address, and are shared by all machines on the network—regardless of their particular subnet. Here, every machine's address on the subnet must have its third byte read 0000 0001. The fourth byte, the host address, is the unique number—the portion we'd mess around with when subnetting. Figure 3.6 illustrates how a network address and a subnet address can be used. The same concepts and practices apply to each subnet created in the network.

FIGURE 3.6

A network address and a
subnet address

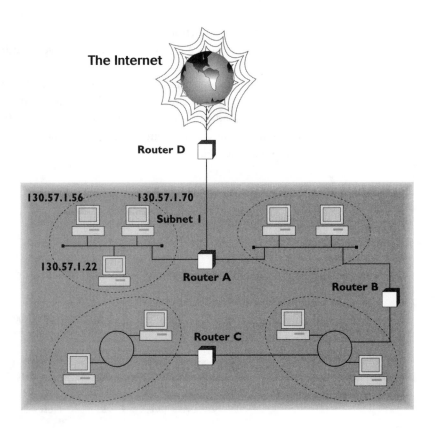

In our Widget, Inc. example, the first two bytes of the subnet mask are ones because Widget's network address is a Class B address formatted Net.Net.Node .Node. Figure 3.7 illustrates these concepts.

The third byte, normally assigned as part of the host address, is now used to represent the subnet address. Hence, those bit positions are represented with ones in the subnet mask. The fourth byte is the only part in our example that represents the unique host address.

The subnet mask can also be denoted using the decimal equivalents of the binary patterns. The binary pattern of 1111 1111 is the same as decimal 255 (see the decimal-to-binary chart in Table 3.3). Consequently, the subnet mask in our example can be denoted in two ways, as shown in Figure 3.8.

All networks don't need to have subnets, and therefore don't need to use subnet masks. In this event, they are said to have a default subnet mask. This is basically the same as saying they don't have a subnet address. The default subnet masks for the different classes of networks are shown in Table 3.4.

FIGURE 3.7

A subnet mask

Subnet Mask Code

1s = Positions representing network or subnet addresses
0s = Positions representing the host address

Subnet Mask for Widget, Inc.

```
IIII IIII. IIII IIII. IIII IIII. 0000 0000
```

Network Address   Subnet   Host
Positions   Positions   Positions

FIGURE 3.8

Subnet mask depiction

Subnet Mask in Binary: `IIII IIII. IIII IIII. IIII IIII. 0000 0000`

Subnet Mask in Decimal: 255 .   255   .   255   .   0

(The spaces in the above example are only for illustrative purposes.
The subnet mask in decimal would actually appear as 255.255.255.0.)

TABLE 3.4

Default subnet masks

Class	Format	Default Subnet Mask
A	Net.Node.Node.Node	255.0.0.0
B	Net.Net.Node.Node	255.255.0.0
C	Net.Net.Net.Node	255.255.255.0

Once the network administrator has created the subnet mask and assigned it to each machine, the IP software views its IP address through the subnet mask to determine its subnet address. The word mask carries the implied meaning of a lens because the IP software looks at its IP address through the lens of its subnet mask, to see its subnet address. An illustration of an IP address being viewed through a subnet mask is shown in Figure 3.9.

Subnet Mask Code

1s = Positions representing network or subnet addresses

0s = Positions representing the host address

Positions relating to the subnet address

Subnet Mask: 1111 1111. 1111 1111. 1111 1111. 0000 0000

IP address of a machine on subnet 1: 1000 0010. 0011 1001. 0000 0001. 0011 1000
(Decimal: 130.57.1.56)

Bits relating to the subnet address

In this example, the IP software learns through the subnet mask that, instead of being part of the host address, the third byte of its IP address is now going to be used as a subnet address. IP then looks at the bit positions in its IP address that correspond to the mask, which are 0000 0001.

The final step is for the subnet bit values to be matched up with the binary numbering convention and converted to decimal. The binary numbering convention is shown in Figure 3.10.

Binary Numbering Convention

Position / Value: ◄— (continued) 128 64 32 16 8 4 2 1

Binary Example: 0   0   0   1 0 0 1 0

Decimal Equivalent: 16 + 2 = 18

In the Widget, Inc. example, the binary-to-decimal conversion is simple, as illustrated in Figure 3.11.

FIGURE 3.11

Binary-to-decimal
conversion

Binary Numbering Convention

Position / Value:	◄— (continued) 128 64 32 16 8 4 2 1
Widget Third Byte:	0 0 0 0 0 0 0 1
Decimal Equivalent:	0 + 1 = 1
Subnet Address:	1

By using the entire third byte of a Class B address as the subnet address, it is easy to set and determine the subnet address. For example, if Widget, Inc. wants to have a subnet 6, the third byte of all machines on that subnet will be 0000 0110. The binary-to-decimal conversion for this subnet mask is shown in Figure 3.12.

FIGURE 3.12

Setting a subnet

Binary Numbering Convention

Position / Value:	◄— (continued) 128 64 32 16 8 4 2 1
Binary Example:	0 0 0 0 0 1 1 0
Decimal Equivalent:	4 + 2 = 6
Subnet Address:	6

Using the entire third byte of a Class B network address for the subnet allows for a fair number of available subnet addresses. One byte dedicated to the subnet provides eight bit positions. Each position can be either a one or a zero, so the calculation is 2^8, or 256. But since you cannot use the two patterns of all zeros and all ones, you must subtract two, for a total of 254. Thus, our Widget, Inc. company can have up to 254 total subnetworks, each with 254 hosts.

Although the official IP specification limits the use of zero as a subnet address, some products do permit this usage. The Novell TCP/IP implementation for NetWare 4 and the Novell MultiProtocol Router (MPR) software are examples of products that do permit zero as a subnet address. This allows one additional subnet number. For example, if the subnet mask was 8 bits, rather than $2^8 = 256 - 2 = 254$, it would be $256 - 1 = 255$.

WARNING Allowing a subnet address of zero increases the number of subnet numbers by one. However, you should not use a subnet of zero (all zeros) unless all the software on your network recognizes this convention.

The formulas for calculating the maximum number of subnets and the maximum number of hosts per subnet are:

$$2^{\text{(number of masked bits in subnet mask)}} - 2 = \text{maximum number of subnets}$$
$$2^{\text{(number of unmasked bits in subnet mask)}} - 2 = \text{maximum number of hosts per subnet}$$

In the formulas, *masked* refers to bit positions of 1, and *unmasked* refers to positions of 0. Figure 3.13 shows an example of how these formulas can be applied.

FIGURE 3.13

Subnet and node formulas

Network Address: 161.11 (class B)

	Network	Subnet	
		Masked	Unmasked
Subnet Mask:	IIII IIII. IIII IIII.	IIIO 0000.	0000 0000
Decimal:	255 . 255 .	224 .	0

The downside to using an entire byte of a node address as your subnet address is that you reduce the possible number of node addresses on each subnet. As explained earlier, without a subnet, a Class B address has 65,534 unique combinations of ones and zeros that can be used for node addresses. If you use an entire byte of the node address for a subnet, you then have only one byte for the host addresses, leaving only 254 possible host addresses. If any of your subnets will be populated with more than 254 machines, you have a problem on your hands. To solve it, you would then need to shorten the subnet mask, thereby lengthening the host address, which benefits you with more potential host addresses. A side-effect of this solution is that it causes the reduction of the number of possible subnets. Time to prioritize!

Figure 3.14 shows an example of using a smaller subnet address. A company called Acme, Inc. expects to need a maximum of 14 subnets. In this case, Acme does not need to take an entire byte from the host address for the subnet address. To get its 14 different subnet addresses, it only needs to snatch 4 bits from the host address ($2^4 - 2 = 14$). The host portion of the address has 12 usable bits remaining, equaling $2^{12} - 2 = 4,094$. Each of Acme's 14 subnets could then potentially have a total of 4,094 host addresses, or 4,094 machines on each subnet.

FIGURE 3.14

Using four bits of the host address for a subnet address

Acme, Inc.

Network Address: 132.8 (Class B; net.net.host.host)

Example IP Address: 1000 0100. 0000 1000. 0001 0010. 0011 1100

Decimal: 132 . 8 . 18 . 60

Subnet Mask Code

1s = Positions representing network or subnet addresses
0s = Positions representing the host address

Subnet Mask:

Binary: 1111 1111. 1111 1111. 1111 0000. 0000 0000

Decimal: 255 . 255 . 240 . 0

(The decimal '240' is equal to the binary '1111 0000.'
Refer to Table 33.3: Decimal-to-Binary Chart.)

Positions relating to the subnet address

Subnet Mask: 1111 1111. 1111 1111. 1111 0000. 0000 0000

IP Address of a Acme Machine: 1000 0100. 0000 1000. 0001 0010. 0011 1100
(Decimal: 132.8.18.60)

Bits relating to the subnet address

Binary-to-Decimal Conversion for Subnet Address

Subnet Mask Positions:	1	1	1	1	0	0	0	0
Position / Value: ← (continue)	128	64	32	16	8	4	2	1
Third Byte of IP Address:	0	0	0	1	0	0	1	0
Decimal Equivalent:				0 + 16 = 16				
Subnet Address for This IP Address:				16				

Subnetting a Class C Network

If you're going to break down your subnets smaller than Class C, then having to figure out the subnet mask, network number, broadcast address, and router address can get kind of confusing. Table 3.5 summarizes how you can break a Class C network down into one, two, four, or eight smaller subnets, with the attendant subnet masks, network numbers, broadcast addresses, and router addresses. We're assuming here that you're starting from a Class C address (the most common), so you'll only be working with the fourth quad. The first three quads have simply been designated x.y.z.

TABLE 3.5 Breaking a Class C network into subnets	Number of Desired Subnets	Subnet Mask	Network Number	Router Address	Broadcast Address	Remaining Number of IP Addresses
	1	255.255.255.0	x.y.z.0	x.y.z.1	x.y.z.255	253
	2	255.255.255.128	x.y.z.0	x.y.z.1	x.y.z.127	125
		255.255.255.	x.y.z.128	x.y.z.129	x.y.z.255	125
	4	255.255.255.192	x.y.z.0	x.y.z.1	x.y.z.63	61
		255.255.255.	x.y.z.64	x.y.z.65	x.y.z.127	61
		255.255.255.	x.y.z.128	x.y.z.129	x.y.z.191	61
		255.255.255.	x.y.z.192	x.y.z.193	x.y.z.255	61
	8	255.255.255.224	x.y.z.0	x.y.z.1	x.y.z.31	29
		255.255.255.	x.y.z.32	x.y.z.33	x.y.z.63	29
		255.255.255.	x.y.z.64	x.y.z.65	x.y.z.95	29
		255.255.255.	x.y.z.96	x.y.z.97	x.y.z.127	29
		255.255.255.	x.y.z.128	x.y.z.129	x.y.z.159	29
		255.255.255.	x.y.z.160	x.y.z.161	x.y.z.191	29
		255.255.255.	x.y.z.192	x.y.z.193	x.y.z.223	29
		255.255.255.	x.y.z.224	x.y.z.225	x.y.z.255	29

For example, suppose you want to chop up a Class C network, 200.211 .192.x, into two subnets. As you see in the table, you'd use a subnet mask of 255.255.255.128 for each subnet. The first subnet would have network number 200.211.192.0, router address 200.211.192.1, and broadcast address 200.211.192.127. You could assign IP addresses 200.211.192.2 through

200.211.192.126, creating 125 different IP addresses. (Notice that heavily subnetting a network results in the loss of a greater and greater percentage of addresses to the network number, broadcast address, and router address.) The second subnet would have network number 200.211.192.128, router address 200.211.192.129, and broadcast address 200.211.192.255.

In case you're wondering, it is entirely possible to subnet further, into 16 subnets of 13 hosts apiece (remember, you always lose three numbers for the network number, router address, and broadcast address) or 32 subnets of 5 hosts apiece, but at that point, you're losing an awful lot of addresses to IP overhead.

Classless Internetwork Domain Routing (CIDR)

Now that we've gotten past some of the finer points of subnet masks, let's elaborate on what you'll see if you ever go to the InterNIC looking for a domain of your own.

The shortage of IP addresses has led the InterNIC to curtail giving out Class A, B, and C addresses. Many small companies need an Internet domain, but giving them a C network is overkill, as a C network contains 256 addresses, and many small firms only have a dozen or so computers they want connected to the Inter-net. For reasons of security, large companies may also want a similarly small presence on the Internet—they may not want the bulk of their computers accessible through the Internet, but would rather keep them confined to an internal network not attached to the outside world. These companies *do* need a presence on the Internet, however—for their e-mail servers, FTP servers, Web servers, and the like—so they need a dozen or so addresses. But, again, giving them an entire 256-address C network is awfully wasteful. However, until 1994, it was the smallest block that the NIC could hand out.

Similarly, some companies need a few hundred addresses—more than 256, but not very many more. Such a firm is too big for a C network, but a bit small for the 65,536 addresses of a B network. More flexibility here would again be very useful.

Because of these types of scenarios, the InterNIC now gives out addresses without the old Class A, B, or C restrictions. The new method used by the InterNIC is called Classless Internet Domain Routing, or CIDR (pronounced "cider"). CIDR networks are described as "slash x" networks, where x represents the number of bits in the IP address range that the InterNIC controls.

If you had a Class A network, then the InterNIC controlled the top 8 bits, and you controlled the bottom 24. If you decided somehow to take your Class A network and make it one big subnet, then what would be your subnet mask? Since all of your A network would be one subnet, you'd only have to look at the top quad to see if the source and destination addresses were on the same subnet. For example, if you had network 4.0.0.0, then addresses 4.55.22.81 and 4.99.63.88 would be on the same subnet. (Please note that we can't actually imagine anyone doing this with a Class A net; we're just trying to make CIDR clearer.) Your subnet mask would then be 11111111 00000000 00000000 00000000 or 255.0.0.0. Reading from the left, you have eight ones in the subnet mask before the zeros start. In CIDR terminology, you wouldn't have a Class A network; rather, you would have a *slash 8* network.

With Class B, the InterNIC controlled the top 16 bits, and you controlled the bottom 16. If you decided to take that Class B network and make it a one-subnet network, then your subnet mask would be 11111111 11111111 00000000 00000000 or 255.255.0.0. Reading from the left, the subnet mask would have 16 ones. In CIDR terms, a B network is a *slash 16* network.

With Class C, the InterNIC controlled the top 24 bits, and you controlled the bottom 8. By now, you've seen that the subnet mask for a C network treated as one subnet is 11111111 11111111 11111111 00000000. Reading from the left, the subnet mask would have 24 ones—or in CIDR terms, a C network is a *slash 24* network.

With CIDR's new flexibility, the InterNIC can, in theory, not only define the A, B, and C type networks, it can offer networks with subnet masks in between the A, B, and C networks. For example, suppose we wanted a network for 50 PCs. Before, the InterNIC would have to give us a C network, with 256 addresses. But now they can offer us a network with subnet mask 11111111 11111111 11111111 11000000 (255.255.255.192), giving us only six bits to play with. Two to the sixth power is 64, so we'd have 64 addresses to do with as we pleased. This would be a *slash 26* network.

Table 3.6 shows how large each possible network type would be.

	InterNIC Network Type	"Subnet Mask" for Entire Network	Approximate Number of IP Addresses
TABLE 3.6 CIDR network types	slash 0	0.0.0.0	4 billion
	slash 1	128.0.0.0	2 billion
	slash 2	192.0.0.0	1 billion
	slash 3	224.0.0.0	500 million
	slash 4	240.0.0.0	250 million
	slash 5	248.0.0.0	128 million
	slash 6	252.0.0.0	64 million
	slash 7	254.0.0.0	32 million
	slash 8	255.0.0.0	16 million
	slash 9	255.128.0.0	8 million
	slash 10	255.192.0.0	4 million
	slash 11	255.224.0.0	2 million
	slash 12	255.240.0.0	1 million
	slash 13	255.248.0.0	524,288
	slash 14	255.252.0.0	262,144
	slash 15	255.254.0.0	131,072
	slash 16	255.255.0.0	65,536
	slash 17	255.255.128.0	32,768
	slash 18	255.255.192.0	16,384
	slash 19	255.255.224.0	8,192

TABLE 3.6 (cont.) CIDR network types	Internic Network Type	"Subnet Mask" for Entire Network	Approximate Number of IP Addresses
	slash 20	255.255.240.0	4,096
	slash 21	255.255.248.0	2,048
	slash 22	255.255.252.0	1,024
	slash 23	255.255.254.0	512
	slash 24	255.255.255.0	256
	slash 25	255.255.255.128	128
	slash 26	255.255.255.192	64
	slash 27	255.255.255.224	32
	slash 28	255.255.255.240	16
	slash 29	255.255.255.248	8
	slash 30	255.255.255.252	4
	slash 31	255.255.255.254	2
	slash 32	255.255.255.255	1

We hope it's obvious that we've included all of those networks just for the sake of completeness, as some of them simply aren't available or reasonable. The slash 0, and some others like the slash 31, just don't make sense. (Slash 31 only gives you two addresses, which would be immediately required for network number and broadcast address, leaving none behind for you to actually use!)

CIDR is a fact of life if you're registering networks with the InterNIC nowadays. With the information in this section, you'll more easily be able to understand what an Internet service provider (ISP) is talking about when it says it can get you a "slash 26" network.

Next we're going to take a look at IP routing with NT and with third-party routers.

CHAPTER

4

IP Routing

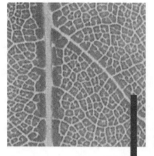

P exists to make it possible for messages to travel from one part of a network to another—but, exactly how does it do this?

Well, to begin, an intranet is made of at least two subnets. The idea of a subnet is built upon the fact that most popular LAN architectures (Ethernet, Token Ring, and ARCNet) are based on something very much like a radio broadcast. Everyone on the same Ethernet segment hears all of the traffic on their segment, just as each device on a given ring in a Token Ring network must examine every message that goes through the network. The trick that makes an Ethernet or a Token Ring work is that while each station *hears* everything, each station also knows how to ignore all messages except for those intended for it.

You may have never realized it, but that means that in a single Ethernet segment, or a single Token Ring ring, there is *no routing*. After sitting through our riveting explanation of the OSI seven-layer network model, you know that much is made of the *Network layer*, which, in OSI terms, is merely the routing layer. Yet a simple Ethernet or Token Ring never has to route. There are no routing decisions to make; as said, everything is heard by everybody. The network adapter on your machine filters out any traffic not destined for you.

Now suppose you have *two* separate Ethernets connected to each other, as you see in Figure 4.1. We've named these two Ethernet segments Rome and Carthage. (We were getting tired of the "shipping" and "finance" examples everyone uses.) The three computers that reside solely in Rome are labeled A, B, and C. Three more computers reside in Carthage, labeled F, G, and H.

FIGURE 4.1

Multisegment intranet

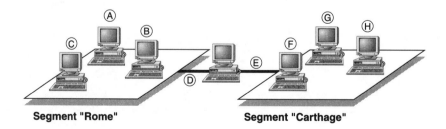

Subnets and Routers

Much of intranet architecture is built around the observation that PCs A, B, and C can communicate directly with each other, as can PCs F, G, and H. Things get a little more complicated when A, B, and C need to communicate with F, G, and H. These two groups *cannot* communicate without some help from the machine containing Ethernet cards D and E. That D/E machine functions as a *router*, a machine that enables communication between different network segments. A, B, C, and D could be described as being in each others' "broadcast range," as could E, F, G, and H. What we've just dubbed a broadcast range is known in intranet terminology as the ubiquitous subnet— a collection of machines that can communicate with each other without the need for routing.

For example, F and H can communicate directly without having to ask the router (E, in their case) to forward the message because they're on the same subnet. A and C can communicate directly without having to ask the router (D, in their case) to forward the message because they're on the same subnet. Because they're not on the same subnet, if B wanted to talk to G, it would have to first send the message to D, asking, "D, please get this over to G."

IP Routers

Now let's return to the computer in the middle. It's part of *both* segments. How in the world do we get one computer to be part of two networks? Well, we do so by putting two Ethernet cards in that computer in the middle. A computer with more than one network card in it is called a *multihomed* computer. One of the Ethernet cards is on the Rome subnet, and the other is on the Carthage subnet. As you've probably figured out by now, each computer on an intranet is called a host in TCP/IP language.

Now, since each Ethernet card must get a separate IP address, the computer in the middle has *two* IP addresses, address D and address E. If a message is transmitted in Rome, then adapter D hears it, but E doesn't. If a message is transmitted in Carthage, then adapter E hears it, but D doesn't.

How would we build an intranet from these two subnets? How could station A, for example, send a message to station G? Obviously, the only way that message will get from A to G is if the message is received on the Ethernet adapter with address D, and then re-sent out over the Ethernet adapter with address E. Once E re-sends the message, G will hear it, since it's on the same network as E—sweet!

In order for this to work, the machine containing boards D and E must be "smart" enough to perform this function of re-sending data between D and E when required. Though these brilliant machines are usually IP routers, with Windows NT, it's possible to use an NT computer—any NT computer, not just an NT Server computer—to act as an IP router, as you'll learn later.

Under IP, the sending machine (A, in this case) examines the address of the destination (G, in this case) and realizes that it doesn't know how to get to it. (We'll explain exactly *how* it knows that in a minute.) Now, if A has to send something to an address that it doesn't understand, then it uses a kind of "catchall" address called the *default router* or *default gateway* address. A's network administrator has already configured A's default router as D, so A sends the message to D. Once D gets the message, it sees that the message isn't destined for itself, but rather for G, and so it re-sends the message from board E.

Routing in More Detail

Now let's look a little closer at how that message gets from A to G. Each computer, as you've already seen, has one *or more* IP addresses. It's important to understand that there is no relationship whatsoever between the address on an Ethernet card and the IP address associated with it. Remember, the MAC address is hardcoded into the card by the card's manufacturer and doesn't ever change. IP addresses are assigned by a network administrator, and can change as the administrator sees fit.

If you examine the IP addresses, you'll see a pattern to them. Rome's addresses all look like 199.34.57.*x*, where *x* is some number, and Carthage's addresses all look like 156.40.10.*x*, where, again, *x* can be any number. The Ethernet addresses follow no rhyme or reason and are grouped by the board's manufacturer. That similarity of addresses within Rome and Carthage is important in understanding routing.

Now, let's re-examine how the message gets from A to G.

1. The IP software in A first asks, "How do I get this message to G—can I just broadcast it, or does it have to be routed?" The way it makes that decision is by finding out whether or not G is on the same *subnet* as A. A subnet is simply a broadcast area. Host A is in essence asking, "Is G part of Rome—a Roman like me?"

2. Station A determines it's on a different subnet from station G by examining IP addresses. Machine A knows its address is 199.34.57.10, and that it must send its message to 156.40.10.50. A has a very simple rule for this little situation: If the destination address looks like 199.34.57.x (where, again, *x* can be any value), then the destination is in the same subnet and requires no routing. On the other hand, 156.40.10.50 is clearly *not* in the same subnet. It comes down to simple matching.

Alternately, if G *had* been on the same subnet, then A would have broadcast the IP packet straight to G, referring specifically to its IP and Ethernet address.

3. So station A determines it can't directly send its IP packets to G. However, since it's been instructed to send G the message, it then looks for a way to do that. When A's network administrator set up A's IP software, she told A the IP address of its *default router*. The default router is basically the address that says, "If you don't know where to send something, send it to me, and I'll try to get it there." A's default router is configured as D.

A then sends an Ethernet frame from itself to D. The Ethernet frame contains this information:

- Source Ethernet address: 14

- Destination Ethernet address: 100

- Source IP address: 199.34.57.10

- Destination IP address: 156.40.10.50

4. Ethernet card D receives the frame and hands it to the IP software running in its PC. The PC sees that the IP destination address doesn't match its own, so the PC knows it must route the packet. Examining the network, it sees the destination lies on the subnet that Ethernet adapter E is on, so it sends a frame out from Ethernet adapter E with this information:

- Source Ethernet address: 100

- Destination Ethernet address: 115

- Source IP address: 199.34.57.10

- Destination IP address: 156.40.10.50

5. G finally gets its packet. By looking at the Ethernet and IP addresses, G clearly sees that although it got this frame from E, the original message really came from another machine—the 199.34.57.10 machine.

That's a simple example of how IP routes, but its algorithms are powerful enough to serve as the backbone for a network as large as the Internet.

There are different kinds of routing algorithms in TCP/IP, and Windows NT only supports the simplest routing approaches: static routes and the Routing Information Protocol (RIP). NT doesn't support the more robust protocols, like the Open Shortest Path First (OSPF) or External Gateway Protocol (EGP). You either need third-party software, or a dedicated hardware router to build large, complex intranets with NT, but it routes adequately within a small to medium-sized intranet.

Routing in Even More Detail

Let's really zoom in on routing and explore how routers communicate, the protocols used, and the different classes of routing protocols that exist.

Routed or Routing?

First, let's talk about the confusion that can set in when discussing the terms *routed* and *routing* protocols:

Routed protocols are used between routers to direct user traffic like IP or IPX. IP and IPX can provide enough information in its network header to enable a router to direct user traffic. Routed protocols specify the type of fields and how they're used within a packet. Packets that are defined as routed protocols can usually send data from end-to-end, that is, complete the path from sending to destination machines.

Routing protocols used between routers only maintain routing tables like RIP, OSPF, or Novell's Link State Protocol (NLSP) and a Cisco proprietary protocol called Interior Gateway Routing Protocol (IGRP). These protocols provide a way of sharing route information with other routers to update and maintain tables. The protocols do not send end-user data from network to network; routing protocols only pass routing information between routers.

Routers can support multiple independent routing protocols and update and maintain routing tables for all routed protocols simultaneously. We can create many networks over the same network media because routed and routing protocols pay no attention to each other's protocols. This bypassing ability is called ships-in-the-night routing. (We didn't make this up, we swear!)

Different Classes of Routing Protocols

The most popular routing protocols can be classified into two basic protocols:

- *Distance vector* understands the direction and distance to any network connection on the internetwork. Distance vector listens to second-hand information to get its updates. In other words, it loves to hear and give gossip!

- *Link-state,* or shortest path first, understands the entire network better then distance vector, and never listens to second-hand information; hence it can make better routing decisions.

Okay then, let's all just use link-state; it seems the best choice—or is it? Let's take a better look at both algorithms, then decide what is or isn't best about both distance vector and link-state.

Distance Vector

What happens when a link drops or a connection gets broken? All routers must update all other routers to let them know to update their routing tables. This is what routing protocols do. However, you may hear people complain about routing protocols taking up their bandwidth with updates. This sometimes happens because of convergence time, not actual problems with the protocol. Convergence is the time it takes for all the routers to update their tables when a reconfiguration, outage, or link drops. No data passes during this time, and a slowdown is eminent. Once completed and all routers in an internetwork are operating with the same knowledge, the internetwork is said to have converged. If convergence did not take place, routers would have outdated tables, and routing decisions based on noncurrent data can be incorrect or wasteful.

Distance vector routing protocols update every 30 seconds. All routers pass their entire routing table to all other routers that they know about.

Let's say you have three routers, A, B and C, as shown in Figure 4.2. Router A has direct connections to networks 1 and 2. Router B has direct connections to networks 2 and 3. Router C has direct connections to networks 3 and 4.

FIGURE 4.2

Distance vector
routing tables

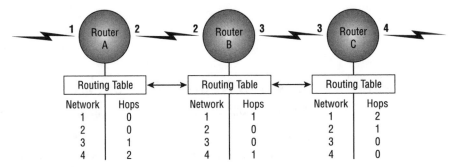

When a distance vector router starts up or gets powered on, it gets to know its neighbors. It learns the metrics (hops) to other routers on each of its own interfaces. As the distance vector network discovery updates continue (every 30 seconds), routers discover the best path to destination networks based on hops from each neighbor. In Figure 4.2, router C knows B is connected to network 1 by a metric of 1; that means it must be a metric of two for router C to get to network 1. Router C will never know the whole internetwork, only what is "gossiped" to it.

Remember convergence? Whenever the network topology changes for any reason, routing table updates must occur by each router sending its entire routing table as a broadcast to all other routers. When a router receives the tables, it compares the table with its own table. If it finds a new network, or what it considers a faster way to get to a network, it updates its table accordingly.

What is the fastest way to a network? Distance vector says, "Less hops, less filling—sign me up!" Well, take a look at Figure 4.3.

Router A is getting to router D through a 56K WAN link. Router B can get to D through a T3. Which is faster? Distance vector says through the 56K pipe! Imagine sending 100MB CAD drawings to a server plugged into a hub going to router D. It would take all day (and night). Why does it do this? Because distance vector uses metrics to make its routing decisions. One hop is better than two, and so on. The solution, of course, is to manually tell router A that the metric to D is three. A will then say, "Two is better than three, let's go!"

One of the problems with distance vector is routing loops, which can occur if the convergence is slow. Let's say network 5 in Figure 4.3 fails. All routers know about network 5 from router E. Router A's tables have a path to network 5 through router B, C, and E. When network 5 fails, router E tells router C, and router C stops routing to network 5 through router E. Routers A, B, and D don't know about network 5 yet and keep sending information. Router C will

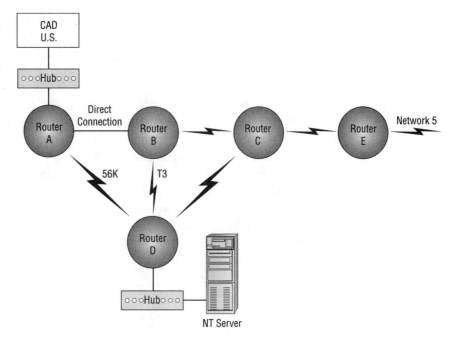

FIGURE 4.3

Distance vector
network decision

eventually send out its update and B and D will stop routing to network 5.
Router A is still not updated. To router A, network 5 is available through router
B to C and then to E with a metric of three.

You still with us? Now comes the fun part!

Router A sends out its regular 30-second message: "Hello, I'm still here, and
these are the links I know about." Router D receives this wonderful news that
network 5 can be reached from router A to B to C and then to E. Router D
sends the information back to router A that network 5 is available through
router D to A to B to C. And router A then tells routers B and C that network
5 is available through router D. So now any packet destined for network 5 will
go to router A to B to C to D and back to A. Gawd, we love this stuff!

Wait, we're not done! What stops this looping?

This continued looping problem is called counting to infinity because each
time a packet passes though a router, the hop count increases. Gossip and
wrong information about the internetwork can cause the looping problem.

One way to solve this problem is to define a *maximum hop count*. Distance
vector uses a hop count of up to 15, so 16 is deemed unreachable. After a loop
of 15 hops, network 5 will be considered down. Yuck.

Another way to solve this problem is something called *split horizon*: Information sent from a router is not sent back to that originating router. This would have stopped router D from sending the updated information it received from A back to A. Split horizon reduces incorrect routing information and reduces routing overhead in a distance vector network.

One more way to avoid problems caused by inconsistent updates is called *route poisoning*. It works like this: When network 5 goes down, router E initiates route poisoning by entering a table entry for network 5 as 16 or unreachable (sometimes referred to as infinite). By poisoning its route to network 5, router E is not corruptible to incorrect updates on how to get to network 5. Router E will keep this information in its tables for many update cycles. It can then trigger an update about network 5 to its neighbors.

Router poisoning and triggered updates will speed up convergence time because neighbor routers do not have to wait 30 seconds (an eternity in computer land) before advertising the poisoned route.

Link-State

The link-state routing algorithm, on the other hand, keeps a more complex table of topology information. Routers using the link-state concept have a complete understanding of all links of distant routers and how they interconnect. Link-state routing uses "hello" packets or link-state packets (LSPs) to tell other routers about distant links. Link-state also uses topological databases, the shortest path first (SPF) algorithm, and of course, a routing table.

Network discovery in link-state has several differences from distance vector:

- First, routers exchange hello packets with one another. This gives a bird's eye view of the entire network, as each router only starts with its directly connected links.

- Second, all routers compile and build a topological database from all the LSPs received from the internetwork.

- Then the SPF computes how to reach each network by finding the shortest path to every participant in the link-state network. Each router creates a tree structure with itself as the root. The results are put together in a routing table, listing the best paths (shortest).

- Finally, the routers can then use the table for switching packet traffic.

Unlike distance vector, link-state understands that for a packet to get from router A to D in the shortest path, the T3 would be faster than the 56K line.

Link-state does not use metrics in its decision to find the best path to an intranetwork. It uses things like bandwidth, congestion on links, and so on.

Link-state routers handle convergence in a completely different way than distance vector: Whenever a topology changes, the router or routers that first understand or become aware of this change send information to all other routers participating in the link-state algorithm, or to a designated router that all other routers can use to update their tables.

A router participating in a link-state network must do the following to converge:

1. Remember its neighbor's name, when it is up or down, and the cost to that router

2. Create an LSP that lists its neighbors' names and costs

3. Send this newly created LSP to all other routers participating in the link-state algorithm

4. Receive LSPs from other routers and update its own database

5. Build a complete map of the internetwork topology from all the LSPs received, then compute the best route to every network destination

Whenever a router receives an LSP packet, the router recalculates the best paths and updates the routing tables.

Some of the problems with link-state are processing power, memory usage, and bandwidth requirements. To run the link-state algorithm, routers must have more power and memory available. This is one reason Microsoft does not support link-state routing in NT. A third-party router like Cisco is designed specifically for this purpose.

In link-state, routers keep track of all their neighbors and all the networks they can reach, all of which must be stored in memory—including various databases, the topology tree, and the routing table!

Dijkstra's algorithm (he's one of the guys who invented this stuff) says a processing task proportional to the number of links in the internetwork times the number of routers in the network will compute the shortest path. Huh? What he means is you need processing power. I'm sorry, your Netware 3.11 router running on 6 megs of RAM with a 386 sx25 just won't cut it.

One other thing to keep in mind is bandwidth requirements. When a link-state router comes online, it floods the internetwork with LSPs. This reduces the bandwidth available for actual data—you remember data, right? The stuff we're actually trying to get from A to B?

The good news is that unlike distance vector, after this initial flooding of the network, link-state routers only update their neighbors about every two hours on average, unless a new router comes online or a link drops. This two hours can be changed to meet bandwidth requirements. Let's say you have 56K links to different continents. Would you use RIP (distance-vector) that updates every 30 seconds, or OSPF (link-state) that can update every 12 hours?

Another great thing about link-state is that routers can be configured to use a designated router as the target for all changes. This router can be contacted by all other routers directly for any network changes, instead of using LSP broadcasts.

What happens if the routers don't get an LSP packet? Or what happens if the link is slow and the network topology changes twice before some routers receive the first LSP? Well, link-state routers can implement LSP time stamps. This would only have to be done in large internetworks. Link-state can also do sequence numbers and aging schemes to avoid inaccurate LSP information.

Comparing Distance Vector to Link-State Routing

There are quite a few major differences between distance vector and link-state routing algorithms. Let's go over a few:

- Distance vector routing gets all its topological data from second-hand information or gossip. Link-state routing obtains a complete view of the internetwork by putting all the LSPs together.

- Distance vector determines the best path by hops or metrics. Link-state uses bandwidth and other information to calculate the shortest path.

- Distance vector updates topology changes in 30-second intervals, resulting in a slow convergence time. Link-state can be triggered by topology change, resulting in a faster convergence time as LSPs are passed to all other routers, or sent to a multicast group of routers.

Link-State Sounds Best? Well...

With routing protocols, no one can say, "This is better than that," for all networks. Routing decisions should not always be based on fastest or cheapest. Multivendor support or standards might outweigh other reasons. Network simplicity, the need to set up and manage quickly and easily, or the ability to handle multiprotocols without complex configurations are other considerations. Many network administrators have prolonged their careers by using proven tried-and-true technologies.

What is best for your network? How about both, or hybrid routing?

Balanced Hybrid

Hybrid, or balanced, routing combines and uses the best of both distance vector and link-state algorithms. Hybrid uses distance vectors with more accurate metric counts to determine the path to an internetwork. Unlike other distance vector algorithms, it can converge quickly, thanks to the use of link-state triggers. Hybrid also uses a more efficient link-state protocol to cut down on required bandwidth, processor, and memory.

Some examples of hybrid protocols are the OSI's IS-IS (Intermediate System to Intermediate System) and Cisco's EIGRP (Enhanced Interior Gateway Routing Protocol).

IP Multicasting

As personal computers have increased in power, that power has turned to running multimedia applications on the desktop. Now, multimedia applications are being designed for use on the network. Applications such as audio and video conferencing and the transmission of live or recorded events using audio and video are only two of the many applications that blend multimedia and the network.

Today's networks are designed to reliably transmit data such as files from point to point. Multimedia places further demands on the network.

First, data such as audio cannot tolerate delays in delivery. A network whose basic task is to move files from one place to another can transmit data packets at an uneven rate. It's usually not a problem if portions of a file arrive slowly or out of order. Multimedia, on the other hand, requires that data packets arrive at the client on time and in the proper order. Real-time protocols and quality of service guarantees on the network address this issue. Second, multimedia requires transmitting large amounts of data over the network and thus uses more of the network's bandwidth than basic network operations such as file transfer. Multicasting addresses this issue.

Unicast, Broadcast, and Multicast

The bulk of the traffic on today's networks is *unicast*: A separate copy of the data is sent from the source to each client that requests it. Networks also support *broadcasting*. When data is broadcast, a single copy of the data is sent to all clients on the network. When the same data needs to be sent to only a portion of the clients on the network, both of these methods waste network bandwidth.

Unicast wastes bandwidth by sending multiple copies of the data. Broadcast wastes bandwidth by sending the data to the whole network whether or not the data is wanted. Broadcasting can also needlessly slow down the performance of client machines. Each client must process the broadcast data whether the broadcast is of interest or not.

Multicasting takes the strengths of both of these approaches and avoids their weaknesses. Multicasting sends a single copy of the data to those clients who request it. Multiple copies of data are not sent across the network, nor is data sent to clients who do not want it. Multicasting allows the deployment of multimedia applications on the network while minimizing their demand for bandwidth.

The MBone, LAN, and WAN

Today, the most widely known and used multicast-enabled network is the Internet Multicast Backbone, or MBone. The MBone is a virtual network consisting of those portions of the Internet, sometimes called multicast islands, in which multicasting has been enabled. Multicasts that must travel across areas of the Internet that are not yet multicast-enabled are sent as unicasts until they reach the next multicast-enabled island. This process is referred to as tunneling.

The MBone has been in place since 1992 and has grown to more than 2,000 subnets. It has been used to multicast live audio and video showing Internet Engineering Task Force conferences, NASA astronauts working in space, and the Rolling Stones in concert. The MBone has successfully demonstrated the practicality and utility of using multicasting to send multimedia across the network.

The hardware for multicasting, chiefly multicast-enabled routers and their software, has reached a point where corporations can take advantage of multicasting on their own LANs and WANs. The technology is of benefit in any scenario where several (or hundreds or thousands) of individuals need the same information. Because such information can be multicast live, multicasting is the ideal method to communicate up-to-date information to a wide audience. For example, sales trends for the week could be presented to all regional sales managers via multicast. Events such as a product introduction or important press conference could also be multicast. Multicasts can also support bi-directional communication allowing, for example, individuals in widely dispersed locations to set up a live conference that includes audio, video, and a whiteboard.

How IP Multicasting Works

Multicasting follows a push model of communications. That is, like a radio or television broadcast, those who want to receive a multicast tune their sets to the station they want to receive. In the case of multicasting, the user is simply instructing the computer's network card to listen to a particular IP address for the multicast. The computer originating the multicast does not need to know who has decided to receive it.

Network Multicasting

Multicasting requires the following mechanisms:

- Clients must have a way to learn when a multicast of interest is available.

- Clients must have a way to signal that they want to receive the multicast.

- The network must have a way to efficiently route data to those clients who want to receive it.

Announcing Multicasts

Multicasts are announced in advance so that clients know when a multicast is available. On the MBone, multicasts are typically announced using the Session Description Protocol (SDP). This protocol supplies clients with all the information they need to receive a multicast, including its name and description, the times it is active, the type of media (audio, video, text, and so on) that it uses, and the IP addresses, ports, and protocol it uses. The announcement information is multicast to a well-known IP address and port where clients running the session directory tool receive this information.

In addition to SDP, there are other ways that multicasts can be announced. For example, on the corporate intranet, multicasts can be advertised using Web pages. Controls embedded in the Web page can then receive the multicast data.

Joining Groups

To signal that they want to receive a multicast, clients join the group to whom the multicast is directed. The Internet Group Management Protocol (IGMP) handles this task.

Multicast groups provide several advantages. Groups are dynamic; clients can join or leave at any time. No elaborate scheme is required to create or disband a group. When a group has no members, it ceases to exist on the network. Groups also scale upward easily because as more clients join a multicast, it becomes more likely that the multicast is already being routed close to them.

When a client joins a group, it initiates two processes: First, an IGMP message is sent to the client's local router to inform the router that the client wants to receive data sent to the group. Second, the client sets its IP process and network card to receive the multicast on the group's address and port. Multicast addresses are Class D IP addresses ranging from 224.0.0.0 to 239.255.255.255. Class D IP addresses map automatically to IEEE-802 Ethernet multicast addresses, which simplifies the implementation of IP multicasting on Ethernet. When a client leaves a group and is the only one receiving the multicast on that particular subnetwork, the router stops sending data to the client's subnetwork, thereby freeing bandwidth on that portion of the network.

Multicast Routing

The bulk of the work that needs to be done to enable multicasting is performed by the network's routers and the protocols they run. Two years ago, major router manufacturers began adding multicasting capability to their routers. Multicasting can be enabled on such routers by simply updating their software and adding memory.

There are several multicast routing protocols in use today: Distance Vector Multicast Routing Protocol (DVMRP), Multicast Open Shortest Path First (MOSPF) protocol, and Protocol-Independent Multicast (PIM). The task of these protocols is to create efficient multicast delivery paths through the network. Multicast routing protocols use varying algorithms to achieve efficiency.

Routed Multicast Data Path

An efficient delivery path implies that multicast data travels only to those clients who want to receive it and takes the shortest path to those clients. If data travels elsewhere through the network, bandwidth goes to waste needlessly. You can visualize the network as a tree structure. The source of the multicast sends data through the branches of the tree. The routers are responsible for sending data down the correct branches to other routers and to the subnetworks where members of a group are waiting for data. Routers prune off branches where no one wants data and graft branches back to the tree when a client in a new subnetwork joins the group. Routers can also stop data from traveling to their own subnetworks when it is not wanted.

Setting Up Routing on NT and Windows Machines

Up to now, we've assumed that all of your Windows NT, Workgroups, and 95 machines had a single default gateway that acted as "router to the world" for your machines. That's not always true, as real-life intranets often have multiple routers that lead a machine to different networks. We've also assumed that your NT network is connected to the Internet, or to your enterprise intranet, via some third-party (Compatible Systems, Cisco Systems, Bay Networks, or whomever) router. That's also not always true, as NT machines can act as IP routers.

Routing problems aren't just *server* problems; they're often workstation problems as well. So, in this section, we'll take on two topics:

- How to set up routing tables on your Windows workstations

- How to use your NT Servers as IP routers

An Example Multirouter Internet

Suppose you had a workstation (whether it's Windows for Workgroups, Windows NT, or Windows 95) on a network with two gateways, as shown in Figure 4.4.

FIGURE 4.4

A workstation on a network with two gateways

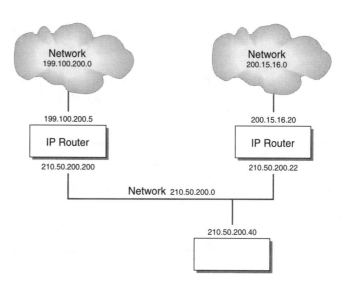

As is the case for most of these diagrams, a multinetwork picture can be cryptic, so here's an explanation of what you are looking at.

First, there are three separate Ethernet segments, three separate subnets. They are all C-class networks, just to keep things clean. Two of the networks are only represented by clouds; thus, the cloud on the left containing 199.100.200.0 is just shorthand for an Ethernet with up to 254 computers hanging off it, with addresses ranging from 199.100.200.1 through 199.100.200.254. Notice that we said 254, not 253, because *there is no default gateway for these subnets.* As there are only three subnets, this is an intranet, not part of the Internet. One side effect of not being on the Net is that you can use the ".1" address for regular old machines. We left the Internet out of this example because we found it confusing when we were first trying to get this routing stuff down. We'll add it later, we promise.

There is also another cloud, to the right, representing a network whose addresses range from 200.15.16.1 through 200.15.16.254—network number 200.15.16.0.

In between is a third subnet with address 210.50.200.0. You see a rectangle representing a PC in the middle which has only one Ethernet card in it, and its IP address is 210.50.200.40. The rectangles on the right and left sides of the picture are routers, computers with two Ethernet cards in them and thus two IP addresses apiece. Each has an address on the 210.50.200.0 network, and each has an address either on the 200.15.16.0 network or on the 199.100.200.0 network.

Adding Entries to Routing Tables: Route Add

Having said that, let's now figure out how to tell the machine at 210.50.200.40 how to route anywhere on this network. Some of the facts that it needs to know are:

- To get a message to the 199.100.200.0 network, send it to the machine at 210.50.200.200.

- To get a message to the 200.15.16.0 network, send it to the machine at 210.50.200.22.

- To get a message to the 210.50.200.0 network, just use your own Ethernet card; send it out on the segment, and it'll be heard.

You tell a workstation how to send packets with the route add command. Simplified, it looks like this:

```
route add destination mask netmask gatewayaddress
```

Here, *destination* is the address or set of addresses that you want to be able to get to. *Netmask* defines how *many* addresses are there—is it a C network with 250+ addresses, something subnetted smaller, or perhaps a "supernet" of several C networks? *Gatewayaddress* is just the IP address of the machine that will route your packets to their destination.

The route add command for the 199.100.200.0 network would look like this:

```
route add 199.100.200.0 mask 255.255.255.0 210.50.200.200
```

This means, "In order to send a message anywhere on the 199.100.200.0 network, send it to the machine at 210.50.200.200, and it'll take care of it."

Just a reminder on subnetting, for clarity's sake: Suppose the network on the upper left wasn't a full C network, but rather a subnetted part of it. Suppose it was just the range of addresses from 199.100.200.64 through 199.100.200.127. The network number would be, as always, the first address (199.100.200.64), and the subnet mask would be 255.255.255.192. The route add command would then look like:

```
route add 199.100.200.64 mask 255.255.255.192 210.50.200.200
```

Anyway, back to the example in the picture. Add a command for the right-hand-side network; it looks like:

```
route add 200.15.16.0 mask 255.255.255.0 210.50.200.22
```

That much will get an NT system up and running.

Understanding the Default Routes

Even if you never type a route add command at a Windows workstation, you'll find that there are routing statements that are automatically generated. Let's look at them. First, we'd need an explicit routing command to tell the 210.50.200.40 machine to get to its own subnet:

```
route add 210.50.200.0 mask 255.255.255.0 210.50.200.40
```

Or, in other words, "To get to your local subnet, route to yourself."

Then, recall that the entire 127.*x.y.z* range of network addresses is the loopback. Implement that like so:

`route add 127.0.0.0 mask 255.0.0.0 127.0.0.1`

This says, "Take any address from 127.0.0.0 through 127.255.255.255 and route it to 127.0.0.1." The IP software has already had 127.0.0.1 defined for it, so it knows what to do with that. Notice the mask, 255.0.0.0, is a simple Class A network mask.

Some NT Internet software uses intranet multicast groups, so the multicast address must be defined. It is 224.0.0.0. It looks like the loopback route command:

`route add 224.0.0.0 mask 255.0.0.0 210.50.200.40`

The system knows to multicast by "shouting," which means communicating over its local subnet.

Viewing the Routing Table

Let's find out exactly what routing information this computer has. How? Well, Windows NT, Workgroups, and 95 workstations have two commands that will show you what the workstation knows about how to route IP packets. Type either **netstat -rn** or **route print** at a command line—the output is almost identical. The netstat command displays the information displayed by route print *plus* any active TCP/IP connections. So use either command—and you will see something like Figure 4.5.

FIGURE 4.5

Sample route print output

Notice that the output of route print is similar to the way you format data in route add. Each line shows a network address, which is the desired destination; the netmask, which indicates how many addresses exist at the desired destination; and the gateway, which is the IP address that the workstation should send its packets to in order to reach the destination. But note two more columns: Interface and Metric. We discussed the meaning of metric values earlier in this chapter, but let's take a closer look at the Interface column.

The Interface Column

Interface asks itself, "Which of my local IP addresses—the ones physically located inside me, like my loopback and all the IP addresses attached to all of my network cards—should I use to get to that gateway?" On this computer, it's a moot point, because it only has one network card in it.

What might this look like on a multihomed machine, like the router on the left-hand side? It has two IP addresses, 199.100.200.5 and 210.50.200.200. A fragment of its route print output might then look like:

Network Address	Netmask	Gateway Address	Interface	Metric
199.100.200.0	255.255.255.0	199.100.200.5	199.100.200.5	1
210.50.200.0	255.255.255.0	210.50.200.200	210.50.200.200	1

There are two networks that the router machine can get to (obviously, or it wouldn't be of much use as a router), and each one has a gateway address, which happens to be the local IP address that the router maintains on each network. But now notice the Interface column: Rather than staying at the same IP address all the way through, this tells the computer, "I've already told you which gateway to direct this traffic to; now I'll tell you which of your local IP addresses to employ in order to get to that gateway in the first place."

Route Print Output Explained

Now that you can decipher each column in the route print output, we'll finish up explaining the output.

The first line is the loopback information, as you've seen before. It's automatically generated on every NT/Workgroups/95 machine running the Microsoft TCP/IP stack. The second and third lines are the manually entered routes that tell your machine how to address the 200.15.16.0 and 199.100.200.0 networks. The fourth line is another automatically generated line, and it explains how to address the 210.50.200.0 subnet, which is the local one. The fifth line refers to 210.50.200.40 itself. The mask, 255.255.255.255, means that these aren't routing instructions to get to an entire network, but rather routing instructions to get to a particular computer. It basically says, "If you need to get data to 210.50.200.40, send it to the loopback address." The result: If you ping 210.50.200.40, then no actual communication happens over the network. The sixth line defines how to do a local subnet broadcast. Again, it doesn't point to an entire network, but rather to the particular subnet broadcast address. The seventh line serves Internet multicasting, as you saw before. And the final address is for something called the *limited broadcast address*, a kind of generic subnet broadcast address.

Adding the Default Gateway

Suppose you wanted to set up our 210.50.100.40 machine. How would you do it? More specifically, you'd ask us, "Which is the default gateway?"

Well, in the TCP/IP configuration screen, you'd obviously be able to supply the information that the IP address should be 210.50.100.40 and the subnet mask should be 255.255.255.0. But what should you use to fill in the Default Gateway field? We mean, there are *two* gateways: 210.50.100.22 and 210.50.100.200. Which should you use?

The answer? *Neither*. A *default gateway* is just another entry in the routing table, but it's not specific like the ones you've met so far; it's a catch-all entry. This network doesn't get to the Internet, and it can only see two other subnets, each with their own routers (gateways), so we left the Default Gateway field blank. And there's an advantage to that.

"Destination Host Unreachable"

If we were to try to ping some address not on the three subnets, like 25.44.92.4, then we wouldn't get the message that the ping had timed out, or experienced an error, or anything of the sort; rather, we'd get a "destination host unreachable" message. That's important: "Destination host unreachable" doesn't necessarily mean that you can't get to the destination host, but it *does* mean that your workstation doesn't know *how* to get to that host—it lacks any routing information about how to get there at all. Do a route print and you'll probably be able to see what's keeping you from getting to your destination.

Building a Default Gateway by Hand

When *would* a default gateway make sense in our network? Well, let's add a connection to the Internet to the network, as shown in Figure 4.6.

FIGURE 4.6

Network with an Internet connection

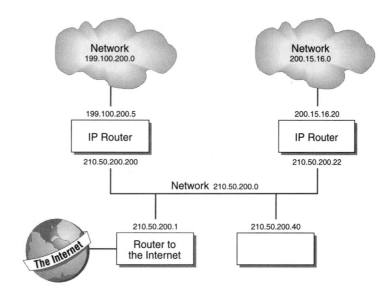

Now we need another route add command—but what should it look like? We mean, what's the generic IP address of the whole Internet?

Believe it or not, there *is* such an address: 0.0.0.0. Think of it as "the network number to end all network numbers." And the network mask? Well, since it doesn't matter *what* address bits match which other address bits—after all, no matter what your address is, you're still on the particular "subnet" which is the entire Internet—the subnet mask is also 0.0.0.0. So the command looks like:

```
route add 0.0.0.0 mask 0.0.0.0 210.50.200.1
```

Handling Conflicts in Routing Information

However, it appears that there are some conflicts here. Look at some of the instructions that you've given the IP software about how to route:

- There's a rule about how to handle the specific address 210.50.200.40: Just keep the message local at 127.0.0.1, no routing.

- There's a rule about how to handle the range from 210.50.200.0 through 210.50.200.255: Shout it out on the subnet, no routing.

- There's a rule about how to handle the range from 199.100.200.0 through 199.100.200.255: Send it to 210.50.200.200.

- There's a rule about how to handle the range from 200.15.16.0 through 200.15.16.255: Send it to 210.50.200.22.

- There's a rule about how to handle *all* Internet addresses: Send the messages to 210.50.200.1.

Here's what we mean about a conflict: Suppose you want to send an IP packet to 200.15.16.33. You have one rule that says, "Send it to 210.50.200.22," and another that says, "Send it to 210.50.200.1." Which rule does the software on your workstation (or server) follow?

Answer: When in doubt, first look for the route with the smallest metric. If there is more than one candidate, then take the *most specific* one—in other words, choose the one with the most specific subnet mask.

In this case, there are two entries in the routing table that point to the destination 200.15.16.33. We haven't shown you their metrics, but both of them require hopping over one router, so each route has metric 2. As their metrics are tied, you look next to the subnet mask. As the 210.50.200.1 route has a very generic subnet mask (0.0.0.0), your machine would ignore it in comparison to the more specific 210.50.200.22's subnet mask of 255.255.255.0.

Suppose workstation 210.50.200.40 wanted to get a message to another machine on the subnet; let's say that its address is 210.50.200.162. Again, there's a routing conflict, as one route entry just says to send it to 210.50.200 .40—in other words, don't route, shout! There's another routing entry—the 0.0.0.0 one again—that says it can also get the IP packet to 210.50.200.162, as it claims it can get any packet *anywhere*. Which to choose? Well, if constructed correctly, an excerpt of the routing table will look something like this:

Destination	Netmask	Gateway	Interface	Metric
0.0.0.0	0.0.0.0	210.50.200.1	210.50.200.40	2
210.50.200.0	255.255.255.0	210.50.200.40	210.50.200.40	1

The first entry is the default gateway. It's got metric 2 because you've got to hop over at least one router to get to the Internet. (In actual fact, it's probably not a bad idea to set this value a bit higher, just to be sure internal IP packets *never* try to get sent over the Internet.) The second entry basically says, "To send data to your local subnet, just say it out loud on your Ethernet card"— again, don't route, shout. As the Internet metric is higher, your machine will know not to try to send a local message by sending it to the default gateway.

One more thing: You wouldn't, of course, want to have to type in those route add commands every time you start up your computer. So you'd use a variation on the route add command; just type **route -p add....** When you add the -p, that entry becomes permanent in your system's routing table.

All Routers Must Know All Subnets

We've talked about how we'd set up our sample network from the point of view of a workstation. It would work, but you can see that it's a real pain to punch in all of those route add statements for each workstation. The answer is to make the routers smarter; *then* you can just pick one router to be the default gateway for the .40 workstation, and the workstation needn't worry about anything. So let's take a minute and see how each of the three routers in this system would be set up.

The first router is the one on the left, that routes between 199.100.200.0 and 210.50.200.0. It must know the following:

- It can get to 199.100.200.0 through its 199.100.200.5 interface.

- It can get to 210.50.200.0 through its 210.50.200.200 interface.

- It can get to the Internet through 210.50.200.1, which it gets to through its 210.50.200.200 interface.

In fact, you would not have to type in routing commands telling it how to get to 199.100.200.0 or 210.50.200.0; assuming it's an NT machine, the NT routing software figures that out automatically. But you can tell it to get to the Internet by setting a default gateway:

```
route add 0.0.0.0 mask 0.0.0.0 210.50.200.1 metric 2
```

The routing software is then smart enough to realize that it should get to 210.50.200.1 via its 210.50.200.200 interface.

The second router, the one on the right, routes between 200.15.16.0 and 210.50.200.0. It can get to both of those networks directly, and, as with the first router, we don't have to tell it about them. But to get to the Internet, it must route packets to 210.50.200.1, and so, like the first router, it should have a default gateway of 210.50.200.1.

Now let's tackle the third router, the machine at 210.50.200.1, which is the Internet gateway. It must know that it should use the Internet as its default gateway. For example, on our Compatible Systems routers, there is a magic address WAN which just means the modem connection to the Internet. We essentially tell it, `Route add 0.0.0.0 mask 0.0.0.0 WAN`, and packets travel to and from the Internet over the modem. The router must then be told of each of the three subnets, like so:

```
route add 210.50.200.0 mask 255.255.255.0 210.50.500.1 metric 1

route add 199.100.200.5 mask 255.255.255.0 210.50.200.200 metric 2

route add 200.15.16.20 mask 255.255.255.0 210.50.200.22 metric 2
```

Using RIP to Simplify Workstation Management

Thus far, we've shown you how to tell your workstations how to exploit routers on the network. In most cases, you won't need to build such large, complex routing tables by hand, and in almost no case will you *want* to build those tables.

Ideally, you shouldn't have to type in static tables; instead, your workstations could just suck up routing information automatically from the nearby routers, using some kind of browser-type protocol. You *can* do such a thing with the Routing Internet Protocol, or RIP.

RIP is an incredibly simple protocol. Routers running RIP broadcast their routing tables about twice a minute. Any workstation running RIP software hears the routing tables and incorporates them into its *own* routing tables. Result: You put a new router on the system, and you needn't punch in any static routes.

RIP is part of the Multivendor Protocol Router package for NT 3.51 users, and ships as part of NT 4. The Microsoft implementation supports both IP and IPX. Routes detected by RIP show up in route print statements just as if they were static routes.

Using an NT Machine As a LAN/LAN Router

In the process of expanding your company's intranet, you need routers. For a network of any size, the best bet is probably to buy dedicated routers, boxes from companies like Cisco Systems, Bay Networks, or Compatible Systems.

Dedicated routers are fast and come with some impressive management tools, neat Graphical User Interface (GUI) programs that let you control and monitor your network from your workstation. But routers have one disadvantage: They're expensive. We haven't seen an Ethernet-to-Ethernet IP router available for less than $2,000. Again, don't misunderstand us: These routers are probably worth what they cost in terms of the ease that they bring to network management and the speed with which they route data. But you might not have the two grand, so you're looking for an alternative.

Your NT machine can actually provide you with an alternative. Any NT workstation or server can act as a simple IP router— all you need is a multi-homed PC (one with two or more network cards installed in it) and NT.

Just open up the Control Panel, open the Networks applet, then the Protocols tab, and the TCP/IP protocol. Click on the Routing tab, and you'll see an option called Enable IP Routing. That's how you turn on NT's routing capability.

Let's see how to set up this router. Imagine you have an intranet that looks like Figure 4.7.

FIGURE 4.7

A sample intranet

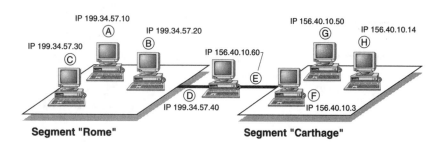

We're going to use the machine that's on both Rome and Carthage as the router. (Actually, there's no choice here, as it's the *only* machine in both TCP/IP domains, and any router between two domains must be a member of both domains.) All you have to do is go to the machine with two Ethernet cards and set up both cards with an IP address. The Enable IP Routing box will no longer be grayed out, and you can then check the box.

Building an IP Router with NT

In cookbook fashion:

Install two network cards (let's use Ethernet for this example) in an NT machine. The NT machine *need not be* an NT Server machine, and, given the cost of NT Server, you're probably better off using a copy of NT Workstation.

1. Configure the Ethernet card on the Rome subnet with an IP address for the Rome subnet. When you are working in the TCP/IP configuration dialog box, you'll notice a single-selection drop-down list box labeled Adapter. You can use that to control which Ethernet card you are assigning to what IP address.

2. Click on the Routing button.

3. Check Enable IP Routing. Notice that the Enable IP Routing box is grayed out unless there are two network cards in your system.

4. Click on OK until you get out of the Control Panel.

The system will reboot, and your router will be active. This will allow an IP router to move traffic from one subnet to another. It will *not*, however, route traffic between three or more subnets.

What do we mean by that last line? Well, the default router software isn't very smart. Look at Figure 4.8, and you'll see what we mean.

FIGURE 4.8

Intranet with three subnets

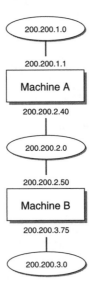

Here, you see an intranet with just three subnets: 200.200.1.0, 200.200 .2.0 and 200.200.3.0. For ease of discussion, let's call network 200.200.1 .0 "network 1," 200.200.2.0 "network 2," and 200.200.3.0 "network 3." The network 1 to network 2 router, machine A, has addresses 200.200.1.1

and 200.200.2.40, and the network 2 to network 3 router, machine B, has addresses 200.200.2.50 and 200.200.3.75.

Once you turn on IP routing in machine A, it's smart enough to be able to route packets from network 1 to network 2, and packets from network 2 to network 1. But if it receives a packet from network 1 intended for network 3, it has no idea what to do about it.

Machine B has the same problem, basically. It knows how to go from network 2 to network 3 and from network 3 to network 2, but it has no idea how to find network 1.

How do you solve this problem? Either with static routes or with RIP. The best answer is probably to put the RIP router on both machine A and machine B, and they will end up discovering each other's routes through the RIP broadcasts. But how would you tell machine A how to find network 3 and how would you tell machine B to find network 1? With static route add commands.

On machine A, tell it about network 3 like so:

```
route add 200.200.3.0 mask 255.255.255.0 200.200.2.50
```

You're saying to this machine, "In order to find network 200.200.3.0, use the IP address 200.200.2.50; it's attached to a machine that can get the packets to that network." For the sake of completeness, you might add the "metric 2" parameter to the end.

On machine B, tell it about network 1 in a similar way:

```
route add 200.200.1.0 mask 255.255.255.0 200.200.2.40
```

Remember that in both cases the "mask" information says, "I'm giving you information about a subnet, but the mask says how useful the information is."

Using an NT Server Machine As an Internet Gateway

Consider this: Your company has purchased a full-time PPP account from some Internet provider. You have your LAN all running TCP/IP with NIC-approved IP numbers. All you need is a machine that will route your local traffic over the Internet when you want to FTP, use e-mail, or whatever.

From a hardware point of view, it's pretty easy: You just need a PC containing both an Ethernet card and a serial port, with a dial-up PPP connection. That machine was essentially doing the job of TCP/IP routing. How do you do that in NT?

The Overview

There are a number of "what ifs" that you have to consider if you want to use your NT machine as a LAN-to-WAN Internet gateway.

The first piece of advice is: Don't, if you can avoid it. In Mark's company, he uses the Compatible Systems mr900i, a terrific box that he picked up for $850. It's very easy to manage, does RIP, is much cheaper than buying a Pentium and a copy of NT, and is as fast as the wind. We'd recommend it as the way to go if you want to hook up your net to *the* Net.

But there are times that he doesn't have access to a dedicated router, and perhaps he'd like to use his NT machine as his Internet router. How does he do it?

Basically, the steps are as follows:

1. Put a network card and a modem in an NT system.

2. Put a static IP address on the network card, but leave off the default gateway.

3. Install RAS and tell it how to dial up to your Internet service provider (ISP). Disable Use Remote Gateway in setting up the connection.

4. Make a change to the Registry (explained later in this chapter).

5. Dial up to the ISP and log in.

6. Use a route add command to tell the system how to route to the Internet.

7. Then tell all the computers on your network to use the IP address of the network card as their default gateway.

The Obstacles

Those steps aren't hard, and we'll do a step-by-step "cookbook recipe" in just a minute. But there *are* two things that will make it a bit difficult to explain how to do this, as it varies from ISP to ISP. They are:

- How you log onto the ISP: simple character-oriented terminal login, the Password Authentication Protocol (PAP), or the Challenge Handshake Authentication Protocol (CHAP)

- How you set the IP address on your dial-up or Frame Relay connection

For more information on these topics, check out *Mastering Windows NT Server 4* (also published by Sybex). We won't go into them in any detail here.

We *did* want to point out, however, that there are differences in how you accomplish those two things.

Login Options

When you attach to an ISP network, you must identify yourself and prove who you are, usually with a password. Most ISPs require that when you dial up to them, you work with a character-based login screen where you type in the account number and password for your network, and that's how we'll describe our example here. You've probably seen something like this before: "Welcome to XYZ Corporation, your on-ramp to the Information Super-highway; please enter your account number and password...." If your ISP works that way, then you can set up a Dial-Up Networking phone book entry that will make a terminal screen appear once you're connected to the ISP. In your Dial-Up Networking phone book, click on Script and you'll see a dialog box like Figure 4.9.

FIGURE 4.9

Telling Dial-Up Networking to pop up a terminal screen so you can enter the ID and password

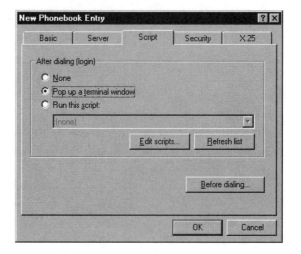

If you have an ISP like this, then you're probably logging into some old UNIX-based portmaster system of some kind. It can be a pain to have to punch in the user ID and password every time you connect to your ISP, so you may want to look into writing a logon script to automate the process. (This is also covered in *Mastering Windows NT Server 4.*)

Some ISPs, however, offer more modern, automated ways to log into their networks. Assuming that you link up to the ISPs with PPP (Point-to-Point Protocol), then the ISP may choose to exploit a couple of extensions to PPP that have become popular: the Password Authentication Protocol (PAP) and the Challenge-Handshake Authentication Protocol (CHAP). Both are protocols allowing your computer to dial up to another computer and pass user ID and password information back and forth automatically, without you having to type that information in. If you have an ISP that supports PAP or CHAP, then click on the None radio button in the Script page and click on the Security page. It looks like Figure 4.10.

FIGURE 4.10

Configuring a PAP or CHAP dial-in

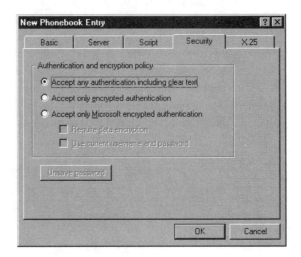

Why this doesn't just have radio buttons labeled PAP, CHAP, and the like is beyond us, but basically here's what to click. If you are dialing into your ISP and authenticating with the Password Authentication Protocol, choose Accept Any Authentication.... If you are using the generic CHAP protocol to authenticate with an ISP, choose Accept Only Encrypted Authentication. If you are dialing up an NT Server, then choose Accept Only Encrypted Microsoft Authentication. Not surprisingly, Microsoft has created its own variation of the standard CHAP protocol called Microsoft-CHAP; clicking on this last button requires it. Again, the value of using PAP or CHAP is that it absolves you of having to write a logon script.

If your ISP is using NT machines, then you're probably in luck; you won't have to do a terminal logon. In most cases, however, terminal logons are still the order of the day. Our advice is that you sit at the NT machine that will be the gateway and just try to get *it* attached to your ISP before going any further; figure out how to get to your ISP as a single dial-up machine before trying to share the connection with your LAN.

Obtaining an IP Address from Your ISP

Then there's the problem of IP addresses over your WAN link. Your dial-up connection has an IP address different from the address on the network card—but *what* address?

Most ISPs that we've arranged PPP connections with have a system whereby they tell the PPP connection what IP address to use automatically, as part of the logon sequence. Even if you have to type in your user name and password by hand, your workstation will get the IP address automatically from the ISP. In our experience, most of the time ISPs just send you a piece of paper telling you to set up your software to use a certain IP address. Dial-Up Networking can accommodate both, as shown in Figure 14.11.

FIGURE 4.11

Dial-Up Networking
TCP/IP settings

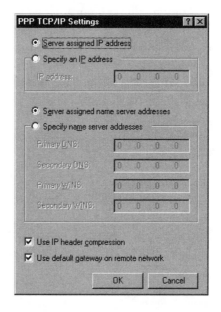

You get this dialog box by editing a Dial-Up Networking phone book entry. Open up the Dial-Up Networking application in My Computer, choose the entry for dialing to your ISP, click on More, then on Edit Entry and Modem Properties. Then click on Server and TCP/IP settings. Note the radio buttons in the group at the top: either Server Assigned IP Address (that's the more common automatic option) or Specify IP Address. And while we're showing this dialog box to you, let us point out that the checkbox at the bottom, labeled Use Default Gateway on Remote Network, is checked by default, as you see in the example screen. In our experience, it's *very* important that you uncheck this box.

Anyway, this how-do-I-get-my-IP-address question is another ISP-specific issue, and another reason why you should dial up and log into your ISP before going any further. The way that most ISPs seem to work, and, again, the way we'll write this example, is that you just tell your PPP software to get an IP address from the ISP and to require a terminal login.

The Recipe

Here are the steps that you use to make an NT workstation or server into a router that will connect your company's network to the Internet. We'll call that computer the gateway machine (when we say that, we're *not* referring to computers from South Dakota; we're just describing that one computer).

In this example, we'll connect our Class C network, 199.34.57.0, to the Internet through our Internet service provider, Digital Express, or, as its customers know it, "Digex." We'll need to know the phone number of Digex (301-555-1212 in this example); our account number (xyzabc123 for this example); and a password (xyzzy).

Our gateway machine is running NT Workstation 4 and contains an Ethernet card as well as a 28.8Kbps modem. If you're setting up NT 3.51, then the procedure will be identical save for one thing: Go to Microsoft's FTP site and get the Multivendor Protocol Router (MPR).

1. On the gateway machine, install IP with static addressing for the network card. Set the network card's IP address (we'll use 199.34.57.1 in this example) with whatever subnet mask makes sense for your network (255.255.255.0 for basic Class C networks).

2. When you're setting up the IP address on the network card, leave the Default Gateway Address field *blank*.

3. Install Dial-Up Networking. Basically you open up the Dial-Up Networking icon in the My Computer folder. If it's the first time you've done that, then it'll automatically install Dial-Up Networking. You must tell it what kind of modem you have and what port it's on. Configure it to dial out only—you won't be receiving calls on this machine, not if it's your constant connection to the Internet. Reboot the system to complete installing Dial-Up Networking. (This is all covered in greater detail in *Mastering Windows NT Server 4.*)

4. In the Registry, go to the key HKEY_LOCAL_MACHINE\System\ CurrentControlSet\Services\RasArp\Parameters and create a new value entry DisableOtherSrcPackets of type DWORD, and

set the value to 0. You will have to create a new value entry, as `DisableOtherSrcPackets` isn't in that key by default.

You do this because this machine will be a router. This command says, "When you forward an IP packet, don't change the 'source' IP address." Otherwise, if machine B forwards a packet to machine C for machine A, then machine B changes the From: part of the IP packet to B's own IP address, with the result that C thinks the message originated with B, not A. Setting this Registry entry to 0 keeps that from happening.

5. Start up Dial-Up Networking, and it'll observe that there are no phone book entries and will prompt you for a first entry; let's make that the dial-up instructions for your ISP. If you already have Dial-Up Networking entries, then just click on New to create another phone book entry. Use the Dial-Up Networking Setup Wizard if you like, or just enter the values directly.

6. Enter a descriptive name and phone number. For our example, we used Digex as the name. The initial screen will look something like Figure 4.12.

FIGURE 4.12

The Basic tab for setting up an Internet connection

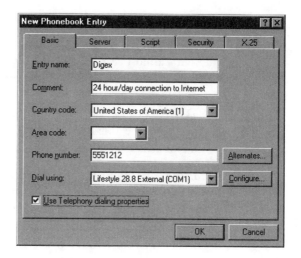

7. Next, tell it that you want a terminal login screen so you can punch in the user name and password whenever you need to reconnect your network to the Internet. Click on Security and choose Accept Any Authentication Including Clear Text. Then choose Script and choose Pop Up a

Terminal Window. Next you need to tell Dial-Up Networking what to expect from the ISP that it's about to dial into, so choose Server, and you'll see a screen like Figure 4.13.

FIGURE 4.13

Setting up the Server tab

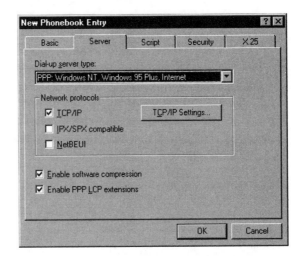

8. Be sure to tell it that you're dialing into a PPP or NT Server server, as that's almost certainly what your ISP is using; PPP is the most common way to set up dial-in UNIX servers. Your ISP *may* use SLIP instead, in which case you would choose SLIP: Internet in the Server field. Check TCP/IP because that's the Internet protocol. Click on TCP/IP Settings and you'll be able to configure whether to get the IP address from the ISP or whether to hard-code it, as mentioned earlier.

9. In the case of our ISP, we chose Server Assigned IP Address. Again, this is something that may be different for your ISP, so if things aren't working, then ask them. In the same way, Use IP Header Compression may work best checked or not checked. It's an option that *you* can enable or disable at your leisure. Which is better for you? In general, for connections slower than 28.8Kbps, turn on IP compression. For a faster system, turn IP compression off. One way to find out is to find a few big files on an FTP site and download them; try it with and without the header compression, and then you'll know which setting is better.

10. Uncheck Use Default Gateway in the TCP/IP Settings dialog box.

11. Now you have to get your system to forward IP packets. Open up the Control Panel, then open Network ➤ Protocols ➤ TCP/IP ➤ Routing, and check Enable IP Forwarding. You now have to reboot.

12. For those of you using NT 3.51, however, you have some more work to do. In NT 3.51, there is still a checkbox labeled Enable IP Routing, but it may be grayed out unless there are two or more network cards present in the Control Panel. That presents a problem, because NT only sees one Ethernet card, so it grays out the routing option. This kind of makes sense because you must have at least two IP addresses to route, but it makes no sense that the IP addresses must be on network cards. NT *ought* to be smart enough to enable forwarding when one IP address is a network card and the other is a RAS/PPP-derived IP address, but it isn't: It *must* see two network cards before it'll enable IP routing.

Or mustn't it? There *is* one sneaky trick that you can do to get the Enable IP Routing box enabled. Just click on Control Panel ➤ Networks ➤ TCP/IP Protocol ➤ Configure, and Advanced. You get the Advanced TCP/IP Configuration screen that you've seen earlier in this chapter. You can actually attach more than one IP address to a network card. So here's the trick to turn on IP routing: Go to your one network card and add a bogus IP address. The Enable IP Routing box will become enabled. Check it. Then remove the bogus IP address, and the Enable IP Routing box will gray out, *but it will stay checked!* Again, NT 4 users needn't worry about this, as you don't have to go through all of this rigmarole to make forwarding work.

13. Once you've rebooted, start up Dial-Up Networking and dial up your ISP. When the terminal screen appears, punch in your user name and password. When you get a message indicating that your session has started, click on Done.

14. Find out what IP address your Dial-Up Networking connection is using. Type **ipconfig** and look for the line that looks like `Ethernet adapter NdisWan6:` or something like that, and the IP address below it is the IP address connected to the outside world. Suppose we find that on our example computer it's `199.34.57.2`.

15. Your system now must know how to find the outside world. Open a command prompt and type **route add 0.0.0.0 mask 0.0.0.0 *x.y.z.a* metric 2**, where *x.y.z.a* is the IP address that you just found for your Dial-Up Networking connection. In our case, we'd type **route add 0.0.0.0 mask 0.0.0.0 199.34.57.2 metric 2**. Now, if you're a RAS expert type, then you're no doubt wondering something like this, "You told me to uncheck Use Default Gateway on Remote System. But the only thing that command does is automatically insert the line `route add 0.0.0.0 mask 0.0.0.0 199.34.57.2` in the routing table. Why then do all the extra work?" Our answer is, try it both ways. We have no idea why, but a Dial-Up Networking box won't route with Use Default Gateway on Remote System. It *will* route if you uncheck the Use Default Gateway... box and enter the `route add 0.0.0.0...` by hand. How do we know? It's how Mark's entire company has been connected to the Internet from time to time—he uses an NT machine as a backup router.

16. Finally, make sure that all of the PCs on your subnet point to the static IP address attached to the network card, not the RAS connection. In our example, all of our machines point to the default gateway `199.34.57.1`.

The machines on your subnet should now be able to ping the outside world.

But If It Doesn't Work...

There are enough pieces to this that you may find you can't get the gateway up first thing. Before you e-mail us asking if we'll troubleshoot your gateway—which is something that's pretty time-consuming and is the sort of thing that will lead us to start talking about hourly rates, if you know what we mean—take the same steps that we would take in troubleshooting your gateway. It has been our experience time and time again that people who can't get the gateway to work have skipped a step or two, causing major frustration on their part. Just take it step by step: First, get the gateway machine talking to the local network, and then get it talking to the Internet, and, finally, get it routing right. Do that, and you'll be surfing in no time.

1. You've got to have honest-to-God approved InterNIC addresses. It's not sufficient to have an approved address for the gateway, and then make up random addresses for your local network. All machines on your network must have IP addresses that you got from your ISP or the InterNIC.

2. Make sure the ISP is prepared to route your new addresses. If their routers aren't ready to accept your packets, those packets will never get anywhere.

3. Load IP on your local area network and make sure it works. Make sure everyone can ping everyone else. Then you know that the first part is functioning perfectly.

4. If you are using NT 3.51, download Service Pack 4 and the Multivendor Protocol Router (MPR). It's on Microsoft's Web and FTP sites. Install these modules on the gateway machine.

5. Set up the NT machine to dial into your ISP. You'll have to play around with the TCP/IP parameter settings in RAS, depending on how your ISP wants you to dial in: Do you preset an IP address? Do you use Van Jacobsen header compression? What's their DNS address? and so on. You'll know you're done when the gateway can ping places in the outside world, FTP to an outside site, and access an outside Web location. Do not try to ping your local network from the gateway yet.

6. Make any necessary changes to the Registry for RAS. The `DisableOtherSrcPackets` that we mentioned earlier may be the only setting you'll have to worry about, but there are two others that you should know:

- The Registry setting to turn on IP routing is in `HKEY_LOCAL_MACHINE\ System\CurrentControlSet\Services\TCP/IP\Parameters`, and is called `IPEnableRouter`. It is of type `REG_DWORD`, and it should be set to 1 to enable IP routing.

- You will sometimes have to modify the value in another Registry parameter named `PriorityBasedOnSubNet`. It is in `HKEY_LOCAL_MACHINE\ System\Current`.

`ControlSet\Services\RasMan\IPCP` is of type `REG_DWORD`. Its value is either 1 or 0. What it does is this: Since your gateway will have a static route to the outside world—a `route add 0.0.0.0`—as well as a static route to your local subnet, the gateway machine could get confused. It could get confused because if it wants to route packets to your local subnet, should it use the `0.0.0.0` route (that is, send it over the modem to the Internet), or should it use the Ethernet connection to your local subnet? We discussed this earlier in the chapter, saying that the IP stack on the gateway will use the most specific route. That's not entirely true. Yes, the NT gateway machine thinks it has two routes to the local subnet, and yes, it will ordinarily take the more specific one. But if RAS sets `PriorityBasedOnSubnet` to 0, then NT will override its normally good judgment, and send traffic destined for the local subnet out the modem. Result: Data never gets to the local subnet. You can troubleshoot that problem like this: If the PCs on your local subnet can ping the gateway machine fine at first, but then after the gateway dials up the Internet, the PCs can no longer ping the gateway, change the `PriorityBasedOnSubnet` value to 1.

7. Remember to do the ipconfig statement and get the IP address assigned to you by the ISP. Then add the static route to the Internet.

Some people have reported to us that they needn't do that at all—they just check the Use Default Gateway on Remote System, and it works fine. (It *hasn't* worked for us, but there may be some quirkiness to our system that makes it not work.)

Make sure that the PCs on the local subnet all refer to the gateway PC as their default gateway, and at this point all your systems should be on the Internet.

Interior and Exterior Routing Protocols

In the Internet world, there are two kinds of routing going on. RIP or your network's static routing tables route IP packets within your company's intranet domain (or perhaps those sleek, shiny Cisco routers do), and the routers in your Internet service provider do another kind of routing. Your routers mainly route data from one side of your company to another, and your ISP's routers mainly route data from one company's network to another company's network. Over the years, these routing processes have become refined into two categories of routers: *interior routers*, like RIP or OSPF, and *exterior routers*.

Exterior routers essentially route from the "border" of one Internet domain to the "border" of another, leading some people to dub them Exterior Border Protocols, or EBPs. The most widely used is probably the Exterior Gateway Protocol, or EGP.

Where would you see something like this? Well, suppose we go to the NIC and get ourselves another Class C network; suppose it's 223.150.100.0. We put it on our 199.34.57.0 network using our NT machines as RIP routers, and the two networks are just pinging one another like mad.

But then we try to ping the outside world from 223.150.100.0. And nothing happens. Why? Because our 199.34.57.0 network only knows about the 223.150.100.0 network because RIP told it. But to get to the outside world would require the complicity of our Internet service provider, and *it* doesn't listen to our RIP routers. If the router in our system that talked to our ISP spoke EGP, then perhaps we'd be okay. But, even then, our ISP *might* not even do EGP; perhaps they do only static routing between customer networks. NT doesn't support EGP.

Well, by now, you're on an intranet in the traditional way. Microsoft adds two possible options to this setup: the Dynamic Host Configuration Protocol (DHCP) and the Windows Internet Naming Service (WINS).

Setting Up TCP/IP on NT with Fixed IP Addresses

Enough talking about intranetting; let's do it, and do it with NT.

Traditionally, one of the burdens of an IP administrator has been that she must assign separate IP numbers to each machine, a bit of a bookkeeping hassle. You can adopt this fixed IP address approach, and in fact there are some good reasons to do it, as it's compatible with more TCP/IP software and systems. It is also possible, however, to have a server assign IP addresses "on the fly" with the DHCP system that we just mentioned.

Some of you will set up your intranet with fixed IP addresses, and some will use dynamic addresses. *Everyone* will use static IP addresses for at least some of your PCs. For that reason, we first want to start the discussion of setting up TCP/IP with just fixed addresses. Then we'll take on dynamic addressing.

Here's basically how to set up TCP/IP on an NT system:

1. Load the TCP/IP protocol.

2. Set the IP address and subnet, default gateway, and DNS server.

3. Prepare the HOSTS file, if you're going to use one.

4. Test the connection with ping.

Let's take a look at those steps, one by one.

Installing TCP/IP Software with Static IP Addresses

You install the TCP/IP protocol (if you didn't choose it when you first installed NT) by opening up the Control Panel, and then choosing the Network icon. You see a dialog box like Figure 4.14.

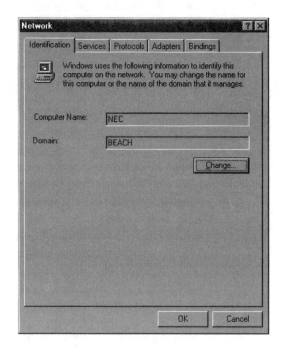

Click on the Protocols tab, and your system will look something like Figure 4.15.

Click on Add and you get a list of protocols that you can add. Select TCP/IP, as shown in Figure 4.16.

Click on OK. The setup routine will then offer you the chance to take the easy way out and have the system automatically set up the TCP/IP protocol using DHCP, which we'll cover later in this book. The dialog box is shown in Figure 4.17.

Click on No, and NT will prompt you for the location of the installation files; point it wherever you keep them. NT will install a bunch of files, and you'll see that the Protocols window now contains TCP/IP. You need to configure it. Click on Close, and NT will rebind all of the protocols, boards, and services, ending up with the TCP/IP configuration property sheet shown in Figure 4.18.

FIGURE 4.15

Protocols tab of Network
property sheet

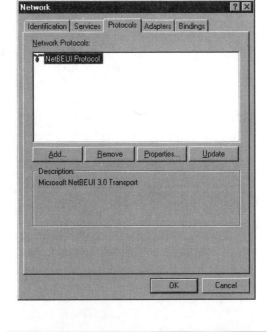

FIGURE 4.16

Add the TCP/IP protocol.

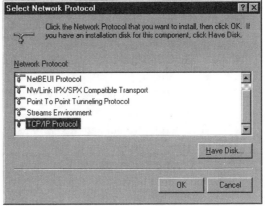

FIGURE 4.17

Choose not to use DHCP.

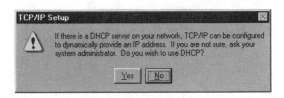

F I G U R E 4.18

TCP/IP configuration
property sheet

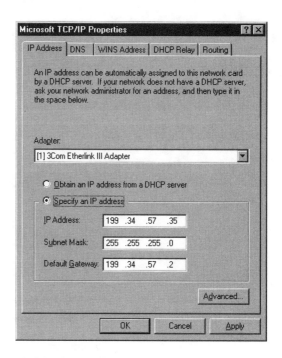

We've already filled in the basic values in that figure—IP address, subnet mask, and default gateway.

First, you put your IP address into the IP Address field. Using the first quad of your address, NT will guess a subnet mask based on your network class—255.0.0.0 for Class A, 255.255.0.0 for Class B, and 255.255.255.0 for Class C. As we indicated in our discussion earlier in this chapter about subnetting, if your network is subnetted *within* its Internet domain, then you have to change the subnet mask.

Once you have the subnet mask in place, you should enter the IP address of your default gateway, the machine on your Ethernet segment that connects to the outside world either via a router, a SLIP, or a PPP connection. To clarify that, Figure 4.19 shows a sample intranet connection.

Suppose you're configuring the machine in the upper left-hand corner of the diagram. You type its IP address into the dialog box that you saw earlier, entering the value **199.34.57.35**. Presuming that your Class C network—since the first quad is 199, it must be a Class C network—is not further sub-netted, then the subnet mask would be 255.255.255.0, and the default gate-way would be the machine with the SLIP connection to the Internet, so you'd enter 199.34.57.2 for the address of the default gateway. (Why didn't we make that gateway machine .1? Just to underscore that it's not necessary to

FIGURE 4.19

An example of a connection to the Internet

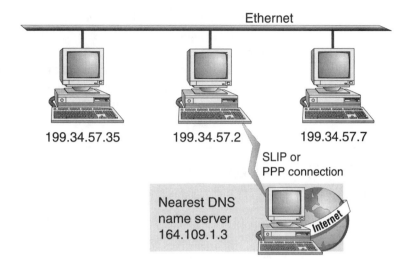

FIGURE 4.19

An example of a connection to the Internet

make the gateway .1; it's just a convention.) Notice the DNS server is at 164.109.1.3. You haven't had a chance to incorporate that information into the TCP/IP setup yet, but you will soon.

Next, click on the DNS tab. You'll see a dialog box like the one in Figure 4.20.

FIGURE 4.20

The DNS configuration screen

The important parts of this screen are the host name, the TCP domain name, name resolution, and DNS search order. Again, we've already filled them in here.

The TCP domain name is your company's domain name, like `exxon.com`, or, if your company is further divided beyond the domain level, perhaps `refining.exxon.com`. The host name is your computer's name, such as marks-computer, printserver, or the like.

WARNING   Don't use underscores in the name, as it seems to render Microsoft TCP/IP nonfunctional.

Next, you tell NT where to find a DNS server. You can use a HOSTS file, DNS name servers, or a combination. If you use a DNS name server or servers, however, then you have to tell NT where the nearest DNS name server is. You can specify one, two, or three DNS servers, and the order in which to search them, in the DNS Service Search Order field. In general, you only include the name of one or two DNS name servers, a primary and a secondary for use in case the primary name server is down.

When that sheet is arranged as you want it, you next want to configure the name resolution system that you use within your enterprise network, a system called the Windows Internet Naming Service, or WINS. Click on the WINS Address tab, and you'll see a page like the one shown in Figure 4.21.

We'll cover WINS in detail later in this book, but for now all you need to understand is that you have one or two NT Servers acting as name resolvers or WINS servers. This dialog box lets you fill in the names of a primary and secondary WINS server.

The Internet uses something called DNS to convert network names to network addresses, as you'll read about in Chapter 9, but now we're saying that we'll *also* use something else called WINS to do what sounds like the same thing. What's going on? In truth, you shouldn't really have to set up WINS at all; NT and Microsoft enterprise networking in general should use DNS for all of its name resolution, but it doesn't. The reason is that Microsoft wanted NT's networking modules to work like the already-existing LAN Manager system, and LAN Manager used a naming system based on its NetBIOS application program interface. A computer's NetBIOS name is the computer name that you gave it when you installed it. When you type **net view \\ajax**, something must resolve \\ajax into an IP address—a NetBIOS-to-IP resolution. WINS does that. In contrast, the rest of the Internet would see a machine called "ajax" as having a longer name, like `ajax.acme.com`. If there were a Web server on ajax, then someone outside the company would have to point her Web browser to `http://ajax.acme.com`,

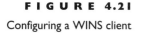

FIGURE 4.21

Configuring a WINS client

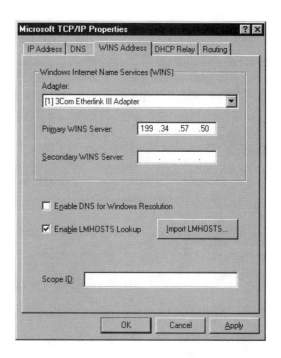

and some piece of software would have to resolve `ajax.acme.com` into an IP address. That piece of software is the socket or WinSock interface, and in either case it will rely upon not WINS but *DNS* to resolve the name. In a few words, then, programs written to employ NetBIOS use WINS for name resolution, and programs written to employ WinSock use DNS for name resolution.

We can probably guess what you're thinking now, and, yes, DNS and WINS should be integrated, and they will be—but not until Cairo, the next version of NT. For now, we'll just have to maintain two different name resolvers. (There is, we promise, much more on the subject of WINS versus DNS name resolution later on in the book, but that's a quick overview.)

Anyway, there's a checkbox labeled Enable DNS for Windows Name Resolution. We wrote the previous two paragraphs so that we could explain this checkbox. As you've read, WinSock-based applications use DNS for name resolution, and NetBIOS applications use WINS. But suppose a NetBIOS-based application cannot resolve a name with WINS—WINS comes back and says, "I don't know who this computer is!" If you check this checkbox, then you are telling your machine, "If WINS fails me on name resolution, let NetBIOS look to DNS to resolve names." If you check it, then some operations may get pretty slow on your system. Consider what happens when you accidentally try an operation on a nonexistent server. Suppose you type **net view \\bigserver** when its real name is \\bigserve. WINS will come back with a failure on the name resolution attempt, but if you have this box checked, then your system will waste even more time asking DNS to resolve the name. On the other hand, some installations have servers with NetBIOS names and use TCP/IP, but do not participate in WINS name resolution. For example, an old LAN Manager/UNIX (LM/X) server will have a NetBIOS name, but it doesn't know to register that name with WINS, as its software was written before Microsoft introduced WINS. Ask a WINS server for the LM/X server's IP address, then, and WINS will come up blank. But *DNS* would know how to find the server. So if you have older Microsoft enterprise networking products that run the TCP/IP protocol, then you may want to check the Enable DNS for Windows Name Resolution box.

You'll enable LMHOSTS if you need the LMHOSTS file; LMHOSTS is a static ASCII file like HOSTS, except that where HOSTS assists in WinSock name resolution, LMHOSTS assists in NetBIOS name resolution. You will almost never use an LMHOSTS file on a modern network. We discuss LMHOSTS later in this book. The NetBIOS scope ID should be left blank for most networks. If you've partitioned your network into NetBIOS scopes, then talk to whomever did it and they can tell you what scope names to use. Otherwise, do not fill anything in here.

Click on OK to return to the Protocols screen, then on Close to close the Network applet. You have to reboot for the changes to take effect.

Just to get started, create your HOSTS file; remember that it goes in winnt\system32\drivers\etc. The file is reread every time a name needs to be resolved, so you needn't reboot every time you change the contents of HOSTS.

Testing Your TCP/IP Installation

Your TCP/IP software should now be ready to go, so let's test it.

TCP/IP has a very handy little tool for finding out whether or not your TCP/IP software is up and running, and whether or not you have a connection to another point—*ping*.

Ping is a program that lets you send a short message to another TCP/IP node, asking, "Are you there?" If it is there, then it says yes to the ping, and ping relays this information back to you. You can see an example of ping in Figure 4.22.

In this figure, we pinged Microsoft or, rather, whatever network Microsoft exposes to the outside world. (Notice it's a Class B network—those Microsoft folks really rate.) The ping was successful, which is all that matters. But *don't* ping Microsoft for your first test; we did that screen shot a

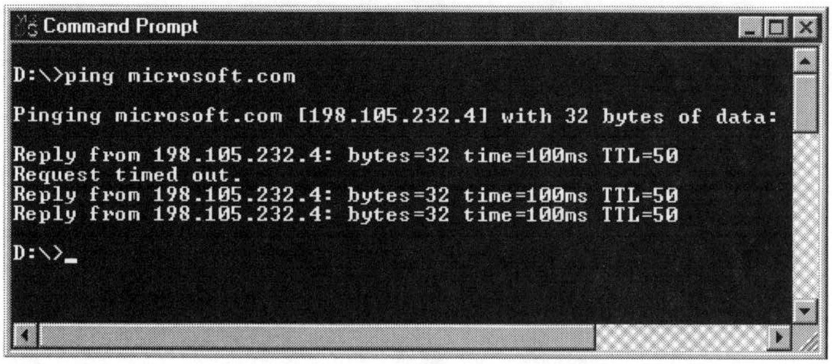

FIGURE 4.22

A sample ping output

```
Command Prompt

D:\>ping microsoft.com

Pinging microsoft.com [198.105.232.4] with 32 bytes of data:

Reply from 198.105.232.4: bytes=32 time=100ms TTL=50
Request timed out.
Reply from 198.105.232.4: bytes=32 time=100ms TTL=50
Reply from 198.105.232.4: bytes=32 time=100ms TTL=50

D:\>_
```

while back, before they put their firewall in. (Pre-firewall, it was actually possible to browse Microsoft's servers from the comfort of your own home, right over the Internet. I can just hear the "oops!" that someone exclaimed over *that* one.) So don't bother trying to ping Microsoft, as their system no longer responds to ping requests anyway. (I guess they couldn't figure out a way to charge for them.) Instead, use ping to gradually test first your IP software, then your connection to the network, your name resolution, and finally your gateway to the rest of your intranet.

Making Sure That TCP/IP Is Set Up Properly

First, test that you've installed the IP software by pinging the built-in IP loopback address. Type **ping 127.0.0.1**, and if that fails, then you know that you've done something wrong in the initial installation, so recheck that the software is installed on your system. This does not put any messages out on the network, it just checks that the software is installed. By the way, that's also what happens if you ping your IP address. For example, in the machine we just installed, pinging 127.0.0.1 does exactly the same thing as pinging 199.34.57.35.

If that fails, then your TCP/IP stack probably isn't installed correctly, or perhaps you mistyped the IP number (if it failed on your specific IP address but not on the loopback), or perhaps you gave the *same* IP number to another workstation.

Ping your gateway to see that you can get to the gateway, which should be on your subnet. In Mark's case, the gateway is at 199.34.57.2, so we type **ping 199.34.57.2**, and all should be well.

If you can't get to the gateway, then check that the gateway is up, and that your network connection is all right. There's nothing more embarrassing than calling in outside network support, only to find that your LAN cable fell out of the back of your computer.

Ping something on the other side of your gateway, like an external DNS server. (Ping Mark, if you like; 199.34.57.1 ought to be up just about all the time.) If you can't get there, then it's likely that your gateway isn't working properly.

Next, test the name resolution on your system. Ping yourself *by name*. Instead of typing **ping 199.34.57.35**, Mark would type **ping nec.mmco.com** (the machine he's on at the moment). That tests HOSTS and/or DNS.

Then, ping someone else on your subnet. Again, try using a DNS name, like mizar.ursamajor.edu, rather than an IP address, but if that doesn't work, then use the IP address. If the IP address works, but the host name doesn't, then double-check the HOSTS file or DNS.

Finally, ping someone outside of your domain, like house.gov (the U.S. House of Representatives) or mmco.com. If that doesn't work, but all the pings inside your network work, then you've probably got a problem with your Internet provider.

If you're successful on all of these tests, it should be set up properly.

After your successful TCP/IP test, take a look at the next section, because Microsoft came out with a new Multi-Protocol Router that runs on NT Server 4.

Microsoft Steelhead

In the Pacific Northwest, some rainbow trout travel from rivers to the open water—large lakes, even saltwater. At that point, they're redubbed Steelhead trout, or, for the Latin lover in the audience, *Oncorhybchus Mykiss*. Anyway, they're still tasty, but they're a fight to catch and even to eat—unless of course, you're really tough, and think bones grating down your throat simply add texture to the meal!

Microsoft's Routing and Remote Access Service (RRAS) is a set of new routing and internetworking capabilities for use with Windows NT Server 4. It enables multi-protocol routing over local area networks and wide area networks, and is the newest version of its Multi-Protocol Routing (MPR) software for Windows NT Server. Before release in June 1997, the product was code-named Steelhead—aptly named, for it really does have a few things in common with the fish. For one thing, MPR software has moved from a very basic routing system that

Microsoft never intended for heavy-duty use—one more suited to the smaller tributaries and woodland streams of most intranets—to (Microsoft claims) enough routing power to take on jobs dedicated routers currently do.

But RRAS does more than make existing NT routing tasks easier; it adds new capabilities like:

- A full complement of protocols for IP and IPX routing (including OSPF and RIP version 2 for IP)

- An intuitive, remote-able graphical user interface and command line interface with scripting capabilities

- An extensible platform with APIs for additional third-party routing protocols, user interface (UI), and management

- Demand-dial routing support

- Secure virtual private networking with Point-to-Point Tunneling Protocol support server-to-server

- Mid-range router performance, at low-end router pricing

All of these features combine to form a way for businesses to deploy routing and virtual private network (VPN) solutions. For example, Steelhead enables the use of the Internet for secure VPN connections between headquarters and branch office locations.

Steelhead can provide WAN connectivity, LAN-to-LAN routing within a building, and other routing functions. It also provides efficient bandwidth utilization and packet filtering capabilities. Steelhead can easily be deployed within an organization's existing router infrastructure. Plus, Steelhead combines the remote access service into a new, more unified RAS/routing service on the server running Windows NT.

Besides being able to work with off-the-shelf LAN and WAN cards, Steelhead includes APIs to enable third-party vendors to add value with additional routing protocols and management capabilities. Steelhead will also enable intelligent, multiport LAN or WAN cards to support certain routing functions on the cards themselves. This eliminates the need to interrupt the server CPU to make a route forwarding decision. As a result, Steelhead's packet forwarding rates should dramatically increase by a factor of three to five, enabling expected packet forwarding rates in excess of 100,000 packets per second.

Of course, this is only good news for MIS managers within small and medium-sized organizations, who will benefit from the increased affordability and added choices available to them in building and managing their internetworking infrastructures. Microsoft's agenda is, of course, to replace your Cisco 7000 series routers with their new MPR.

Management   Steelhead offers a comprehensive, intuitive graphical user interface which provides a whole bunch of monitoring and administrative functions for all routers, LAN or WAN interfaces, and packet-filtering features. Steelhead also furnishes a command line user interface.

RASR   RAS Restartable file copy automatically begins retransferring a file upon reconnection whenever your RAS connection has been lost—really! Anyone who's ever been at the mercy of a modem has probably had the nefarious experience etched into memory: A nearly complete, lengthy file transfer is aborted because the remote connection was prematurely disabled before the transmission was complete. Restartable file copy will help keep us all out of therapy. It remembers the status of the file transmission and continues the transfer from exactly that point once reconnected—very cool. Also, if you double-click on an icon to open a file, and if that file is only accessible over the dial-up connection, Dial-Up Networking will automatically initiate the call.

PPTP   Steelhead also includes support for Point-to-Point Tunneling client-to-server and server-to-server. Huh? Well, the Point-to-Point Tunneling Protocol (PPTP) provides a way to use public data networks such as the Internet to create a virtual private network connecting remote machines with servers. PPTP offers protocol encapsulation to support multiple protocols like IP, IPX, and NetBEUI via TCP/IP connections, plus data encryption for privacy, making it safer to send information over nonsecure networks. This technology extends the capacity of RAS to enable remote access and securely extend private networks across the Internet without the need to change the client software.

IP/IPX Packet Filtering   Steelhead supports a variety of inbound and outbound packet-filtering features. These features provide an important measure of network security. Here's a list of filtering options:

- TCP port

- UDP port

- IP protocol ID

- ICMP type

- ICMP code

- Source address

- Destination address

Steelhead also supports a similar level of packet filtering for IPX packets. Here's a list those options:

- Source address

- Source node

- Source socket

- Destination address

- Destination node

- Destination socket

- Packet type

Security   Since Microsoft Proxy Server can't filter IP/IPX packets, Steelhead can be used in conjunction with Microsoft Proxy Server to provide an even higher level of network security and performance. Also, Microsoft Proxy Server reduces network costs and bandwidth needs by caching frequently visited Internet or intranet sites. See Chapter 16 for more information on Microsoft Proxy Server.

The Test Spawning Ground

Since all that was available at press time was the Steelhead beta software, which Microsoft released as RRAS, that's what we tested. The scenario we played with was basic, what Microsoft calls "home-office LAN" in the Steelhead documentation.

Suppose you have a small business (or a small part of a large business), and you want to connect your local LAN to the Internet over a dial-up connection. You could always do this with NT, but you've got to admit that it was a little painful. Steelhead makes it easier for the NT Server to act as your LAN/WAN Internet router. The solution isn't perfect, but it is an improvement.

We started with a Class C network, or CIDR block of addresses, from our ISP. To set up a router with NT, we also needed the following:

- A machine with at least 32MB of RAM

- NT Server 4

- Service Pack 2 (SP2)

- Steelhead beta 2

- A modem

- ISDN or other RAS capable connection

- A network card

Other PCs on our local network have network cards, and we had to configure them with IP addresses from the block our ISP provided.

First, we set up all the PCs on the LAN with the ISP-provided IP addresses. This step is important: Each machine must have a separate and distinct, honest-to-God Internet address. Do not make up addresses, and do not use the nonroutable addresses. (A lot of people e-mail us looking for help in setting up their routers, and surprisingly often the problem turns out to be that they just made up some IP addresses out of the blue.)

Next, we set up the NIC on the router PC and gave it an ISP-supplied address. The router PC eventually ends up with two IP addresses, one for the NIC and another for the RAS connection to the ISP. We installed a fresh copy of NT Server 4 on the router machine from the distribution CD, but we didn't install RAS because Steelhead removes RAS before installing. We pointed all the PCs' default gateways to the IP address on the router PC's NIC. Then, we made sure that all the PCs on the LAN could ping each other. With that done, we knew the LAN worked properly.

We then installed SP2 on the router PC; yes, that's SP2, because SP3 didn't work with Steelhead and our dial-up configuration. (Microsoft fixed this problem for the final release, and RRAS requires SP3.) Then we installed Steelhead. It arrived as one .exe file, but expanded to several files that installed with the command `mprsetup <directory>`, where `<directory>` is the directory in which those files reside. The setup program offers checkboxes to let Steelhead handle network connections, routing, and dial-up connections; we checked them all, and the system restarted.

Next, we logged on at the server, opened up Dial-Up Networking (DUN), and figured out how to connect to our ISP. We weren't worried about routing yet; we just wanted to get the NT Server to successfully dial up the ISP and establish a Point-to-Point Protocol (PPP) connection so that we could ping and run Internet Explorer, etc., from the NT Server. We had to noodle around with the IP parameters to make a PPP connection with our ISP work well. And when we say "noodle," we mean it. Our ISP had a specific FAQ on connecting with RAS and DUN, and some recommended settings were dead wrong. If tech support from your ISP is like tech support from most ISPs—that is to say, highly unsupportive—plan on missing a few meals while messing with the DUN parameters. If you use a full-time connection such as a Frame Relay Access Device (FRAD), look to tech support for that device. In this case, don't buy the FRAD until you speak to both your ISP and the FRAD maker to be sure that someone will be around to help get you up and running.

You'll also need to experiment to find out how to automate your dial-in. With ordinary DUN, you can just tell NT to pop up a terminal window that lets you type in your username and password. But RRAS won't let you do that. Your ISP has to support Password Authentication Protocol (PAP) or Challenge-Handshake Authentication Protocol (CHAP), or you'll need to write a login script. Now's the time to get the bugs out of this procedure, before you start worrying about routing. In our case, our ISP supported PAP, so authentication wasn't a problem.

Once you figure out all that ISP configuration stuff, write it down, and keep the information in a safe place. Now you're ready to route.

If you've tried to make an NT Server act as a LAN and WAN IP router, you know that at this point, you must typically make a handful of Registry changes and reboot. But with RRAS, this stage is easy downstream swimming.

RRAS has an administrative tool called Routing and RAS Administrator; you'll find it in the Administrative Tools group. Here's a summary of some common administrative tasks you can perform in Routing and RAS Administrator:

- Adding a demand-dial interface

- Granting RAS clients dial-in permissions

- Adding a routing protocol

- Adding interfaces to a protocol

- Deleting interfaces from a protocol

- Managing RAS servers

At this point, Steelhead didn't know about the modem, so we had to build the WAN link. We right-clicked on the Ethernet interface to get the Add Interface option. That action kicked off the Demand Dial Interface Wizard, which looks a lot like the Wizard that helps create new phone book entries. A couple of clicks in, and we found a screen which tells Steelhead that we're using this modem as a dial-up IP router. The next few screens are similar to ordinary New Phonebook Entry Wizard screens. The last screen let us set filters.

There is one final step before routing. The router knows that an Ethernet interface and a demand-dial interface exist, but it doesn't know anything about the demand-dial interface—for example, what IP addresses can the router access through this dial-up interface? RRAS needs a static route to get to the Internet. To add a static route, we clicked on the plus sign next to IP Routing and right-clicked on the Static Routes line. That step gave us an Add Static Route option, plus a dialog box.

We filled in the values: The first two are trivial because this connection will be a gateway to the Internet, and the Internet's network address is 0.0.0.0 and subnet mask is 0.0.0.0. We also had to fill in a gateway address, the one an ISP assigns to you when you dial in. Your router must have the same dial-in IP address as the gateway address, as near as we can tell. When you get a CIDR block or Class C network from your ISP, make sure the ISP always assigns the same address when you dial in. We filled in the metric of 2, because our connection has a hop across the router to get to the Internet. If you set the metric to 1, you might not be able to route within your local network.

Next, we needed to wake up the demand-dial connection. We went to a PC on our network and tried to ping a location, such as www.microsoft.com. Cool stuff happened. From across the Ethernet, our NT Server router got the clue that it needed to dial up, and it did. At this point, we were live on the Net using an NT Server as a router. The connection takes a couple of minutes to get set up, so your first few pings might fail. We usually set a big timeout, like:

```
ping www.microsoft.com -w 10000
```

What's the Catch?

Other than the two pitfalls we've mentioned so far—you must end up with the same IP address all the time on the demand-dial interface, and you need to use either PAP/CHAP or an authentication script—how does the rest of RRAS work? For the application we explored here, we give Steelhead a grade of "C," because sometimes it worked more like a bottom-feeder. The modem connection sometimes dropped for no apparent reason in the middle of transferring data. Steelhead, our ISP, or perhaps line noise was at fault. Other times, the connection stayed up, but the Steelhead router stopped responding to external pings. The router was sometimes smart enough to reconnect—but not *always*. Like its real-life namesake, Steelhead sometimes dropped right off the line—the connection just went "poof." The off-hook light on the modem turned off, but the Routing and RAS Admin program showed the connection still up—go figure! Other times, we had to drop the connection manually and force it to reset before we could get packets to route correctly.

All in all, Steelhead isn't as hands-off as we'd like. But it is a big improvement over messing around with Registry parameters. And our old method of making NT act as a LAN/WAN router isn't kosher in the eyes of Microsoft tech support, meaning if you can't make it work, you're high and dry. Presumably, that lack of support won't be true with RRAS.

We'd like to see a throughput measure built into the tool, but Perfmon's RAS counters let you watch those statistics. And the user interface is a bit clumsy. For example, we had to fumble around just to dump the IP routing table from the GUI, although the familiar route print command works just as well as it ever did. And best of all for the stodgy old command-line types, from the command line, you can use routemon to do everything that you can do from the GUI.

To figure out whether the problem was the router or the ISP, we re-implemented the Class C network connection to the ISP with a dedicated router, the Micro Router 900i (MR900i) from Compatible Systems. The MR900i is reasonably priced (about $850 discounted) and comes with an Ethernet connection and a serial port—a nice basic LAN-to-WAN router. It doesn't do OSPF or port filtering (or at least the one we own doesn't; Compatible Systems' Web site shows that later models do), but you can do single-seat management of multiple Compatible routers through a Windows program that comes with the router. Rebuilding the network with the Compatible router was a snap—no hitches—and the PCs on the network were able to access the Internet without trouble for big and small jobs. This result suggests that the instability resides in the Steelhead software.

Trolling for More

Well, suppose you're concerned about security in your intranet. In that case, RRAS is quite a catch. Virtual Private Networks (VPNs) offer one approach to Internet security. They let you use the Internet as a big, private LAN. PPTP lets you do that trick, but for the best PPTP security, the router machine must also be the PPTP server. RRAS' higher performance means that you can use an NT machine as your LAN/WAN router even on a T1 connection, and that machine can also act as a PPTP server.

Or you might choose to open your network to the Internet, but protect it from people using NetBIOS over TCP (NBT) to penetrate your network. In that case, filter TCP and UDP ports 135 through 139. Under IP Routing/Summary, right-click on the WAN link and choose IP Configuration to get a dialog box that lets you filter particular ports from particular locations. With precise control like that, you can, for example, filter out port 25 from a particular IP address, denying that address the ability to send Internet mail to mail servers inside your network.

As the network gets bigger, walking around to all the NT Server machines to administer the ones acting as routers can get old. But the Routing and RAS Admin tool can control any Steelhead router from one location. Large networks can't handle the chatty nature of the Routing Information Protocol (RIP), so you'll welcome RRAS's OSPF protocol support. Both RIP and OSPF are dynamic routing algorithms that discover routes through your network rather than requiring static routing.

Test the Water

RRAS takes NT's routing capabilities and moves them forward considerably. First, it runs faster than the built-in IP routing software and might now be good enough to replace some dedicated routers. Second, single-seat management makes RRAS more practical to manage. Third, taking NT's LAN/WAN routing capabilities out of the closet and making them officially supported tools is incredibly significant not only for Internet users but also for ISPs who want to move from a UNIX-based network to an NT-based network. Add the PPTP and packet-filtering capabilities, and RRAS is actually pretty cool.

Now that you know an incredible amount about routing with NT TCP/IP, let's move on to Host Names and Resolution with Microsoft NT in our next chapter.

CHAPTER

5

Host Names and Resolution

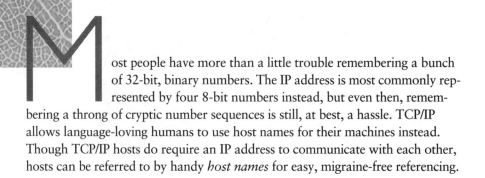

ost people have more than a little trouble remembering a bunch of 32-bit, binary numbers. The IP address is most commonly represented by four 8-bit numbers instead, but even then, remembering a throng of cryptic number sequences is still, at best, a hassle. TCP/IP allows language-loving humans to use host names for their machines instead. Though TCP/IP hosts do require an IP address to communicate with each other, hosts can be referred to by handy *host names* for easy, migraine-free referencing.

Host Names Defined

A host name is an assigned identifier called an *alias* that's used to designate a specific TCP/IP host in a logical way. This alias can be any string of up to 256 characters of almost any type. A single host can have many host names which may be the same, or different, from that system's NetBIOS name—something we'll discuss in Chapter 6. These aliases allow a given machine to be referenced by name, function, or anything else that makes the light of recognition burn brightly in the mind of the user.

Host names are similar to NetBIOS names in that their functional uses are the same. For example, a host name such as "Hal" may be resolved to the IP address 160.1.92.26. As we already know, that IP address can then be resolved to a hardware address, fully identifying the device. It works the same with NetBIOS. Highly noteworthy is the fact that UNIX machines, as well as some others, don't use NetBIOS names. Using TCP/IP utilities to reference a UNIX host will allow you to access the host using the IP address. UNIX has always been TCP/IP based, and TCP/IP has been specifically tailored to fit the needs of this operating system. However, Microsoft has been backward-fitting their operating systems to function with TCP/IP with much success. The NetBIOS names used by Microsoft are intended to function under the guidance of different protocols which use a different naming convention, both for user and program-oriented communication.

To a UNIX-based machine, the naming function for both user and program communication may be referenced by anything that is an equivalent to what it's used to seeing. For instance, a UNIX utility like FTP will allow you to contact a host by its host name, domain name, or IP address. To demonstrate this, suppose that you were on the Internet with a UNIX workstation. If you desired to retrieve files from Microsoft's FTP site, you could open `ftp.microsoft.com`, or access it by entering its IP Address—whichever you prefer.

The Host Naming Hierarchy

TCP/IP has full support for host naming, which is organized into a hierarchical structure. Each host belongs to a domain, and each domain is classified further into domain types; `microsoft.com` is a commercial organization—the "com" standing for "commercial" (see Figure 5.1).

FIGURE 5.1

Domain name hierarchy

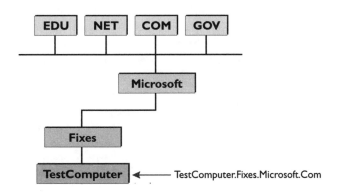

You can tell immediately what type of group you are dealing with by the suffix following the organization name. The chart shown in Figure 5.2 lists some common types of organizations suffixed in this manner which you may come across as you explore TCP/IP though the Internet.

FIGURE 5.2

Internet top-level
domain names

Domain Name	Meaning
com	Commercial organization
edu	Educational institution
gov	Government institution
mil	Military group
net	Major network support center
org	Organization other than those above
int	International organization

There are also domain names for countries. Some examples include:

de   Germany (Deutschland)

it   Italy

nz   New Zealand

us   United States

The format of a host name with a domain name is:

HostName.DomainName

Your computer will refer to a Domain Name System server to resolve names listed in the hierarchy. Domain names require a DNS—a computing service, like UNIX, that requires a *server daemon*, which is a program for UNIX that runs in the background, just like a TSR does for DOS. A DNS provides a centralized online database for resolving domain names to their corresponding IP addresses. The base-names like "Microsoft" in `microsoft.com` are registered by the Stanford Research Institute Network Information Center, or SRI International/SRI NIC, so that they're kept unique on the Internet.

Domain Names

Though IP addresses are useful in that they're precise and handy for subnetting, they're obviously tough to remember, and as said, people generally prefer referring to stuff with words over strings of numbers. This being the case, TCP/IP allows us to group one or more TCP/IP networks into groups called *domains*. These groups share a common name like `microsoft.com`, `senate .gov`, `army.mil`, or `mit.edu`. Domain names are descriptive categories created by Internet authorities to indicate generic types of organizations.

Subdomain Names

Domains can be further subdivided into *subdomains*. These are arbitrary names assigned by a network administrator to further differentiate a domain name. Think of them as network nicknames. The format of a host name with both subdomain and domain names is:

HostName.SubdomainName.DomainName

Both the domain and subdomain names serve as additional descriptors for a machine. Here are a few other examples of these names:

- `ftp.microsoft.com`

- `nic.ddn.mil`

- `internic.net`

There are three ways for host names to be mapped to IP addresses:

- HOSTS tables

- Domain Name System (DNS)

- Network Information Services (NIS)

The following sections explain techniques for mapping host names to their corresponding IP addresses and also explain how TCP/IP connects the language names—the *host* names—to the IP addresses. How is it that can we sit at our PCs and get the information we need to find another host called `archie.au`, when archie's all the way on the other side of the world in Australia?

Simple—with HOSTS, DNS, NIS, and later in this book, WINS. The process of converting a name to its corresponding IP address is called *name resolution*. How does it work? Read on.

Resolving Host Names

Before ARP (Address Resolution Protocol) can be used to resolve the IP address to a hardware address, a host name must first be resolved to the IP address. The name resolution methods are similar to those used in NetBIOS resolution processes, as you'll see in Chapter 6. Microsoft TCP/IP can use any of six methods to resolve host names. The first three resolution methods, WINS, Local Broadcast, and the LMHOSTS file, will be discussed in greater detail later in this book. The Local Host Name, DNS, and the HOSTS file are the remaining three. In this chapter, we'll be focusing on the last two, the DNS and the HOSTS file methods, as they're applied in the UNIX world, and also explore how they translate into the Microsoft environment. The methods that Windows NT can use to resolve a host name are configurable.

Standard Resolution

- **Local Host Name:** The name of the local configured machine as it relates to the destination host. It's typically used for loopback, or recursive, connections.

- **HOSTS File:** A table stored in a local file and used to resolve host names to IP addresses. It conforms to Berkeley Software Distribution's version 4.3 UNIX's host file. This file is most commonly used with the TCP/IP utilities, FTP, Telnet, Ping, etc., to resolve a host's name. It may be used to address a computer by an alias, and in many cases, be placed on multiple computers of varying platforms for host resolution purposes.

- **Domain Name System (DNS):** A cornerstone in the UNIX world, and is found on systems running the DNS service daemon. It's commonly employed for the resolution of host-name-to-IP addresses. This file can be thought of as a networked host file.

Specific Resolution

- **Local Broadcast:** An announcement made on a local network requesting the IP address for the system assigned to a specific NetBIOS, or host name. It is commonly referred to as a B-node broadcast.

- **Windows Internet Name Service:** Commonly implemented as a WINS, this type of name resolution service corresponds to RFC 1001/1002, and delivers NetBIOS or host name resolution from a server that's running it.

- **LMHOSTS file:** A table that's stored in a local file and used to resolve NetBIOS or host names to IP Addresses on remote networks. It's similar to the HOSTS file discussed in detail next, but offers some functions we'll discuss more in Chapter 6 on NetBIOS.

Resolution via the HOSTS File

Before getting down into the skinny on the host name resolution process, it's important to examine in more detail a few particulars regarding the HOSTS file.

The HOSTS File

The HOSTS file is an ordinary text document that can be created or modified using any text editor. It's used by Ping and other TCP/IP utilities to resolve a host name to an IP address on both local and remote networks. Each line with a host name or alias can only correspond to one IP address. Because the file is read from top to bottom, duplicate names will be ignored, and commonly used names should be placed nearer the top for speedier access. Older implementations of TCP/IP with Windows NT maintained the case-sensitivity associated with UNIX, but this is no longer the case (pun intended). An entry can be any valid string of up to 256 characters, with comments placed to the right of a pound (#) sign.

On an NT server, the host table file is located in \%systemroot%\system32\ drivers\etc. On a UNIX system, it is located in, and named, /etc/HOSTS. The format for the host table is:

IPAddress HostName Aliases Comments

Highly important computer syntax rules relevant to host tables include the following:

- Any number of blanks and/or tab characters can separate items.

- The pound (#) sign designates the beginning of a comment.

- Any software that references a host table will not read anything from the # symbol to the end of line.

Here's an example of a host table:

```
129.31.78.2      ACCT-2
123.90.11.4      SALES-AS400 SALES
110.171.64.73    VAX-ADM VAX ADM
110.20.51.3      ACME #Located in Chicago
127.0.0.1        LOCALHOST #Loopback
```

Another file that's similar to a host table is the networks table. This file contains the names and addresses of networks that you want your software to know about. On an NT server, the host table file is located in \systemroot\ system32\drivers\etc. On a UNIX system, this file is located and named /etc/ networks. As with the host table, anything that follows a # symbol is considered a comment.

The format for the networks table is:

NetworkName NetworkAddress Aliases

Here's an example of a networks table:

ACCT-2	167.31
SALES	132.90
VAX-ADM	171.110
ACME	110
ARPANET	46 ARPA
LOOPBACK	127

Since entries in a network table are fingering entire networks, they only depict the network portion of an IP address. Alternately, a host table depicts the entire IP address of a particular host.

Ah, but now comes the really rotten part of HOSTS tables: You have to put one of these HOSTS files on *every single workstation*. That means that every single time you change any one person's HOSTS file, you have to go around and change *everybody's* HOSTS files. Every workstation must contain a copy of this file, which is basically a telephone directory of every machine in your subnet. A total pain, yes, but simple. If you're thinking, "Why can't I just put a central HOSTS file on a server and do all my administration with *that* file?" then what you're really asking for is a *name server*, and we'll show you two of them, the Domain Naming System (DNS) and the Windows Internet Naming Service (WINS), in lots more detail later in this book.

HOSTS is reread every time your system does a name resolution; you needn't reboot to see a HOSTS change take effect.

The HOSTS File Resolution Process

The HOSTS file has long been used for name resolution purposes as implemented with TCP/IP on most UNIX HOSTS. Since a host can have multiple names, the HOSTS file will commonly contain listings of the local host 127 .0.0.1 as well as other aliases by which the machine may be known when it's referenced by other systems. The HOSTS file will be checked for all host name resolutions, including those for itself.

Resolution begins when a command is issued requesting resolution. This command can be either machine or user generated. The system will initially check the destination name against its own. If a match is found, it's a done deal—the name's been resolved. However, in some cases, like when the required destination turns out to be on a remote system, or if the request is actually an alias for itself, the system will proceed to check the HOSTS file for a match. If no match is found, and the HOSTS file is the only configured method for resolution, an error will be spawned and sent back. If a match is achieved, the IP address is then used to resolve the destination's IP address to a hardware address with ARP, and the destination host is found. If the destination host is on a remote network, ARP obtains the hardware address of the proper router (default gateway), and the request is then forwarded to the destination host. In Figure 5.3, a user has typed **Ping Alta** from the Aspen host with IP address 160.1.24.3. Aspen first looks into its HOSTS file and finds an entry for Alta at 160.1.29.7. If the name isn't found in the HOSTS file, an error is generated reading, "No such host." If Aspen has talked with Alta before, the hardware address will be in Aspen's ARP cache. If not, host Aspen will then ARP for the hardware address for the workstation, Alta.

FIGURE 5.3

Resolving names with a HOSTS file

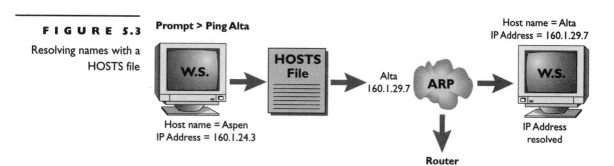

At this point, this process is identical to NetBIOS resolution. We keep comparing the two resolution methods because it's very important for you to understand their similarities and differences. A local machine will resolve to its hardware address, while a remote machine will resolve to the hardware address of the proper default gateway. No local cache is used with host name resolution.

Configuring the HOSTS File

1. Open the following file:

   \%systemroot%\system32\drivers\etc\HOSTS

2. Read the instructions at the beginning of the HOSTS file for adding entries.

3. Go to the end of the file and type in an additional entry.

Example: `161.71.201.22 NTincharge`

4. Save the file as **HOSTS**.

Resolution via DNS

HOSTS is a pain, but it's necessary if you want to communicate within your subnet using host names. How does IP find a host name outside of your subnet or outside of your domain?

Suppose someone at `exxon.com` wanted to send a file to `mmco.com`. Surely the `exxon.com` HOSTS files don't contain the IP address of Mark's company, and vice versa?

To take a fictitious example, how would TCP/IP find a machine at some software company named "macrosoft"? How would IP figure out that a host named, say, `database.macrosoft.com` really has an IP address of, say, `181.50.47.22`?

Within an organization, name resolution can clearly be accomplished by the HOSTS file. Between domains, however, name resolution is handled by DNS. If you're only running a private intranet, then *you* perform the function of name manager instead of the central naming clearinghouse for the Internet, InterNIC Registration Services. As we discussed in Chapter 3, there's a hierarchy of names, a hierarchy created specifically to make it simple to add names to the network quickly. After all, with 20 million Internet users, can you imagine having to call the NIC every single time you put a new user on one of your networks? It would take months and all of our remaining forests to get the paperwork done. Instead, the NIC created DNS, of which you see only a small portion. The NIC started off with the six initial naming domains we mentioned earlier in this chapter: `edu`, `net`, `com`, `mil`, `org`, and `gov`. For example, there is a domain on the Internet called `whitehouse.gov`; you can send e-mail to the President that way, at `president @whitehouse.gov`. There are also root domains like `.fi` for sites in Finland, `.uk` for sites in the United Kingdom, and so on.

Although Windows NT doesn't provide a daemon or a server service to behave as a DNS in version 3.51, it does allow itself to act as a client machine. A DNS can be thought of as a networked version of the HOSTS file. In computing environments, such as UNIX, the DNS provides a central reservoir used to resolve Fully Qualified Domain Names (FQDNs) to IP addresses.

As shown in Figure 5.4, resolution begins with the issuing of a command requiring resolution. Again, the command can originate from either a machine

or a user. In our example, we show a user-originated command: `Ping Alta`
`.Fixes.Microsoft.Com`. The DNS receives a request for the IP address of the
host system, Alta. If found, the DNS will reply with the matched address. If no
match is found, or the DNS server does not respond to requests made at pro-
gressive intervals of 5, 10, 20, 40, 5, 10, and 20 seconds, an error will be generated (assuming that DNS is the only configured host name service). If a match
is achieved, the IP address is then used by the client to resolve the destination's
IP address to a hardware address with ARP. Remember... A local machine—a
destination host located on the same subnet as the sending host—will resolve
to its hardware address, while a destination for a remote host will resolve to
the hardware address of the default gateway.

FIGURE 5.4

Resolution with DNS

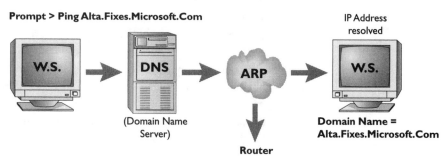

A Windows NT machine can be configured to use DNS through the procedure outlined below:

Configuring Domain Name Server Support on a Windows NT Server

1. Open the Control Panel and select Network.

2. Select the Protocols tab and click on TCP/IP Protocol, then the Properties Button. Select the DNS tab.

3. Type in your system's primary host name (additional ones may be added
as aliases in a HOSTS file) in the Host Name box. The default is the
name of the Windows NT machine. Assuming you have a domain, enter
it, making sure to include its proper extension (i.e., `.com`, `.edu`, `.gov`).

4. Type in the name of the DNS server in the DNS Search box. The order
of priority can be set using the order buttons.

5. Type in the domain suffix that you would like added to your host name. A total of six may be added to search your internetwork. The order of priority can be set using the order buttons.

6. Choose OK.

Additionally, you may set up TCP/IP to use DNS for NetBIOS by clicking on Enable DNS for Windows Networking in the WINS Address tab.

Network Information Services (NIS)

Another mechanism for mapping host names to IP addresses is Network Information Services (NIS). NIS servers can be created for a domain. These NIS servers contain databases called *maps*, which provide host-name-to-IP-address translation. Their databases can also contain user and group information. The major difference between NIS and DNS is that an NIS server covers a smaller area. NIS servers relate only to an internally contained group of computers, as in a private network, not to the entire Internet.

The Microsoft Method

Windows NT can be configured to resolve host names using either the HOSTS file or a DNS. If one of them fails, the other is there for fault tolerance to provide backup. Microsoft's implementation of TCP/IP under Windows NT supports all forms of resolution mentioned earlier: WINS, B-node broadcasts, and LMHOSTS. In Figure 5.5, we show a system configured to support all forms of name resolution.

Such a system would follow this search order:

1. Beginning with a command requiring host name resolution, (i. e., `Ping`, `Telnet`, `FTP`, etc.), the local machine's host name will be checked for a match. In the example shown in Figure 5.5, this would be `Ping Alta`. If a match is found, no further action is required, and no network traffic is created.

FIGURE 5.5

Microsoft's method of resolving host names

Prompt > Ping Alta

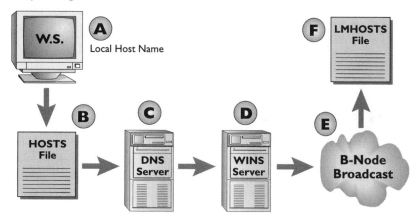

2. If the name isn't found, the next step would be to review the HOSTS file on the local machine. Again, if a match is found, no futher action is required, and no network traffic is created.

3. If the name isn't found, the next strategy will be to attempt resolution though the DNS. If no response is received from the DNS machine, repeat requests will be sent in intervals of 5, 10, 20, 40, 5, 10, and 20 seconds, progressively. If your system is configured for DNS, and the unit is offline or down, all other systems using DNS in some form will experience a considerable slowdown—so much so that they may appear to have crashed while attempting to resolve the name.

4. If the DNS server was offline, or is unable to resolve the name for some reason, a check is run on the NetBIOS name cache, followed by three attempts to get the WINS server to resolve the name.

5. If none of the attempts in step 4 successfully resolve the host name, three B-node broadcasts are then sent out.

6. If this is also unsuccessful, the final step is to search the LMHOSTS file. This action is very similar to, and corresponds to, the behavior of a Microsoft Enhanced B-node system.

If all of these resolution attempts fail, an error will be returned. Since the name can't be resolved, the only remaining way to communicate with the unresolved machine will be to use its specific IP address.

The action path of host name resolution closely resembles that of NetBIOS name resolution. The key difference between them is that NetBIOS name resolution methods generate less network traffic, whereas host names are resolved by standard UNIX methods.

Some Common Problems

There are several problems associated with host name resolution. Commonly, Ping is used to verify entries. This works extremely well unless a different client has the IP address, resulting in the dismal fact that you are actually checking the wrong machine. There is a great degree of similarity between the following list of pitfalls plaguing host name resolution and those experienced with NetBIOS name resolution.

HOSTS/DNS Does Not Contain a Name

Like the search for Atlantis, you just can't find something if it isn't there. If the name doesn't exist, the system can't find it. Quite often, companies will implement DNS as a solution. It's important to remember that if your system is configured for the wrong DNS, you won't be successful in resolving the filename, and therefore will also fail to resolve the host name to an address. This same predicament occurs when backup copies of the HOSTS file are created, but the wrong one is modified.

HOSTS Contains a Misspelled Entry

People who tell you not to let little things bug you have never had a really bad case of the flu. Little things are capable of great pain and destruction, and host name resolution can fail because of something as simple as a tiny spelling error in a command or entry in the HOSTS file. Be sure to back up the HOSTS file before making changes. HOSTS files can become really humongous, containing legions of entries—a fairly horrible thing to encounter at 3:00 A.M. when it's oh so easy to make mistakes like typos in IP addresses or host names. These entries just won't work if the host names are spelled incorrectly.

HOSTS Entry Has the Wrong IP Address

Most often, it's not that the IP address is wrong in the HOSTS file or DNS, so much as the host's IP address has changed. If this is the case, then you are trying to reach a host at an IP address that either no longer exists, or has been reassigned elsewhere. When you come across this problem, be sure to verify that you really do have the right IP address. Commonly, in our busy world, when systems are moved and IP addresses are changed, details like the HOSTS file are overlooked. Sure, the DNS was changed, and a memo was sent to management, but if the numbers don't match, your memo was a lie. If you change a machine's IP address, pay close attention to these numbers—sometimes the only way to know for sure is to check the host itself. This applies to a wrong IP address attached to a DNS server.

HOSTS File or DNS Contains Repeat NetBIOS Name Entries

Once the host name has been found with an IP address, there is no need to search any further. The systems involved consider the name to be resolved. Unfortunately, if the IP address recorded in the file is an old one, and the correct entry located below it contains the right one, the proper system will never be reached. Make sure you have only one up-to-date entry for each host name entered in the file.

E-Mail Names: A Note

If you've previously messed around with e-mail under TCP/IP, then you may be wondering something about these addresses. After all, you don't send mail to `mmco.com`, you send it to a name like `mark@mmco.com`, which is an e-mail address. The way it works is this: A group of users in a TCP/IP domain decide to implement mail. In order to receive mail, a machine must be up and running, fully ready to accept mail from some other subnet or domain. Since mail can arrive at any time of day, this machine must be up and running all the time. That seems to indicate that it would be a dumb idea to get mail delivered straight to your desktop. So, instead, TCP mail dedicates a machine to the responsibility of mail whose tasks include receiving mail from the outside world, holding that mail until you want to read it, taking mail that you wish to send somewhere else, and routing that mail to the appropriate mail router. The name of the most common TCP/IP mail router program is *sendmail*. The name of the protocol used most commonly for routing e-mail on the Internet is the Simple Mail Transfer Protocol, or SMTP.

Unfortunately, Microsoft did not include an SMTP router program in either the workstation or the server version of NT, so you either have to hook up to an existing mail router in order to get Internet mail, or you have to buy a third-party mail product to work under NT.

You can see how mail works in Figure 5.6.

FIGURE 5.6

The interrelationship of host names, e-mail names, and the Internet

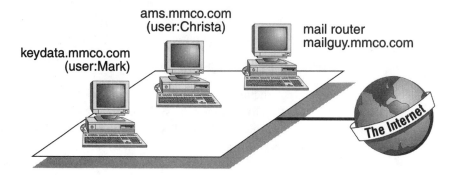

In this small domain, we've got two users, Mark and Christa. (One of the great things about the Internet is that you don't need that pesky Shift key on your keyboard.) Mark works on `keydata.mmco.com`, and Christa works on `ams.mmco.com`. Now, suppose Christa wants to send some mail to her friend Corky, executive director of Surfers of America; Corky's address is `corky@surferdudes.org`. Christa fires up a program on her workstation, which is called a *mail client*. The mail client allows her to create and send new messages, as well as receive incoming messages. She sends the message and closes her mail client. Notice that her mail client software doesn't do routing—it just lets her create, send, and receive messages.

The mail client has been configured to send messages to the program sendmail, which is running in this subnet on `mailguy.mmco.com`. Mailguy is kind of the post office (in Internet lingo, a *mail router*) for this group of users. Sendmail on `mailguy.mmco.com` stores the message, and it then sends the message off to the machine with the DNS name `surferdudes.org`, trusting IP to route the message correctly to Corky at Surfers of America.

Additionally, sendmail knows the names Christa and Mark. It is the workstation that is the interface to the outside world *vis-à-vis* mail. Note, by the way, that DNS has no idea who Mark or Christa are; DNS is concerned with host names, not e-mail names. It's DNS that worries about how to find `mailguy.mmco.com`.

A bit later, Corky gets the message and sends a reply to Christa. The reply does *not* go to Christa's machine `ams.mmco.com`; instead, it goes to `mailguy.mmco.com`, because Corky sent mail to `christa@mmco.com`. The mail system sends the messages to `mmco.com`, but what machine has the address `mmco.com`? Simple: We give `mailguy.mmco.com` an alias, and mail goes to it.

Eventually, Christa starts up the mail client program once again. The mail program sends a query to the local mail router `mailguy.mmco.com`, saying, "Any new mail for Christa?" There *is* mail, and Christa reads it.

Getting onto an Intranet

So far, we've talked quite a bit about how an intranet works and the type of stuff you can do with an intranet, but we haven't told you enough yet to actually get *on* an intranet—whether it's your company's private intranet, or *the* Internet.

- You can connect to a multi-user system and appear to the Internet as a dumb terminal.

- You can connect to an Internet provider via a serial port and a protocol called either the Serial Line Interface Protocol (SLIP) or the Point to Point Protocol (PPP), and appear to the Internet as a host.

- You can be part of a local area network that is an Internet subnet, and then load TCP/IP software on your system, and appear to the Internet as a host.

Each of these options has pros and cons, as you'll see. The general rule is that in order to access an intranet, all you basically have to do is to connect up to a computer that is already on an intranet.

Dumb Terminal Connection

This is a common way for someone to get an account that allows access to *the* Internet. For example, you can get an account with Performance Systems Inc. (PSI), Delphi, or Digital Express, to name a few Internet access providers.

Delphi, for example, has computers all around the U.S., so to get onto the Internet all you need to do is simply run a terminal emulation package on your system and dial up to their terminal servers. This kind of access is often quite cheap, at least in the U.S.: $25 per month is common. If you wanted to do this with NT, then you needn't even run TCP/IP on your NT machine. Instead, you'd merely need to put a modem on your system and use Terminal to dial up to your Internet access provider.

Now, understand: This is just a *terminal* access capability that we've gotten, so it's kind of limited. Suppose, for example, that we're in Virginia, and we connect to the Internet via a host in Maine. From the Internet's point of view, we're not in an office in Virginia; instead, we're located wherever the host we're connected to is—in this case, Maine. It follows then that any requests we make for file transfers wouldn't go to Virginia—they'd go to our host in Maine.

Now, that can be a bit of a hassle. Say we're at my Virginia location, logged onto the Internet via the Maine host. We get onto Microsoft's FTP site, and grab a few files, perhaps an updated video driver. The FTP program says, "I've got the file," but the file is now on the host in Maine. That means we're only halfway there, because we now have to run some other kind of file transfer program to move the file from the host in Maine to our computer in Virginia.

SLIP/PPP Serial Connection

A somewhat better way to connect to a TCP/IP-based network—that is, an intranet—is by a direct serial connection to an existing intranet host. If you use PCs, then you may know of a program called LapLink that allows two PCs to share each other's hard disks via their RS232 serial ports; SLIP/PPP are similar ideas. An intranet may have a similar type of connection called a SLIP or PPP connection. The connection needn't be a serial port, but it often is. SLIP is the Serial Line Interface Protocol, an older protocol that can be thought of as the *simple* line interface protocol. There's really nothing to SLIP—no error checking, no security, no flow control. It's the simplest protocol imaginable: Just send the data, then send a special byte that means, "This is the end of the data." PPP, in contrast, was designed to retain the low overhead of SLIP, and yet to include some extra information required so that more intelligent parts of an intranet—devices like routers—could use it effectively. The Point to Point Protocol works by establishing an explicit link between one side and another, then uses a simple error checking system called a *checksum* to monitor noise on the line.

Which protocol should you use? A good basic rule is that SLIP doesn't provide error checking but uses less overhead, and PPP provides error checking and uses more overhead. Therefore, when using error-correcting modems, use SLIP. On noisy lines and without error-correcting modems, use PPP.

NT supports both PPP and SLIP via Remote Access Services.

LAN Connection

The most common way to connect to an intranet is simply by being a LAN workstation on a local area network that is an intranet subnetwork. Again, this needn't be *the* Internet—almost any LAN can use the TCP/IP protocol suite.

This is the connection that most NT Servers will use to provide TCP/IP services. Microsoft's main reason for implementing TCP/IP on NT is to provide an alternative to NetBEUI, as NetBEUI is quick and applicable to small networks, but inappropriate for large corporate networks. In contrast, TCP/IP has always been good for intranetworking, but one could suffer tremendously considering speed. That's not true anymore. For example, a quick test of TCP/IP versus NetBEUI on a workstation recently showed network read rates of 1250K/sec for NetBEUI and 833K/sec for TCP/IP, and write rates of 312K/sec for NetBEUI and 250K/sec for TCP/IP. Again, TCP's slower, but not by a lot. And NetBEUI *doesn't go over routers*.

Terminal Connections versus Other Connections

Before moving on to the next topic, we'd like to return to the difference between a terminal connection and a SLIP, PPP, or LAN connection. In Figure 5.7, you see three PCs on an Ethernet attached to two minicomputers, which in turn serve four dumb terminals.

FIGURE 5.7

When Internet connections involve IP numbers and when they don't

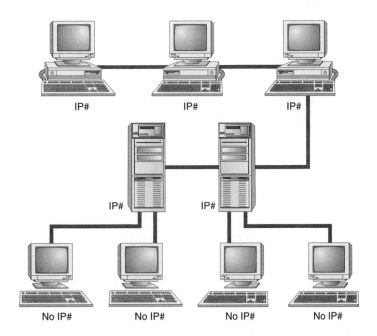

The minicomputer-to-minicomputer link might be SLIP or PPP, or then again they might be LAN-ed together. Notice that only the *computers* in this scenario have intranetwork protocol (IP) addresses. Whenever you send mail to one of the people on the PCs at the top of the picture, it goes to the mail server and then to that person's PC. If you were to scrutinize the IP addresses— most of the time, you won't—then you'd see that each person had a unique IP address. In contrast, the people at the *bottom* of the picture get their mail sent to one of the minicomputers, and so, in this example, each pair of terminals shares an IP address. If Shelly and George in your office access your company's intranet through terminals connected to the same computer, then a close look at mail from them would show that they have the same IP address. But, if you think about it, you already knew that; if you send mail to george@mailbox.acme .com and to shelly@mailbox.acme.com, then the machine name to which the mail goes is the same; it's just the user names that vary.

So, in summary: If you want to get onto *the* Internet from a remote location, then your best bet is to sign up with a service that will bill you monthly for connect charges, like Delphi. To attach to a private intranet, you need to dial up to a multi-user computer on that intranet, or you need a SLIP or PPP connection, or you have to be on a workstation on a LAN that's part of that intranet. You then need to talk to your local network guru about getting the software installed on your system that will allow your computer to speak TCP/IP so that it can be part of your intranet.

CHAPTER

6

NetBIOS Name Resolution

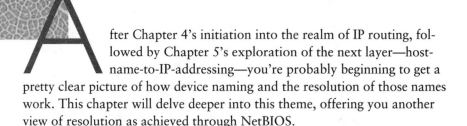

fter Chapter 4's initiation into the realm of IP routing, followed by Chapter 5's exploration of the next layer—hostname-to-IP-addressing—you're probably beginning to get a pretty clear picture of how device naming and the resolution of those names work. This chapter will delve deeper into this theme, offering you another view of resolution as achieved through NetBIOS.

NetBIOS Naming

In everyday conversation, when people refer to the place where the U.S. President lives, most would simply say, "The White House," rather than refer to his actual address of 1600 Pennsylvania Avenue. Furthermore, it would indeed be a rare bird who would reference the White House by noting its lot number as defined in a city planning grid for Washington, D.C.

It's the same with computer programs, especially those that human beings interact with. That's because for us, it's just easier to recall and keep track of a name, as opposed to an impersonal and nondescript number. This given, a logical name is referred to as a *NetBIOS name*. A NetBIOS name may be up to 15 characters in length, with an additional 16th character which internally represents the service or application that was utilized to enter the name.

When communicating with each other, systems such as Windows NT, Windows for Workgroups, LAN Manager, and LAN Manager for UNIX use NetBIOS names rather than IP addresses. NetBIOS names are generally registered when a service or application requiring use of NetBIOS is started up. A good example is Windows NT, in which the NetBIOS name is registered during the initialization phase of the server or workstation that's running it.

NetBIOS naming is widely used in Microsoft's suite of operating systems. In Windows NT, the NetBIOS name can be viewed by typing **nbtstat -n** or through the Control Panel, under Network icon. It can also be accessed in the registry under:

```
\\HKEY_LOCAL_MACHINE\SYSTEM\CurrentControlSet\Control\
ComputerName\ComputerName
```

Another common use for NetBIOS names in Windows NT is command line entries which enable connections through File Manager by using the *UNC* (Universal Naming Convention) with the net command. This naming scheme serves to make connectivity management more simple and efficient. Let's say you wanted to see exactly which shared directories were available on a certain NetBIOS computer named Bill. On a Windows NT computer, you'd begin by entering the command prompt **net view \\Bill**. If all goes well, from there you'd see that there's also a shared directory appropriately named Share. To connect to this directory, you would type **net use z: \\Bill \Share**. You'd then find yourself privy to all directories located therein.

The Name Resolution Process

Before ARP (Address Resolution Protocol) can be used to resolve an IP address to a hardware address, a NetBIOS name must first be resolved to that IP address. Again, looking to the White House analogy, suppose you'd like to send a letter to the U.S. President. To make it possible for your note to reach him, you'd need to resolve the name "White House" to its actual, physical location of 1600 Pennsylvania Ave., Washington, D.C., plus the zip code. To find the proper address information, you could look in a telephone book, ask a buddy, or call a government office. NetBIOS names are resolved much the same way, and just as in the above scenario, there are several ways to accomplish that goal. These possible resolution avenues can be sorted into two categories: *standard resolution* and *specific resolution*. Under Windows NT, all the methods by which resolution may be achieved are configurable.

Standard NetBIOS Resolution

Standard NetBIOS name resolution, which is the process of mapping a NetBIOS name to an IP address, is done dynamically by Windows NT. Standard resolution comes in these three forms:

- **Local Broadcast:** A request sent out on a local network announcing a specific device's NetBIOS name with the goal of discovering its IP address. Commonly referred to as a B-node broadcast.

- **NetBIOS Name Cache:** A listing comprised of both locally resolved names and names, other than local ones, that have been recently resolved.

- **NBNS, or NetBIOS Name Server:** Commonly implemented as a WINS, this type of name resolution conforms to RFC 1001/1002, performing NetBIOS naming resolution from a server that's running it.

Specific NetBIOS Resolution

Alternately, specific resolution is a manual process. It is the Microsoft-specific NetBIOS name resolution method for building a set of tables, and referring to them for resolution. As with standard resolution, specific resolution also comes in three different varieties:

- **LMHOSTS file:** A table stored in a local file used in resolving NetBIOS names to IP addresses on remote networks. Though similar to the HOSTS file listed below, it offers further functionality that'll be explained more thoroughly later in the chapter.

- **HOSTS file:** Remember our discussion in Chapter 5 about the table stored in a local file used to resolve host names to IP addresses? This file conforms to BSD UNIX, version 4.3's HOSTS file. Because of its versatility—it's at home on many different platforms—this is the file most commonly used with the TCP/IP utilities, FTP, Telnet, and Ping for host name resolution. It may additionally be used to address a computer by an alias.

- **Domain Name Server (DNS):** Here's another one we discussed earlier. It's also common in the UNIX world, and used for resolving a host name to an IP address. This file can be functionally thought of as a networked HOSTS file.

NetBIOS over TCP/IP Node Types

As is certainly apparent by now, there exist different modes and means by which NetBIOS names can be resolved. Just as in other forms of problem resolution, the process chosen implies, and sometimes determines, the tools that must be used. For example, when faced with a numbingly boring T.V. show, we may: (A) turn off the tube, or (B) fall asleep. If we opt for choice A, we'll either use hands, fingers, and a remote control, or legs and feet, a wheelchair, etc., to personally deactivate it. Option B would require mentally tuning it out and closing our eyes. Similarly, the modes by which a client resolves a host address are also different and named accordingly. Collectively, there are five modes for resolving names, of which four are defined by RFC 1001/1002, and one by LMHOSTS as specified by Microsoft. They are as follows:

- B-node (broadcast)

- P-node, or, peer-to-peer

- M-node (mixed)

- H-node (hybrid)

- Microsoft Enhanced B-node

B-Node (Broadcast)

Operating in this mode resolves and registers names via the broadcast of UDP datagrams. On small networks, this works well. However, as the networking environment grows, UDP data broadcasting both increases traffic and falls short of achieving its goal when routing is introduced. Typically, routers won't pass broadcasts, creating the undesirable consequence of only local systems receiving messages. One way around this is to configure the router to pass B-node broadcasts. Unfortunately, the vast amount of traffic generated by doing so quickly defeats the whole purpose of having a functional network in the first place, and therefore is not recommended.

P-Node, or Peer-to-Peer

This method of operation provides an effective and efficient means for resolving names directly from a NetBIOS Name Server (NBNS) such as WINS, with only one major drawback: The WINS IP address must be specified at each client. This can lead to major issues if the IP address is ever changed or the server goes offline. Microsoft does provide for a secondary server, but this causes a performance reduction while waiting for the primary server to time out. Also, since broadcasts aren't used, local communication isn't possible in the event a WINS server is unavailable as specified in the TCP/IP configuration at each host.

M-Node (Mixed)

This method is a composite mode wherein a client behaves as both a B-node and a P-node system. In the event the system is unable to find the IP address of a given destination machine via the broadcast mode, it'll switch to using the NBNS P-node method to directly resolve the name.

H-Node (Hybrid)

H-node is a combination of B-node and P-node. Here, we see the inverse operation of the M-node mode, and by default, an H-node functions as a P-node. Using H-node, a system will first query the NBNS, only sending a broadcast as a secondary name resolution strategy.

Microsoft Enhanced B-Node

When Microsoft TCPI/IP is initialized, it'll load the #PRE portion of the LMHOSTS static map file into the address cache. During operation, a Microsoft Enhanced B-node system first attempts to resolve names by checking the address cache before a broadcast is sent out. The system will only issue a broadcast if the name isn't found in the cache. If these efforts are unsuccessful, the system will examine the LMHOSTS file directly to achieve resolution as a last resort.

NetBIOS Name Registration, Detection, and Discharge

We can choose to have our names listed in the telephone book, to look and see if we're listed in it, and if desired, to remove our names from it. NetBIOS naming is similar in this respect. All modes of NetBIOS over TCP/IP use a form of registration and duplicate detection, and all discharge obsolete or otherwise unwanted names. Operations such as these are commonly resolved through broadcasts, or by contacting a NetBIOS name service. There are three ways NetBIOS names are registered, released, and discovered as part of the NetBIOS name resolution process. They are:

- **Name registration:** As a NetBIOS over TCP/IP host starts up, it registers its name through a NetBIOS name registration request. If the designated name is found to be a duplicate, the host, or NetBIOS Name Server to which the client is registering, will counter with a negative name registration response. An initialization error will result.

- **Name detection:** When communicating between NetBIOS, a name query request is issued for resolution. Depending on how the request was issued, either the host which possesses that name or the NetBIOS Name Server will reply with a positive name query response.

- **Name discharge:** At the conclusion of a NetBIOS over TCP/IP host-assisted session, the NetBIOS name that the system has used is discharged. This prevents the system from issuing negative name registration responses resulting from duplicates when later attempts are made to register that same name by a different system. This catharsis takes place when the unit is either taken offline or workstation service ends.

B-Node: NetBIOS Names Resolved Locally

The steps listed below are crucial in understanding NetBIOS name resolution, and why it functions the way it does. A solid grasp of how NetBIOS names are resolved when the destination host is on the local network will equip you with much more than answers to basic questions—it provides a foundation for understanding later topics which evolve from it. The process for achieving the resolution of NetBIOS names on the local network is shown in Figure 6.1 and described below:

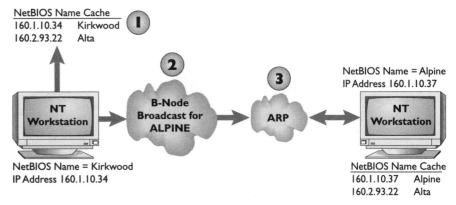

FIGURE 6.1

Illustrating how a local NetBIOS name is resolved to an IP address using a B-node broadcast

DOS Prompt > NET USE K: \\Alpine\public

NetBIOS Name Cache
160.1.10.34   Kirkwood
160.2.93.22   Alta

NetBIOS Name = Alpine
IP Address 160.1.10.37

NT Workstation

B-Node Broadcast for ALPINE

ARP

NT Workstation

NetBIOS Name = Kirkwood
IP Address 160.1.10.34

NetBIOS Name Cache
160.1.10.37   Alpine
160.2.93.22   Alta

1. Systems operating in B-node mode initiate a command with a NetBIOS requirement like `net use k: \\Alpine\public`. To prevent costly name-resolution transactions, the system will first check the local address cache. If the name is found there, adding traffic to the network, and thereby reducing its speed and efficiency, can successfully be avoided. If no match is found, the system moves on to step 2.

2. At this stage, name query broadcasts are sent out on the local network carrying the request for the destination's NetBIOS name.

3. The broadcast is received by all systems on the local network. They will all begin to check to see if their name matches the one broadcasted. If the owner is found, that device will prepare a name query response. This

response is sent out as soon as ARP resolves the hardware address of the system that initiated the name query. As the requesting system receives the positive response, a NetBIOS connection is established.

> Recall that, typically, routers won't pass broadcasts, resulting in only the local systems getting the message. Broadcasts that are passed increase network traffic, thereby decreasing performance. Because of this, even though many routers can support broadcasts, the function is usually disabled.

Enhanced B-Node: NetBIOS Names Resolved Remotely

When a host resides on a remote system, a local broadcast will still be issued in an attempt to resolve the name. If the broadcast is passed by the router, the request will be answered and processed in the same manner as a local B-node resolution request. If this effort fails, the LMHOSTS file is examined in a further attempt to locate the specific address (see Figure 6.2).

FIGURE 6.2

Resolving remote NetBIOS names

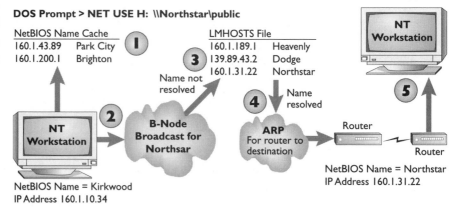

1. Systems operating in Enhanced B-node mode initiate a command with a NetBIOS requirement—again, as an example: `net use h: \\NorthStar\ public`. As in regular B-node mode, the system checks the local address cache, looks no further if found, and moves on to the next step if this endeavor is unsuccessful.

2. Again, as in non-enhanced B-node mode, at this stage, the system broadcasts a name query request on the local network looking for `\\NorthStar`.

Assuming the destination system resides on another network, and the mediating router won't pass B-node broadcasts, the resolution request will again fail, requiring things to proceed to step 3.

3. Here, the LMHOSTS file is searched, and the corresponding entry is found: NorthStar, IP address 160.1.31.22. The address is resolved.

4. Once the IP address is revealed to the requesting remote system, the local routing table is consulted for the most efficient path to it. If one isn't found, an ARP request is made to obtain the hardware address of the default gateway. Whenever a remote address is identified, it will be sent to the gateway for delivery. Since the gateway is used frequently, its hardware address is usually acquired from the local cache. Alternately, if it's not present in the cache, it can be located via broadcast.

5. A response is sent out as soon as ARP resolves the hardware address of the router. When the response is received by the requesting system, a NetBIOS connection is established.

Resolving NetBIOS Names with a NetBIOS Name Server

Now we're going to take a look at how name resolution works when using a NetBIOS Name Server (NBNS). A common implementation of an NBNS is a WINS (Windows Internet Name Service) server. An NBNS is highly flexible, so these servers enjoy wide usage. They'll function in P-node, M-node, as well as H-node modes of NetBIOS over TCP/IP. Another reason for their popularity is that using an NBNS extends better performance than does traditional broadcast resolution. See Figure 6.3 on how NetBIOS names are resolved to an IP address using a NetBIOS name server.

FIGURE 6.3

Resolving names with a NetBIOS Name Server

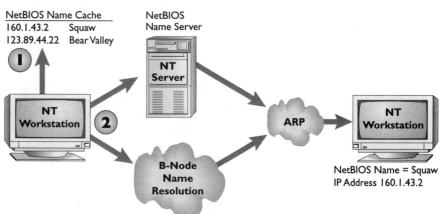

As in prior examples, the process of resolving a NetBIOS name begins with entering a command that triggers the initiation of it, e.g., net use, net view, etc. It also parallels previous methods in the following ways:

1. **Net use L: \\SquawValley\public**. The system will explore the local address cache to try to resolve the name.

   - If found, resolution is achieved, and the ARP process will commence for the additional resolution of the hardware address.

   - The object of things functioning thus is to avoid creating any additional traffic on the network.

   - In this mode of operation, no matter what's done, the local cache will always be checked before any further resolution efforts are begun.

2. Depending on the mode by which TCP/IP is configured, the step that comes next varies. Following is a list organizing these special circumstances.

   - **P-node (peer to peer)**: After step 1 collectively fails to resolve the name, a request is sent directly to the NetBIOS name server. If found, the identified name is returned in a response to the requesting system.

   - **M-node (mixed)**: If step 1 fails to resolve the name, the steps outlined for B-node broadcasts are followed. If this strategy also misfires, the host will then attempt to resolve the NetBIOS name as if it were configured as a P-node.

   - **H-node (hybrid)**: Again, as with M-node, should step 1 attempts prove unsuccessful, the steps detailed earlier in the section for P-nodes are then followed. If these also flop, the host will then attempt to resolve the NetBIOS name as if it were a B-node—by using a broadcast.

3. As soon as the host name is resolved, as in steps 1 or 2, ARP is used to determine the hardware address.

NetBIOS Name Resolution in Action

Microsoft's implementation of TCP/IP under Windows NT supports all forms of resolution mentioned earlier. If your system has been configured in this fashion, you would then find that Microsoft has designated that name searches follow this sequence (see Figure 6.4).

FIGURE 6.4

The Microsoft method of resolving NetBIOS names

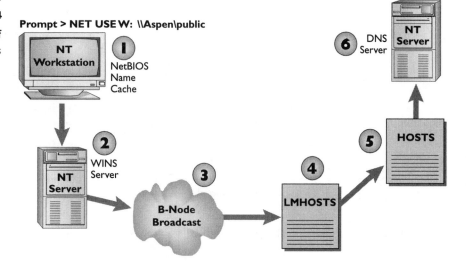

1. The process begins by entering a command initiating NetBIOS name resolution, such as **net use w: \\Aspen\public**. At this point, the local address cache will be checked for the destination host.

2. Assuming the name wasn't found, the next step is to contact the WINS server following the process outlined under P-node in this chapter.

3. If the WINS server was unable to locate the name, or if it did, and identified it as unavailable, Microsoft's TCP/IP would then issue a B-node type broadcast.

4. If the broadcast fails to hit paydirt, the next step is to search the LMHOSTS file. The action taken corresponds to that of a Microsoft Enhanced B-node system.

5. At this point, the HOSTS file, which resides on the local hard drive, will be examined.

6. The last gasp efforts that will be made are done though DNS. If the DNS machine is ignoring you and not responding, a repeat request will be sent to

it at intervals of 5, then 10, 20, 40, 5, 10, and 20 seconds. If your system's configured for DNS, and the unit has crashed or is offline, all systems on the network that are using DNS in some form or another will experience a considerable operational slowdown. The delay can be so pronounced, systems can appear to have crashed while resolving the name. This sinister effect is most commonly seen with Windows for Workgroups, and isn't nearly as nasty with Windows NT. NT's process managing is much more efficient.

If all attempts at resolution fall short of the target, an error message will be sent in reply. However, it should be pointed out here that Microsoft's implementation provision for name resolution is not only tenacious, it's efficient. Its system's sequence of resolution strategies prioritize in such a way that it chooses first the quickest method, requiring the minimum cost in network overhead. Also important to note is that once resolution is achieved, no further steps are taken—it does not simply complete a predetermined process, it monitors that process, only doing that which is required to accomplish success, and no more.

NetBIOS Resolution Locally via LMHOSTS

LMHOSTS is a static table that's stored in a local file used to resolve NetBIOS names to IP addresses on remote networks. Just like any other table, LMHOSTS has a specific format, and supports special functions based on the commands entered therein. Functionally, LMHOSTS offers the following:

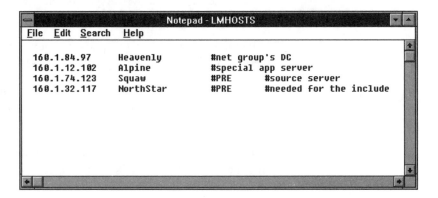

- Name resolution, when called upon.

- A single entry for names-to-IP addresses. All other following entries will be ignored if the same NetBIOS name is used in combination with a different IP address.

To avoid constant reboots for changes in the LMHOSTS file, entries can be manually loaded by typing **nbtstat -R**. Note that the -R is case sensitive.

- The ability to load the IP addresses of frequently accessed host machines into memory by using the #PRE remark after the entry. This is a handy little feature for reducing network traffic, since it warrants that no broadcasts need to be made to access the host. The information intended for the lines with the #PRE remark is loaded when NetBIOS over TCP/IP is initialized.

- Domain validation, account synchronization, and browsing by adding #DOM to an entry line.

All statements in Microsoft TCP/IP32 that begin with a # sign are treated as comments.

- Support for old LMHOSTS files originating from older implementations of Microsoft TCP/IP, such as LAN Manager.

- On Windows NT systems, maintenance of LMHOSTS in %SystemRoot%\ system32\drivers\etc. (Default directory is WinNT. If installed from an upgrade, it will be in the previous versions of Windows directory.)

NetBIOS Resolution Networked via LMHOSTS File

As mentioned earlier, Microsoft has created enhanced flexibility with their implementation of TCP/IP. Conforming to this standard is the expanded functionality regarding LMHOSTS. Microsoft has added features to LMHOSTS, like the unprecedented ability to use it within a networked, or centralized, configuration. This not only makes the file readily accessible and easily amended and expanded, but facilitates and simplifies the entire TCP/IP management process.

A networked LMHOSTS file can be added to a local LMHOSTS file by adding #INCLUDE to the beginning of the line that precedes the file you desire to add.

The following graphic illustrates how to use a networked LMHOSTS file:

```
=                     Notepad - LMHOSTS                      ▼ ▲
 File  Edit  Search  Help
                                                              ▲
   160.1.84.97     Heavenly        #net group's DC
   160.1.12.102    Alpine          #special app server
   160.1.74.123    Squaw           #PRE     #source server
   160.1.32.117    NorthStar       #PRE     #needed for the include

 #INCLUDE \\localsrv\public\lmhosts
 #INCLUDE \\rhino\public\lmhosts

   160.1.55.23     Dodge           #Worthless server


                                                              ▼
 ◄ ►                                                        ► 
```

Windows NT 4 automatically examines the LMHOSTS file prior to users logging on. Because the NetBIOS Helper service starts at boot-up, when it doesn't yet have a user name to retrieve the LMHOSTS file from a remote system, a null user name is substituted. Unlike Windows NT 3.1, version 4 must be specifically configured to support null user names.

Shared LMHOSTS files should be accessible by all users. To make a share accessible by a null user, use REGEDT32 to modify:

\HKEY_LOCAL_MACHINE\SYSTEM\CurrentControlSet\Services\
LanmanServer\Parameters\NullSessionShares

On a new line in NullSessionShares, type the name of the share for which you want null session support, such as **Public**. This complete, you can now activate it by either rebooting, or stopping and then starting, the Server service.

This process sounds rather long, however in practice, these steps go by rather quickly.

An alternative to modifying the Registry is to manually run the nbtstat -R command to include the remote LMHOSTS files. Depending on your requirements, you could place this command in a batch file such as a login script, if used, or place an icon in the startup group to automate a manual process. The best approach is to either modify the Registry, or place the file in a login script.

Block Inclusion

The LMHOSTS file has one final feature that we haven't yet discussed—block inclusion. This is a special, last resort, reconnaissance-type feature that enables you to spy into another system's LMHOSTS file and look up unresolved names.

The only time block inclusion is used is after all other LMHOSTS search path possibilities have been exhausted. If the system is unable to find the name you desire resolved in the local cache, and additionally fails through use of any #PRE tags and pre-existing file entries to the block inclusion, only then should you use block inclusion.

A block inclusion is designated by placing #begin_alternate and #end_alternate at the beginning and ending of the block, respectively. During a search, the first system listed in the inclusion block is checked for a match to a requested name. Whether that name is successfully resolved or not, no additional systems will be searched in the block unless that first system is unreachable, and perhaps offline. Only then would the next entry in the inclusion block be read. Lines that are typically found in the block inclusion are usually started with #include, which designates a remote system. When deciding whether or not to search LMHOSTS files recorded in a block inclusion, keep in mind that this feature exists more for purposes of fault tolerance than it does for facilitating group searches. Doing multiple recursive searches may progressively lead to longer and longer resolution times as your list grows.

Speaking of performance, when initially designing the LMHOSTS file, it's very important to keep in mind that the names of the most commonly used systems should be placed at the top of the file, and all #PRE entries at the bottom. Since the LMHOSTS file is read from top to bottom, doing this will help you to find your more commonly accessed machines more quickly. The #PRE entries can be ignored after TCP/IP initializes.

The following graphic is an example of an LMHOSTS file with block inclusion:

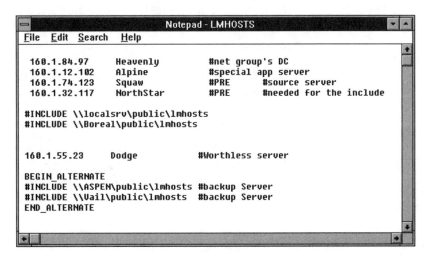

NetBIOS Name-Resolution Headaches

Just as it is with so many things (too many?) in this ol' world, you have to follow certain guidelines in order for things to operate smoothly. For example, if, like so many people, you fail to change your car's oil every 3,500 miles, you spend far too much time with your mechanic, and bring about premature death to your car. It's much the same with the LMHOSTS file, as it is with TCP/IP in general. Not understanding or following guidelines and proper procedure,1 and failing to maintain things well, cause problems. Here are a few common ones:

Case Study #1: A Horse with No Name—When NetBIOS Names Cannot Be Resolved

We know you'll be absolutely stunned to hear that when a NetBIOS name can't be resolved, it's usually because a user has forgotten that a specific entry is required for each device that needs to be resolved by the system that's been asked to resolve it. For instance, a company that uses both a WINS server and LMHOSTS file may find that they can only access some of their computers when their WINS server is taken offline. Why? Because the WINS server was nicely up-to-date—knowing all servers, but the LMHOSTS file wasn't.

The Moral of the Story Ignore it, and it will go away... maintain it, and it's here to stay.

Case Study #2: Spell-Check

...or the case of mistaken identity. It is amazing how many times people will add a host name containing a one (1), and replace it with a lower case L (l), or the Roman Numeral one (I). As with host names, the way a NetBIOS name is spelled in the system is exactly the way it must be entered when trying to resolve it.

The Moral of the Story Don't get creative with host names—keep 'em the same.

Case Study #3: Return to Sender—No Longer at This Address

Usually it's not that the IP address is entered wrong in the LMHOSTS file, but that the host's IP address has changed. If it has, then you are trying to reach a host at an IP address that either no longer exists, or has now been reassigned. It's important to be sure—verify that you really do have the right IP address.

During a big undertaking, such as the movement of an entire network system, or when IP addresses on HOSTS are changed, small things, like LMHOSTS files, are commonly overlooked. Sure, the DNS was changed, memos were e-mailed to management, etc., but even the most efficient folks can make mistakes. Pay close attention to the numbers— sometimes the only way to know is to check the host itself.

The Moral of the Story   Make your list, and check it twice.

Case Study #4: Sorry—I Thought You Were Someone Else

As we've pounded into you, once the name has been found, accompanied by its corresponding IP address, there's no need to search any further. Resolution has been achieved. Unfortunately, if the name listed in the file is associated with the wrong, or more commonly, obsolete IP address, the correct entry below it will never be reached. Just as you're sometimes judged by the company you keep, so are computers!

The Moral of the Story   Don't procrastinate—stay up to date. Make sure that you have only one, *current* entry for each NetBIOS name.

Words to the Wise

Debugging problems in TCP/IP is easy if you have a clear understanding of each individual part's function. While each element and its role is pretty straightforward stuff, trying to put it all together to grasp the Big Picture can be difficult and confusing. Small, simple details can grow to become really big problems if overlooked, or are otherwise hidden from you. For instance, suppose a certain host was moved, and another device was put in its place using the same IP address. When pinging diagnostically, you'd get the impression that the server was up and running. However, what's really happening is that the address is no longer representing the server you think it is—you're not talking to the server, you're talking to some mysterious other machine! All in all, understanding how all the pieces of the TCP/IP puzzle fit together, paying attention to details, and considering an action's consequences will make you better able to both prevent problems before they occur, and equip you with solutions to solve them when they do.

Next we're going to take a look at using Dynamic Host Configuration Protocol to give dynamic IP addresses to our HOSTS.

CHAPTER

7

Microsoft NT TCP/IP with DHCP

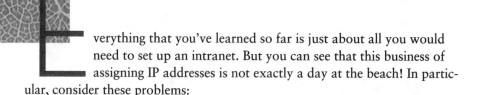

Everything that you've learned so far is just about all you would need to set up an intranet. But you can see that this business of assigning IP addresses is not exactly a day at the beach! In particular, consider these problems:

- Wouldn't it be nice not to have to keep track of which IP addresses you've used and which ones remain?

- And how do you assign a temporary IP address to a visiting computer, like a laptop?

Looking at these problems—and possible solutions—leads toward an understanding of DHCP and how to install it.

Simplifying TCP/IP Administration: BootP

As an administrator, it's great to have a little list...a list of PCs and IP addresses—kind of a master directory of which IP addresses have been used so far. Obviously, you'd have to consult it when putting TCP/IP on each new computer.

Enter Murphy's law. It's unfortunate that you just never seem to have that list handy when you need it. One way to deal with this is to start keeping this list of computers and IP addresses on one of your servers, in a kind of common HOSTS file. This serves two purposes: First, it tells you what IP addresses were already used, and second, it gives you a HOSTS file to copy to the local computer's hard disk.

However, that's kind of a hassle too. Why on earth should we have to manually tend to what is clearly a rote, mechanical job—you know, the kind of job that computers are good at!

The Internet world agreed and invented a TCP/IP protocol called BootP, which became DHCP, as you will see. With BootP, a network administrator would first collect a list of MAC addresses for each LAN card. MAC, or Media Access Control, addresses are unique 48-bit identifiers for each network card.

Next, the administrator would assign an IP address to each MAC address. A server on the company's intranet would then hold this table of MAC address/IP address pairs. Then, when a BootP-enabled workstation would start up for the day, it would broadcast a request for an IP address. The BootP server would recognize the MAC address from the broadcaster, and would supply the IP address to the workstation.

This was a great improvement over the static IP addressing system we've described so far. The administrator didn't have to physically travel to each workstation to give them their own IP addresses; she needed only to modify a file on the BootP server when a new machine arrived or if it was necessary to change IP addresses for a particular set of machines.

Another great benefit of BootP was that it provided protection from the "helpful user." Suppose you have user Tom, who sits next to user Dick. Dick's machine isn't accessing the network correctly, so helpful user Tom says, "Well, *I'm* getting on the net fine, so let's just copy all of this confusing network stuff from my machine to yours." The result was that both machines ended up with identical configurations—including identical IP addresses, so now neither Tom *nor* Dick can access the network without errors! In contrast, if Tom's machine is only set up to go get its IP address from its local BootP server, then setting up Dick's machine identically will cause no harm, as it will just tell Dick's machine to get *its* address from the BootP server. Dick will get a different address (provided that the network administrator has typed in an IP address for Dick's MAC address), and all will be well!

DHCP: BootP Plus

BootP's ability to hand out IP addresses from a central location is terrific, but it's not dynamic. The network administrator must know beforehand what all of the MAC addresses of the Ethernet cards on her network are. This isn't *impossible* information to obtain, but it's a bit of a pain (usually typing **ipconfig /all** from a command line yields the data). Furthermore, there's no provision for handing out temporary IP addresses, like an IP address for a laptop used by a visiting executive.

DHCP improves upon BootP in that you just give it a range of IP addresses that it's allowed to hand out, and it just gives them out first-come, first-served to whatever computers request them. If, on the other hand, you want to maintain full BootP-like behavior, then you can; it's possible with DHCP to pre-assign IP addresses to particular MAC addresses too.

With DHCP, you only have to hard-wire the IP addresses of a few machines, like your BootP/DHCP server, and your default gateway.

Let's take a look at how to get a DHCP server up on your network so the IP addresses will start getting handed out dynamically. Then we'll explore how DHCP works.

Installing and Configuring DHCP Servers

DHCP servers are the machines that provide IP addresses to machines that request access to the LAN. DHCP only works if the TCP/IP software on the workstations is *built* to work with DHCP—if the TCP/IP software includes a *DHCP client*. NT includes TCP/IP software with DHCP clients for Windows for Workgroups and DOS. NT workstations and Windows 95 workstations are already DHCP-aware.

To get ready for DHCP configuration:

- Have an IP address ready for your DHCP server—this is one computer on your network that *must* have a hard-wired IP address.

- Know which IP addresses are free to assign. You use these available IP addresses to create a pool, or *scope,* of IP addresses.

To start up DHCP configuration:

1. Open the Control Panel and the Network applet, and click on the Services tab.

2. Click on Add.

3. Select Microsoft DHCP Server, and click on OK. You'll be prompted, as always, for the location of the files. An information dialog box will appear and instruct you to change any IP addresses on your network card(s) to static addresses. Click on OK.

4. The DHCP software will install. Click on the Close button, and the binding operations will begin. After a while the hard drive activity stops. You'll see a screen like Figure 7.1. Here you specify a static IP address.

FIGURE 7.1

The Microsoft TCP/IP Properties dialog box

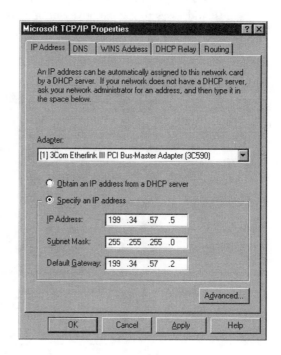

5. Once the system has rebooted, you'll find a new icon in the Administrative Tools group, the DHCP Manager. Start it up, and you'll see a screen like Figure 7.2.

FIGURE 7.2

DHCP opening screen

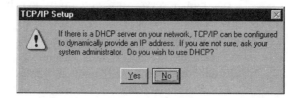

Not much to look at now, as there are no scopes set up yet. Scopes? What's a scope? Let's find out…

DHCP Scopes

In order for DHCP to give out IP addresses, it must know the range of IP addresses that it can give out. You tell it with a *scope*. You have to create a scope for your DHCP server, and you do that by clicking on Scope, and Create…. You'll see a screen like the one shown in Figure 7.3.

FIGURE 7.3

Create Scope dialog box

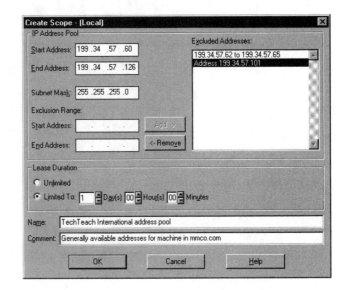

A scope is simply a range of IP addresses—a specific pool from which they can be drawn. In the example shown, we've created a scope that ranges from a .60 address to a .126 address. Another fine use for scopes: You can assign a scope to each subnet serviced by your DHCP servers, and yes, it *is* possible for one DHCP server to handle multiple subnets. We'll also show you how to get more than one server to act as a DHCP server (for the sake of fault tolerance) in a minute.

Getting back to actually setting up a scope: Note that the dialog box's title is Create Scope (Local). That's because you can control a DHCP server from another NT machine, as is the case with so many NT network functions.

You should also note that we've filled in the Start Address, End Address, Lease Duration, Name, and Comment fields. Let's see why...

Start Address and End Address specify a range of possible IP addresses to give out. As said, we've offered the addresses from the .60 address through the .126 address for that IP pool. That's 67 addresses, which is a sufficient amount for a respectable Class C network. Another valid way to go about that is to offer all 250-odd addresses, then exclude particular addresses with the Exclusion Range field.

The Name and Comment fields are used mainly for administering scopes later. The Lease Duration field has Unlimited checked by default, but don't *you* use that—the alternative "one day" option is the better one. Click on OK, and you'll see a dialog box like Figure 7.4.

FIGURE 7.4

Activating a new scope

Click on Yes, and it will be immediately available. The DHCP Manager will then look something like Figure 7.5.

FIGURE 7.5

DHCP Manager with an active scope

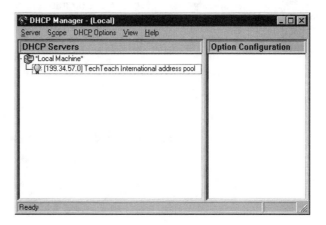

Note the lighted light bulb: that indicates an *active* scope. But you're not done yet. DHCP can provide default values for a whole host of TCP/IP parameters, including these basic items:

- Default gateway

- Domain name

- DNS server

- WINS server (DHCP calls it a WINS/NBNS server)

Remember that you had to manually type all that stuff in when you assigned fixed IP addresses? Well, DHCP lets you specify some defaults, making it an even more attractive addressing alternative. Just click on DHCP Options, and you'll see options called Global, Scope, and Default.

Click on Global to modify options that don't change from subnet to subnet, like the domain name or the DNS and WINS server addresses.

Click on Local to modify options that are relevant to particular subnets, like the address of the default gateway (which DHCP, for some perverse reason, calls the Router).

If you set an option like Domain Name, or WINS Server via DHCP, but also specify a value for that option in the client PC in the Control Panel ➤ Network Protocol ➤ TCIP ➤ Properties, then the value you set in the Control Panel overrides the DHCP settings.

Most of the settings are global, so click on Global, and you'll see a dialog box like the one shown in Figure 7.6.

FIGURE 7.6

Setting DHCP global options

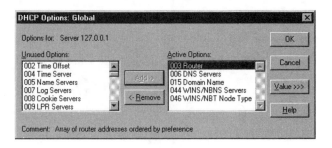

Now, despite the fact that there seem to be bushels of sadly unused parameters, mutely begging to be used, *don't*. Even though they exist, the Microsoft DHCP *clients* don't know how to use any options save the ones we just mentioned. They're just parts of Windows, DOS, Windows 95, and NT that know how to get IP addresses from a DHCP server. Microsoft included the other things just to remain compatible with BootP. Again, the five we adjusted were:

- **DNS Servers**; here we named our two DNS servers.

- **Domain name**, in this case, `mmco.com`.

- **WINS/NBNS Servers**, with the addresses of the WINS servers (which we'll cover soon). Setting this requires that you also set...

- **WINS/NBT Node Type**, a cryptic-looking setting that you needn't worry about, except for to set it to 0x8; that makes WINS run best. We'll explain node types in the upcoming discussion on WINS.

- **Router** (by going over to the Local settings), which is, again, the DHCP equivalent of the Default Gateway option in the TCP/IP setup screen.

We did this by highlighting the option we wanted to use, then clicking on Add. Then, we can click on Value and Edit Array. For example, say we wanted to make our default gateway `199.34.57.2`. We'd click on Router, then Edit Array. We'd then get a dialog box that looks like Figure 7.7.

FIGURE 7.7

Setting the default router address

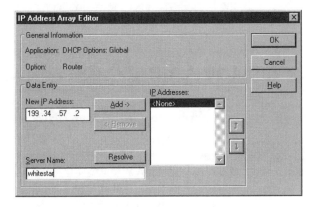

Notice that the original default value is 0.0.0.0, which is a meaningless address in this context. We entered 199.34.57.2 and clicked on Add, but didn't stop there. Next, we clicked on 0.0.0.0 and clicked on Remove. *Then* we clicked on OK.

Do the same thing with the domain name and the DNS router, and you're set. The DHCP Manager now looks like Figure 7.8.

FIGURE 7.8

The DHCP manager

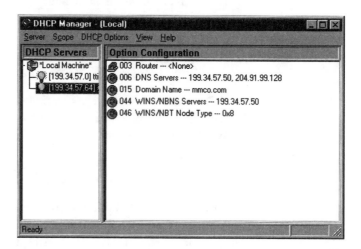

Note the different icons for the global settings and the local settings. Close up the DHCP Manager, and your server is set up. You don't even need to reboot.

DHCP on the Client Side

Now that you've set up DHCP on a server, how do you tell clients to use it? Simple. The Windows for Workgroups TCP/IP 32-bit software has DHCP configuration as an installation option, as does the latest Microsoft Client software for DOS and Windows. If you want to find out what IP address a client machine has, go to that machine, open up a command line, and type **ipconfig /all.** On a Windows 95 workstation, click on Start and Run, and then type **WINIPCFG** and press Enter.

DHCP in Detail

That's setting up DHCP. But how does it work and, dismally, why does it sometimes *not* work?

DHCP supplies IP addresses based on the idea of *client leases*. When a machine (a DHCP client) needs an IP address, it asks a DHCP server for that address. A DHCP server then gives an IP address to the client, *but only for a temporary period of time*—hence the term *IP lease*. You might have noticed that you can set the term of an IP lease from DHCP; it's one of the settings in Scope ➤ Properties.

The client then knows how long it's got the lease. Even if you reboot or reset your computer, it'll remember the lease that's active for it, and how much longer it's got on that lease.

On a Windows 3.*x* machine, that information is kept in dhcp.bin in the Windows directory. On a Windows 95 machine, it's in HKEY_LOCAL_MACHINE\System\ CurrentControlSet\Services\VxD\DHCP\Dhcp-info*xx*, where *xx* is two digits. If you wish to enable or disable the error messages from the DHCP client on a Windows 95 machine, it's the value PopupFlag in the key HKEY_LOCAL _MACHINE\System\CurrentControlSet\Services\VxD\DHCP; use 00 00 00 00 for false, or 01 00 00 00 for true.

If your PC had a four-day lease on a certain address, and you rebooted two days into its lease, the PC wouldn't just blindly ask for an IP address. Instead, it would go back to the DHCP server that it got its IP address from, and request the same IP address it had before. If the DHCP server were still up, then it would acknowledge the request, letting the workstation use the IP address. But what if the DHCP server had its lease information wiped out through some disaster? Well, if no one else is using the address, it would go ahead and give the IP address to the machine. If, on the other hand, the address is in use by another machine, the DHCP server would send a *negative acknowledgment*, or *NACK*, back and make a note of that NACK in the Event Log. In a perfect world, your workstation would be smart enough to start searching around for a new DHCP server— but this is Earth, and sometimes workstations aren't what they should be.

188 Chapter 7 · Microsoft NT TCP/IP with DHCP

Like BootP, DHCP remembers which IP addresses go with what machine by matching up an IP address with a MAC (Media Access Control, i.e. Ethernet address).

This leads to the following tip:

Do not set the leases to Infinite. This seems like a cool way to easily assign fixed IP addresses. The first time a system logs on, it gets an IP address, and all seems well, but there are two problems with this. The first one's minor: What if you have to reinstall your DHCP server, but didn't back up the Registry where the DHCP database lives? Your system would proceed to spend a lot of time NACKing innocent PCs. The second one's worse: What if you want to reconfigure your network? Suppose you have 200 people in two departments on the same subnet. You decide to divide them up into two subnets. Half of the users of the old subnet will now be on a new subnet, requiring a whole new set of IP addresses. Obviously you have to create a new scope, but creating the new scope is easy. The *problem* is, how do you force a new IP address on the people in the new subnet? Their leases never expire, so they never really give the DHCP server a chance to assign them new addresses. (Well, it would, but only after lots of NACKing and plenty of systems that will randomly refuse to communicate with anything.) So, keep yourself sane by setting the lease to a few days. You can then enforce changes to your subnet structure automatically through the DHCP servers.

Let's expand on that a bit. Suppose you know that on November 1 you're going to take your 200.1.1.x subnet and break it up into 200.1.1.x and 200.1.2.x. Now, with old static IP addresses, you'd be faced with the prospect of having to go to every single workstation and change its IP address by hand. With DHCP, however, you don't have to do that.

Instead, here's the process. Suppose you give out 10-day leases. Nine days before November 1, reduce the lease length to nine days. The next day, reduce the leases to eight days, and so on. On October 31, reduce lease length to just a few hours. Then, after hours, do the physical partitioning of your subnets—install the routers and isolate the machines for the new subnet on the 200.1.2.x side—and create the new 200.1.2.x scope on your DHCP server—piece of cake!

Getting an IP Address from DHCP: The Nuts and Bolts

A DHCP client gets an IP address from a DHCP server in four steps:

1. A *DHCPDISCOVER* broadcasts a request to all DHCP servers in earshot, requesting an IP address.

2. The servers respond with *DHCPOFFER* of IP addresses and lease times.

3. The client chooses the offer that sounds most appealing and broadcasts back a *DHCPREQUEST* to confirm its acceptance of the IP address.

4. The server handing out the IP address finishes the procedure by returning with a *DHCPACK*—an acknowledgment of the request.

Initial DHCP Request: DHCPDISCOVER

First, a DHCP client sends out a message called a *DHCPDISCOVER* saying, in effect, "Any DHCP servers out there? If so, I want an IP address." This message is shown in Figure 7.9.

FIGURE 7.9

DHCP step 1: DHCPDISCOVER

DHCP
client

Enet addr: 00CC00000000
IP addr: 0.0.0.0

"Is there a DHCP server around?"

IP address used: 255.255.255.255 (broadcast)
Ethernet address used: FFFFFFFFFFFF (broadcast)
Transaction ID: 14321

DHCP
server

Enet addr: 00BB00000000
IP addr: 210.22.31.100

You may be wondering how a machine can communicate if it doesn't have an address. Well, it does so through a different protocol than TCP—namely, UDP, the User Datagram Protocol. It's not a NetBIOS or NetBEUI creature; it's all TCP/IP-suite stuff.

Now, to follow all of these DHCP messages, there are a couple of things to watch. First of all, we're showing you both the Ethernet addresses (Token Ring addresses for those of you using Token Ring) and the IP addresses, because they tell somewhat different stories. Also, there is a "transaction ID" attached to each DHCP packet that's quite useful. The transaction ID makes it possible for a client to discern exactly *what* the server is responding to in the first place, as well as understand the response itself.

In this case, notice that the IP address to which the message is sent is 255.255 .255.255. That's the generic address for "Anybody on this subnet." Now, 210 .22.31.255 would also work, assuming that this is a Class C network that hasn't been subnet-ted, but 255.255.255.255 pretty much always means, "Anyone who can hear me." If you set up your routers to forward broadcasts, then 255 .255.255.255 will be propagated all over the network; 210.22.31.255 would not. Notice also the destination Ethernet address, FFFFFFFFFFFF. That's the Ethernet way of saying, "Everybody—a broadcast."

DHCP Offers Addresses from Near and Far

Any DHCP servers within earshot—that is, any that receive the UDP datagram—respond to the client with an offer, a proposed IP address, like the one shown in Figure 7.10. Again, this is an offer, not the final IP address.

This offering part of the DHCP process is essential because it's possible for more than one DHCP server to hear the original client request. If every DHCP server just thrust an IP address at the hapless client, then it would end up with multiple IP addresses, addresses wasted in the sense that the DHCP servers would consider them all taken, and so they couldn't give those addresses out to other machines.

Worse yet, what if a DHCP server from another subnet gave an IP address to our client? Wouldn't that put the client in the wrong subnet? DHCP keeps that from happening via BootP forwarding. The original UDP message, "Are there any DHCP servers out there?" is a broadcast, and most routers don't forward those. If DHCP requests don't go over routers, then you would need a DHCP server on every subnet, a rather expensive scenario.

The BootP standard got around this by defining RFC 1542, a specification whereby routers following RFC 1542 would recognize BootP broadcasts, and forward them to other subnets. The feature must be implemented in your

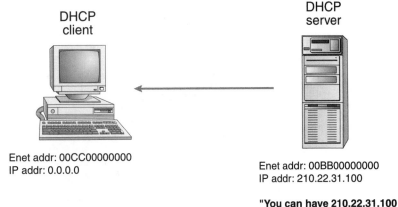

DHCP
client

DHCP
server

Enet addr: 00CC00000000
IP addr: 0.0.0.0

Enet addr: 00BB00000000
IP addr: 210.22.31.100

**"You can have 210.22.31.100
for two days."**

IP address used: 255.255.255.255 (broadcast)
Ethernet address used: 00CC00000000 (directed)
Transaction ID: 14321

routers' software, and it's commonly known as (you've got it) BootP forwarding. Of course, when an NT machine acts as an IP router, it implements BootP forwarding.

Assuming that you have routers that support BootP forwarding, the original DHCP request will reach all of them. But how do we keep a DHCP server in an imaginary subnet 200.1.2.x from giving one of its available addresses in 200.1.2.x to a PC sitting in some other imaginary subnet like 200.1.1.x? Simple. When the router forwards the BootP request, it attaches a little note to it that says, "This came from 200.1.1.x." The DHCP server then sees that information, and so it only responds if it has a scope within 200.1.1.x.

Anyway, notice that to the higher-layer protocol (UDP) this is a broadcast, while the lower-layer Ethernet protocol behaves as though it is not, and the Ethernet address embedded in the message is the address of the client, *not* the FFFFFFFFFFFF broadcast address. Notice also that the transaction ID on the response matches the transaction ID on the original request.

Picking from the Offers

The DHCP client then looks through the offers that it has and picks the one that's best for it. If there are multiple offers that look equally good, it picks the one that arrived first. Then it sends another UDP datagram, another broadcast, shown in Figure 7.11.

FIGURE 7.11

DHCP step 3:
DHCPREQUEST

DHCP
client

DHCP
server

Enet addr: 00CC00000000
IP addr: 0.0.0.0

Enet addr: 00BB00000000
IP addr: 210.22.31.100

**"Can I have the 210.22.31.100 IP address,
and thanks for the other offers, but no thanks."**

IP address used: 255.255.255.255 (broadcast)
Ethernet address used: FFFFFFFFFFFF (broadcast)
Transaction ID: 18923

It's a broadcast because this message serves two purposes. First, the broadcast *will* get back to the original offering server if the first broadcast got to that server, which it obviously did. Second, this broadcast is a way of saying to any *other* DHCP servers who made offers, "Sorry, folks, but I'm taking this other offer."

Notice that both the Ethernet and the IP addresses are broadcasts, and there is a new transaction ID.

The Lease Is Signed

Finally, the DHCP server responds with the shiny, new IP address, which will look something like Figure 7.12.

It also tells the client its new subnet mask, lease period, and whatever else you specified (gateway, WINS server, DNS server, and the like). Again, notice it's a UDP broadcast, but the Ethernet address is directed, and the transaction ID matches the previous request's ID.

You can find out what your IP configuration looks like after DHCP by typing **ipconfig /all**. It may run off the screen, so you may need to add |**more** to the line. This works on DOS, Windows for Workgroups, and NT machines. You can see a sample run of ipconfig /all in Figure 7.13.

Windows 95 machines have a graphical version of ipconfig called winipcfg.

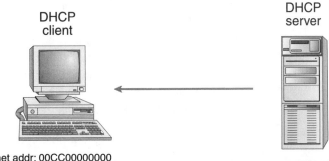

FIGURE 7.12
DHPC step 4: DHCPACK

DHCP
client

DHCP
server

Enet addr: 00CC00000000
IP addr: 0.0.0.0

Enet addr: 00BB00000000
IP addr: 210.22.31.100

**"Sure; also take this subnet
mask, DNS server address,
WINS server, node type,
and domain name."**

IP address used: 255.255.255.255 (broadcast)
Ethernet address used: 00CC00000000 (directed)
Transaction ID: 18923

FIGURE 7.13
Run of `ipconfig`

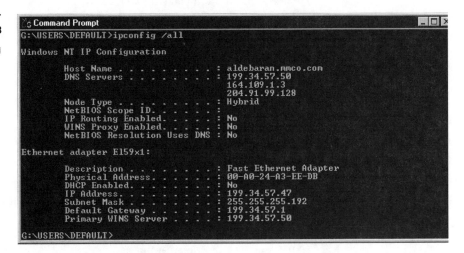

```
Command Prompt                                                    _ □ ×
G:\USERS\DEFAULT>ipconfig /all

Windows NT IP Configuration

        Host Name . . . . . . . . . : aldebaran.mmco.com
        DNS Servers . . . . . . . . : 199.34.57.50
                                      164.109.1.3
                                      204.91.99.128
        Node Type . . . . . . . . . : Hybrid
        NetBIOS Scope ID. . . . . . :
        IP Routing Enabled. . . . . : No
        WINS Proxy Enabled. . . . . : No
        NetBIOS Resolution Uses DNS : No

Ethernet adapter E159x1:

        Description . . . . . . . . : Fast Ethernet Adapter
        Physical Address. . . . . . : 00-A0-24-A3-EE-DB
        DHCP Enabled. . . . . . . . : No
        IP Address. . . . . . . . . : 199.34.57.47
        Subnet Mask . . . . . . . . : 255.255.255.192
        Default Gateway . . . . . . : 199.34.57.1
        Primary WINS Server . . . . : 199.34.57.50

G:\USERS\DEFAULT>
```

Lost Our Lease! Must Sell!

What happens when the lease runs out? Well, when that happens, you're supposed to stop using the IP address. But that's not likely to happen.

When the lease is half over, the DHCP client begins renegotiating the IP lease by sending a DHCP request to the server that originally loaned its IP address. The IP and Ethernet addresses are both specific to the server.

The DHCP server then responds with a DHCPACK. The benefit of this is that the DHCPACK contains all of the information that the original DHCPACK had—domain name, DNS server, etc. That means you can change the DNS server, WINS server, subnet mask, and the like, and the new information will be updated to the clients periodically, but at no more than 50 percent of the lease time.

Now, if the DHCPACK doesn't appear, then the DHCP client keeps resending the DHCP request out every two minutes until the IP lease is 87.5 percent expired. (Don't you wonder where they get these numbers from?) At that point, the client just goes back to the drawing board, broadcasting DHCPDISCOVER messages until someone responds. If the lease expires without a new one, the client will stop using the IP address, effectively disabling the TCP/IP protocol on that workstation.

If you've messed with the DHCP servers, then you know the renewal process can sometimes seem to get bogged down a bit. In that case it's a good idea to force a workstation to restart the whole DHCP process by typing **ipconfig /renew**. That'll often clear up a DHCP problem.

Even with an infinite lease, however, a DHCP client checks back with its server whenever it boots. Therefore, you can often change from infinite to fixed leases by just changing the lease value at the server. You would then have to stop and restart the DHCP service.

Designing Multi-DHCP Networks

Clearly the function of the DHCP server is one that shouldn't rest solely on the shoulders of one server, so how can you put two or more DHCP servers online to ensure a little fault tolerance?

Microsoft seems a bit confused about how to go about providing multiple DHCP servers for a given subnet.

In one document, *Windows NT 3.5 Family Upgrade Course*, they say several things. First, "There is NO mechanism in DHCP that allows two or more DHCP servers to coordinate the assignment of IP addresses from overlapping IP address pools."

No argument there. If you had two different DHCP servers on the same subnet, and they both thought that they could give out addresses 202.11.39 .10 through 202.11.39.40, then there would be nothing keeping the first server from giving address 202.11.39.29 to one machine, while simultaneously the other server was giving out that same 202.11.39.29 address to another machine—yikes!

But then, they go on to demonstrate two different machines running DHCP server, and each machine has a different scope—both scopes taken from a single subnet.

This leaves us two options:

- Create two DHCP servers and give one 80 percent of the IP addresses, and the second one 20 percent. If one goes down, at least 20 percent of the registrations would get re-registered. If your IP scopes are set to default (three days), that's enough time to get a PC up and running. Twenty percent of the IP range should be sufficient to take care of any requests until you get the PC back online.

- Create a second DHCP server with the exact same scopes, but don't activate them. If your main server goes down, then you can activate the scopes, and no one will ever be able to tell the server went down.

Using the DHCP Relay Agent

Windows NT Server 4 includes as part of the Multi-Protocol Router (MPR) component the ability to be an RFC 1542-compliant DHCP relay agent. This component, when used in conjunction with either static or dynamic IP routers, relays DHCP messages between DHCP clients and servers on different IP networks.

When a dynamic client computer on the same subnet as the DHCP relay agent requests an IP address, that request is forwarded to the subnet's DHCP relay agent. In turn, the DHCP relay agent is configured to forward the request directly to the correct computer running the Windows NT Server DHCP service. The computer running the Windows NT DHCP service returns an IP address directly to the requesting client.

But We Don't Really Want to Do This

The DHCP relay agent is only necessary when you have old routers that will not forward BootP requests. Cisco, Bay, and 3Com can all forward BootP requests, but not by default. For example, in a Cisco router, you must put a configuration line in each Ethernet interface telling the UDP BootP packet where the DHCP server is located. The Cisco interface would then look something like this:

```
ip dhcp-server 150.150.28.215
ipx routing 0060.5c5c.c119
!
interface Ethernet0
 ip address 150.150.28.221 255.255.252.0
 ip helper-address 150.150.28.215
 ipx network 2100 encapsulation SAP
 media-type 10BaseT
!
interface Ethernet1
 ip address 150.150.40.221 255.255.252.0
 ip helper-address 150.150.28.215
 ipx network 40100 encapsulation SAP
 media-type 10BaseT
!
interface Ethernet 2
ip address 150.150.44.221 255.255.252.0
ip helper-address 150.150.28.215
ipx network 44100 encapsulation SAP
media-type 10BaseT
!
```

Notice that regardless of the IP address of the interface and what subnet it is part of, it forwards all UDP BootP packets to 150.150.28.215. That's the DHCP server located on subnet 28, on interface 0.

Here's how it does it:

The client comes online and sends a DHCP request packet. Remember, the workstation doesn't have an IP address yet, so it sends along a UDP packet with its hardware address. The router interface receives the packet and discards the frame. It then sees it is a UDP BootP packet, and knows to forward the packet to 150.150.28.215 because of the IP helper-address 150.150.28.215 in the interface configuration. The router then puts a source address of the network it came from (for example, 150.150.40.0), and sends a frame out with the destination of the DHCP server to interface 0.

The DHCP server receives the UDP packet, and notices its source is from network 150.150.40.0. The server then checks to see if there are any defined scopes for subnet 150.150.40.0—a function of the NT DHCP server. If a scope is defined, and an address is available, it will take any available IP address from the pool, and send it on back to its default gateway. Hopefully, that should be the router interface it came from (150.150.28.221\interface 0). Upon receiving the packet, the router sends it to the appropriate subnet, where the client then receives its new IP address.

But what happens if the DHCP's default gateway is not 150.150.28.221 or interface 0? If there is more then one router on your network, which interface do you specify in the default gateway of your NT DHCP server?

You can choose more then one interface for the default gateway; however, packets will only be sent to the first one listed. This may cause you to wonder why you can choose more than one default gateway.

Well you see, the default gateway will only choose the second IP address listed if the first one listed won't respond to an ARP broadcast. Basically, it's there for backup purposes. Okay, so how then do you transmit to multiple subnets through multiple routers? This is where your NT education comes in—remember `route add`?

First, go to a DOS prompt and type:

```
route print
```

This will provide you with an output of all known IP interfaces, plus the routes with which to get to them.

Then, put in a static mapping of all known addresses, making sure you use -p in the `route add` command to make it permanent. For example, to get to network 150.150.40.0, at the NT DHCP server, you'd type:

```
route add -p 150.150.40.0 mask 255.255.252.0 150.150.28.221
```

This says, "Add a static route to network 150.150.40.0 using interface 150.150.28.221." The DHCP server will then send all responses headed for network 40 over to 150.150.28.215, or interface 0. That router will receive the packet and proceed to ship it on over to network 40.

So, Did You Get All That?

Since you're about half-way to becoming an NT TCP/IP wizard now, here's a quiz. The router configuration above was cut and pasted from a Cisco router at one of our clients in San Jose, California. We added static routes, just like we suggested, so to see if you have been paying attention, analyze the following:

The address at the client is 150.150.0.0 255.255.252.0. How many subnets and how many hosts on each subnet?

Give up? We hope not! Check Chapter 3 for subnetting information if you get stuck.

Okay, the answer is...

In a Class B network, the first two octets in a subnet cannot be used for subnetting; this leaves us the third and fourth octet. We are only using the third, however. Break 252 into binary: How many *1*s are there for subnets?

252 = 11111100 = 6 bits for subnetting. This leaves two bits on the third octet for workstations, plus eight more on the fourth octet.

So, we get 62 subnets each with 1,022 hosts. Good job!

Again, check Chapter 3 if you're still confused.

DHCP and the ipconfig Utility

Well, as you can see, TCP/IP is indeed wonderfully flexible, offering its users legions of opportunities for customization. It's completely routable, and supports many internal functions. NetBEUI, on the other hand, is non-routable, and virtually nonconfigurable, but traditionally, TCP/IP hasn't been plug and play. What's plug and play? That simply means that when a software or hardware item is installed (plugged in), it configures itself. (You can play without further ado.) DHCP has changed all this. TCP/IP users now enjoy unparalleled ease in implementing it, but unfortunately, as invention and progress often simplify things, they also tend to author whole new sets of problems. Suppose, for whatever reason, you need to find out about the IP address, subnet mask, and default gateway to which your system has been assigned. Well, Microsoft has created a command line utility called ipconfig. When ipconfig is executed, it'll display all the basic, can't live without it, IP information you most often need to concern yourself with:

- IP address
- Subnet mask
- Default gateway

If only things were that simple! Nope—sad, but true, knowing this basic stuff may fail to do the trick when it comes to situations like the blood-pressure-increasing inability to resolve a NetBIOS name. The good news is that Microsoft thought of that one. Should this dismal yet commonplace event happen to you, proceed by typing **ipconfig /all**. This will access the advanced listing information you need, plus additional beneficial and potentially curative information such as:

- Your system's host name
- NetBIOS node type (B-node, P-node, M-node, H-node)
- The assigned NetBIOS scope ID
- The IP address(es) of designated DNS servers
- NetBIOS resolution via DNS enabled status
- The IP address(es) of designated WINS servers
- IP routing's enabled status
- WIN Proxy's enabled status
- DHCP's enabled status
- The Network Adapter's description
- The hardware address of the Network Adapter

Renewing a Lease through ipconfig

As discussed earlier in this chapter, a DHCP lease is automatically renewed (most of the time) when 50 percent of the lease time gets used up. In the same vein—adhering to the same availability proviso—one can also renew a DHCP client's IP address lease manually via the ipconfig utility by executing ipconfig /renew. This can be especially critical when a DHCP server goes down, and you wish to maintain a new lease once that server's brought back up—and this happens more than one might think. For example, suppose you were upgrading the server and intended to have it down more than half of your client's lease period. Here's when ipconfig /renew hits a homer. With this cool little command, you can schedule a time for the server to be up, making it possible for all your users to renew their leases (still done through a DHCPREQUEST, by the way).

Releasing a Lease through ipconfig

Aside from renewing leases, you'll likely need to cancel them. For example, if you want to move a system from one subnet to another, that system's IP address, subnet mask, and default gateway will probably all need to be changed. As a result, the machine's old information becomes obsolete, requiring lease cancellation. Typing **ipconfig /release** from the command line will generate a DHCPRELEASE message, and immediately cause all TCP/IP functioning on that client to cease.

Additionally noteworthy is the fact that the DHCPRELEASE message isn't automatically generated when you shut down a DHCP client. So, if one of your users is going to the Bahamas, resulting in their system's extended dormancy, **ipconfig /release** again comes in handy. Releasing their lease gives the server an opportunity to assign the lucky sap's IP address to some less fortunate being's computer.

Maintaining the DHCP Database

There are three basic functions for maintaining the DHCP database: backup, restore, and compact. In most cases, you'll only be performing backups occasionally, and compacting the database on a weekly basis, or less. Only volatile, problematic, or extremely complicated network environments will require more vigilance on your part. To a degree, some functions described in this section are automatic. For example, if the system detects a corrupted database, it will automatically revert to its backup. Should this occur in a neglected network where no backup exists—it's curtains, folks! The following procedures are essential for ensuring your network's health, and optimizing its performance. A solid understanding of this section will help you prevent problems and preserve your sanity, as well as that of those who depend on you.

Backing Up a DHCP Database

Suppose one of your servers that gave out three-day leases crashed, and that it was your only DHCP server.

Once you determine the server can't be saved, you decide to zap the disk and start over. In a few hours, you rebuild the server, re-create a scope, and activate the scope, so all the client machines can get their IP addresses. You see a fair number of error messages for a few days, because all of those clients still think they have leases on IP addresses for up to three days—but now, the DHCP server doesn't know anything about that. The clients start requesting that their DHCP licenses be renewed, and the new DHCP server sends them NACK (negative acknowledgment) messages, saying, in effect, "Nope, sorry pal, but you can't use the IP address you just requested an extension for!"

At that point, the DHCP client is supposed to initiate the DHCPDISCOVER process all over again—however, it usually doesn't work. You have to go to the workstation and type the **ipconfig /all** command.

The way to avoid all of this is to simply back up the DHCP database now and then. Best of all, DHCP does that automatically. Every hour, DHCP makes a backup of its database.

You can make DHCP back up the database less often or more often with a Registry parameter. In HKEY_LOCAL_MACHINE\System\CurrentControlSet\services\DHCPServer\Parameters, look for (or create) a value entry called BackupInterval of type REG_DWORD. Enter the value (in hexadecimal, of course) in minutes. The smallest value you can enter is five minutes, and the largest is 60 minutes, which (at least on our machines) appears to be the default, despite the fact that the *Resource Kit* claims it's 15 minutes.

The database (in WINNT\system32\DHCP) consists of several files:

- Dhcp.mdb, which is the actual DHCP database.

- System.mdb, which every Microsoft document describes as, "Used by DHCP for holding information about the structure of the database" (must be a secret, huh?)

- Jet.log, which is a transaction log. The value of logs is that the database using them (DHCP, in this case, but lots of other database systems use them) can use log information to find out what changes have been made recently. This allows the database to repair itself, in some cases.

You don't really *need* to log changes in the DHCP database. There's an option to not log changes, which, if you choose it, will speed up DHCP. Plus, if you must restore a DHCP server, then you get just the last database and no previous logging information. What does all that mean for you? Well handily, you can set the database to back itself up every five minutes, meaning that if you lost the DHCP server, and restored the backup without the Jet log, then you'd only have lost five minutes. You can shut off Jet logging by going to the dhcpserver\Parameters key in the Registry just mentioned and setting the value DatabaseLoggingFlag to 0 (zero).

- Dhcp.tmp is a "hanger-on," a file that DHCP uses to store temporary information.

- The backup process also keeps a Registry key, HKEY_LOCAL_MACHINE \System\CurrentControlSet\services\dhcpserver\Configuration, which it stores in a file called DHCPCFG.

By default, the DHCPCFG file goes into \winnt\system32\DHCP\backup. The rest of the files go into \winnt\system32\DHCP\backup\jet.

Restoring a DHCP Database

What we just took a couple pages to tell you was basically that (1) You should back up your DHCP database, and (2) It happens automatically every hour anyway.

But how do you *restore* a DHCP database in the wake of disaster?

In true NT fault-tolerant fashion, DHCP will check itself for internal problems whenever it starts up. If it detects a problem, it automatically restores from the backups.

If, on the other hand, DHCP doesn't seem to recognize the problem, you can force it to restore from the backups by setting a value named RestoreFlag to 1 (it's another Registry entry in dhcpserver\parameters), stopping the DHCP service, and restarting it.

And if all else fails, you can always stop the DHCP service and copy the backups to the DHCP directory. But *before* you stop the DHCP service, copy the backups somewhere. Why? When you stop the DHCP service, DHCP *backs up its database,* meaning that if DHCP's database is corrupted and you shut down DHCP, it will just back up its rotten, corrupted self.

Then go into DHCP options and click on Reconcile Database to make sure the database is internally consistent.

Compacting Your DHCP Database

Windows NT Server 4 is designed to automatically compact the DHCP database, so normally you shouldn't need to run this procedure. However, if you're using Windows NT Server versions 3.51 or earlier, then after DHCP has been running for a while, the database might need to be compacted to improve DHCP performance. You should compact the DHCP database whenever it approaches 30Mb.

You can use the Jetpack utility provided with any Windows NT Server version to compact a DHCP database. Jetpack is a command-line utility that is run in the Windows NT Server command window.

Compacting the Database

1. Stop the DHCP server though Control Panel ➤ Services ➤ Microsoft DHCP Server or by typing **net stop dhcpserver** at a command prompt.

2. Change to the DHCP directory *systemroot*\system32\DHCP, and run **Jetpack dhcp.mdb temp_file.mdb**.

3. Finally, restart the DHCP server either by rebooting from Control Panel ➤ Services ➤ Microsoft DHCP Server or typing **net start dhcpserver** at a command prompt.

The temp file name is not important. Once Jetpack has completed compacting the database, the temp_file (regardless of name) will have its contents copied back to the dhcp.mdb file, and will then be deleted.

DHCP Files

Knowledge of what files you're working with, and how they perform with a DHCP server, can be useful knowledge indeed, so we've included this little resource. This list includes filenames and brief descriptions, and should help you get a good picture of the DHCP database:

- **Dhcp.mdb**: This is the main DHCP database file. It's arguably the most important file in the DHCP directory that you'll work with.

- **Dhcp.tmp**: This file is used internally by the DHCP server for temporary storage while running.

- **Jet.log/jet*.log**: These are transaction log files which can be used in a jam by DHCP to recover data.

- **System.mdb**: A storage file used by the DHCP server to track the structure of the database.

Now that you can give clients an IP address dynamically, how do you keep track of IP addresses in relating to their host names? If you're using the NetBIOS interface, you can use Windows Internet Naming System (WINS) to translate between host name and IP addresses. Let's take a look at WINS in the following chapter.

CHAPTER

8

WINS

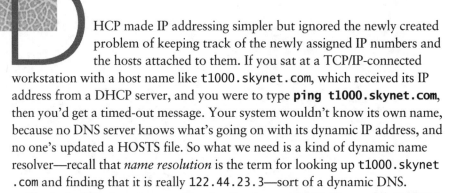

DHCP made IP addressing simpler but ignored the newly created problem of keeping track of the newly assigned IP numbers and the hosts attached to them. If you sat at a TCP/IP-connected workstation with a host name like `t1000.skynet.com`, which received its IP address from a DHCP server, and you were to type **ping t1000.skynet.com**, then you'd get a timed-out message. Your system wouldn't know its own name, because no DNS server knows what's going on with its dynamic IP address, and no one's updated a HOSTS file. So what we need is a kind of dynamic name resolver—recall that *name resolution* is the term for looking up `t1000.skynet.com` and finding that it is really `122.44.23.3`—sort of a dynamic DNS.

That's the Windows Internet Naming Service, or WINS. Now, while DHCP is part of a wider group of BootP-related protocols, this one is mainly Microsoft's, and that's a problem. WINS is a name resolution service that's pretty much only recognized by Microsoft client software (NT, Windows for Workgroups, DOS, and presumably OS/2 clients eventually).

With NT 5, a dynamic DNS will be available for workstations running the WinSock API instead of the NetBIOS interface, but only if the workstations are running TCP/IP. This will make WINS obsolete unless you're running IPX or NetBEUI. If, however, you are running NT 3.51 or 4, WINS is needed for name-to-IP-address resolution.

WINS/DNS Integration

In Windows NT 4, Microsoft's implementation of DNS is tightly integrated with WINS. This allows non-WINS clients to resolve NetBIOS names by querying a DNS server. Administrators can now remove any static entries for Microsoft-based clients in legacy DNS server zone files in favor of the dynamic WINS/DNS integration. For example, if a non-Microsoft-based client wants to get to a Web page on an HTTP server that's DHCP/WINS enabled, the client can query the DNS server, the DNS server can query WINS, and the name can be resolved and returned to the client. Previous to the WINS integration, there was no way to reliably resolve the name because of the dynamic IP addressing.

WINS is, therefore, only half of the answer to the name resolution problem, albeit an important half. We'll take that up in this chapter and look at DNS alternatives in the next chapter.

What WINS is *really* good for is administering NetBEUI networks over routers. What does that mean? Well, to find out, let's look more closely into names on an NT network using TCP/IP.

Names in NT

Here is one of the most common questions we get asked about NT and TCP/IP:

"I've got an NT server on one subnet, and some Windows for Workgroups machines on another subnet. There's a router between them. I can *ping* the NT server from the Windows for Workgroups machine, but I can't see the NT machine on my browse list, and I can't net use to it. How can this be?"

The short answer:

"Ping relies upon the WinSock programming interface, and the browse list and net use rely on the NetBIOS interface. As WinSock and NetBIOS work differently, it's entirely possible that there are situations where one would work and the other would fail—this happens to be one of them. What you have to do is to help out NetBIOS a bit with either a file called LMHOSTS or a service called WINS."

The specifics take a little longer to explain; that's the purpose of this chapter.

Consider the following two commands, both issued to the same server:

```
ping server01.bigfirm.com
```

and

```
net use * \\server01\mainshr
```

In the ping command, the server is referred to as `server01.bigfirm.com`. In the net use command, that same server is called `server01`. The difference is important.

Why Two Different Names?

The ping command is clearly a TCP/IP/Internet kind of command. You can't run it unless you're running TCP/IP, and, as a matter of fact, it's a valid command on a UNIX, VMS, Macintosh, or MVS machine, so long as that machine is running a TCP/IP protocol stack.

In contrast, net use is a Microsoft networking command. You can do a net use on an NT network no matter what protocol you're running, but the command usually won't be valid on a UNIX, VMS, or Macintosh. In general, Microsoft networking is pretty much built to work on PCs. (Yes, we know, NT is architecture-independent, so you could find an Alpha, a MIPS, or a PowerPC machine using net use commands, but on the whole, NT is an Intel *x*86 operating system—at this writing—and we haven't seen announcements of an NT/390 for the IBM mainframe world, NT VAX for the Digital world, or NT SPARC for the Sun world.)

The difference is in the network application program interface (API) that the application is built atop. Ping was built on top of the common PC implementation of TCP/IP Sockets, the *WinSock* interface. Building Ping atop sockets was a good idea, because then it's simple to create a ping for any operating system, as long as there's a sockets interface on that computer. In fact, people use basically the same source code to create pings for the PC, UNIX machines, VMS machines, or Macs. The `server01.mmco.com` is a DNS name, so for a ping to recognize `server01 .mmco.com`, you'd need a DNS name resolver—a client code that knows how to talk to DNS servers—on your network. We'll talk about how to do that in Chapter 9.

In contrast, net use was built on top of the NetBIOS API. You may recall that NetBIOS is a protocol and a very simple one at that. As Microsoft has been selling the software to do net use commands since 1985, the net command has been built—and is still built—to sit atop NetBIOS. The `\\server01` name is a NetBIOS name, rather than a DNS name. That implies that to make net use work, you'd need a NetBIOS name resolver or a NetBIOS name server—which is exactly what WINS is, as you'll see in the next few pages.

If the `server01.mmco.com` versus `\\server01` distinction still isn't clear, then think of the APIs as communications devices. Telephones and the mail service are communications devices also, so we'll use them in an analogy. Ping's job is to communicate with some other PC, and net use also wants to communicate with some PC. But Ping uses WinSock (the telephone) and net use uses NetBIOS (the mail). If you use the telephone to call a friend, that friend's "name," as far as the phone is concerned, may be something like (222) 555-2121. As far as the mail is concerned, however, the friend's "name" might be Phil Jones, 1234 Main Street, Anytown, U.S.A, 12345. Both are perfectly valid "names" for your friend Phil, but they're different because different communications systems need different name types.

NetBIOS atop TCP/IP (NBT)

The NetBIOS API is implemented on the NetBEUI, IPX/SPX, and the TCP/IP protocols that Microsoft distributes. That makes Microsoft's TCP/IP a bit different from the TCP/IP you find on UNIX, for example, because the UNIX TCP/IP almost certainly won't have a NetBIOS API on it. It'll probably only have the TCP/IP Sockets API on it. (Microsoft's TCP/IP also has Sockets in the form of the WinSock API.)

NetBIOS on the Microsoft implementation of TCP/IP is essential, because if the TCP/IP *didn't* have a NetBIOS API on it, then you couldn't use the net use, net view, net logon, and similar commands to allow your PC-based workstation to talk to an NT server. Instead, the closest thing you would be able to find that would do the job of net would be something called *NFS*, the *Network File System*, but it wouldn't replace all of the functions of net. Microsoft's NetBIOS on TCP/IP even has a name—NBT.

So the server's name, so far as NetBIOS or NBT is concerned, is `server01`, and its name, so far as WinSock is concerned, is `server01.bigfirm.com`. You can run programs that either call upon NBT or WinSock, but you have to be sure to use the correct name.

Name Resolution Issues: Why DNS Isn't Always the Best Answer

Once NBT has a NetBIOS name or WinSock has a fully qualified domain name (FQDN), they have the same job: resolve that name into an IP address. So computers on a Microsoft-based network that uses TCP/IP need some kind of name resolution.

How about the obvious one—DNS? DNS clearly *could* do the job, so Microsoft could have designed NBT to do its name resolution via DNS. But it didn't, for several reasons:

- First of all, Microsoft isn't the only player in the NBT world. The whole idea of putting a NetBIOS interface atop a TCP/IP stack started, believe it or not, way back in 1987, before DNS was even invented!

- Second, DNS is nifty in many ways, but it's not dynamic in NT version 4. What that means in English is that every time you put a new computer on your network, you'd have to trot on over to the machine that was running the DNS server, type in the new computer's name and IP address, and then you'd have to stop the DNS server and restart it to get DNS to recognize the new name. Something more automatic would definitely be more desirable.

- Third, Microsoft didn't even ship a DNS server with NT as of NT version 3.51, and the beta NT 4 DNS server was absolutely terrible. Only in the final release of NT 4 is it workable, so they couldn't really *require* people to set up a DNS server, could they?

NetBIOS name resolution over TCP/IP is, then, not a simple nut to crack. Many people realized this, and so there are two Internet RFCs on this topic: RFC 1001 and 1002.

B-Nodes, P-Nodes, and M-Nodes

The RFCs attacked the problem by offering options.

Option No. 1: B-Nodes

The first option was sort of simplistic: Just do broadcasts. A computer that used broadcasts to resolve NetBIOS names to IP addresses is referred to in the RFCs as a *B-node*. To find out who server01 is, then, a PC running B-node software would just shout out, "Hey! Anybody here named server01?"

Simple, yes, but fatally flawed: Remember what happens to broadcasts when they hit routers? As routers don't rebroadcast the messages to other subnets, this kind of name resolution would only be satisfactory on single-subnet networks.

Option No. 2: P-Nodes

The second option was to create a name server of some kind and to use that. Then, when a computer needed to resolve a name of another computer, all it needed to do was send a point-to-point message to the computer running the name server software. As point-to-point messages *do* get retransmitted over routers, this second approach would work fine even on networks with routers. A computer using a name server to resolve NetBIOS names into IP addresses is said to be a *P-node*.

Again, a good idea, but it runs afoul of all of the problems that DNS had. *What* name server should be used? Will it be dynamic? The name server for NetBIOS name resolution is, by the way, referred to as a NetBIOS Name Server, or NBNS.

Option No. 3: M-Nodes

The most complex approach to NetBIOS name resolution over TCP/IP is the *M-node*, or *mixed* node. It uses a combination of broadcasts and point-to-point communications to an NBNS.

When Microsoft started out with TCP/IP, they implemented a kind of M-node software. It was "point-to-point" in that you could look up addresses in the HOSTS file, or in the LMHOSTS file, and if you had a DNS server, then you could always reference that. Other than those options, Microsoft TCP/IP was mainly B-node prone, which either limited you to single-subnet networks, or required that you repeat broadcasts over the network, thereby clogging it up. Clearly, some kind of NBNS was needed, and the simpler it was to work with, the better. As the RFCs were silent on the particulars of an NBNS, vendors had license to go out and invent something proprietary and so they did—several of them, in fact, with the result that you'd expect: None of them talk to each other.

Where WINS Comes In

WINS is simply Microsoft's proprietary NBNS service. What makes it stand out from the rest of the pack is Microsoft's importance in the industry. They've got the clout to create a proprietary system and make it accepted widely enough so that it becomes a *de facto* standard, and as there is no doubt an RFC or two on WINS out there, perhaps WINS will become the *de rigueur* standard as well.

Benefits of Using WINS

Here's a short list of the evidence in favor of WINS:

- Dynamic database maintenance to support computer name registration and resolution.

- Centralized management of NetBIOS name database.

- Reduction of IP broadcast traffic in the internetwork, while allowing the clients to locate remote systems easily across local or wide area networks.

- The ability for the clients (Windows NT 3.5 or newer, Windows for Workgroups 3.11, Windows 95) on a Windows NT Server-based network to browse remote domains without a local domain controller being present on the other side of the router.

- On a Windows NT network, the ability to browse transparently across routers (for domains that span multiple subnets). To allow browsing without WINS, the network administrator must ensure that the users' primary domain has computers with Windows NT Server or Windows NT Workstation on both sides of the router to act as Master browsers. These computers need correctly configured LMHOSTS files with entries for the domain controllers across the subnet.

Microsoft client software with WINS actually doesn't implement B-nodes, P-nodes, or M-nodes; rather, Microsoft uses what they call an *H*, or *Hybrid* node. But wait a minute; isn't M-node a hybrid? Yes. Both M-nodes and H-nodes (and note well that at this writing, M-nodes are RFCed and H-nodes aren't) use both B-node and P-node, but the implementation is different.

- In M-node, do a name resolution by first broadcasting (B-node) and then, if that fails, communicate directly with the NBNS (P-node).

- In H-node, try the NBNS first. If it can't help you, then try a broadcast.

The difference is merely in order of operation.

Understanding the NBT Names on Your System

A major part of the NetBIOS architecture is its lavish use of names. A workstation attaches up to 16 names to itself. Names in NetBIOS are either group names, which can be shared—workgroups and domains are two examples—or normal names, which can't be shared, like a machine name. As you'll soon see that WINS keeps track of all of these names, you may be curious about what all of them *are*—so let's take a minute and look more closely into your system's NetBIOS names.

You can see the names attached to your workstation by opening a command line from a Windows for Workgroups, Windows 95, or NT machine, and typing **nbtstat -n**. You get an output like this:

```
Node IpAddress: [199.34.57.53] Scope Id: []
        NetBIOS Local Name Table
    Name         Type       Status
    ---------------------------------------------
    MICRON133   <00> UNIQUE   Registered
    ORION       <00> GROUP    Registered
    MICRON133   <03> UNIQUE   Registered
    MICRON133   <20> UNIQUE   Registered
    ORION       <1E> GROUP    Registered
    MARK        <03> UNIQUE    Registered
```

In this example, the ORION group names are Mark's workgroup and domain. MICRON133 is Mark's personal machine's name, and MARK is, well, Mark's name—notice that NetBIOS registers not only the machine name, but the person's name as well. You can see the list of registered names on any computer in your network by typing **nbtstat -A <IP address>**, where the -A *must* be a capital letter.

But why is there more than one MICRON133? Because different parts of the Microsoft network client software each require names of their own, so they take your machine name and append a pair of hex digits to it. That's what the <00>, <20>, and the like are—suffixes controlled by particular programs. For example, if some other user on the network wanted to connect to a share named STUFF on this computer, she could type **net use * \\micron133\stuff**, and the redirector software on her computer would then do a NetBIOS name resolution on the name MICRON133<00>, as the <00> suffix is used by the redirector. Table 8.1 summarizes suffixes and the programs that use them.

T A B L E 8.1 Examples of machine names	**Unique Names**	**Where Used**
	<computername>[00h]	Workstation service. This is the "basic" name that every player in a Microsoft network would have, no matter how little power it has in the network.
	<computername>[03h]	Messenger service
	<computername>[06h]	RAS server service
	<computername>[1Fh]	NetDDE service; will only appear if NetDDE is active, or if you're running a NetDDE application. (You can see this by starting up Network Hearts, for example.)
	<computername>[20h]	Server service; name will only appear on machines with file/printer sharing enabled.
	<computername>[21h]	RAS client service
	<computername>[BEh]	Network monitor agent
	<computername>[BFh]	Network monitor utility
	<username>[03h]	Messenger service; any computer running the Messenger service (which is just about any MS networking client) will have this so that users can receive net send commands.

T A B L E 8.1 (cont.) Examples of machine names	**Unique Names**	**Where Used**
	\<domain name>[1Bh]	Primary domain controller
	\<domain name>[1Dh]	Master browser

GROUP NAMES		
Group Names	**Where Used**	
\<domain name>[00h] or \<workgroup name>[00]	Domain name; indicates that the computer is a member of the domain and/or workgroup. If a client is a member of a workgroup whose name is different from a domain, then no domain name will be registered on the client.	
\<domain name>[1Ch]	PDCs and BDCs would share this; if a machine has this name registered, then it is a domain controller.	
\<domain name>[1Eh] or \<workgroup name>[1Eh]	Used in browser elections, indicates that this computer would agree to be a browser. Will only show up on servers. (Potential browser.)	
MSBrowse	Domain Master browser	

No matter what kind of computer you have on a Microsoft enterprise network, it'll have at least one name registered: *\<computer name>*[00]. Most computers also register *\<workgroup>*[00], which proclaims them as a member of a workgroup. Those are the only two names you would see if you had a DOS workstation running the old LAN Manager network client without the Messenger service, or a Windows for Workgroups 3.1 (not 3.11) workstation that had file and printer sharing disabled.

Most modern client software would also have the Messenger service enabled and so would have *\<computer name>*[03] and *\<user name>*[03] registered as well.

Adding file and/or printer sharing capabilities to a computer would add *\<computer name>*[20]. Servers all agree to be candidates for browse master by default, so unless you configure a machine to *not* be a candidate for browse mastering, then *\<workgroup name>*[1E] will appear on any machine offering file or printer sharing. If the machine happens to be the browse master, it'll also have *\<workgroup name>*[1D] as well. Workstations use the [1D] name to initially get a list of browse servers when they first start up—they broadcast a message looking to see if the [1D] machine exists, and if it does, then the [1D] machine presents the workstation with a list of potential browsers.

Browse masters also get the network name [01][02]__MSBROWSE__[02] [01] as well—it's a group name, and only the *Master* browsers are members. Master browsers use that name to discover that each other exists.

Master Browsers versus Domain Master Browsers: A Note

This topic is a little out of order, and it is covered completely in Chapter 10, but it's a topic that is relevant to TCP/IP, network names, and browsing, so this seemed the least "out of order" place to put it.

For a moment, let's consider browse lists under NT. Most of the messages that drive the browsing services in Microsoft enterprise networking are broadcasts. As routers don't generally pass broadcasts, what does that imply for an intranet made up of multiple segments—but only one NT domain?

Without WINS, each subnet ends up having its own browser elections, and each subnet has its own Master browsers as a result. NT centralizes the browse information by dubbing one of these Master browsers the Domain Master browser (DMB). Again, this isn't "domain" in the TCP/IP sense, it's "domain" in the NT sense. The reason DMBs exist is to support browsing of an NT domain that's split up over two or more subnets. Even if your NT domain is only situated on a single subnet, it'll still end up with a DMB. DMBs register the name <*domain*> [1B], and there will, again, be one per NT domain. There can be many DMBs within a single TCP/IP domain, because there can be as many NT domains in a TCP/IP domain as you like.

Name Resolution before WINS

Clients written prior to WINS, or clients without a specified WINS server, try to resolve a NetBIOS name to an IP address with a number of methods. The tools they'll use, if they exist, are:

- A HOSTS file, if present

- Broadcasts

- An LMHOSTS file, if present

- A DNS server, if present

You met HOSTS before—it's just a simple ASCII file. Each line contains an IP address, at least one space, and a name. LMHOSTS does everything that HOSTS does—it can completely replace HOSTS—and it does a bit more besides. While HOSTS is generally a basic TCP/IP standard from years ago,

LMHOSTS is a Microsoft modification that lets you do things such as identify a primary domain controller (PDC) for an NT domain or tell the system to load a part of LMHOSTS from a central location every time you log on, allowing an administrator to keep the fast-changing information in a central location. For example, supposing that you had a server called Fido at 210.10.22.33 that was the primary domain controller on a domain named Browsers, you'd just add the following line to your LMHOSTS file:

```
210.10.22.33 fido #DOM:browsers
```

Then, when a workstation wanted to obtain a browse list for Browsers, the workstation's LMHOSTS file would tell it to go to 210.10.22.33 for the browse list.

Anyway, if you set up a Microsoft network client and do not specify a WINS server, and also do not check Enable DNS for Windows Networking, your client will be what Microsoft calls a "modified B-node." These clients first look in the HOSTS file, if it exists. If the entry they're looking for isn't there, the computer will look in LMHOSTS. If they still can't get the name resolved, they broadcast a request for a response from <*computername*>[00]. It's a UDP broadcast. They try that three times, and if there's still no answer, they give up.

If you specify a DNS server in your TCP/IP client configuration, once again, your computer will go first to HOSTS for name resolution, and if that doesn't work, it'll contact the DNS server you specified in the configuration. Where the LMHOSTS file figures in varies with the client type; in fact, if you're running Windows 95, then LMHOSTS is ignored altogether when you're using a DNS server. If DNS can't help your computer, then the client software will turn to a UDP broadcast as a last resort.

How WINS Works

You've seen that the world before WINS was a rather grim place, where everyone shouts, and many questions (well, resolution requests) go unanswered. Now let's look at what happens with WINS.

WINS Needs NT Server

To make WINS work, you must set up an NT Server machine (it won't run on anything else, including NT Workstation) to act as the WINS server. The WINS server then acts as the NBNS server, keeping track of who's on the network and handing out name resolution information as needed. A very cool thing about how WINS works is the way in which it collects name information. If your workstation wants to be able to address name resolution questions to a WINS server, it must first introduce itself to the WINS server. In the process, WINS captures the IP address and NetBIOS name of that workstation, augmenting the WINS database further!

WINS Holds Name Registrations

Basically, when a WINS client (the shorthand term for "any PC running a Microsoft enterprise TCP/IP network client software designed to use WINS for NBT name resolution") first boots up, it goes to the WINS server and introduces itself. It knows the IP address of the WINS server because you either hard-coded it right into the TCP/IP settings for the workstation, or the workstation got a WINS address from DHCP when it obtained an IP lease.

That first communication is called a *name registration request.* In the process of registering its name with a WINS server, the workstation gets the benefit of ensuring that it has a unique name. If the WINS server sees that there's another computer out there with the same name, it'll tell the workstation, "You can't use that name." The name registration request and the acknowledgment are both directed IP messages, so they'll cross routers. And when a workstation shuts down, it sends a "name release" request to the WINS server telling it that the workstation will no longer need the NetBIOS name. That name is then available for the WINS server to register it for some other machine.

WINS Failure Modes

But what if something goes wrong? What if you try to register a name that some other workstation already has, or if a workstation finds that the WINS server is unavailable?

Duplicate names are simple—instead of sending a "success" response to the workstation, the WINS server sends a "fail" message in response to the workstation's name request. That workstation then will not consider the name registered, and doesn't include it in its NetBIOS name table—an nbstat -n will not show the name.

But if a workstation can't find the WINS server when it boots up, then the workstation simply stops acting as a hybrid NBT node and reverts to its old ways as a Microsoft modified B-node. This means it depends largely on broadcasts, but will also consult HOSTS and LMHOSTS if they're present.

It's My Name, but for How Long?

Like DHCP, WINS only registers names for a fixed period of time called the *renewal interval*. By default, it's four days (96 hours), and there will probably never be a reason for you to change that. Forty minutes seems to be the shortest time that WINS will accept.

In much the same way that DHCP clients attempt to renew their leases early, WINS clients send name *refresh* requests to the WINS server before their names expire—*long* before. According to Microsoft documentation, a WINS client attempts a name refresh very early after it gets its names registered—after only one-eighth of the renewal interval has elapsed. Our tests show that it's actually *three*-eighths, but that's not terribly important. The WINS server will usually reset the length of time left before the name must be renewed again. This time is sometimes called the "time to live," or TTL. Once the client has renewed its name *once*, however, it doesn't renew it again and again every time one-eighth of its TTL elapses. Instead, it only renews its names at one-half of TTL intervals.

Installing WINS

Installing WINS is much like installing all the other software that we've installed elsewhere in this chapter and in the book.

When you're planning how many WINS servers you need and where to put them, bear in mind that you need not put a WINS server on each subnet—one of the great features of WINS. However, it *is* a good idea to have a second machine running as a secondary WINS server, just for fault tolerance's sake. Remember that if a workstation comes up and can't find a WINS server, it reverts to broadcasting, limiting its name resolution capabilities to its local subnet, and causing it to do a lot of shouting. This adds traffic to the subnet, and is not a good thing. Why would a WINS client *not* find a WINS server if there's a working WINS server present? Normally, the client would, but in a small percentage of cases, the WINS server might be too busy to respond to that client in a timely manner and cause the client to give up on the server. *This* is where having a secondary server comes in handy. If you have a backup domain controller, then put a WINS server on that machine as well. The WINS software actually doesn't use a lot of CPU time, so it probably won't affect your server's performance unless you have thousands of users all hammering on one WINS server. If *that's* the case, we recommend dedicating a computer solely to WINSing.

To get a WINS server set up, follow these directions:

1. Open the Control Panel.

2. Within the Control Panel, open the Networks applet.

3. Click on the Services tab.

4. Click on the Add button.

5. Choose the Windows Internet Name Service.

6. Tell the program where to find the files on your CD-ROM or whatever drive you used to install NT.

7. Click on the Close button.

The system will want to restart; let it. Once your server has rebooted, you'll find a new icon in the Administrative Tools group, the WINS Manager. Start it up, and it will look like Figure 8.1.

FIGURE 8.1

The initial WINS Manager screen

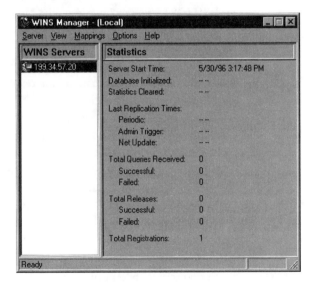

Static Entries

The first thing you should do on your WINS server is inform it of the machines on your subnet that have hard-coded IP addresses. You do that by clicking on Mappings, then Static Mappings. You'll then see a dialog box like the one shown in Figure 8.2.

FIGURE 8.2

The Static Mappings table

Many nodes on a network, such as a server running UNIX, aren't capable of registering a name with the WINS server. These names might be resolved from an LMHOSTS file, or by querying a DNS server, but a better solution would be to enter the name-to-IP-address mapping statically in the WINS server. This accomplishes two things. First, it allows nodes to resolve the name with a query to the WINS server without having to resort to secondary resolution methods. This results in faster name resolution. Second, it prevents the WINS server from allowing another node to dynamically register the name.

Static entries may be entered interactively or by importing an LMHOSTS file. They are never released and they are never overwritten by dynamic entries.

In Figure 8.2, you see that we've added the IP addresses for two devices with predefined IP addresses. Just click on Add Mappings, and you'll get a dialog box that lets you add IP addresses and host names as static values. If you have an existing HOSTS file, you can click on Import Mappings, and the program will take that information to build a static-mapping database.

Backing Up

Be a good scout—back your stuff up! Doing so is the hallmark of the seasoned, "been there—done that," commemorative-hat-wearing network professional. It is an aspect of the WINS database not to be ignored. Always keep a backup copy of all information entered when configuring the server. This backup becomes automatic after a 24-hour period lapses, and after a backup directory has been specified. To specify your backup directory, follow these steps:

1. From the WINS Manager, Select Mappings ➤ Backup Database. You'll see a dialog box asking you for a directory. The default location is \Users\Default, which we suppose will work as well as any other. It'll end up creating a directory called \Users\Default\WINS_bak, which will include three files: jet.log, system.mdb, and wins.mdb.

2. Under Directories, select *systemroot*\system32\WINS.

3. Cancel Perform Incremental Backup and choose OK.

The WINS Manager window will appear, followed by a message box indicating the backup was completed successfully.

4. Choose OK.

5. Switch to File Manager, then select *systemroot*\system32\WINS.

6. View the contents of the WINS_bak directory, then exit File Manager.

In addition to backing up the database, you should also back up all the Registry entries. You do that by:

1. Running the Registry Program REGEDT32.

2. Then, open `HKEY_LOCAL_MACHINE\SYSTEM\CurrentControlSet\ Services\WINS`.

3. Choose Save Key from the Registry menu.

4. Type in the path to where the WINS files are backed up.

Restoration

Restoration ensures that reliable data is served. If the WINS server determines upon initialization that its data is corrupt, it'll automatically revert to the backup. You can manually force the WINS server to restore the database in two ways. The first way is by selecting Restore Database from the WINS Manager Mapping menu, and specifying the path where the backup directory is located. The second way is begun by deleting jet*.log, winstmp.mdb, and system.mdb from the *systemroot*\system32\WINS directory. That done, proceed to copy system.mdb from the Windows NT server distribution CD-ROM to the *systemroot*\system32\WINS directory. Finally, copy wins.mdb from the backup directory to *systemroot*\system32\WINS.

This is how to go about restoring the WINS database:

1. First, go to WINS Manager.

2. From the Mappings menu, choose Restore Local Database. The Select Directory to Restore dialog box will then appear.

3. Under Directories, select *systemroot*\\system32\\WINS, then choose OK.

The WINS Manager window will then appear, followed by a message box indicating the restore was completed successfully.

4. Choose OK.

5. Use Control Panel Services ➤ Services ➤ Windows Internet Name Service or a command prompt to start the Windows Internet Name Service.

So, to summarize what you should do to be able to rebuild a WINS server: Tell the WINS server where to do backups, and it'll do them automatically every day. And when you make changes to WINS settings, save the part of the Registry that holds the settings. Most importantly, be sure to run a secondary WINS server—then you don't really have to worry about backing up your WINS database at all, as you have two machines working in parallel.

WINS services are totally independent of NT domain security, as is DHCP. A WINS server can serve workstations throughout your network. In fact, if your network is connected to the Internet and doesn't have a firewall, you could actually *publish* your WINS server address, and other networks across the Internet could share browsing capabilities! (Whether or not you'd *want* to do that is another issue.)

Compacting

This management function is executed by running the Jetpack.exe utility. This program should be run periodically when the database grows over 30MB in size to keep the database efficient. The size of the database depends on both the number and the type of entries in it. A unique or group entry uses only 50 to 70 bytes to record it, but an Internet group or multihomed entry will use a whopping 50 to 300 bytes, depending on the number of IP addresses associated with them. On top of that, there are about 50 to 100 bytes of overhead needed to track time stamps and the other information that supports each entry. To compact a database, follow the steps below:

1. First, stop the WINS server though Control Panel ➤ Services ➤ Windows Internet Name Service or by typing **net stop WINS** at a command prompt.

2. Change to the WINS directory, *systemroot*\\system32\\WINS, and run **Jetpack wins.mdb temp_file.mdb** instead.

Once Jetpack has completed compacting the database, the temp_file (regardless of name) will have its contents copied back to the wins.mdb file, and will then be deleted.

3. Finally, restart the WINS server either by rebooting from Control Panel or Server Manager, or by typing **net start WINS**.

Below is a list of some of the files you'll be working with along with some information on how they perform in relation to the WINS server.

- **Jet.log/jet*.log**: This file contains transaction log files which may be used by WINS to recover data if necessary.

- **System.mdb**: This is a storage file that is used by the WINS server to track the structure of the database.

- **Wins.mdb**: This is the main WINS database file. It's the most important file you'll work with in the WINS directory. You'll most likely find yourself performing all maintenance operations with this file.

- **Winstmp.mdb**: This temporary file is used and created internally by the WINS server. In the event of a crash, this file doesn't have to be removed.

Database Replication

Unlike DHCP servers that don't communicate with each other, WINS servers can be configured to replicate their database entries, sharing them with each other so that all servers across the network have synchronous name information. This also facilitates communication between WINS clients that have registered with different WINS servers. As an example, suppose your system has registered with the WINS server "Alpine" (see Figure 8.3), and your buddy's system registers with the WINS server "Aspen." Not only will these systems enjoy full communication, they'll be able to resolve the names directly for each other because the WINS database is replicated between servers. This feature is not automatic, and requires configuration to become operative. When it has been, replication is automatically triggered any time the database changes (for example, when names are registered and/or released). To configure a WINS server to function in this manner, it must be ordained as either a push or pull partner.

FIGURE 8.3

Determining whether a WINS server is a push or pull partner

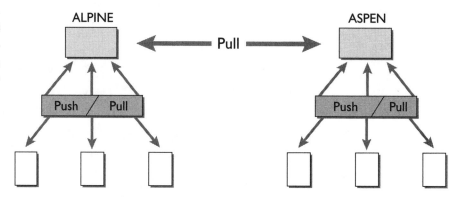

Push or Pull Partners

Push partners are WINS servers that function by sending update notices to pull partners whenever changes are made. Pull partners—also WINS servers—function by sending out requests to push partners, asking them for entries more recent than their current listings when they want to update their database contents. WINS servers can be defined as both push and pull, ensuring that the most up-to-date information is registered. Only new listings added since the last time an update occurred will be replicated—not the entire database. To get a picture of this, take a peek at Figure 8.3.

Determining If a Server Is a Push or Pull Partner

WINS database replication types can be determined by how a WINS server is used and by the architecture of the network. If your network spans multiple sites across slow links, you'll want your servers to pull each other for updates. This is because pull requests can be predetermined to occur at specific times (like during lunch or late evening) when the network's traffic is likely to be light. Alternately, if the links are fast, your concerns would have less to do with traffic, and your servers should be ordained as push partners. If you choose to set the server as a push, it's often a good idea to go ahead and configure it as both push and pull. By doing so, you'll be ensuring yourself that you're in possession of the most up-to-date WINS entries available.

In all, there are four ways in which replication takes place:

- Once configured as a replication partner, each server will automatically pull updates during initialization at startup.

- As a pull partner, the machine will query other WINS servers for updates at a chosen and specified time.

- As a push partner, the machine will advertise its updates when it reaches its threshold for number of changes. Both the threshold and the update interval are user definable.

- Finally, WINS databases may be manually replicated though the WINS Manager.

Conflicts Detected during Replication

Name conflicts are normally handled at the time of name registration. However, it's possible for the same name to be registered at two different WINS servers. This would happen if the same name were registered at a second WINS server before the database from the first WINS server had been replicated. In this case, the conflict will be noted and resolved at replication time.

Conflict at replication can be:

- Between two unique entries

- Between a unique entry and a group entry

- Between two group entries

A multihomed entry is a unique entry with multiple addresses.

Conflict between Unique Entries

How do you resolve conflicts between unique entries? Well, first take the following into account:

- **State of the entries:** Database entries can be in active, released, or tombstone states. The replica either can be in the active or tombstone state.

- **Ownership of the entries:** Your WINS server may or may not own the database entry.

- **Addresses of the entries:** The addresses of the entries can be the same or different.

What about two replicas with the same or different IP addresses? The replica in your database will be overwritten by the new one, no matter if the addresses match or not—*unless* the replica in that database is active, and the new one's a tombstone. So if that's the case, the replica in the database won't be overwritten by the new one *unless* they're both owned by the same WINS server.

What happens if there's a conflict between an owned entry and replica with the same IP address? The replica supersedes your database record *unless* it's active, and the replica's a tombstone. In that case, the database record's version ID will be incremented so the record will be reproduced at replication time.

Okay—but what about conflicts between an owned entry and replica with *different* IP addresses? Unless the database record's active, it'll be replaced by the replica, but if the replica's a tombstone, the database record's version ID will again be incremented so as to be reproduced at replication time. If the replica's also active, the database record's node will be challenged to find out if it still has the name. If so, the replica's node will be sent a Name Conflict Demand which will force the node to put that name into a conflict state.

What if there's a conflict between unique and group entries? When the conflict is between a unique entry and a group entry, the group entry will be kept. If the unique entry isn't in the released or tombstone state, and is owned by the WINS server, it will ask the node in the unique entry to release the name.

What about hostilities between two Special Group entries? Again, the database record will be replaced by the replica unless it's active, and again, if it is, its version ID will be incremented so it gets propagated at replication time. If the replica is also in the active state, the database record's member list will be updated, adding any members found in the replica that aren't already included. Extra members won't be admitted if the list of members in the active state totals more than twenty-five.

Conflicts Involving a Multihomed Record

What if a multihomed replica conflicts with a tombstone or released entry in the database? Well, unless the entry is a normal group in the released state, it will be replaced with the replica. It's the same as the scenarios where a non-multihomed entry conflicts with a released normal group entry.

But what if a tombstone multihomed replica clashes with an active database entry that's owned by the same machine? The database entry will simply be replaced; however, if the active database entry is a replica owned by a different machine, it won't be. If the active database entry happens to be a unique entry owned by the local WINS server, its version ID is incremented to cause propagation.

The same holds true if an *active* multihomed replica clashes with an *active* unique/multihomed replica in the local database with the same owner—it'll be replaced. If the owner's different, it won't be. But if the entry in the database is owned by the local WINS server, and if the members of the record (one member if it's a unique record) is a subset of the members in the replica, the database record's version ID will be incremented to propagate it, and its time stamp will be changed. The local record's addresses will be challenged if the replica's members aren't a subset. If the challenged node doesn't respond, making the challenge a success, the database record will then be replaced. If the challenged node responds, it will be told to release the name from all addresses before the database record is replaced with the replica.

As with prior scenarios, if a multihomed replica clashed with an active group entry in the database, the entry in the database's version ID will be incremented to cause propagation.

Lastly, if a non-multihomed replica clashes with a nonactive multihomed record in the database, the database record will be replaced, as it would be if it clashes with an active multihomed entry in the database held by the same owner. But if the multihomed entry in the database is a replica owned by a different machine, it won't be. Again, if it's a unique record owned by the local WINS server, the addresses in the multihomed record will be challenged. If all challenges are successful, the database record is replaced, but if any challenge fails, release requests for the name then will be sent to the addresses in the database record before the database record is updated.

Scavenging

Scavenging is a method for maintaining the correct state information within the database. At boot time, the Scavenging Timer is started for a period equal to half the renewal interval. After half the renewal interval has elapsed, scavenging occurs for the first time, and all scavenging actions occur except for tombstone deletion. Tombstones will only be deleted after at least three days have passed since boot to allow sufficient time for their replication. Scavenging will reoccur at half the renewal interval, or may be initiated manually.

Cleanup

It's probably becoming pretty apparent by now that most of the data managed by WINS machines is maintained automatically, with the option for the network administrator to intervene at certain times. Often, it's best to leave the majority of management functions to the internal system control of the WINS server, unaided by us humans. Controlling a WINS server pretty much comes down to setting things up, adding names, and removing them when necessary. There are some exceptions, though. The related duties of database backup, restoration, and compression are definitely going to suffer without good ol' fashioned human support. Understanding that the name registration process is automatically handled by each WINS client may lead you to wonder about its opposite function—that of removing obsolete or incorrect names from the database.

Most of the database cleanup is accomplished automatically by controls set though the Configuration menu in the WINS Manager program. Once in, you'll be presented with a configuration screen listing four different timers:

- **Renewal Interval:** This delimits the intervals at which a WINS client is cued to renew its name with the WINS server. It's similar to the DHCP lease period discussed in Chapter 7. The default setting for this value is four days, or 96 hours.

- **Extinction Interval:** This sets the period of time between an entry being marked to be released and its subsequent extinction. Names are marked "release" when a WINS client terminates its session, changes its name, etc. At this point, the entry is considered deleted, but it's not automatically removed from the database. The default setting for this value is also four days, or 96 hours.

- **Extinction Time-Out:** This option describes the time elapsed between an entry being marked as extinct, and when that entry is removed, or "zapped." This setting is the Lysol of database cleanup. The default setting for this value is again four days or 96 hours, but it can also have a minimal value set for one day.

- **Verify Interval:** This sets the frequency at which a WINS server verifies that the entries it doesn't own are still active, i.e., those depicting shared information from other servers. Both the default and minimal settings for this value equal 24 days, or 576 hours.

That's not all folks—there are two more options involved in the whole push or pull configuration fest. Let's say you want your server to pull other WINS servers for any new database entries, or other replication related stuff upon initialization. To do this, select the Initial Replication box located under Push Parameters, inside of which you'll find the spiffy option to set a retry count. This is like a replication insurance policy that ensures important changes are made even if your server is extremely busy, or temporarily unreachable. However, it's generally effective to simply push changes upon initialization, notifying other available WINS servers of changes when your server starts up. Since, in most cases, the servers that are up have more current information than those that are down, you may want to consider using both these methods. One final thing on push parameters—you can also set updates to automatically occur upon any IP address change. This is a highly mutable area, since when an entry is changed, it's often because DHCP has assigned a new address to it, or because the device has been moved to a different subnet.

If you're professionally managing this server, you should also select the Advanced button from the WINS Manager configuration panel to display additional options. This will reveal the additional control opportunities described in the list below.

- **Logging Enabled**: Turns on WINS server database event logging. As the name suggests, whenever changes are made to the database, they're recorded in the log.

- **Log Detailed Events**: Specifies whether log entries are to be short and sweet or long-winded. It's used to add potentially telling details in the log, which can become quite handy when troubleshooting. Be warned, however... nothing worthwhile in life is free! There's an abundance of overhead associated with this function that can turn your Porsche of a network into a Volvo. Steer clear of this one if speed and performance tuning are your goals.

- **Replicate Only with Partners**: Determines whether your WINS server will communicate with other servers with which it's not already configured to push or pull entries. This is a really cool feature if you're running separate networks that shouldn't be communicating with each other. This function is enabled by default.

- **Backup on Termination**: As the name implies, automatically backs up the database when WINS Manager is closed.

- **Migrate On/Off:** Replaces static information with the dynamic variety if a conflict occurs. For example, if you've made static entries, and the information you entered eventually changes, the WINS server will cause the database entries to "migrate" from static (S) to active/dynamic (A). A better name could be "evolve." If you're upgrading systems to Windows NT, use this option.

- **Starting Version Count (hex):** Specifies the highest version ID number for the database. Usually, you will not need to change this value unless the database becomes corrupted and needs to start fresh.

- **Database Backup Path:** A local, non-network directory to which the WINS database will be backed up. This variable will be used along with automatic restore if the database is ever corrupted.

Maintaining the WINS Database

Now that you know the ins and outs on configuring replication partners, we'll give you the skinny on database control. The WINS Manager provides you with the tools you need to list, filter, and control name mappings. You'll learn to use them, as well as gain insight into what's involved in these processes.

To open and view the contents of the WINS database:

1. **Startup:** Open the WINS Manager, and select Show Database from the Mappings menu. Call mappings on the currently selected WINS server will then be displayed.

2. **Filter:** To streamline and arrange the scope of displayed mappings, select Show Only Mapping from Selected Owner from the Display Options box. Then select an owner from the Owners list, and choose a sort order. The options for determining the sort order can be established by IP Address, Computer Name, Expiration Date, Version ID, or Type. This function can be used independently of whether a filter is applied or not. You can also customize the filter by using the Set Filter button. This will specify a limited range of mappings for names and IP addresses.

3. **Information:** This allows you to examine the information you've entered. Notice each line entry is designated by a little computer icon indicating a unique name, or by a computer with an echo trail denoting a group, Internet group, or multihomed computer. You'll notice the registered

NetBIOS name, located to the right of the symbol and followed by the IP address, plus a checkmark under *A* for active/dynamic, or *S* for static mapping. If you see an ominous little cross (like one on a tombstone) appear in the *A* column, it means the entry is doomed on death row, and will soon be deleted. The cross icon never appears for static entries because they're immortal and permanent. The remaining information consists of the Expiration Date equaling the current WINS server time, plus the TTL and the Version ID—a unique hexadecimal number used to determine how fresh an entry is when communicating with other WINS servers.

4. **Removal:** If you're seeking to delete a certain WINS server, plus all related database entries owned by it, choose it from the Select Owner list, and click on the Delete Owners list.

5. **Exit:** Click on the Close button to exit back to the WINS Manager main menu.

WINS Proxy Agents

Using an NBNS (NetBIOS Naming Server) like WINS can greatly cut down on the broadcasts on your network, reducing traffic and improving throughput. But, as you've seen, this requires the clients to understand WINS; the older network client software just shouts away as a B-node would.

WINS can help those older non-WINS-aware clients with a *WINS proxy agent*. A WINS proxy agent is a regular old network workstation that listens for older B-node systems helplessly broadcasting, trying to reach NetBIOS names that (unknown to the B-node computers) are on another subnet.

To see how this would work, let's take a look at a very simple two-subnet intranet, as shown in Figure 8.4.

FIGURE 8.4

An example of a two-subnet intranet

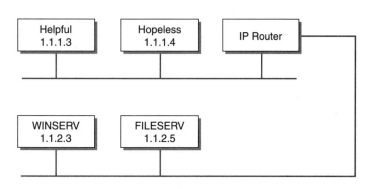

Here, you see two Class C subnets, `1.1.1.0` and `1.1.2.0`, with a router between them. On `1.1.1.0`, there are two workstations. One's a WINS-aware client named Helpful which is also running a WINS proxy agent. The other is an old B-node client named Hopeless which is not WINS-aware. On `1.1.2.0`, there are a couple of servers, a machine acting as a WINS server and a regular old file server.

When Hopeless first comes up, it'll do a broadcast of its names to ensure that no one else has them. The machine that it really should be talking to, of course, is WINSERV, but WINSERV can't hear it. Helpful, however, hears the B-node broadcasts coming from Hopeless and sends a directed message to WINSERV, telling it that there's a workstation named Hopeless trying to register some names.

WINSERV looks up those names to ensure that they don't already exist. If they *do* exist, then WINSERV sends a message back to Helpful, saying, "Don't let that guy register those names!" Helpful then sends a message to Hopeless, saying, "I'm sorry, but *I* already use the name Hopeless." That keeps Hopeless from registering a name that exists on another subnet.

Assuming that Hopeless names do *not* currently exist in the WINSERV database, WINSERV does *not* register the names. Putting a WINS proxy agent on `1.1.1.0` doesn't mean the non-WINS clients will have their names registered with WINS. That means it's okay to have the same NetBIOS name on two different computers, so long as they're both B-node clients and are on different subnets.

Suppose then that Hopeless does a `Net Use d: \\fileserv\files`—in that case, the name `\\fileserv` must be resolved. Assuming that Hopeless does not have a HOSTS or LMHOSTS file, Hopeless will start broadcasting, saying, "Is there anyone here named FILESERV? And if so, what's your IP address?" Helpful will intercede by sending a directed IP message to WINSERV, saying, "Is there a name registered as FILESERV, and what is its IP address?"

WINSERV will respond with the IP address of FILESERV, and Helpful will then send a directed message back to Hopeless, saying, "Sure, I'm FILESERV, and you can find me at `1.1.2.5`." Now Hopeless can complete its request.

WARNING   Make sure there is only *one* WINS proxy agent per subnet! Otherwise, two PCs will respond to HOPELESS, causing—how do the manuals put it? Ah yes—"unpredictable results."

New Stuff in NT 4 WINS

Burst Mode

Events like many WINS clients coming online for the first time, and the WINS server being started with a clean database, are when the burst handling parameter comes in handy. It's used to temporarily maintain a steady state in the WINS server. Why? Because these situations result in a large amount of name registration and name refresh traffic occurring en masse, and WINS servers currently store only 25,000 name registrations and refresh queries in their queues at maximum before they start dropping queries. Here's where burst parameter comes in: With it, the WINS server can be configured to send success responses to those clients whose requests have been abandoned. The server's responses have TTLs that serve to slow down the refresh rate of the barrage of clients, and thereby regulate the burst of WINS client traffic. The elegant result is a steady state being reached a lot quicker.

Great! But how do you configure the burst parameter? Well, it's enabled by creating the "BurstHandling" key under the HKEY_LOCAL_MACHINE\System\ CurrentControlSet\Services\WINS\Parameters key and setting the value to 1. You do this by:

```
Name: BurstHandling
Type = REG_DWORD
Value: 0 or 1
Default = 0
```

Hitting the Wall, and Working through It—Administering WINS through a Firewall

For remote WINS administration, set up an initial session to port 135, followed by another session to some random port above 1024. Why? Because the WINS administrator uses "dynamic endpoints" with a remote procedure call (RPC), and you can't make Internet firewalls pass this traffic when the port's not consistent. In Windows NT 4, system defaults for dynamic port appropriation are defined in the Registry.

A list of all ports available (or not available) from the Internet should be defined in the Registry to allow you to administrate WINS through a firewall remotely. You do this with the following keys, found under:

`HKEY_LOCAL_MACHINE\Software\Microsoft\Rpc\Internet`

- **Ports:** Delimits a set of IP port ranges comprised of either all the ports available from the Internet or all the ports that aren't available. Each string either represents a solitary port or a set of ports, and will look like "1050-2000" or "1994". The RPC run time will regard the whole configuration invalid if any entries are outside the range of zero to 65535, or if any string can't be interpreted. Type in:

`REG_MULTI_SZ - (set of IP port ranges)`

- **PortsInternetAvailable:** The *Y* and *N* stand for (surprise) yes and no. If the ports listed in the Ports key enjoy a *Y* status, that means you're looking at all the Internet-available ports on that machine. If it's *N*, the ports listed in the Ports key equal unavailable Internet ports. Type in:

`REG_SZ - Y or N (not case-sensitive)`

- **UseInternetPorts:** Designates the system default policy. If it's *Y*, the processes that'll be using the default are assigned ports from those in the Internet-available ports set. If *N*, they're only assigned ports out of the set of intranet-only ports. Type in:

`REG_SZ - Y or N (again, not case-sensitive)`

How Does WINS Check for Consistency?

Even though it's possible to periodically check the WINS database for consistency in Windows NT 4, consistency checking is a very network intensive thing that consumes a lot of cycles on the WINS server. This is because WINS replicates all records for the owner whose records are being checked by another WINS machine so it can ascertain if its database is in synch with it. Good ol' common sense and discretion is the key when selecting the values for the different parameters below. The important thing to keep in mind and carefully consider here is your existing network configuration. How many WINS servers, WAN/LAN lines between them, and how many WINS clients are you working with, etc.? The answers will imply the best values for these parameters for your individual situation. You do this by creating the "Consistency-Check" key under:

HKEY_LOCAL_MACHINE\System\CurrentControlSet\Services WINS\Parameters

The following values are options you can create under this key:

- **TimeInterval:** Delimits the time interval when WINS will do a consistency check. Its default is 24 hours. Type in:

REG_DWORD -(*Number of Seconds*)

- **SpTime:** Pinpoints the exact time in *hh:mm:ss* format that the first consistency check will be done. Successive ones will be done periodically at TimeInterval seconds. Its default is: 2:00:00 (2 AM). To set it, you type in:

REG_SZ *hh:mm:ss*

- **MaxRecsAtATime:** You guessed it—this limits the maximum number of records that'll be replicated in each consistency check cycle. WINS does consistency checks on each WINS owner's records. So, when it finishes checking one, it'll either go on to the next on its list, or stop, depending on how the MaxRecsAtATime value is set. Its default is 30000. To set this one, type in:

REG_DWORD (*Number of Recs*)

- **Name: UseRplPnrs:** If this is set to anything but a zero value, WINS will only contact its pull partners when doing consistency checks. If the owner with records that need to be checked *is* a pull partner, then great—it'll be used. Otherwise, some random pull partner will be. To set it, type in:

DWORD 0 or *non-zero value*

WINS never ever deletes records in its database if the partner with which it's verifying them isn't the owner. This isn't computer courtesy, it's because WINS has no idea which database is more current.

WINSCHK—Huh?

There's a new tool in the Windows NT 4 Resource Kit bag of tricks—
WINSCHK. It's a command-line utility that checks name and version
number inconsistencies that can crop up in WINS databases. It also monitors replication activity, plus authenticates replication topology in an
enterprise network—a very cool, particularly useful tool indeed! With
WINSCHK, you can not only check and resolve WINS database replication issues remotely, you can also pinpoint some of the most common
problems that cause database inconsistencies—and all by running this little
gem in a central location! It supplements WINSCL with options geared
towards flagging potential causes for database inconsistencies, including
these likely demons:

- Asymmetric replication topologies

- High communication failures

WINSCHK recognizes both of these and responds by giving you a warning.
It also helps monitor replication activity by allowing you to:

- Check for version number inconsistencies

- Check up on the state of one or more names in various WINS databases
  in your network

WINSCHK can be used in interactive or noninteractive mode, and when it's
in the latter, it keeps a log of all its activities in the local directory (winstst.log).
You can choose to monitor WINS activity in the background, too. Doing this
will cause all logs to be dumped into monitor.log. Here's a list of WINSCHK
options:

- **0: Toggle the interactive switch.** The default value is Interactive. All
  status messages will be logged into winstst.log, and if the Interactive
  switch is on, it permits you the option of having status messages printed
  on the command window.

- **1: Test for names (in names.txt) against WINS servers (in servers.txt).**
  It tests for N names against M servers. A quick tool to check for consistency between various WINS servers, this utility is driven by two flat
  files that you can revise with your favorite text editor. The IP address of
  a starting WINS server from which a list of all the replicating WINS

servers is built up to query is in the file servers.txt. The file names.txt holds a list of NetBIOS names to query and may contain multiple Net-BIOS names—one per line—that need to be checked. The names you'll see in this file follow this format: <name>*<16th byte>, for example, FOOBAR*20, and names must be in upper-case. This utility will run the list of NetBIOS names querying each WINS server, check for consistency of addresses, and report mismatched IP addresses, plus any instances of "name not found." It'll also tattle on nonresponsive WINS servers.

■ **2: Check for version number consistencies.** This is how you get the owner address—version number maps (through an RPC function)—from different WINS servers so you can check how consistent their databases are. You do this by making sure a WINS server always has the highest version number for the records it owns—higher than all other WINS servers populating the network.

Here's what it'll look like:

```
   A    B    C      <--- list of owners

A 100   80   79     <-- mapping table retrieved from A

B 95    75*  65     <---mapping table retrieved from B

C 78    45   110    <---mapping table retrieved from C
```

An intersection B with B flags a problem requiring fixing.

■ **3: Monitor WINS servers to detect communication failures between WINS servers.** This has two versions in which it can be run: once or continuous, with the latter running every three hours by default. Since it generates a lot of network activity, we recommend not running this option too often. It monitors WINS servers periodically to ensure that the primary and backup aren't down at the same time, and logs its activity in monitor.log. It also retrieves WINS statistics periodically, ensuring that replication failures aren't happening consistently. No matter what, the administrator is alerted to the situations it detects.

- **4: Verify replication configuration setup.** This option checks the Registry of a WINS server to both make sure each partner is pull and push, and that there's a defined pull interval. It'll check into this for each partner, covering the entire network (and therefore you), and flags any weird partner relationships it finds.

- **99: Exit this tool.**

Designing the WINS Infrastructure

For an enterprise network environment often spanning the globe via a routed network, you need NetBIOS connectivity. NetBIOS name spaces are flat, each of them has to be unique, and you need something to convert the NetBIOS name to an address. As described in RFC 1001 and RFC 1002, WINS is Microsoft's implementation of a NetBIOS name server, furnishing a distributed database for NetBIOS names and their corresponding addresses. Local WINS servers will replicate the entries (NetBIOS name/IP address pairs) that WINS clients have registered to them to other WINS servers, ensuring that NetBIOS names are unique, and making local name resolution possible.

What about WINS System Convergence Time?

An important consideration indeed! For your specific configuration, use the worst-case scenario—the longest it could possibly take to get a new entry in a WINS server database replicated to all the others. Since you've allowed a better than good chunk of time for your convergence to occur, you've guaranteed that name queries for a new name will be successful. If ample time isn't allowed, you'll run the risk that clients might be unable to find the new, or recently modified, machine. To see how this works, take a look at Figure 8.5.

Here you see a client registering its name in WINS_C. Since other clients can query WINS_C for this name, they can get the IP address but at this moment, if they query the *other* WINS servers (A, B, and D), they won't get a positive response—not until the entry is replicated to A, B, and D. When the push update count threshold (as configured on C) is exceeded, or when the pull replication interval (15 minutes, as configured on A) expires, replication from WINS_C to WINS_A will then take place. A guarantee that the entry will be replicated can only be had when the pull replication interval expires. And even then, name queries to WINS servers B and D may still be unsuccessful. However, after 15 minutes, it's guaranteed the entry will have been replicated to WINS server B, and

FIGURE 8.5

WINS convergence

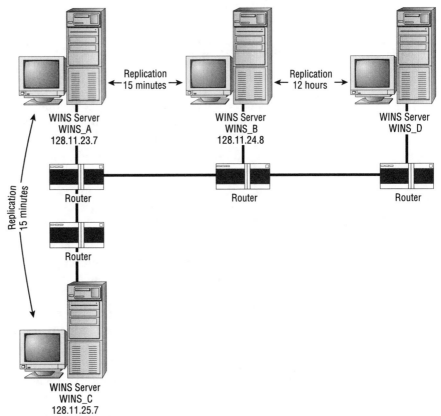

after 12 hours, it's guaranteed to have been replicated to WINS server D. In this configuration, the convergence time is twice 15 minutes plus 12 hours, or 12.5 hours. It's possible for name query requests to succeed before the convergence time has passed, but the entries would have to be replicated over some shorter path than your "worst-case" path. Also, if an update count threshold was passed before the replication interval expired, the result would be an earlier replication of the new entry. Remember, the longer the replication path, the longer the convergence time. Our example of 15 minutes between sites is pretty short by reality's standards, while 12 hours is actually rather long—even when hopping continents. The wisest choice in setting these intervals really depends on individual network requirements, and is mostly a result of the design choices that created it.

And It All Comes Down to Fault Tolerance

We know it sounds cliché, but bear with us—there are basically two types of failures:

1. A WINS server crashing or being stopped for maintenance

2. Network failures where links go down or routers fail

In our example in Figure 8.5, a WINS_A or WINS_B failure would cause the network to become segmented, and entries would no longer be replicated between WINS_C and WINS_D. Other clients would be unable to connect to the updated machines because the IP address/name no longer matched for updated clients. But suppose you added replication between WINS_B and WINS_C—that would improve the configuration if WINS_A fails. The same goes for adding replication between WINS_D and WINS_C in the event WINS_B fails.

But why stop there? Why would you only add replication between those servers and not the rest? Because failures of the links between WINS_A, B, and C are already covered by the underlying router network which would reroute the traffic should that occur—that's why. Although not the most elegant, efficient scenario when compared to a healthy network, WINS replication will still continue uninterrupted. But any failure on the link between WINS_B and WINS_D would segment the WINS configuration. Additionally, failures on the B-D link would bring other network traffic to a grinding halt, so you'd want to have an on-demand backup link between WINS_D and WINS_C. Then you're covered, and your WINS replication traffic would simply be rerouted by the underlying router infrastructure.

Okay, great—but what if the routers fail—what then? Yes, true—in our example, the routers are all single points of failure, and if one of them failed, it would segment the WINS configuration for sure. A good, generally accepted approach is to look at two simultaneous failures, analyze what their consequences would be, prioritize those, and proceed to come up with backup plans accordingly.

And don't panic—a segmented WINS configuration is not as catastrophic as it sounds. Most of the time, your clients can still resolve the names to addresses, and local WINS servers and/or broadcasts can take care of most of the name resolution. The only gimpy spot has to do with updated or new remote entries—they, of course, would be unknown. Remember, entries aren't dropped at scavenging time when the owning WINS cannot be reached, WINS service can be installed on some other machine, and the database backups can be restored on that new machine.

Now that we've worked through DHCP and WINS, let's move on to the next chapter and take a look at the future of Microsoft TCP/IP.

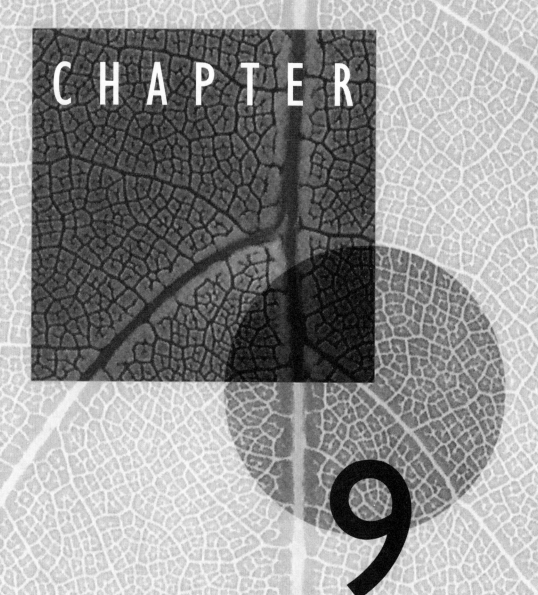

CHAPTER

9

DNS in the New NT World

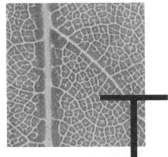

he onset of Enhanced Directory Services for the Windows NT
operating system is coming to us soon in a later release of Windows NT, and the Domain Name System (DNS) server will be
much more important than it was in any prior Windows NT release. DNS will
completely replace WINS. Because of this, installing and designing effective
DNS implementations today will help tremendously when tomorrow's need to
migrate to the next version of Win-dows NT materializes.

The use of DNS in the Microsoft Windows NT 4 operating system is currently optional. The DNS service that ships with Windows NT 4 is there if
you want to use it, but there's presently nothing in Windows NT Directory
Services that requires you to do so. If you opt to use DNS, this chapter will
show you how to do just that—but it won't stop there. Our focus will be on
how best to design your DNS infrastructure in preparation for that imminent
release of Windows NT Enhanced Directory Services (DS).

Because of DS, we're soon to experience a Windows NT paradigm shift. Until
now, groups using Windows NT within a given company could happily move
about within their own Private Idahos, laying out domains, assigning user
accounts, and creating trusts, shares, etc. Windows NT groups just didn't have
to concern themselves with the Directory Services world because X.500, DNS,
and the like were typically and traditionally the worry of a different group. But
Enhanced DS will change all that—and it's slated to be included in the next
major version of Windows NT! With it, these two groups will have to collabo-
rate. Why? Because Enhanced DS will be rather like X.500, and it'll use DNS to
ferret out the servers that provide these Directory Services. So… pay attention!
This is a very important chapter that will give groups using Windows NT insight
into the other Directory Services that are available. Consider this chapter to be
about foreign relations—its purpose is to promote an understanding of each
group's needs to ensure a smooth migration to Enhanced Directory Services.

Toward this goal, we'll first define the DNS technology—important for
anyone new to DNS. We'll then take a look at the Microsoft-specific DNS and
talk about why the Microsoft DNS solution is the correct choice for a Microsoft

or mixed environment. Next we'll be configuring DNS architectures—critical for anyone about to design a DNS solution—and last, we'll talk about the future of Windows NT with DNS.

Where Did DNS Come From?

In the late 1970s there were only a handful of networked computers, and all of the computer name-to-address mappings were contained in a single file called HOSTS. This was stored at the Stanford Research Institute's Network Information Center (SRI-NIC). Whenever anybody wanted to update their HOSTS file, they would download the latest HOSTS file from Stanford. This actually worked for a while, until more computers got on the network, and managing the HOSTS file went ballistic. Bandwidth being pretty limited back then, Stanford got overloaded. One of the biggest problems centered around the HOSTS file being a flat name structure, requiring all computers across the whole Internet to have a unique name. The ARPANET was created to find the solution to this problem (along with a few others), which led to DNS, a distributed database using a hierarchical name structure.

According to Dr. Paul Mockapetris, principal designer of DNS, the original design goal for DNS was to replace this cumbersome, singularly administered HOSTS file with a lightweight distributed database that would allow for hierarchical name space, distribution of administration, extensible data types, virtually unlimited database size, and reasonable performance.

The Domain Name System is a set of protocols and services on a TCP/IP network which allows users of the network to utilize hierarchical, user-friendly names when looking for other hosts (computers) instead of having to remember and use their IP addresses. This system is used extensively on the Internet and in many private enterprises today. If you've used a Web browser, Telnet application, FTP utility, or other similar TCP/IP utilities on the Internet, then you have probably used a DNS server.

The DNS protocol's best-known function is mapping user-friendly names to IP addresses. For example, suppose the FTP site at Microsoft had an IP address of 157.55.100.1. Most people would reach this computer by specifying ftp.microsoft.com instead of its human-being-alienating IP address. Besides being easier to remember, the name is more reliable. The numeric address could change for any number of reasons, but that name can remain in spite of the change.

The most popular implementation of the DNS protocol BIND was originally developed at Berkeley for the 4.3 BSD UNIX operating system. The name BIND stands for Berkeley Internet Name Domain. The primary specifications for DNS are defined in Requests for Comments (RFCs) 974, 1034, and 1035.

How DNS Works

DNS's job is to translate computer names into IP addresses. This is done by a hierarchical client/server-based distributed database management system. DNS works at the Application layer of the OSI reference model and uses TCP and UDP at the Transport layer.

DNS uses clients called *resolvers* and servers called *name servers*. Client machines (resolvers) send a UDP packet to servers (name servers) for lower overhead, and use TCP if abridgment of the returned data occurs.

Resolvers pass name requests between applications and name servers that query the name server, looking for a World Wide Web site. Netscape Navigator and Internet Explorer have the resolver built into the application.

Name servers receive queries from resolvers and resolve host names to IP addresses.

Microsoft DNS

All right. That said, what's up with Microsoft DNS anyway, and why should you use it? Well, we'll start by telling you what it's not. First of all, know that the Microsoft DNS server isn't a port of the Berkeley BIND code. The Big M made up its collective mind to not port the BIND code in favor of writing their very own fully RFC-compliant code that's compatible with BIND instead. Why? Because, ever mindful of growth, they were trying to make it easy to add stuff like performance enhancements later. It's a really good thing that the Microsoft DNS server isn't the code that was shipped in the Windows NT Resource Kit—if you used that utility, trusting that you could actually perform trouble-free zone transfers, you know why! But fear not, the DNS server service in Windows NT 4 has been totally rewritten—it's not just the fumigated version—and rest assured that RFC compliance has been viciously tested. Yes folks, it *all* works, even the zone transfer part!

So what exactly *is* the Microsoft DNS server? Well, in accordance with the whole RFC thing, if an RFC-required feature isn't found in the Microsoft DNS product, it's considered a bug, so, primarily, the DNS server in Windows NT 4 is an RFC-compliant implementation of DNS. Because of this, it not only sustains all standard resource record types, it both creates and uses standard DNS zone files. Additionally, it can interoperate with other DNS servers, and includes the DNS diagnostic utility nslookup and the UNIX utility dig—the definite article and standard of standards. Microsoft DNS doesn't stop there either—it goes above and beyond what's specified in RFCs, with features like DNS Manager (a graphical administration utility) that greatly eases administrative burdens, and dynamic updates through tight integration with WINS.

Let's expand on that…with Microsoft's DNS, network admins now have freedom of choice—the option to turn off traditional DNS systems and choose the Microsoft Windows NT implementation instead. This gives you the ability to remove static entries for the Microsoft-based clients in the traditional DNS server zone files and opt for the WINS/DNS dynamic integration. Here's what we mean: Suppose you have a non-Microsoft-based client that wants to get out to a Web page on some HTTP server that's DHCP/WINS enabled. All that client would have to do is query the DNS server. That server then queries WINS, and the name's resolved and returned to the client. Because of dynamic IP addressing, before WINS integration you couldn't reliably resolve that name—nice touch, huh!

Microsoft DNS supports RFCs 1033, 1034, 1035, 1101, 1123, 1183, and 1536.

A Closer Look at DNS

Let's go back to DNS for a minute. A Domain Name System is composed of a distributed database of names that establishes a logical tree structure called the *domain name space*. Each node or domain in that space is named and can contain subdomains. Domains and subdomains are grouped into zones to allow for distributed administration of the name space (we'll talk about zones more in a bit). The domain name identifies the domain's position in the logical DNS hierarchy in relation to its parent domain by separating each branch of the tree with a period (.). Figure 9.1 shows a few of the top-level domains, where the Microsoft domain fits, and a host called Tigger within the `microsoft.com` domain. If someone wanted to contact that host, they would use the fully qualified domain name (FQDN) `tigger.microsoft.com`.

FIGURE 9.1

DNS hierarchy

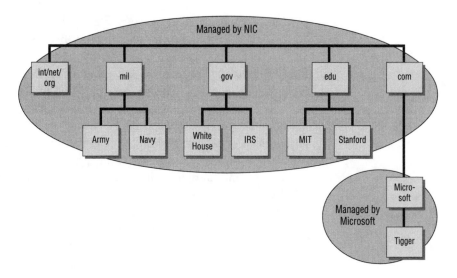

DNS Servers and the Internet

The root of the DNS database on the Internet is managed by the Internet Network Information Center (`http://www.internic.com`). The top-level domains were assigned organizationally, and by country. These domain names follow the International Standard 3166. Two-letter and three-letter abbreviations are used for countries, and various abbreviations are reserved for use by organizations, as shown in the following examples.

DNS Domain Name	Type of Organization
com	Commercial (for example, `globalnet.com` for Globalnet System Solutions Corporation)
edu	Educational (for example, `mit.edu` for Massachusetts Institute of Technology)
gov	Government (for example, `whitehouse.gov` for the White House in Washington, D.C.)
int	International organizations (for example, `nato.int` for NATO)
mil	Military operations (for example, `army.mil` for the Army)

DNS Domain Name	Type of Organization
net	Networking organizations (for example, `nsf.net` for NSFNET)
org	Noncommercial organizations (for example, `fidonet.org` for FidoNet)
de	Germany (Deutschland)
it	Italy
nz	New Zealand
us	United States

The Skinny on Domains

Each node in the DNS database tree, along with all the nodes below it, is called a *domain*. Domains can contain both hosts (computers) and other domains (subdomains). For example, the Microsoft domain `microsoft.com` could contain both computers, such as `ftp.microsoft.com`, and subdomains, such as `sales.microsoft.com`, which could and most likely do contain hosts such as `appserver.sales.microsoft.com`.

In general, domain names and host names have restrictions in their naming which only allow the use of characters *a–z*, *A–Z*, *0–9*, and – (dash or minus sign). The use of characters such as the / (slash), . (period), and _ (underscore) is not allowed. We've had many a problem with clients creatively naming their hosts DHCP_1 and DHCP_2. These unfortunately named NT Servers could not be registered with DNS.

Zones

Finally… it's time to enter the DNS Zone. A *zone* isn't some spaced-out individual, it's a portion of the DNS namespace whose database records exist and are managed in a particular zone file. A single DNS server can be configured to manage one or multiple zone files. Each zone is anchored at a specific domain node—referred to as the zone's *root domain*. Zone files don't necessarily contain the complete tree (that is, all subdomains) under the zone's root domain. For a comparison of domains and zones, take a look at Figure 9.2. What are you looking at? Well, in this example, `microsoft.com` is a domain, but the entire domain isn't controlled by one zone file. Part of the domain is actually broken off into a separate zone file for `sales.microsoft.com`.

Breaking up domains across multiple zone files may indeed be necessary to either distribute management of the domain to different groups, or to ensure efficiencies in data replication—zone transfers—which will be discussed soon.

Never ever confuse a zone with a domain. A zone is a physical file composed of resource records that defines a group of domains. A domain is a node in the DNS namespace and all subdomains below it.

FIGURE 9.2

Domains and zones

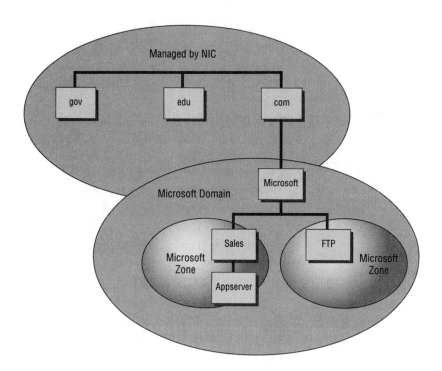

Name Servers

DNS servers store information about the domain namespace and are referred to as name servers. Name servers generally have one or more zones for which they are responsible. The name server is then predictably said to have *authority* for those zones.

When you configure a DNS name server—as we shall soon see with the "NS" record—you're essentially telling it who all of the other DNS name servers are in the same domain.

Primary, Secondary, and Master Name Servers

A *primary name server* is a name server that gets the data for its zones from local files. Changes to a zone, such as added domains or hosts, are carried out at the primary name server.

Secondary name servers get the data for their zones from another name server across the network that's the specific zone's authority. The processes of obtaining this zone information—the database file—across the network is referred to as a *zone transfer*.

There are three reasons to have secondary servers within an enterprise network. Those reasons are:

- **Redundancy:** Though this is usually something to avoid, it's prudent here. You need at least two DNS name servers serving each zone—a primary, and at least one secondary for (you guessed it) fault tolerance. As is true for other scenarios where fault tolerance is your goal, your strategic machines involved should be as independent as possible—that is, on different networks, etc.

- **Remote locations:** You should also have secondary servers (or other primary servers for subdomains) in remote locations that have a large number of clients. You wouldn't want a whole legion of clients having to communicate across slow links for name resolution, would you?

- **Reduce load on the primary:** Having secondary servers present reduces the load on your primary server.

Since information for each zone is stored in separate files, this primary or secondary designation is defined at a zone level. In other words, a given name server may be a primary name server for some zones and a secondary name server for others.

When defining a zone on a name server as a secondary, you must designate a name server from which it will obtain that zone information. The source of zone information for a secondary name server in a DNS hierarchy is referred to as a *master name server*, and it can either be a primary or secondary name server for the requested zone. When a secondary name server starts up, it contacts its master name server and initiates a zone transfer with it.

Use secondary servers as master servers when the primary is overloaded, or when there is a more efficient network path between "secondary to secondary" versus "secondary to primary."

Forwarders and Slaves

When a DNS name server receives a DNS request, it attempts to locate the requested information within its own zone files. If this fails because that server isn't authoritative for the domain requested, it must then communicate with other DNS name servers to resolve the request. Since, on a globally connected network, a DNS resolution request outside a local zone typically requires interaction with DNS name servers located outside of the company on the public Internet, it's a good idea to selectively enable specific DNS name servers in your company for this type of wide-area communication.

To address this issue, DNS allows for the concept of *forwarders*—specific DNS name servers selected to carry out wide-area communications across the Internet. All other DNS name servers within the company are configured with the IP addresses of the DNS name servers designated as forwarders to use them for this purpose. You do this configuration on a per server basis, not a per zone basis!

When a server that's configured to use forwarders receives a DNS request that it's unable to resolve through its own zone files, it passes the request along to one of the designated forwarders. The forwarder then carries out whatever communication is necessary to resolve the request, and returns the results to the requesting server, which, in turn, sends back the results to the original requester. If the forwarder is unable to resolve the query, the DNS server attempts to resolve the query on its own as it normally would.

Slaves are DNS servers that have been configured to use forwarders and have also been configured to return a failure message if the forwarder is unable to resolve the request. Slaves make no attempt to contact other name servers if the forwarder is unable to satisfy the request.

Caching-Only Servers

Although all DNS name servers cache queries that they've resolved, *caching-only servers* are DNS name servers whose only job is to perform queries, cache the answers, and return the results—they aren't authoritative for any domains, and only contain information which they have cached while resolving queries.

When trying to determine when to use such a server, bear in mind that when these servers initially start up, they possess no cached information, because they have to build up a store of it over time as they service requests. However, if you're dealing with a slow link between sites, there's much less traffic sent across that link, because these servers don't perform zone transfers.

Name Resolution

There are three types of queries that a client can make to a DNS server: *recursive, iterative,* and *inverse.* During our little talk on name resolution, keep in mind that a DNS server can be a client to another DNS server at the same time.

Recursive Queries

In a recursive query, the queried name server is petitioned to respond with the requested data, or with an error stating that either data of the requested type or the domain name specified doesn't exist. The name server *cannot* just refer the querier to a different name server.

Queries of this type are typically done by a DNS client (a resolver) to a DNS server. Also, if a DNS server is configured to use a forwarder, the request from this DNS server to its forwarder will be a recursive query.

Iterative Queries

In an iterative query, the queried name server gives back the best answer it currently has to the querier. This type of query is typically by a DNS server to other DNS servers, and happens after it has received a recursive query from a resolver.

You've Got That IP Address, Now What about the Host Name?

Instead of supplying a name and then asking for an IP address, the client first needs to provide the IP address before it asks for the name. Since there's no direct correlation in the DNS namespace between the domain names and the associated IP addresses they contain, only a thorough search of all domains could guarantee striking gold.

A special domain, in-addr.arpa., in the DNS namespace was created to help get us all through this little catch. Nodes in the in-addr.arpa domain are named after the numbers in the dotted-octet representation of IP addresses, but since IP addresses get more specific from left to right, and domain names get less specific from left to right, the order of IP address octets must be reversed when building the in-addr.arpa tree. With this arrangement, administration of lower limbs of the DNS in-addr.arpa tree can be given to companies as they are assigned their Class A, B, or C subnet address.

Once the domain tree is built into the DNS database, a special pointer record is added to associate the IP addresses to the corresponding host names. In other words, to find a host name for the IP address 157.55.89.2, the resolver would query the DNS server for a pointer record for 2.89.55.157.in-addr.arpa. If this IP address was outside the local domain, the DNS server would start at the root and sequentially resolve the domain nodes until arriving at 89.55.157.in-addr.arpa, which should contain the resource PTR record for 2 (that is 157.55.89.2).

Caching and Time to Live

When a name server is processing a recursive query, it may be required to send out several queries to find the definitive answer. The name server caches all received information during this process for a period of time specified in the returned data, known as the time to live (TTL). Its duration is set by the name server administrator of the zone that contains the data. If yours is a volatile network that changes a lot, smaller TTL values will help ensure that data about your domain is more consistent across that network. But there's a catch—teensy TTLs also increase the load on your name server. Once data is cached by a DNS server, it starts decreasing the TTL (that is, begins a count-down) from its original value, so it'll know when to flush the data from its cache. If a query comes in that can be satisfied by this cached data, the TTL that's returned with it equals the current amount of time left before flush time. Client resolvers also have data caches and honor the TTL value so that they too know when to flush.

DNS Files

Most DNS systems must be configured by editing text files, but as hinted at before, with Microsoft DNS, as with all Microsoft Windows-based products, there's a very cool interface to make that experience less odious than in times past. The new administration interface makes it a lot easier to configure both local and remote Microsoft DNS servers, and the DNS administrative tool configures the RFC-compatible text files for you. Time to pop that cork!

Even though the spiffy graphical user interface gives you the ability to modify the DNS files without an editor, you should still know the makeup of the DNS system configuration files. In RFC-compliant DNS systems, several files define the DNS system configuration and database. These files include the database, cache, reverse lookup, and 127 reverse lookup files. These files, explained in detail in the coming section, also exist in the Windows NT 4 DNS, and they too are RFC compliant.

The Database File

A database file or zone file is the file which contains the *resource records* for the part of the domain for which the zone is responsible. Some of the common resource records are discussed below. Windows NT 4 supplies a file, called place.dns, as a template to work with. It's wise to edit and rename this file the same as the zone it represents before using it on a production DNS server, because it's the file that will be replicated between masters and secondaries.

The Start of Authority

The first record in any database file is the Start of Authority (SOA) Record.

```
IN SOA <source host> <contact e-mail> ( <ser. no.> <refresh
time> <retry time> <expiration time> <TTL> )
```

source host   The host on which this file is maintained.

contact e-mail The Internet e-mail address for the person
                    responsible for this domain's database file.

Instead of writing the @ symbol in the e-mail name as you would normally do, you must replace the @ with a . (period) when placing it in the zone files. In other words, the e-mail address mark@mmco.com would be represented as mark.mmco.com in the zone file.

serial number   The "version number" of this database file that
                    should increase each time the database file is changed.

refresh time   The elapsed time (in seconds) that a secondary server will wait between checks to its master server to see if the database file has changed, and a zone transfer should be requested.

retry time   The elapsed time (in seconds) that a secondary server will wait before retrying a failed zone transfer.

expiration time   The elapsed time (in seconds) that a secondary server will keep trying to download a zone. After this time limit expires, the old zone information will be discarded.

time to live   The elapsed time (in seconds) that a DNS server is allowed to cache any resource records from this database file. This is the value that is sent out with all query responses from this zone file when the individual resource record doesn't contain an overriding value.

In order for a resource record to span a line in a database file, parentheses must enclose the line breaks.

In a zone file, the @ symbol represents the root domain of the zone (mmco.com in the following examples). The "IN" in the following records is the class of data. It stands for Internet. Other classes exist, but none of them are currently in widespread use.

Any domain name in the database file which is not terminated with a . (period) will have the root domain appended to the end.

Example:

```
@  IN SOA  nameserver1.mmco.com. mark.mmco.com. (
       1; serial number
   10800; refresh [3 hours]
    3600; retry [1hour]
  604800; expire [7 days]
   86400 ); time to live [1 day]
```

Setting the server's refresh interval is a balance between data consistency (accuracy of your data) and your network's load.

The Name Server Record

This lists the name servers for this domain, allowing other name servers to look up names in your domain.

```
<domain> IN NS <nameserver host>
```

Example:

```
@ IN NS  nameserver2.mmco.com.
@ IN NS  nameserver3.mmco.com.
```

The Mail Exchange Record

This record tells us what host processes mail for this domain. If multiple mail exchange records exist, the resolver will attempt to contact the mail servers in order of preference from lowest value (highest priority) to highest value (lowest priority). By using the example records that follow, mail addressed to bob@mmco.com is delivered to bob@mailserver0.mmco.com first, if possible, and then to bob@mailserver1.mmco.com if mailserver0 is unavailable.

```
<domain> IN MX <preference> <mailserver host>
```

Example:

```
@    IN MX  1  mailserver0
@    IN MX  2  mailserver1
```

The Host Record

A host record is used to statically associate hosts names to IP addresses within a zone. It should contain entries for all hosts which require static mappings, including workstations, name servers, mail servers, etc. These are the records which make up most of the database file when static records are used.

```
<host name> IN A <ip address of host>
```

Example:

```
tigger      IN A  157.55.89.102
nameserver2 IN A  157.55.89.12
mailserver1 IN A  157.55.89.15
```

The Local Host Record

A local host record allows lookups for localhost.mmco.com to return 127.0.0.1.

```
localhost  IN A  127.0.0.1
```

The CNAME Record

These records are sometimes called *aliases* but are technically referred to as *canonical name* (*CNAME*) entries. These records allow you to use more than one name to point to a single host.

Using canonical names makes it nice and easy to do stuff like host both an FTP server and a Web server on the same machine.

```
<host alias name> IN CNAME <host name>
```

Example:

Assume that www.mmco.com and ftp.mmco.com are on the same machine. Your zone file would then have the following entries in it, and look something like:

```
FileServer1  IN A      157.55.89.41
FTP          IN CNAME   FileServer1
www          IN CNAME   FileServer1
```

But what if you decide to move the FTP server service away from the Web service? Well, all you'd have to do is change the CNAME in the DNS server for FTP, and add an address record for the new server like this:

```
FTP          IN CNAME   FileServer2
FileServer2  IN A       157.55.89.42
```

The Cache File

The cache file contains host information needed to resolve names outside the authoritative domains, and contains names and addresses of root name servers. For users on the Internet, the default file provided with the Microsoft DNS service should suffice. For installations *not* connected to the Internet, the file should be replaced to contain the name servers authoritative for the root of your private network.

For a current Internet cache file, see:

```
ftp://rs.internic.net/domain/named.cache
```

Example:

```
; DNS CACHE FILE
;
; Initial cache data for root domain servers.
;
; YOU SHOULD CHANGE:
; -Nothing if connected to the Internet. Edit this file only
;  when update root name server list is released.
;   OR
; -If NOT connected to the Internet, remove these records and
;  replace with NS and A records for the DNS server authoritative
;  for the root domain at your site.
; Internet root name server records:
;  last update: Sep 1, 1995
;  related version of root zone: 1995090100
;
; formerly NS.INTERNIC.NET
.          3600000 IN NS A.ROOT-SERVERS.NET.
A.ROOT-SERVERS.NET.  3600000  A  198.41.0.4
; formerly NS1.ISI.EDU
.          3600000  NS B.ROOT-SERVERS.NET.
B.ROOT-SERVERS.NET.  3600000  A  128.9.0.107
; formerly C.PSI.NET
.          3600000  NS C.ROOT-SERVERS.NET.
C.ROOT-SERVERS.NET.  3600000  A  192.33.4.12
; formerly TERP.UMD.EDU
.          3600000  NS D.ROOT-SERVERS.NET.
D.ROOT-SERVERS.NET.  3600000  A  128.8.10.90
; formerly NS.NASA.GOV
.          3600000  NS E.ROOT-SERVERS.NET.
E.ROOT-SERVERS.NET.  3600000  A  192.203.230.10
; formerly NS.ISC.ORG
.          3600000  NS F.ROOT-SERVERS.NET.
F.ROOT-SERVERS.NET.  3600000  A  39.13.229.241
; formerly NS.NIC.DDN.MIL
.          3600000  NS G.ROOT-SERVERS.NET.
```

```
G.ROOT-SERVERS.NET.   3600000   A   192.112.36.4
; formerly AOS.ARL.ARMY.MIL
.         3600000   NS H.ROOT-SERVERS.NET.
; End of File
```

The Reverse Lookup File

This is a database file used for reverse lookups in particular IP DNS zones of host names when supplied with the IP numbers. The reverse lookup file allows a resolver to provide an IP address and request a matching host name. It contains SOA and name server records similar to other DNS database zone files, plus pointer records.

This DNS reverse lookup capability is an important one because some applications provide a way to implement security based on the connecting host names. What does this mean? Well, if a client tries to link to a Network File System (NFS) volume with this security arrangement, the NFS server would then contact the DNS server, and do a reverse-name lookup on the client's IP address. If the host name returned by the DNS server isn't in the access list for the NFS volume, or if the host name isn't found by DNS, then the NFS mount request would be denied. This reverse lookup capability is often used for troubleshooting reasons as well, but we're not going to go there quite yet.

Here are a couple example zones for different IP class networks.

Example Class C zone:

`100.89.192.in-addr.arpa`

Example Class B zone:

`55.157.in-addr.arpa`

The Pointer Record

Pointer records provide a static mapping of IP addresses to host names within a reverse lookup zone. IP numbers are written in backward order and `in-addr` `.arpa.` is appended to the end, creating the pointer record. For example, looking up the name for `157.55.89.51` requires a pointer record (PTR) query for the name `51.89.55.157.in-addr.arpa`.

```
<ip reverse domain name> IN PTR <host name>
```

Example:

```
51.89.55.157.in-addr.arpa.   IN PTR   mailserver1.mmco.com.
```

The Arpa-127.rev File

This is yet another database file. It's for the `127.in-addr.arpa.` domain and is used for reverse lookups of IP numbers in the 127 network, such as `localhost`. The only things in this file that change are the SOA and NS records.

The BIND Boot File

Although the boot file isn't actually defined in RFCs and isn't needed to be RFC compliant, it *is* described here. We wanted to be thorough. This file is actually a part of the BIND-specific implementation of DNS. Microsoft DNS can be configured to use a boot file if you're going to administer it through changes to the text files instead of using the DNS Administrator GUI.

The BIND boot file controls the startup behavior of the DNS server. Commands must start at the beginning of a line, and no spaces may precede commands. Recognized commands are: `directory`, `cache`, `primary`, `secondary`, `forwarders`, and `slave`. The syntax for this file is as follows:

Directory Command   Specifies a directory where other files referred to in the boot file can be found.

```
directory <directory>
```

Example:

```
directory c:\winnt\system32\dns
```

Cache Command   Specifies a file used to help the DNS service contact name servers for the root domain. This command and the file it refers to *must* be present. A cache file suitable for use on the Internet is provided with Windows NT 4.

```
cache   . <filename>
```

Example:

```
cache . cache
```

Primary Command   Specifies a domain for which this name server is authoritative and a database file that contains the resource records for that domain (that is, zone file). Multiple primary command records could exist in the boot file.

```
primary  <domain>  <filename>
```

Example:

```
primary mmco.com mmco.dns
primary sales.mmco.com sales.dns
```

Secondary Command   Specifies a domain for which this name server is authoritative and a list of master server IP addresses from which to attempt downloading the zone information—rather than reading it from a file. It also defines the name of the local file for caching this zone. Multiple secondary command records could exist in the boot file.

```
secondary <domain> <hostlist> <local filename>
```

Example:

```
secondary test.mmco.com 157.55.89.100 test.dns
```

Forwarders Command   Specifies another server that's willing to try resolving recursive queries on behalf of the system.

```
forwarders <hostlist>
```

Example:

```
forwarders 157.55.89.100 157.55.89.101
```

Slave Command   Specifies that the use of forwarders is the only possible way to resolve queries. Can only follow a forwarders command.

```
slave
```

Example:

```
forwarders 157.55.89.100 157.55.89.101
slave
```

Setting Up a Small Domain with DNS Manager

There's a lot to know about running a DNS server, but since with many small domains you can get away with just a few basics, we'll start the "how-to" part of the DNS story with pointers on setting up a DNS server under NT 4 for a small imaginary domain. For those of you still using 3.5, we'll follow that up with the nuts and bolts of using the DNS Manager, and then offer some ideas on making the DNS Manager work better under NT 4.

Suppose you'd like to set up a domain named bowsers.com. Its Class C network number is 210.10.20.0. It has just a few machines important enough to need entries in DNS:

- The mail server for bowsers.com is a machine named retriever .bowsers.com, at 210.10.20.40.

- The Web server for bowsers.com is a machine named www.bowsers .com, at 210.10.20.20.

- That same 210.10.20.20 machine is also the FTP server, and we want it to respond to the name ftp.bowsers.com.

- There is a machine that acts both as a major file server for the organization and as the primary domain controller; it's named bigdog.bowsers .com, at 210.10.20.100.

- The DNS server runs on collie.bowsers.com, and it has IP address 210.10.20.55.

The first thing to do is to load the DNS service. You'd go to the actual collie.bowsers.com machine and install the DNS service there. Open the Control Panel, start the Network applet, and click on Services. Then click on the Add button and choose the Microsoft DNS Server, as you see in Figure 9.3.

The system will reboot. Look in Administrative Tools, and you'll find the DNS Manager. Start it up, select DNS ➤ New Server, and fill in the address of the local machine; of course, 127.0.0.1 works just as well. You'll see a mostly blank screen, as you see in Figure 9.4.

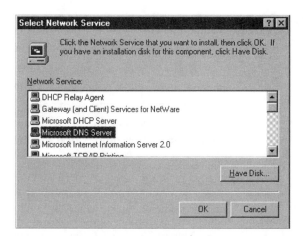

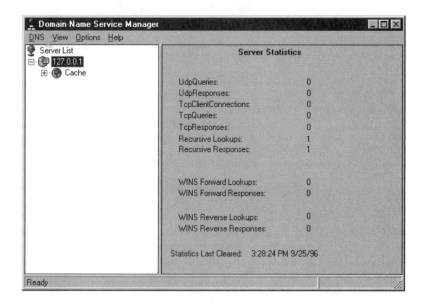

We're going to create a whole new zone, so start by choosing DNS ➤ New Zone. Click on Primary and the Next button, and then fill in the name of the zone, and you'll see a screen like the one in Figure 9.5.

Note that we didn't type in **bowsers.com.dns**—the Wizard created that field. We had to tab down to the Zone File field for our machine to create it. When you click on Next, the Wizard will say it has all the information it needs, and to click on Finish. Do this. It will then set up the DNS Manager, as you see in Figure 9.6.

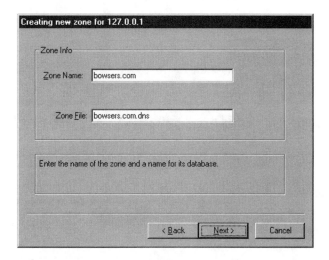

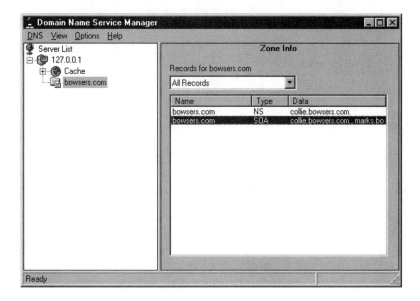

The Wizard has automatically done a few things:

- First, it created an NS record, which identifies this machine—`collies .bowsers.com`—as the name server, the DNS server for this domain.

- Second, it created a Start of Authority (SOA) record. The SOA record is essential, because it defines some basic parameters about the zone.

Before going any further, we'll need to create a zone for the *reverse* DNS lookups. As the `bowsers.com` zone lives in the C network `210.10.20.0`, you must create another zone for reverse lookups. It must be named `20.10.210 .in-addr.arpa`. (Note the *reverse* numbering of the quads, which *is* correct in this file.) Click on the server (`127.0.0.1`, in this example), choose DNS ➤ New Zone, and make it a primary zone. Then click on Next, and in the Zone Name field type **20.10.210.in-addr.arpa** (we had to tab down to the Zone File field for our machine to create it), and click on Next and Finish. Your DNS server will then look like the screen shown in Figure 9.7.

FIGURE 9.7

DNS server with both forward and reverse lookup zones

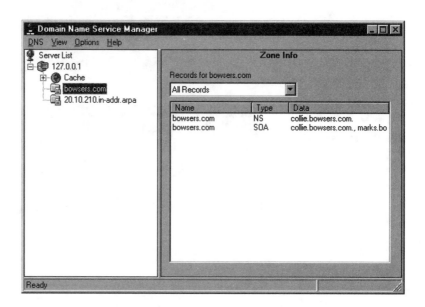

Now let's insert a record each for retriever, www, bigdog, and collie. Right-click on `bowsers.com`, and choose New Record. Fill in the name and IP address, and you'll see a dialog box like the one in Figure 9.8.

Note that we *didn't* enter `collie.bowsers.com`, just **collie**. The checkbox makes sure there is a reverse entry created at the same time. Notice the dialog box indicates that you're creating an A record—that's the correct name for a name record. There are other types as well—you've already met the NS and SOA records. The DNS Manager screen now looks like the one in Figure 9.9.

FIGURE 9.8

Creating a name record
for collie

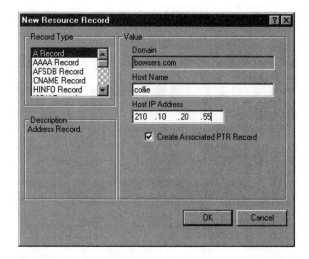

FIGURE 9.9

DNS Manager showing
the new collie entry

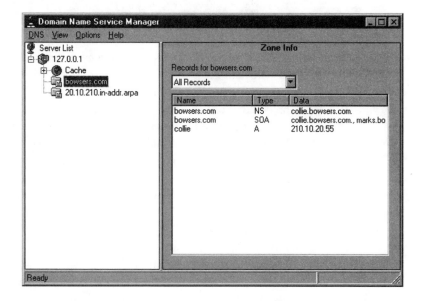

Click on the reverse lookup domain 20.10.210.in-addr.arpa, and you'll
see an entry there also (you may have to press F5 to update the display), as
you see in Figure 9.10.

Note that a reverse lookup record is a pointer record (PTR) type. You enter
the records for retriever, www, and bigdog the same way.

FIGURE 9.10

DNS Manager showing
the reverse lookup
entry for collie

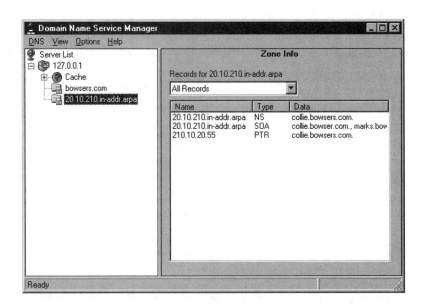

Next, we need an MX (Mail Exchange) record to tell our DNS server where
to send mail addressed to `bowsers.com`. As we've said, the actual mail server in
`bowsers.com` is at `retriever.bowsers.com`. That means if you have a user
named Rex on the network you could e-mail him at `rex@retriever.bowsers`
`.com`. You would have to use the whole name of the mail server so that the
Internet mail system could figure out which machine is the "post office."

But you'd prefer to be able to send mail to `rex@bowsers.com`; however, there
is no one machine named `bowsers.com`. So how do you get mail addressed to
`rex@bowsers.com` automatically redirected to a machine named `retriever`
`.bowsers.com`? With an MX-type DNS record. Right-click on the `bowsers.com`
zone and choose New Record and then choose MX. We've filled in the dialog
box, as you can see in Figure 9.11.

Notice that the Domain field is grayed out—you can't change it. Under
Host Name (Optional) we have *not* filled in a name. That's because the Host
Name field says, "What computer should this computer be the mail exchange
agent *for*?"

You see, if you wanted to, you could create one mail exchange agent for
one specific computer. For example, suppose you filled in **bigdog** here. That
would mean whenever someone sent mail to *somename*@`bigdog.bowsers`
`.com`, it would be redirected to `retriever.bowsers.com`. By leaving this

FIGURE 9.11

Setting up retriever as the
mail exchange agent

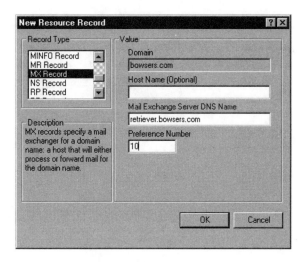

blank, we're saying that whenever someone sends mail to *somename*@bowsers .com, this mail goes to retriever. So, fill in retriever's name as the mail agent, and set the Preference Number to **10**.

A preference number allows you to specify a number of machines to act as mail exchange agents. You could set up mail software on bigdog and have its server as a kind of "emergency" mail server. If you set its preference number value higher than that of retriever, DNS would know to send mail to retriever unless retriever were down, in which case the mail would go to bigdog.

Next, we need www.bowsers.com to respond to a second name, ftp.bowsers .com. We can do that with a CNAME type record. Create the record as usual by right-clicking on the bowsers.com zone, selecting New Record, and then choosing CNAME type. We've filled in the dialog box, as you see in Figure 9.12.

From now on, www.bowsers.com will respond to requests for ftp.bowsers .com. Notice that you don't enter the whole name for the alias, just the leftmost part. Your DNS screen should look something like the one in Figure 9.13.

Well, by now, your DNS server should be up. But how to check it? With a diagnostic tool called nslookup, that's how. It's a command-line utility—one of those old cryptic UNIX types. If DNS is a server, think of nslookup as a simple diagnostic client. It'll talk to any DNS server and let you make simple queries, queries that mimic an outside computer trying to resolve a name.

FIGURE 9.12

Creating a CNAME for
ftp.bowser.com

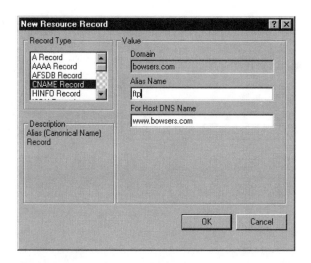

FIGURE 9.13

Bowsers.com is now
open for business

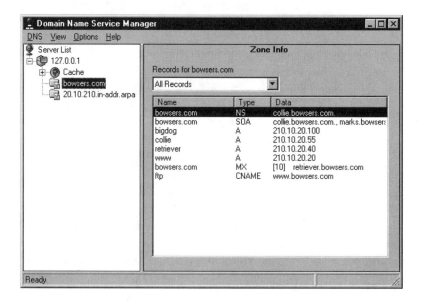

When you type **nslookup,** it responds with a > prompt. These are the commands we'll use:

- **server 210.10.20.55** tells nslookup which DNS server to read its data from. Since we're testing collie at 210.10.20.55, we'll point the server there.

- **ls -d bowsers.com** says, "List everything you know about bowsers.com."

- **set type mx** and **bowsers.com** say to show the mail exchange records for bowsers.com.

- **exit** exits nslookup.

You can see the session in Figure 9.14.

A complete success! There's just one more thing to do and you're finished—enable the dynamic WINS/DNS link. From the main DNS Manager screen, right-click on bowsers.com and choose Properties. You'll see a property sheet like the one in Figure 9.15.

We've clicked on the WINS Lookup tab, checked Use WINS Resolution, and filled in the address of a WINS server. Click on OK, and the connection is made. You should do the same thing for the reverse lookup domain as well. Now just get your ISP to refer to your DNS server, and you're running your own name service.

FIGURE 9.15

Enabling WINS linkage

We don't use the WINS/DNS link. Why? Well, because our ISP's DNS servers could no longer understand our DNS server once we turned it on. This is probably some DNS quirk, and quite annoying at that—Microsoft can hardly claim the UNIX world should change their software to match Microsoft's—right?

Now, for a network based on NT Server 4, this is mostly what you'll need to know. But if you're still running 3.51, then you'll first have to download some software from Microsoft, and you'll have to learn about *bind files,* the UNIX approach to DNS servers.

Setting Up DNS on NT 3.51

You can find the DNS server on the CD that comes with the NT Resource Kit in the i386\inet directory. Failing that, you can FTP to `rhino.microsoft` `.com`, logging on with the user name **dnsbeta** and the password **dnsbeta**. "Anonymous" won't work here, so don't use your Web browser; just use the FTP client that comes with NT.

Once you're on the FTP site, you see a file at the root named contents.txt, and directories named "63" and "files." Apparently, the last one to appear, 63, contains build 63 of the DNS beta. If there *is* a newer version, then you won't see 63; you'll obviously see a higher number. These files contain the things that won't change much from version to version. Within the 63 directory will be subdirectories for each of the four processor platforms. As always, you only need the files that are specific to your particular server, whether it's a PowerPC, Alpha, MIPS, or Intel *x*86 machine.

Get all of the files in the appropriate subdirectory of 63, and all of the files in files, and then disconnect from the FTP server.

In the directory where you put all of the files is a file called install .bat; run it. It will copy the DLLs into their proper places. Look in the Control Panel under Services, and you'll see that you have a new entry, the Domain Naming Server Service. Do not start the DNS server yet, as you have some files to set up.

The Setup Files

The 3.51 DNS service relies on a number of ASCII text files:

- BOOT contains basic information about where the other files reside. It *must* go in the \winnt35\system32\drivers\etc directory.

- Arpa-127.rev contains information required to allow DNS to be able to resolve the name "localhost" into 127.0.0.1 and to allow DNS to be able to resolve 127.*x*.*y*.*z* to "localhost" for any values of *x*, *y*, and *z*. In general, you won't touch it.

- Cache tells DNS where to find the Internet "root servers," the top of the DNS hierarchy.

- You need at least one file with the names of your computers along with their specified IP addresses. You can call it anything that you like, because you direct DNS to find it with a line in BOOT that we'll introduce you to later. For example, Mark chose to put the list of names for his domain, mmco.com, into a file called mmco.nms. (He could have called it mmco .com, but he didn't want NT mistaking it for an executable file.)

- You have at least one file with a name like arpa-202.rev which contains the *reverse* DNS references. The name is built up out of arpa-x.rev, where *x* is the left-most quad of your network. In Mark's case, his network is 199.34.57.0, so he called the file arpa-199.rev. DNS knows to go looking for this file because, again, you point DNS to the rev file in the BOOT file, as we'll show you soon.

Let's take a look at the files.

The BOOT File

Like the other configuration files, BOOT is an ASCII text file. It must be placed in the winnt35\system32\drivers\etc directory. In the BOOT file, you specify these things:

- In which directory would you like to place the other DNS data files?

- What is the name of the file that contains the names of the Internet root servers?

- For what domain will this DNS server resolve names?

- For what IP address range will this DNS server do reverse name resolution?

Here's an example of a DNS file, which will be explained in just a moment.

```
directory  C:\dns
cache . cache
primary mmco.com.  mmco.nms
primary 127.in-addr.arpa arpa-127.rev
primary 57.34.199.in-addr.arpa arpa-199.rev
```

The comments have been removed to keep the file short, but you can add a comment to any DNS file by prefixing it with a semicolon.

The first command, directory, tells DNS that the other files were put into the directory C:\dns. There must be a space between "directory" and "C:\dns".

The second command points to the file containing the names of the Internet root servers. Microsoft provides a file that works just fine, and they call it cache. There's really no reason to change its name, so the command cache means, "You find the Internet root name servers' names in a file called 'cache' (that's the second 'cache'), in the C:\dns directory."

Next, the *primary* statements define what this DNS server is good for. Its job will mainly be to convert mmco.com names to 199.34.57.x names, convert 199.34.57.x IP addresses into mmco.com names, and also it'll reverse-resolve any local host address references. The primary mmco.com. mmco.nms line says, "If someone needs information about any computer in the mmco.com domain, then you can find that information in the file mmco.nms, which is in the C:\dns directory." Note the extra period on "mmco.com."; don't leave it off your domain name. The primary 127.in-addr.arpa arpa-127.rev means, "If you're ever asked to reverse-resolve any number from 127.0.0.0 through 127 .255.255.255 (the range of loopback addresses), then look in the file arpa -127.rev, which is in the C:\dns directory." The primary 57.34.199.in-addr .arpa arpa-199.rev line means, "If you ever have to do a reverse name resolution for 199.34.57.0 through 199.34.57.255, then look in the file named arpa-199.rev, which is in C:\dns."

Hey—what's that last primary statement mean? What's 57.34.199? After looking at it a time or two, you've probably noticed that it is 199.34.57 backwards. Since the last two primary commands are for *reverse* DNS resolution, the names go in backward. You should specify the level that the DNS server will be authoritative for here. For example, primary 199.in-addr.arpa x.rev would mean, "Any reverse DNS request starting with '199' can be resolved with 'x.rev,'" and that's definitely *not* what you'd want to do here—Mark's only got 199.34 .57.0, not 199.132.22.0 or 199.99.55.0, or whatever. Just to provide another example, primary 22.140.in-addr.arpa revs .rev would mean, "DNS server, you're responsible for addresses 140.22.0.0 through 140.22.255.255, and you'll find the reverse DNS information for that range in the file revs.rev, which is in C:\dns."

Now that the BOOT file's in place, let's move to the files in C:\dns. *Do not* touch the arpa-127.rev file or the cache files that ship with the DNS service; just use them as provided.

The DNS Name Resolver File

Next, we have to create the file that tells the DNS server how to convert PC names to IP addresses. Now, as mentioned before, you don't have to do that for every computer on the network; but you *should* do it for the ones with the static IP addresses—like servers, in particular. Suppose there's an Internet mail server named mailserve.mmco.com on Mark's network at 199.34.57.20, and a time server named timeserve.mmco.com at 199.34.57.55; those will be the machines whose addresses we must worry about. We'll put the DNS service on a machine named eisa-server.mmco.com, at 199.34.57.50. Remember that we chose to call the file with the names mmco.nms. Let's start off with a look at it, with the comments removed.

```
@    in   soa   eisa-server.mmco.com. mark.mailserve.mmco.com. (
              1996021501    ; serial [ yyyyMMddNN]
              10800      ; refresh [ 3h]
              3600      ; retry [ 1h]
              691200      ; expire [ 8d]
              86400 )     ; minimum [ 1d]
```

```
$WINS 199.34.57.32
@ in ns eisa-server.mmco.com.
@ in mx 10 mailserve
localhost in a 127.0.0.1
mailserve in a 199.34.57.20
timeserve in a 199.34.57.55
```

The first part is the Start of Authority record, a bit of boilerplate that you can just type right in. The only things inserted were the name of the machine running the DNS server (`eisa-server.mmco.com.`) and where to find Mark (`mark@ mailserve.mmco.com`). Notice two syntactic oddities that you'd better follow, *or else*. If you don't, DNS won't work. First, add an extra period to the end of the full name of the name server, or DNS will automatically append `mmco.com` to the name. If we'd entered **eisa-server.mmco.com** instead of **eisa-server .mmco.com.**, then DNS would think that the name server was running on a machine named `eisa-server.mmco.com.mmco.com`. The second oddity is the format for Mark's e-mail address—remember DNS wants you to replace the @ with a period, hence the e-mail name `mark.mailserve.mmco.com`.

Notice also the first indented line, the one that starts with "19960215..."— it's the *DNS serial number*. Since Mark's Internet service provider gets name information about his company from his name server, and because his ISP doesn't want to have to read what could be a monstrous DNS list every time it's asked to resolve a name, this serial number tells the outside ISP whether or not things have changed since the last time the ISP looked at Mark's domain's DNS server. The number can be anything at all; just make sure that you change it every time you change the file.

We repeat: Be sure to change the serial number line in your SOA record every time you change any of the data in the DNS database. Mark didn't, and it took him two weeks to figure out why his updated name information was being ignored by his ISP.

Next is a command that you won't find in any other DNS server: the $WINS command. That tells Microsoft's DNS server, "If you're asked to resolve a name, but cannot find it in the static listing, then ask the WINS server at 199.34 .57.32 to resolve it." You can specify multiple WINS servers by listing them on the $WINS line, separated by semicolons.

Following that line is the line that names the name server or DNS server for this domain. It seems a bit redundant—after all, you wouldn't be reading this file if you didn't know who was the name server for this domain—but it's required. The format is just "@ in ns '*name of your DNS server.*'" The ns stands for *name server*. The in means, "This is information used by an intranet."

After that goes an MX (mail exchange) record. An MX record makes it possible for someone to send mail to joeblow@bigfirm.com when in actual fact there is no single machine called bigfirm.com; rather, bigfirm's got a machine named mailserve.bigfirm.com. The MX record translates mail addresses from a generic domain name to a specific machine name. An MX record looks like "@ in mx 10 '*name of your mail server.*'" You can add particular MX records for particular machines, but it's not necessary. For example, what happens if someone sends mail not to mark@mmco.com, but to mark@timeserve.mmco.com? Well, nothing happens, basically; timeserve isn't prepared to receive mail, and so the message will just be lost. But Mark *could* idiot-proof the system a bit by adding MX records to every single DNS entry, so no matter what machine an outsider tried to send mail to, the mail would end up at mailserve.

Next is the listing of machines and IP addresses. Each record looks like "*machinename* in a *IP address*," where *machinename* is just the left-most part of the name, rather than the fully qualified domain name. For example, a machine on Mark's network called mwm66.mmco.com would have a record that looked like "mwm66 in a 199.34.57.66" if its IP address were 199.34.57.66. Remember, the *in* part is for *intranet*. The *a* part means this is an *address* record. You also need a localhost reference, as you see in the example. Microsoft provides a sample name file in a file called place.dom. In it, they also show you how to create an alias for an FTP and a WWW site, but it's just as easy to type in a file like the one above.

The Reverse Name Resolution Files

As mentioned earlier, DNS isn't too terribly bright about using the information that you give it; although it knows that mypc.mmco.com is 199.34.57.43, it still can't seem to figure out that given the IP address 199.34.57.43, it should reverse-resolve the DNS name mypc.mmco.com. So you have to help it out with the reverse DNS files.

In our example, we told the DNS server in the BOOT file that it could reverse-resolve addresses in the 199.34.57.0 network, and that information was in a file called arpa-199.rev. It looks like the following, again with the comments removed:

```
@  IN SOA eisa-server.mmco.com. mark.smtphost.mmco.com. (
                1    ; serial number
                10800  ; refresh [3h]
                3600  ; retry  [1h]
                691200 ; expire [8d]
                86400 ) ; minimum [1d]
@ in ns eisa-server.mmco.com.
32 IN PTR eisa-server.mmco.com.
50 IN PTR mailserve.mmco.com.
55 IN PTR timeserve.mmco.com.
35 IN PTR sdg90.mmco.com.
```

It looks a lot like the mmco.nms file that we just created, with a few differences. It starts off with a Start of Authority record just like the mmco.nms file. There is, again, a pointer to the local name server, eisa-server.mmco.com. Then there are references to the IP addresses of machines in the mmco.com domain. Notice that since the DNS server only looks in here to resolve names looking like 199.34.57.*something*, you need only specify the last quad on the IN PTR lines.

Notice also that there's no $WINS statement; that's important. For some reason, this WINS-to-DNS dynamic link can do DNS name resolution, but not reverse resolution. That's why there's an extra entry, for a machine named sdg90.mmco.com; it attaches to an FTP site that double-checks who you are before letting you on by requesting a reverse DNS resolution. It sees that someone's attaching from 199.34.57.35, but it needs to be sure that the DNS name is also sdg90.mmco.com. As sdg90 gets its IP address from the DHCP server, we needed to put a specific address into this file so that the DNS server could reverse-resolve the address for that particular PC. (How can we be so sure that sdg90 gets 199.34.57.35? We reserved the address for it in DHCP.)

As your DNS server must also be able to reverse-resolve loopback addresses, you have an arpa-127.rev, but, as already said, don't touch it; it's fine out of the box from Microsoft.

Now all you have to do is to start up the service, point all of your workstations to that machine for DNS resolution, and you have your very own dynamic DNS server. It's still a bit flaky, but it's often useful, and no doubt the final version will be cleaner.

Once the DNS service is up and running, you can point workstations to it: When they need the name of a DNS server, just fill in the IP address of your NT machine running the DNS server. And ask your ISP to tell its DNS server to pull its address resolution information off your DNS server.

WARNING   The DNS server beta ran well until we installed NT 3.51 Service Pack 3; if you can avoid that Service Pack, then you just might want to do that.

Migrating from an NT 3.51 DNS Server to an NT 4 DNS Server

You just read that NT 3.51 DNS servers store their data in a set of ASCII files called *bind* files. What we haven't told you is that the NT 4 DNS server stores its data in the Registry. How can you get a 4 DNS server to read a set of bind files from a 3.51 installation, so that you can forgo having to retype piles of names?

Here's our recipe:

1. Take all of the bind files and put them into \winnt\system32\dns; they *must* be there, or the 4 DNS server can't find them.

2. Install the DNS service.

3. Before creating any zones, right-click on the server and choose Properties. Click on the Boot Method tab, and choose Boot from BootFile.

4. Click on OK.

5. Stop the DNS Service.

6. Restart it.

It should now see your bind files. At this point, we recommend switching back to Boot from Registry and stopping, then starting, the service.

Name Resolution Sequence under WinSock

Everything's just peachy now that you know how to configure DNS and WINS, right? Well, maybe not—you just may be faced with a troubleshooting dilemma or two in reference to name resolution. Perhaps you try to FTP to a site inside your organization, but you can't hook up. Even though you know that `ftp.goodstuff.acme.com` is at one IP address, your FTP client keeps trying to attach somewhere else. You've checked your DNS server, of course, and its information is right. Oh my! What to do?

Review: WinSock versus NBT

Remember first that there are two kinds of name resolution in Microsoft TCP/IP networking: WinSock name resolution and NetBIOS name resolution. A `net view \\`*somename* needs NetBIOS over TCP name resolution, or NBT name resolution. In contrast, FTP is like Ping, an Internet application, and it uses WinSock name resolution. So, to troubleshoot a name resolution problem, you have to follow what your client software does, step by step.

Examining Network Traces

When once faced with a problem like this, we turned to the Microsoft documentation for help, but there wasn't much detail there. So, we ran a network monitor and issued ping commands to computers that didn't exist, to see the sequence of actions that the network client software tried in order to resolve a name. The HOSTS and LMHOSTS files do not, of course, show up in a network trace, so we inserted information into those files that didn't exist on the DNS or WINS servers, and then tried pinging again, to demonstrate where the HOSTS and LMHOSTS files sit in the name resolution hierarchy. Pinging for a nonexistent "apple," we found that the name resolution order proceeds as shown in Figure 9.16.

Step by step, it looks like this:

1. First, consult the HOSTS file, if it exists. If you find the name you're looking for, stop.

2. Next, if there's a specified DNS server or servers, then query them. First, query "apple." NT machines then query `apple.mmco.com`, tacking on the domain name; Windows 95 workstations don't do the second query.

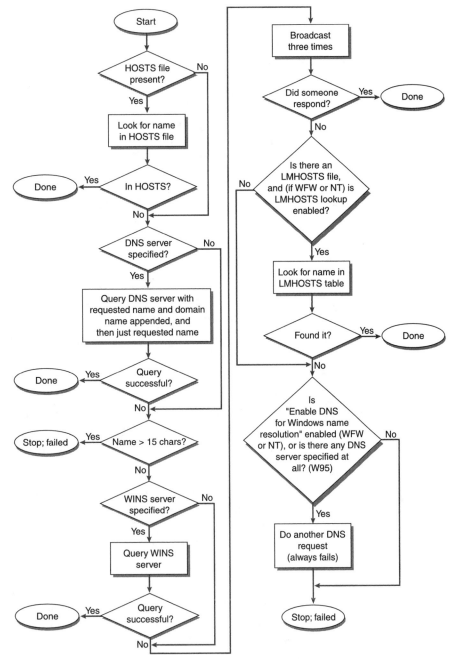

This happens whether or not the box Enable DNS for Windows Name Resolution, found in the Advanced Microsoft TCP/IP Configuration dialog boxes of NT 3.51 and Windows for Workgroups, is checked. If DNS has the name, then stop.

3. After that, the client looks to see if the name has 16 or more characters. If it does, then the process stops—a failed name resolution attempt. Notice that this means that *LMHOSTS cannot resolve FQDNs longer than 15 characters*—yipes—quite a scary little limitation if you depend on LMHOSTS!

4. Next, if there's a specified WINS server or servers, then query the WINS server(s). The name WINS looks for is "`apple <00>`," the name that *would* be registered by the Workstation service, if the apple machine existed.

5. If that fails, then do three broadcasts looking for a machine with NetBIOS name "`apple <00>`," requesting that it identify itself and send back its IP address. Again, this would succeed with a workstation running some NetBIOS-over-TCP/IP client, even a relatively old one, as it would have registered the "`apple <00>`" name already, if only on its own name table. Unfortunately, this only works if the machine is on the same subnet.

6. If the name still hasn't been resolved, read the LMHOSTS file. (Under NT 3.51 and Windows for Workgroups, do not do this if the box labeled Enable LMHOSTS Lookup is unchecked. If it is, skip this step.) As with the earlier steps, stop if you find a match, keep going if not.

7. If you're running an NT or Windows for Workgroups machine with the box Enable DNS for Windows Name Resolution checked, then you've instructed your system to do a DNS lookup every time a WINS lookup fails. If that box is checked, then a second and last DNS lookup will happen. If, on the other hand, you *don't* have the Enable DNS box checked, then there's nothing left to do.

Look at that sequence: HOSTS, DNS, WINS, broadcast, LMHOSTS, and DNS again. This is a bit surprising for a couple of reasons. First, it seems that every unsuccessful name resolution results in broadcasts, the *bête noire* of those of us trying to keep the network traffic to a minimum. Our guess is that the broadcasts aren't part of an according-to-Hoyle IP stack, but Microsoft just threw them in for good measure and the WINS query as well. Then, if you've checked Enable DNS for Windows Name Resolution, the client software performs a DNS lookup as a matter of course after any failed WINS lookup; unfortunately, that leads to a redundant DNS lookup here. In short, if your Windows 95 workstation knows of a DNS server, it'll use that DNS server when doing both DNS and NetBIOS name resolutions.

Yes, the broadcasts are a pain, but they *would* be of benefit when you tried to execute a TCP/IP command on a computer in your network and wanted to use the shorter NetBIOS name rather than the longer DNS name, for example, apple instead of `apple.mmco.com`.

What happened on the workstation that couldn't access the FTP site? There was an old HOSTS file sitting in the Windows directory that pointed to a different IP address, an older IP address for the FTP server. HOSTS is read before anything else, so the accurate information on the DNS or WINS servers never had a chance.

There is an explicit Enable DNS for Windows Name Resolution checkbox in Windows for Workgroups and NT 3.51 clients, but how do you control whether or not DNS gets into the act on a Windows 95 client? You can't, at least not entirely. Where Workgroups and NT 3.51 separate the options about whether to specify a DNS server, and whether or not to use that DNS server as a helper when resolving NetBIOS names (that's what "Enable DNS for Windows Name Resolution" means), Windows 95 just doesn't seem to do that.

Controlling WINS versus DNS Order in WinSock

Now, what we just showed you is the order of events by default in NT or Windows 95 clients. But if you feel like messing around with the way that WinSock resolves names, you can. As usual, let us take this moment to remind you not to mess with the Registry unless you know what you're doing!

Look under HKEY_LOCAL_MACHINE\System\CurrentControlSet\Services\ TCPIP\ServiceProvider in the Registry, and you see a HostsPriority, DNSPriority, and NBTPriority value sets. They are followed by hexadecimal values. The lower the value, the earlier that HOSTS, DNS (and LMHOSTS), and WINS (and broadcasts) get done. For example, by default, DNS' priority is 7D0 and WINS' is 7D1, so DNS goes before WINS. But change DNS' priority to 7D2, and WINS does its lookup and broadcast *before* the client interrogates the DNS server.

Again, we're not sure *why* you'd want to do this, but we threw it in for the sake of completeness, and for the enjoyment and recreation of those who delight in undocumented features.

Name Resolution Sequence under NetBIOS

Having looked at the steps that the system goes through to resolve a DNS name, what happens when the system attempts to resolve a NetBIOS name? Again, it's an involved process, but, in general, the factors that affect how NBT resolves names are:

- Is the workstation an NT 3.51 or Windows 95 workstation?

- Is LMHOSTS enabled?

- Is DNS enabled to assist in Windows (NetBIOS) name resolution?

- Is the network client software WINS-aware?

Summarized, the name resolution sequence appears in Figure 9.17.

The same components that went into WinSock name resolutions contribute to NBT resolutions, but in a slightly different order. The NBT name resolver uses the following steps; if any succeed, then it stops looking.

1. The first part is the WINS client, if the client software is WINS-aware. If WINS is disabled under Windows 95, or if there is no WINS server specified in Workgroups or NT 3.51, then the client skips this step.

2. If WINS isn't being used, then the client does three broadcasts. For example, `net view \\apple` causes three broadcasts looking for a workstation with the name apple registered, rather than `apple.mmco.com`, or the like.

3. Next, if LMHOSTS is enabled—and it appears that LMHOSTS is *always* enabled on Windows 95 clients (but must be enabled with the Enable LMHOSTS checkbox for NT 3.51 and Workgroups), then the client looks up the name in LMHOSTS. Surprised? When doing NBT name resolutions, LMHOSTS gets consulted *before* HOSTS, a reversal over WinSock name resolutions.

For LMHOSTS to be of help here, it must specify NetBIOS names, not fully qualified domain names. For example, if you have a workstation named `rusty.acme.com` at `212.11.41.4`, but you want to do a `net view \\rusty`, then the line in LMHOSTS should look like this:

```
212.11.41.4 rusty
```

Not `rusty.acme.com`, just `rusty`.

FIGURE 9.17

Name resolution sequence
under NetBIOS

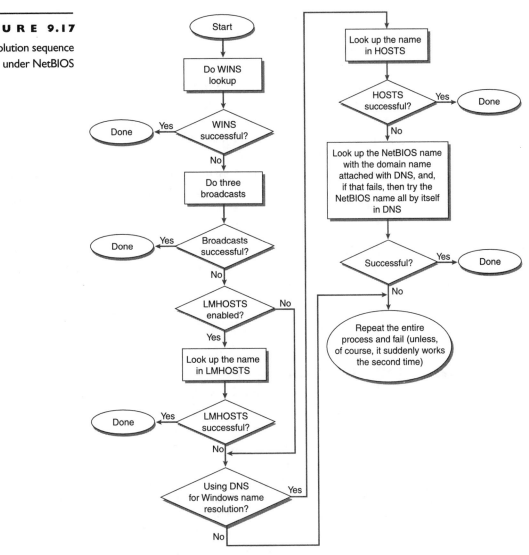

4. If you've checked *Enable DNS for Windows Name Resolution* in Workgroups or NT 3.51, or if you have specified a DNS server in Windows 95,
then the workstation's client software will look at HOSTS. If HOSTS
can't help, it will interrogate the DNS server (or servers, as you can specify
up to four DNS servers).

The NT/Workgroups clients and the 95 clients use DNS differently. The NT/Workgroups clients do a DNS query for the name with the domain name appended to it, and then a DNS query of just the name. For example, if your domain is `acme.com`, and you're doing a `net view \\myserver`, then an NT workstation will ask DNS first to resolve the name `myserver.acme.com`. It automatically adds the domain name for the first resolution. Then, if the DNS server can't resolve the name with the domain name attached, the client will request that the DNS server just resolve "myserver."

In contrast, the Windows 95 client software only asks the DNS server to resolve the name with the domain name appended. In our example, a Windows 95 workstation would ask DNS to resolve `myserver.acme.com`, but would not ask about "myserver."

5. The last part is *really* strange. If the client software is the NT client, (not the Workgroups or Win95 clients), and if it's been unsuccessful so far, then it goes back and does it all over again. Maybe it hopes things will work the second time around.

You've seen how WinSock and NBT resolve names; now you're ready to look at the "battle of the network names."

What If DNS and WINS Conflict?

Here's a question we get in class sometimes. It's here mainly as a review of what you've read so far.

WINS will generally have accurate name information for your local domain, at least among the WINS-aware machines, as it gets its naming information from the horse's mouth, so to speak. You can't *use* a WINS name server unless you *contribute* a bit of information—i.e., address information about yourself. DNS, in contrast, gets its information from people typing data into ASCII files, so the data *could be* wrong. That leads students to the following question.

What if you have a Microsoft networking client that's not only WINS-aware, but also uses a DNS server—in that case, which name service does the workstation query first? Suppose you have a machine named `ollie.acme.com` whose IP address is `207.88.52.99`. Not only does WINS know of ollie, DNS does too—but suppose DNS incorrectly thinks that ollie's IP address is `207.88.52.100`. Type **ping ollie.acme.com**, and what will happen? Will the system look to the `.99` address, or the `.100` address?

Do you see how to answer this question? First, ask yourself, "Is this a Win-Sock or an NBT name resolution request?" As the application is Ping, the answer is WinSock. Go to the WinSock name resolution flowchart, and you see that the DNS server gets first crack at answering the name resolution request.

Now, that was the answer for a WinSock resolution, but what about an NBT resolution? For example, suppose we open up a command line and type **nbtstat -a xyz.nyoffice.mmco.com**. What will happen?

This is kind of a trick question. First of all, understand that nbtstat takes a *NetBIOS* name as a parameter, and we've specified a WinSock name. An NBT resolution will fully gag on that `xyz.nyoffice.mmco.com` name, as it's way over 15 characters, so it truncates it after the fifteenth character, and does an NBT name resolution on `xyz.nyoffice.mm`.

There's a lot more to network name resolution on NT networks than you might guess when you first look into this, as you can see, but now you're equipped with all the information that you need to tackle the enigma of, "Machine X says it can't see machine Y."

A New Day Dawns

As said, soon Windows NT will come with an Enhanced Directory Services implementation, and a whole new way to deal with domains, users, groups, and trusts. In the brave new Windows NT world, Enhanced DS domains will directly map to DNS domains, and administration for groups and users will be the duty of Organizational Units in the directory. These glittering new Enhanced DS domains will predictably be a lot better than the dusty domains of today.

A major point is that in the Enhanced Directory Services network, DNS will be the primary locator service. To find other hosts on the network and servers running the DS service, Enhanced DS clients will use DNS, in a similar way that clients running Windows NT 4 use WINS today.

Let's canvass some future Enhanced Directory Services concepts and the new standards that will soon change DNS, exploring first what a solid prospective DNS/DS design may look like. We hope this will indicate how best to design your network now, to be ready for future migration. (We actually know a guy who sits home on the weekend reading RFCs, so we've included some Web pages that list them, in case you're like him.)

Dynamic DNS

Windows NT 4 includes two name-to-IP-address mapping services—WINS and DNS. One key difference between the two is that WINS accommodates *dynamic* registration of NetBIOS names and associated IP addresses, but DNS names and associated IP addresses must be *statically* entered into the DNS service database.

Static registration of name-to-IP-address information is not a good thing in the Windows NT/Windows 95 operating systems. Why? Because in all but very small Microsoft network installations, machines don't have static IP address assignments. Machines generally use DHCP to obtain an IP address assignment each time they initialize.

A proposal for dynamic registration of DNS information is under consideration by the IETF (Internet Engineering Task Force). You can download the specification from `http://ds.internic.net/internet-drafts/draft-ietf-dnsind-dynDNS-09.txt`.

With DNS "dynamic update," a client machine, having obtained its assigned IP address from DHCP, can use a standard protocol to dynamically register its DNS name and IP address in the DNS database. In the Windows NT 4 time frame, it was determined that dynamic update shouldn't be implemented due to the fluid status of the specification, and because of scalability concerns. The current dynamic DNS proposal is based on a "pull from single master" replication model and, consequently, if the single master is down or unreachable, dynamic updates just don't happen. Microsoft favors a multiple master arrangement similar to WINS, that would allow registrations to continue without a single point of failure.

In the long run, using DNS dynamic update is better than using Windows NT 4 DNS-WINS integration for the following reasons:

- DNS-WINS integration doesn't enable efficient DNS reverse lookup (resolution of IP address to DNS name). Reverse lookup is used for security purposes by Internet WWW (World Wide Web) and firewall services. Due to the recent proliferation of such services, the need for efficient DNS reverse lookup is significantly on the rise. If DNS dynamic update was used instead of WINS integration, the problem goes "poof."

- DNS-WINS integration doesn't enable a proper "primary-backup" relationship between Microsoft and non-Microsoft DNS name servers. This is due to the fact that non-Microsoft DNS name servers aren't capable of WINS lookup. For migration purposes, you'd want to install Microsoft DNS servers as backups of non-Microsoft DNS primary servers. If DNS dynamic update was used instead of WINS integration, again, the problem vaporizes.

- Non-Microsoft hosts don't register in WINS, and therefore cannot "dynamically register" in DNS. DNS dynamic update is an IETF standard. If implemented (by Microsoft), non-Microsoft hosts (that support the DNS dynamic update standard) could dynamically register in the Microsoft DNS, and Microsoft hosts could dynamically register in a non-Microsoft DNS, as long as it supports the DNS dynamic update standard.

- WINS registration isn't secure and has no reasonable means of becoming so. The IETF has worked to complete a standard for adding a security feature to DNS dynamic update. Some companies have already decided to forego a standard and have simply rolled their own security implementation.

- Microsoft-based clients can't register with any of the current versions of dynamic DNS, and dynamic DNS servers can't replicate their dynamic data to other non-dynamic DNS servers.

- In current implementations of dynamic DNS, the primary is a single point of failure. All of the clients must register their names and IP addresses with this machine, so if it's down, no updates to the DNS database can occur.

IPv6 (IPng)

IPv6 is defined in RFC 1883 (`http://ds2.internic.net/rfc/rfc1883.txt`). This protocol used to be referred to as "IP Next Generation" or "IPng." IP version 6 (IPv6) is a new version of the Internet Protocol designed as a successor to IP version 4 (Ipv4, RFC-791). The current header in IPv4 hasn't been changed or upgraded since the 1970s! The initial design, of course, failed to anticipate the growth of the Internet and eventual exhaustion of the Ipv4 address space.

Ipv6 is an entirely new packet structure which is incompatible with IPv4 systems. The changes from IPv4 to IPv6 fall into the following categories:

- **Expanded addressing capabilities:** IPv6 has 128-bit source and destination IP addresses. With approximately 5 billion people in the world and using a 128-bit address, there are 2^{128} addresses, or almost 2^{96} addresses per person! An IPv6 valid IP address will look something like this:

  `3F3A:AE67:F240:56C4:3409:AE52:220E:3112`

  IPv6 uses 16 octets; when written, it is divided into eight octet pairs, separated by colons and represented in hex.

- **Header format simplification:** The IPv6 headers are designed to keep the IP header overhead to a minimum by moving nonessential fields and option fields to extension headers that are placed after the IP header. Anything not included in the base IPv6 header can be added through IP extension headers placed after the base IPv6 header.

- **Improved support for extensions and options:** IPv6 can easily be extended for unforeseen features through the adding of extension headers and option fields after the IPv6 base header. Support for new hardware or application technologies is built in.

- **Flow labeling capability:** A new field in the IPv6 header allows the preallocation of network resources along a path so that time-dependent services such as voice and video are guaranteed a requested bandwidth with a fixed delay.

With the onset of this new standard, changes will need to be made to the DNS protocol. RFC 1886 (`http://ds2.internic.net/rfc/rfc1886.txt`) defines these changes, which include a new resource record type to store an IPv6 address, a new domain to support lookups based on an IPv6 address, and updated definitions of existing query types that return Internet addresses as part of additional section processing. The extensions are designed to be compatible with existing applications and, in particular, DNS implementations themselves.

Current support for the storage of Internet addresses in the DNS cannot easily be extended to support IPv6 addresses since applications assume that address queries return 32-bit IPv4 addresses.

Incremental Transfers—Multimaster Replication

Incremental Transfer serves to permit the propagation of changes to a DNS database quickly, and Windows NT 4 doesn't support it—not yet. This protocol's specialty is the reduction of latency and the quantity of data sent during a zone transfer. It accomplishes this in two ways:

- Notification is used to reveal changes in a zone file to servers and is achieved by the NOTIFY extension of DNS (Microsoft DNS support NOTIFY in Windows NT 4). To find out more about the NOTIFY specification, look up the Internet draft at `http://ds.internic.net/internet-drafts/draft-ietf-dnsind-notify-07.txt`.

- Zone propagation has been refined to send only changed information—a lot better than sending out the whole shebang as is currently the practice! To look into this further, check out the Internet draft at `http://ds.internic.net/internet-drafts/draft-ietf-dnsind-ixfr-06.txt`.

Dynamic data replication will work much like WINS works today, except instead of replicating a whole bunch of unnecessary data to each and every server like WINS does, the data will be kept within the zone itself.

Secure DNS

You might be thinking that as DNS becomes so critical to the operational part of Internet infrastructure, we'll all need a lot more in the way of security than is currently available. You're right—a defined method of security *will* need to be put in place to assure data integrity and authentication. Extensions to the DNS are described in the IETF-DRAFT *DNS Protocol Security Extensions—30 January 1996*. They provide these services to security-aware resolvers or applications through the use of *cryptographic digital signatures*—what? Well, these are included in secured zones as resource records, and in many cases, security can still be provided even through non-security-aware DNS servers.

Extensions also provide for storage of authenticated public keys in the DNS. This storage of keys can support general public key distribution service as well as DNS security. The stored keys enable security-aware resolvers to learn the authenticating key of zones in addition to those for which they are initially configured. And keys associated with DNS names can be retrieved to support other protocols. If that weren't enough, provision is even made for a variety of key types and algorithms. In addition, the security extensions provide for the optional authentication of DNS protocol transactions. For more on this, see `http://ds.internic.net/internet-drafts/draft-ietf-dnssec-secext-09.txt`.

In current implementations of dynamic DNS, the vendors had to come up with their own security protocol because of the lack of a defined standard. Be careful if you use one of these products, because it may become incompatible with future ones when a specification is finally defined!

Migration…from Where?

So, how's it all going to happen? To find out, let's first take a look at the migration process to Enhanced Directory Services. New Enhanced DS domains will be fully interoperable with Windows NT Server domains. This means that existing Windows NT Server domains will be able to trust Enhanced DS domains, just as they trust other Windows NT Server domains today. Enhanced DS servers will also be able to function as backup domain controllers. This interoperability will allow the upgrade to Enhanced DS server to occur in an orderly manner, while allowing existing Windows NT Server-based servers to work without modification—pretty clean!

And what's more, the Enhanced DS administration model won't be forced down the throats of administrators until they're ready to use it. What do we mean? Well, even with Enhanced DS servers on the network, you'll be able to maintain all account information in the Windows NT Server domain, using the current Windows NT Server administration tools. In other words, you'll be able to deploy Enhanced DS servers without righteously screwing up your network!

As Enhanced DS servers are deployed, you can begin to store user account information on them while simultaneously continuing to store and administer those accounts in and from the Windows NT Server domain. That means you'll be able to migrate account information to an Enhanced DS server in an incremental fashion as you gain confidence in their stability and capability—a feel-good feature for you and your company. Once your new Enhanced DS servers are well-established, you'll be able to maintain all account information on them, using the Enhanced DS tools. Furthermore, for non-Enhanced DS clients, the new kids on the block will continue to look and act just like Windows NT Server 4.*x*-based servers (even a feel-good feature for your machines, too—wow!).

Once all client and server transitions are complete, the Enhanced DS environment will be the everyday environment for both end users and system administrators. And, the transition enabled by the interoperability between and integration of Windows NT Server and Enhanced DS will allow you and your organization to make an easy transition to the unified and global namespace provided by Enhanced DS—as said, all without disrupting the day-to-day operations of the network.

What Happens to IPX and NetBEUI?

Even though the Microsoft direction is distinctly heading toward TCP/IP, (true for most other networking vendors as well), there'll still be support for NetBEUI and IPX. Should you choose to use IPX and NetBEUI in the coming version of Windows NT, you'll have to use NetBIOS, but if you choose TCP/IP instead, NetBIOS won't be a required part of the picture.

Well, What about NetBIOS Names?

Obviously, you'll maintain the need to use NetBIOS name resolution on your network as long as you have applications that require NetBIOS names. When you begin the exodus to Enhanced DS, you'll need to find out all of the applications (services and so forth) that require NetBIOS, and come up with a host name migration plan for each.

Finding DCs in an Enhanced Directory Services Environment

Along the route to a genuine Windows NT Enhanced Directory Services environment—one devoid of NetBIOS—you'll follow a required migration path that embraces the use of all three standards for supporting backward compatibility with traditional NetBIOS systems.

When machines running the new Windows NT Enhanced Directory Services start up, they'll use a present WINS protocol for registering NetBIOS names with their WINS servers, and their A record, or records with their DNS server. Thus, Windows NT NetBIOS and DNS name-to-IP-address mappings will be accessible to all machines using Windows NT Enhanced DS, plus those still using Windows for Workgroups, Windows 95, etc.

At startup, Windows NT Enhanced DS servers that contain the Directory Services Database will do the same, plus they'll also register an additional record with the DNS server delimiting location, the DS access protocols supported, and transport protocols, etc. Here's an example of what an Enhanced Directory Services domain controller may register:

```
globalnet.nt.mmco.com              A   123.123.123.123
domain-controllers.nt.mmco.com     A   123.123.123.123
```

This provides other Enhanced Directory Services workstations with the information they need to find domain controllers and validate their security credentials.

Things You Can Count on for the Future

Microsoft will adopt a "secure" dynamic DNS solution, and the clients will automatically register with the DNS. There will also be a process for using DNS to locate the closest Directory Services domain controller.

The next revision of Directory Services will assume that DNS domains map to DS domains.

Where There Is No Vision...

Here are a few dos and don'ts for creating solid, future-oriented DNS solutions. Follow them, and thou shall not perish.

- If there are servers within a site, then there must be a DNS server within that site, too.

- Create a DNS zone for each Windows NT 4 domain.

- Every site DNS server should be a primary for the site-specific DNS domain and a secondary for the parent DNS domain.

- Windows-based clients should be registered in a site-specific DNS domain.

- Servers running Windows NT Server should be registered in a master DNS domain.

Now that we are ready for WinSock resolution in the new NT 5, let's move on to the next chapter, where we talk about NT internetwork browsing.

CHAPTER

10

Internetwork Browsing
and Domain Functions

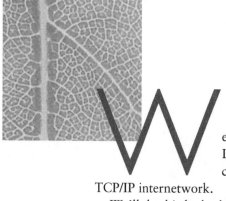

ell, we've covered NetBIOS name resolution using the LMHOSTS file and WINS and DNS, so now we'll discuss how browsing for NetBIOS resources occurs in a TCP/IP internetwork.

We'll do this by looking at the Microsoft NT browsing service in terms of collection, distribution, and servicing of client requests. We'll also go over some problems involved with browsing an IP internetwork, and how to solve them with the LMHOSTS file and WINS.

A Browsing Brief

Before you can share something, you must first be aware of it, know how to find it, and obtain it. Browsing plays an important role in both finding and sharing currently available network resources. By providing a list of these resources, the computer browser service works to free most of the network's computer population from the burden of individually maintaining their own. This saves time and memory because this resource list is only distributed to a few, specially designated machines.

Let's say you want to print something. Before you can, you need to locate and connect to a printer on your network. Without the help of a browser, your system would be reduced to a door-to-door solicitor, petitioning each system along the network corridor about what resources it has available until finally finding what it needs. Your system must then record and maintain that information for future use. All this would take up lots of CPU time, while reducing available memory on your workstation.

NT's browsing service reduces costs and adds efficiency in terms of network overhead. To find a particular resource, your workstation can simply contact the network's designated browser instead of generating network traffic by searching on its own to find the treasure you're after.

But How Do They Work?

Here's a step-by-step outline of basic browser service behavior and operation:

1. After startup, every machine running a browser service checks in with the Master browser of their domain or workgroup. They're required to do so even if they don't have any shared resources to offer their group. Sometimes, under Windows NT, a system will possess hidden administrative shares like "c$".

2. Like any introduction, the client's first time contacting the Master browser is special. The first time the client tries to locate its available network resources, it asks the Master browser for a list of backup browsers.

3. The client then asks for a list of network resources from one of the backup browsers.

4. The backup browser then provides the client with a list of domains and workgroups, plus a list of local servers appointed for the client's particular workgroup or domain.

5. The client's user then picks a local server, domain, or workgroup in order to view another list of available servers.

6. Finally, the client's user chooses a server to look for the right machine with which to establish a session for using their desired resource. The user then contacts that server.

Browser Forms and Functions

The task of providing a list of network resources to clients is broken down into various roles, which are carried out by the corresponding computer.

- **Master browser:** The machine that builds, maintains, and distributes the master list of all available network resources (known as a *browse list*).

- **Preferred Master browser:** A system specially cast and designated to play the role of Master browser by a network administrator. At startup, this system arrogantly proclaims itself to be the network's Master browser. If it finds another machine trying to horn in on its rightful network position in its absence, the Preferred Master browser will force an "election" between itself and the upstart. Networks not being democracies, these elections most often result in the Preferred Master browser reclaiming its throne. The only exception to this being if that "little upstart" machine also happens to be a *primary domain controller (PDC)*. PDCs always function as the Master browser of the domain—their reign is not to be challenged.

- **Backup browser:** These systems act as relay stations. They receive copies of the browse list from the Master browser, and upon request, distribute them to clients.

- **Potential browser:** This is a system that has the capacity of becoming a browser, but isn't one, and won't become one unless specifically commanded to do so by the Master browser.

- **Nonbrowser:** This computer is configured so that it won't maintain a browser list. These are most often client systems.

Windows NT Workstation, Windows NT Server, Windows for Workgroups, and Window 95 computers can perform the Master browser and backup browser roles. However, only a Windows NT Server acting as a PDC can perform the Domain Master browser role.

Browser Criteria

Browser criteria serve as a means of determining the hierarchical order of the different types of computer systems in the workgroup or domain. Each browser computer has certain criteria, depending on the type of system it is. These criteria include:

- The operating system

- The operating system version

- Its current role in the browsing environment

The following is a hypothetical list of computers in a domain. They're presented in the order in which they would win an election, and organized into three criteria categories.

Criteria Category #1: Operating System

- Windows NT Server that is the PDC

- Windows NT Server

- Windows NT Workstation

- Windows 95

- Windows for Workgroups

Criteria Category #2: Operating System Version

- 4

- 3.51

- 3.5

- 3.1

Criteria Category #3: Current Browser Role

- Preferred Master browser

- Master browser

- Backup browser

- Potential browser

This criteria ranking is observed and referred to during an election. These elections are held to determine which computer should be the Master browser if the current Master browser becomes unavailable.

The Browser Election

As the name implies, the Master browser oversees the entire browsing environment. There's only one Master browser for each domain or workgroup. In a domain that spans subnets, there's a Domain Master browser. If the computer that's designated as the Master browser shuts down for any reason, another computer needs to be selected to be the Master browser. This is done through a browser election, which ensures that only one Master browser exists per workgroup or domain. An election is instituted when any of the following events occur:

- A client computer can't locate a Master browser.

- A backup browser attempts to update its network resource list, and can't locate the Master browser.

- A computer that's been designated as a Preferred Master browser comes online.

Configuring Browsers

To determine whether a Windows NT computer will become a browser, the browser service looks in the Registry when the computer initializes for the following parameter:

`\HKEY_LOCAL_MACHINE\SYSTEM\CurrentControlSet\Services\`
`Browser\Parameters\MaintainServerList`

For performance tuning and optimization purposes, it's possible to both configure and prevent a computer from becoming a browser.

The MaintainServerList parameter can contain the following values:

Parameter	Value
No	This computer never participates as a browser server.
Yes	This computer becomes a browser server. At startup, this computer attempts to contact the Master browser to get a current browse list. If the Master browser cannot be found, the computer forces one to be elected. This computer either is elected as the Master browser or becomes a backup browser. Yes is the default value for Windows NT Server domain controller computers.
Auto	Depending on the number of currently active browsers, this computer may or may not become a browser server. It's referred to as a potential browser. This computer is notified by the Master browser as to whether it should become a backup browser. Auto is the default value for Windows NT Workstation and Windows NT Server—nondomain controller computers.

Browser Announcements

Master browsers and backup browsers each have their own roles to play in the operation of the browsing environment. Browsers need to communicate with each other and must provide service to client computers. When a computer that's running the server service comes online, it must inform the Master browser that it's available. The computer does this by announcing itself on the network.

Servers

Each computer periodically announces itself to the Master browser by broadcasting on the network. Initially each computer announces itself once per minute. As the computer stays running, the announcement time is extended to once every 12 minutes. If the Master browser hasn't heard from a computer after three announcement periods elapse, it'll remove the computer that hasn't kept in touch from the browse list.

Important! This means that there could be a 36-minute delay between the time a server goes down and the time that server is removed from the browse list. Computers appearing in the list could possibly be unavailable.

Backup Browsers

In addition to announcing themselves, backup browsers contact the Master browser every 15 minutes to obtain an updated network resource (browse list), and a list of workgroups and domains. The backup browser caches these lists and forwards them to any clients that send out a browse request. If the backup browser can't find the Master browser, it forces an election.

Master Browsers

Master browsers also periodically announce themselves to backup browsers with a broadcast. When backup browsers receive this announcement, they refresh their Master browser name with any new information.

Master browsers receive announcements from the following systems:

- Windows NT 4/3.51 Workstation

- Windows NT 4/3.51 Server

- Windows NT 3.1 Workstation

- Windows NT 3.1 Advanced Server

- Windows 95

- Windows for Workgroups

- LAN Manager systems

Master browsers will return lists of backup browsers to these systems for their local subnet:

- Windows NT 4/3.51 Workstation

- Windows NT 4/3.51 Server

- Windows NT 3.1 Workstation

- Windows NT 3.1 Advanced Server

- Windows 95

- Windows for Workgroup clients

When a system starts, and its MaintainServerList parameter is set to Auto, the Master browser is responsible for telling the system whether to become a backup browser or not.

The list of resources that the Master browser maintains and returns to the backup browsers is limited in size to 64K of data. This limits the number of computers that can be in a single workgroup or domain browse list to 2,000–3,000 computers.

Cruising an Internetwork

Many a problem can arise when trying to browse around networks that require a hop or two across routers to reach. A big reason for this is because Master browsers receive notices via B-node broadcasts—and as you've learned, routers won't let those pass through to different subnets. Also, domains that span routers are very prevalent in TCP/IP internetworks. On Microsoft networks, the browser service relies heavily on NetBIOS name broadcasts for getting information from connecting systems. Microsoft has come up with two great solutions for machines with that ol' Travelin' Jones—one dependent on WINS, and the other on the LMHOSTS file.

On the Wing with WINS

Recall that WINS solves the whole NetBIOS broadcast jam by dynamically registering names. Machines running WINS maintain and store all that name-related stuff (like IP addresses) in their databases where the information is readily available to the remote TCP/IP hosts that require it when contacted to establish communications. WINS clients, configured to operate compatibly with a WINS server, automatically register their names with them upon startup. This makes clean, broadcast-less identity referencing routinely available to all—except, of course, non-WINS clients, which we'll be discussing next. For a visual reference to what we've been talking about, see Figure 10.1.

FIGURE 10.1

Browsing with WINS

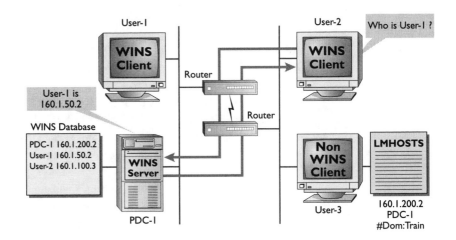

If you happen to be running the client component Windows for Workgroups with TCP/IP-32, you'll have to replace the VREDIR.386 file with the one supplied on the Windows NT Server 3.5x distribution CD.

The LMHOSTS File and Domain Functions

Non-WINS clients can be internetwork browsing's problem children. The fact that non-WINS clients register using B-node broadcasts presents a major problem if the system designated as the domain's Master browser is somewhere over the rainbow on a different subnet. Why? Simple—its registration broadcast won't be forwarded. On the client end of things, receiving messages that the browser service isn't available or viewing empty resource lists are also potential pitfalls.

To address these dilemmas, Microsoft added a pair of tags to the LMHOSTS file: #PRE, and #DOM. These tags enable the non-WINS client to communicate with a domain controller to do three very important things:

- Register with it

- Verify a user account

- Change passwords

Because user validation is required to operate login scripts and user profiles, and because broadcasts are used for replication of the domain database, special care should be used when configuring domain controllers when there isn't a WINS server around. To ensure your non-WINS clients will function well, be sure an entry is added for each domain controller present in the domain. Domain controllers that are also non-WINS machines should have a listing of all other domain controllers in their databases. This'll prove very handy if one of the servers is ever promoted to primary domain controller at any point in the future.

LMHOSTS file entries on each subnet's Master browser must first list the IP address, followed by the domain browser's NetBIOS name. Then come the tags, #PRE and #DOM, followed by the domain name. They should look something like this:

```
137.37.9.9 master-browser_name #PRE #DOM: domain-name
137.37.9.10 domain-controller_name #PRE #DOM: domain-name
```

Domain Functions

The #PRE tag tells TCP/IP to preload the resolution information into memory, while the #DOM tag alerts the client machine that it has reached a domain controller. #DOM is significant for directing data during broadcasts. These addresses indicate to the router to forward broadcasts to certain addresses. All this means that you're essentially making a broadcast and then directing it to a special place, so the #PRE tag must always precede the #DOM tag. See Figure 10.2 for a visual illustration of LMHOSTS in action.

Certain tasks executed by Windows NT network services will cause broadcasts to be sent out to all computers located within a Microsoft domain. For instance, when logging into a domain or changing a password, a broadcast will be transmitted to the domain to find a domain controller able to authenticate

FIGURE 10.2

Using LMHOSTS to browse across subnets

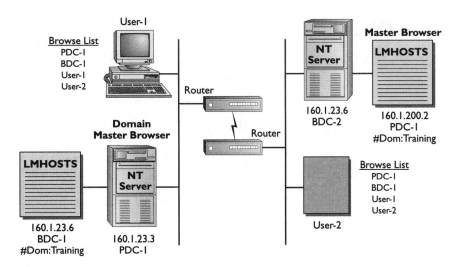

the logon request, and/or change the user's password. Another situation that'll induce broadcasts is when a domain controller replicates the domain user account database. To do this, the primary domain controller sends a broadcast out to all backup domain controllers that populate the domain, directing them to request a replication of updated changes made in the domain accounts database. (See Figure 10.3.)

FIGURE 10.3

Non-WINS clients domain functioning in an internetwork

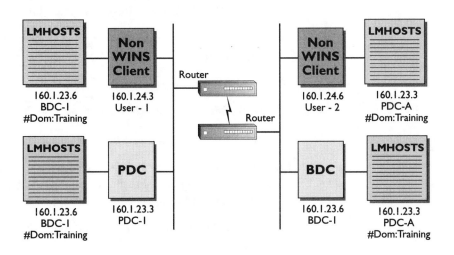

Remember that for Windows for Workgroups, the presence of a Windows NT server domain is required for WAN browsing, since Workgroups do not define a domain controller. For a Windows for Workgroups client to be capable of WAN browsing, it must first log onto a domain.

Configuring the LMHOSTS File

1. First, prepare your LMHOSTS file with the appropriate entry to log onto another computer on your domain.

2. Stop the WINS server service. From the command prompt, type **net stop wins**.

3. From the command prompt, verify that you have no existing connections to your other computer. Type **net use \\othercomputername\ ipc$ /d**. (Replace \\othercomputername with the name of your computer).

4. Purge the NetBIOS name cache. Type **nbstat -R** and then press Enter (the *R* must be in upper case).

5. Try to browse by typing **net view \\othercomputername**.

6. Notice the error that occurs when a remote host does not exist in the LMHOSTS file or when the entry is invalid.

7. Use Notepad to create a file in the \winnt\system32\drivers\etc directory named LMHOSTS.

8. Add the following entry to the file:

    `IP_Address  othercomputername  #PRE  #DOM:domain`

9. Save the file, and then exit Notepad.

10. Now, you're going to add the LMHOSTS file mapping for the other computer's domain controller to the NetBIOS name cache for browsing and logon validation.

11. Clear the NetBIOS name cache and load #PRE entries. Type **nbstat -R** and then press Enter.

12. View the NetBIOS name cache. Type **nbstat -c** and then press Enter.

13. Notice the entry that appears. Hopefully, it's your other computer!

14. Start the WINS server service by typing **net start wins** from the command prompt.

Let's go on to the next chapter and talk about how to implement NT in heterogeneous environments.

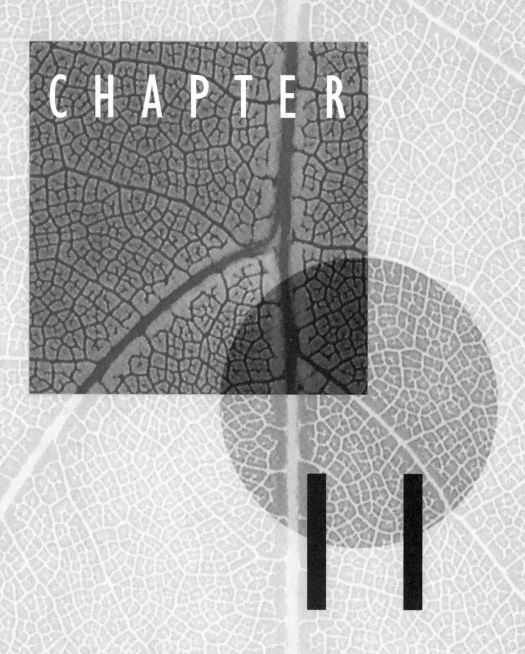

CHAPTER

11

Connectivity in Heterogeneous Environments

As discussed in Chapter 1, TCP/IP affords an extremely high degree of flexibility when operating within a diverse environment populated with many different platforms. The fundamental benefit of using TCP/IP is that it provides the wonderful ability to smoothly connect to, and interoperate with, different types of hosts. Disparate systems, such as VAX, Macintosh, UNIX, mainframes, etc., all use TCP/IP. Within each set of diversified systems, there exist subsets of systems that are more TCP/IP-oriented than others—for instance, all machines running UNIX, such as Sun workstations, SunOS, IBM's AIX, AT&T's System 5, etc. For systems like these, mutual, common ground is found in the interface of the tools that allow them to interoperate. These systems and their shared, correlative functions are what we're going to focus on in this chapter. For example, we'll show you how a NetBIOS-based host is able to achieve fluid communication with dissimilar systems whose only parallel is the fact that they're using TCP/IP as their communication protocol.

Here's a list of stuff to keep in mind while you're reading through this chapter:

- Dissimilar communication environments

- Communication between NetBIOS and foreign host systems

- Software requirements for achieving communication with Microsoft operating systems

- Usage of TCP/IP utilities as provided by Microsoft

- The Windows NT FTP server

- TCP/IP printing issues

Making Connections

As we said, TCP/IP provides a flexible means by which dissimilar computing environments may effectively communicate with each other. Without thinking in terms of a network, think of two systems communicating through asynchronous modems. Regardless of what operating systems these two systems may be running, they can "talk," provided they do so using the same parameters and protocols for communication. TCP/IP serves as an organizational model by establishing a set mode of communication despite differences in the operating system in use. Here's a sample list of some common operating systems that can use TCP/IP to interoperate for file and print services:

- Apple Macintosh
- DEC VAX systems
- DOS systems with TCP/IP
- IBM mainframes (among others)
- Internet objects
- LAN Manager
- NFS HOSTS
- OS/2 systems with TCP/IP
- TCP/IP-based printers
- Windows 95
- Windows NT
- Windows for Workgroups
- UNIX-based systems

The only requirements for connecting between these disparate operating systems are that they're running TCP/IP as their communication protocol and using their respective utilities and services in some specific ways that we'll describe later in the chapter.

A Microsoft client such as Windows NT, Windows 95, or Windows for Workgroups can interoperate with an RFC-compliant, NetBIOS-based, SMB (Server Message Block) server using the Windows Redirector. It accomplishes interoperation through use of standard Windows commands over a common set of communication protocols like TCP/IP or NetBEUI. Two examples of machines that can operate in this manner are a UNIX host that's running LAN Manager for UNIX, and a DEC VAX running Pathworks. Both of these operate similarly to Windows NT systems running on non-Intel platforms.

TCP/IP Utilities and the Windows NT Command

Many of the TCP/IP-based networking features are built directly into Windows NT. The type of network function you're attempting to perform will also determine whether you'll be using a Windows NT internal function or a TCP/IP utility. The chosen function will further define the requirements for carrying it out. Here are a few network truisms to abide by while working with Windows NT and TCP/IP commands:

- The same protocol must be used on both systems attempting communication with each other for connectivity and communication to result.

- Network connections from a command line are achieved through the net use command.

- Applications on other systems are accessed though Windows NT's native environment, and are processed at the client (distributed) rather than processed by the server host (centralized).

- Windows NT can use NetBIOS names—not just IP address names—to communicate via the net use and net view line commands. This is done for reasons of maintaining compatibility with other protocols, like NetBEUI, that don't use IP addresses and don't accommodate the overhead of additional program processing well.

- The NetBIOS scope parameter must match all other hosts' scope parameters. This allows NetBIOS networks to be divided and organized. Systems set for one scope don't communicate with those set for another scope. Therefore, two systems can have the same NetBIOS name as long as they're using different scopes.

- Remote hosts—those located on other subnets—must be resolved by a supported method such as WINS, LMHOSTS, etc.

How to Interoperate with an RFC-Compliant NetBIOS Host

When Windows NT isn't attempting to communicate with an RFC-compliant NetBIOS-based host (Windows for Workgroups, Windows 95, Windows NT, LAN Manager, LAN Manager for UNIX, etc.), but is trying to talk to a foreign TCP/IP system, different rules apply. While it's true that a number of common functions work great within a common realm, they're not understood and shared among foreign hosts that use tools uniquely and specifically defined for their way of communicating. Here are some ins and outs to know when communicating with foreign TCP/IP hosts:

- You must use TCP/IP—NetBEUI won't talk to TCP/IP and neither will IPX or any other non-IP protocol.

- Only commands supported by the specific TCP/IP utility, such as FTP, Telnet, etc., may be used to communicate with the foreign system.

- Applications that are accessed on the foreign system are run centrally at the foreign system—not at your local system. This is because different systems use different compilers, CPU commands, and memory instructions which are generally not platform-independent.

- TCP/IP utilities can either use the host name or the IP address.

- Both local and remote host names that are used in TCP/IP utilities must be resolved in the HOSTS file, DNS, WINS, B-node broadcast, or in the LMHOSTS file.

There's a distinct difference in how TCP/IP communication is established between similar and foreign hosts. While these differences may seem trivial, they're important to understand. Grasping these similarities and differences will greatly assist you later in debugging and configuring large TCP/IP environments.

TCP/IP Utilities the Microsoft Way

TCP/IP utilities follow their own specific set of rules. This conformity provides for standardization and ease of use when moving from one machine to the next through various operating systems. Microsoft provides FTP, LPD, LPQ, LPR, REXEC, RSH, RCP, Telnet, and TFTP TCP/IP utilities. The majority of the commands presented here are similar in implementation to their UNIX-based counterparts. And yes, just like UNIX, they're usually case-sensitive. They can be divided into three categories:

- Command utilities: REXEC, RSH, and Telnet

- Transfer utilities: RCP, FTP, TFTP, and WWW

- Printer utilities: LPD, LPR, and LPQ

Command Utilities

REXEC (Remote Execution)

The Remote Execute connectivity command will run a process on a remote system equipped with the REXEC server service. The REXEC service is password protected. Only upon receiving a valid password will this function proceed. The command format is as follows:

```
REXEC host {-1 username} {-n} command
```

This command line is broken down like this:

host	Specifies the host name or IP address of the system that is not the default.
-1 username	Specifies a valid user on the remote system when this is not the default.
-n	Redirects the input for REXEC to null, if you don't want input.
command	Specifies the execution line you wish to run on the host.

RSH (Remote Shell)

The Remote Shell utility allows a user to issue a command to a remote host without logging into it. Password protection isn't provided; however, the designated user name must exist in the .rhosts file on the UNIX server that's running the RSH daemon. This command is commonly used with UNIX systems for executing program compilers. The command format looks like this:

```
RSH host {-1 username} command
```

host	Specifies the host name or IP address of the system where the remote commands are run.
-1 username	Designates a valid user on the remote system when this is not the default. (it must be in an .rhosts file located in the user's home directory).
command	The UNIX command to be run on the remote host.

Telnet

The Telnet connectivity command initiates terminal emulation with a remote system running a Telnet service. Telnet provides DEC VT 100, DEC VT 52, or TTY emulation through the connection-based services of TCP. With this program, users can remotely execute any command as if they were sitting right in front of the host. Telnet has similarities to Novell's Rconsole utility, but can also be thought of as a text-based network version of Symantec's PC Anywhere remote control utility, because it's limited to those machines (a workstation or server) running a Telnet server program. The Telnet program requires TCP/IP on both the client and server, and requires an account set up on the server being contacted. Microsoft Windows NT doesn't provide the server process, but it does provide a client interface. Security is furnished by the requirement of a user name and password identical to those used when logging into the system directly. Telnet sometimes serves up a full graphical display beyond text. If this occurs, it's usually a form of X Window.

If you've installed TCP/IP and connection utilities from Windows NT, you have access to the Telnet program. To establish a connection, simply type **Telnet**, plus the destination name or IP address. If no destination is specified, the Telnet terminal screen will be displayed. At this point, choose Remote System from the Connect menu. The Connect dialog box will appear. Then, in the Host Name box, type the host name or IP address of the Telnet server, and choose Connect. When logging onto the Telnet server, enter your user account and the corresponding password. You'll then be able to talk to the remote host as though you were sitting there in front of it.

By default, Telnet uses port 23. Depending on the service, SMTP, FTP, Telnet, Time, Login, Whois, BootP, etc., can be redirected by a command line, through which you can use a different port. (A port specifies the remote port you want to connect to, providing compatibility with applications.) This is very handy for talking to other services—for example, direct communication to an SMTP mail port 25. You would type **Telnet host 25** to connect SMTP with an Internet mail server.

Using Telnet for Remote Login

In the early days of TCP/IP and intranetting, people's first concern was getting onto other people's computers. For instance, suppose we worked at the John Von Neumann Supercomputing Center, and we had written a fantastic celestial motion simulator—a program that could compute the location of thousands of planets, planetoids, and comets in the solar system. Suppose also that we had developed this with government money, and so the Feds wanted to offer this simulator to everyone. Well, how does one get to this simulator?

In all likelihood, to get to this program, you'd have to come to the Von Neumann center. That's true for two reasons. First, we developed it on a supercomputer for a good reason—it's too darn big to fit anywhere else. Stick it on a normal computer, and it would take weeks to get an answer to a simple question like, "When will Jupiter and Mars next be near to each other and high in the night sky?" The second reason is that we're back in the early days of intranetting, recall, and in those days programs were generally specific to the machines that they were built on. Moving this program to another computer would be a pain in the neck, even *if* we were willing to put up with the slower speed. So it seems that the most likely way to offer this service to everyone is to put some modems on the Von Neumann system and allow anyone to dial into the system to access this program. And, in fact, things like that have been done—but they end up generating awfully large phone bills for the people on the other side of the country.

Telnet solves this problem. It lets you work on the terminal or computer on your desk and access other hosts just as if you were there on-site—in the case of the Von Neumann center, just as if you were right at Princeton, New Jersey, where the center is located. Now, there *is* no publicly available astronomical simulator at Von Neumann, not at least as far as we know, so we can't show you anything like that. What we *can* show you is Archie, an essential Internet tool.

Seeing What's Out There: Using Archie

As we'll discuss later, the Internet is a very big source of information, from recipes to rutabaga farming tips to religion, which leads to the question, "How do I know what's available on the Internet?" There are three main ways to find out what's on the Internet, and one is Archie. There are a large number of computers—*hosts*, they're called—on the Internet that hold files that are available for public downloading and use. How would you find out about the existence of these things? Ask Archie.

Site	Location
archie.rutgers.edu	Northeast United States
archie.sura.net	Southeast United States
archie.unl.edu	Western United States
archie.ans.net	The Internet backbone
archie.mcgill.ca	Canada
archie.funet.fi	Europe
archie.doc.ic.ac.uk	United Kingdom
archie.au	Australia and Pacific Rim

Archie is available on several servers around the world. It's best to hook up to the Archie server closest to you to minimize network traffic. For example, there is quite limited data transfer capability to England, so, although using the UK Archie server might seem cosmopolitan, it's a fairly inconsiderate thing to do if you're intranetting from the US. We'll hook up to Archie at archie.unl .edu at the University of Nebraska.

We'll do the Telnet login from the command line. Once the session is active, however, we'll automatically be shifted to the NT Terminal program. We remotely log onto Archie at the University of Nebraska by typing **telnet archie.unl.edu**.

After some introductory things, we get a prompt that says Login:. We respond by typing **archie**. For the password, type in your e-mail address. Now, not every Telnet site will require a login. Some just drop you right into the middle of the application. Others may require that you get an account for their service, and they may charge you money for using whatever service they're pur-veying over the Net—that's fair game. Expect to see more and more services on the Internet that are for-pay—the Net is slowly going commercial. Anyway, we get a prompt that says `unl-archie>`, indicating that when we type something now, making a request for information, then that request is being processed by the computer running Archie at the University of Nebraska. Typing **help** at the command line, and then **?**, displays a list of valid subtopics at the current level. Type **.** (period) to go up one level. Let's see what we find if we search for Microsoft. After logging in, type **prog microsoft**. The search shows us:

```
##############################################################################

      #    # ###### ###### ######    #    ##### #   #    #
      ##   # #      #     # #    #    #    # #   ##  #   # #
      # #  # #      #     # #    #    #   #   #  # # #  #   #
      #  # # #####  ######  ######   #    #   # # #   # #
      #   ## #      #     # #   #     #######  #   # # #######
      #    ## #      #     # #    #    # #   # #   # #     #
      #     # ###### ###### #     # #    #    # ##### #   # #     #
```

      Welcome to the ARCHIE server at the University of Nebraska
- Lincoln

      If you need further instructions, type help at the unl-
archie> prompt.

```
##############################################################################
```

Bunyip Information Systems, 1993
Terminal type set to `ansi 24 80'.
`erase' character is `^?'.
`search' (type string) has the value `sub'.
unl-archie> prog Microsoft

Host ftp.ugcs.caltech.edu   (131.215.134.135)
Last updated 11:44 8 Sep 1994

      Location: /pub/elef/texts/misc
        FILE   -rw-r--r--   4500 bytes 14:13 25 Jul 1994
startrek_n_microsoft.txt

Host dime.cs.umass.edu   (128.119.40.244)
Last updated 08:51 4 Aug 1994

```
    Location: /pub/vision
       FILE    -rw-r--r--      115 bytes   18:05  2 Aug 1994
plz_send_microsoft_space_simulator

Host terminator.rs.itd.umich.edu    (141.211.164.2)
Last updated 10:33  4 Aug 1994

    Location: /www-public/projects/directory-yp/ypdemo/
keyword.index
       FILE    -rw-r--r--     1042 bytes   03:03 22 Jul 1994
Microsoft-Mail.html
       FILE    -rw-r--r--      570 bytes   03:03 22 Jul 1994
Microsoft-Word.html

unl-archie>
```

Notice that every group of information starts off with host; that's important, as that's the name of the place that we'd have to go to get the files we found by searching for Microsoft. Then there's a filename. The parts in front of it are exactly *where* the file is. If you're a PC user, then you may, at first glance, think that you recognize the subdirectory usage, but look again! Instead of backslashes, which DOS uses to separate subdirectory levels, UNIX uses *forward* slashes!

Anyway, now that we've found some cool information about Microsoft, we'll quit Archie by typing **quit**. The message, Connection closed by foreign host, is from our computer to us. It says that the Archie computer at Nebraska—which it calls the *foreign host*—has stopped talking to us.

Non-Standardization Problems

In general, Telnet works fine with computers of all kinds. But some host computers just plain won't talk to you unless you're an IBM 3270-type dumb terminal, so there is another program, tn3270. Tn3270 is a variation of Telnet that emulates an IBM 3270 full-screen type terminal. The main thing to know about tn3270 is that 3270-type terminals have a *lot* of functions about them. Not all implementations of tn3270 are equal, so don't be totally shocked if you Telnet to an IBM site using tn3270, work for a while, and get a message, Unexpected command sequence–program terminated. It means that your tn3270 couldn't handle some command that the IBM host sent it. And IBM terminal emulation can be a real pain in the neck when it comes to key mapping. On the IBM terminal is a set of function keys labeled PF1, PF2, and so on. As there are no keys labeled like that on a PC or a Mac, what key should you press to get PF4, for instance? Well, it's Esc-4 on some implementations of tn3270, F4 on some others, and there doesn't seem to be any real agreement either on what the key is, or what the key should be. Make sure that you have the documentation for your tn3270 somewhere around before you start Telnetting to an IBM host.

tn3270 is not shipped with NT.

Why Use Telnet?

What is Telnet good for, anyway? Several things. First, it is the way to access a number of specialized basic information services. For instance, many large libraries put their entire card catalog on Telnet servers. University researchers can then look for an item and request it through interlibrary loan. Another example can be found by Telnetting to InterNIC. The InterNIC keeps track of all registered IP addresses on the Internet. Just type **Telnet internic.net**, and you're in:

```
UNIX(r) System V Release 4.0 (rs1)


*****************************************************************************
* -- InterNIC Registration Services Center   --
*
* For wais, type:                    WAIS <search string> <return>
* For the *original* whois type:     WHOIS [search string] <return>
* For referral whois type:           RWHOIS [search string] <return>
*
* For user assistance call (703) 742-4777
# Questions/Updates on the whois database to HOSTMASTER@internic.net
* Please report system problems to ACTION@internic.net
*****************************************************************************
Please be advised that use constitutes consent to monitoring (Elec Comm
Priv Act, 18 USC 2701-2711)
```

```
6/1/94
We are offering an experimental distributed whois service called referral
whois (RWhois). To find out more, look for RWhois documents,a sample
client and server under:
gopher: (rs.internic.net) InterNIC Registration Services ->
        InterNIC Registration Archives -> pub -> rwhois
        anonymous ftp: (rs.internic.net) /pub/rwhois
Cmdinter Ver 1.3 Sun Jun 22 15:37:39 1997 EST
[ansi] InterNIC >
```

Another use for Telnet might be a commercial firm that wants to offer an online ordering service: You just log on, browse the descriptions of the items available, and place an order electronically. A third, somewhat technical, reason for using Telnet is that it can be used as a debugging tool. Using Telnet, you can essentially impersonate different applications, like FTP and mail.

The final reason for using Telnet is simply its original reason for existence: remote login to a service on a distant host. That has become a feature of much less value than it was when it first appeared, largely because of the way that we now use computers. Twenty years ago, you would have had a dumb terminal on your desk. Today, you are likely to have a computer on your desk, a computer with more computing power than a mainframe of 20 years ago. We are less interested today in borrowing someone else's computing power than we are in borrowing their information—with their permission, of course. Specifically, we often seek to transfer files to and from other computers over an intranet. For that reason, we'll consider transfer utilities next.

Transfer Utilities

RCP (Remote Copy)

RCP is used to copy files between local and remote UNIX hosts or between two remote hosts. The Remote Copy tool is used in a similar manner as FTP for copying files, except it doesn't require user validation. Like RSH, the designated user name must exist in the .rhosts file located on the UNIX server that's running the RCP daemon. It's also commonly used with UNIX systems. The command format is as follows:

```
RCP {-abhr}{host1.}{user1:}source {host2.}{user2:}path/
destination
```

Host1/host2 is the name, or IP address, of the destination or source system. If the host .user: portion is omitted, the host is assumed to be the local computer.

User1/User2 specifies valid users that exist on the destination and source systems (user names must be in the .rhosts file), and source/destination is the full path designating where files are copied.

The switch options are as follows:

-a Set by default, this option sets transfers to ASCII, and specifies for translation UNIX/DOS text formatting for cr-1f (carriage return/linefeed, DOS hex 0d 0a) and 1f (linefeed, UNIX hex 0a).

-b Sets transfers to binary with no translation.

-h Sets the transfer of hidden files.

-r Recursively copies the contents of all subdirectories of the source to the destination. Both the source and destination must be directories. It's equal to the DOS /S command with XCOPY.

FTP

The File Transfer Protocol is used to copy files to and from a system running an FTP server over TCP, and is therefore quite obviously connection-oriented. The host may be UNIX, VAX, Windows NT, or any other system running an FTP server process. Although this utility uses both user and password protection, it can be configured to allow anonymous usage. Unlike Telnet, Microsoft does provide a daemon or server service for FTP to run. In most Internet applications, when using FTP with "anonymous" as a user ID, an e-mail account is used as the password, as it can be logged to show an audit trail.

If you've installed TCP/IP and connection utilities with Windows NT, you already have the FTP program. Because no icon is created from a command prompt, type **ftp** and the destination name or IP address.

The command line with options is:

    ftp {options} host command

If no destination host is specified, the FTP terminal screen will appear. When it does, type **open** to establish your connection. As with Telnet, you'll then be prompted for a login name and password. Once connected, you have a variety of options available to you. You can view these options by typing **help** or **?**. Doing so will yield the following information:

!	DOS shell to command prompt. Type **Exit** to return.
?	Command listing or **?** Command displays the command description. It works the same as **help**.
append	Allows you to add to a file.
ASCII	Sets the transfer mode type to ASCII. Used for text files.
bell	Inserts a little beep when the command is completed.
Bye	Closes an FTP session, and exits the FTP program.
Binary	Sets the transfer mode type to Binary. Used for files other than text.
cd	Changes directory on FTP server (must include a space following **cd**, also uses **..** (double dots) for going back a directory, and **/** for specifying root.
close	Closes an FTP session.
debug	Toggles the debug mode.
delete	Removes a remote file.
dir	Lists a directory of files—similar to **ls -l** in UNIX).
disconnect	Closes an FTP session.
get	Retrieves a file.
Glob	Toggles meta-character expansion of local filenames.
hash	Toggles printing # (hash signs) for each data block transferred.
help	Command listing or **help** *Command* displays the command description. Same as **?**.
literal	Sends arguments, verbatim, to the remote FTP server. A single FTP reply code is expected in return.
lcd	Changes directory locally.
ls	Lists a directory of files. (Use **ls -l** for all information.)
mdelete	Removes multiple remote files.

mdir	Provides a directory of multiple remote directories.
mget	Downloads multiple files from a remote system.
mkdir	Makes a directory on the remote system.
mls	Provides a directory of multiple remote directories.
mput	Uploads multiple files to a remote system.
open	Begins an FTP session.
prompt	Toggles interactive prompting on multiple commands.
put	Uploads a file.
pwd	Prints a working directory (like cd in DOS).
quit	Exits the FTP session.
Quote	Sends arguments, verbatim, to the remote FTP server. A single FTP reply code is expected in return. Quote is identical to Literal.
recv	Downloads a file.
rename	Renames a file.
rmdir	Removes a directory.
remotehelp	Gets a help listing from the FTP server.
send	Uploads a file.
status	Shows the current status of FTP connections.
trace	Toggles packet tracing.
type	Sets the transfer type.
user	Sends new user information.
verbose	Toggles the verbose mode.

As you can see, there are a ton of commands, and while it's not important to memorize them, you should be aware of their existence and how to find them. Many new GUI FTP programs have been created by third parties in an effort to simplify the FTP process. However, most FTP systems use the same commands in a manner that complies to the standard.

To get really into FTP, flip over a page and look under "The FTP Server—Installation and Configuration."

TFTP

The Trivial File Transfer Protocol, also discussed in detail in Chapter 2, is equal to FTP without security. Using UDP to communicate in place of TCP, this program will communicate with a host running the TFTP server software. As with Telnet, Microsoft only provides the client portion of TFTP. The server part must come from a third-party source or be used from another operating system such as a UNIX server. The command format is as follows:

```
TFTP [-i] host [GET | PUT] source [destination]
```

-I	Specifies binary image transfer mode, also called octet. If –i is omitted, the file is transferred in ASCII mode.
source/ destination	Is the full path designating where files are copied to and from.
get	Transfers destination (specifies where to transfer) on the remote computer to source (specifies what file to transfer) on the local computer.
put	Transfers source (specifies what file to transfer) on the remote computer to destination (specifies where to transfer) on the local computer.

WWW

Web browsers such as Microsoft Internet Explorer and Netscape Navigator use HTTP to transfer pages of data from a Web server. The WWW follows a client/server model and uses the HTTP protocol between the client and the server.

System requirements for the client:

- **A Web browser:** There are several World Wide Web clients available, some of which can be freely downloaded from the Internet.

System requirements for the server:

- **The World Wide Web service:** The server responds with the status of the transaction, successful or failed, and the data for the request. After the data is sent, the connection is closed and no state is retained by the server. Each object in an HTTP document requires a separate connection.

Web browsers support the following data transfer benefits:

- **Web browsers support many data types:** A Web browser can automatically download and display text files and graphics; some can even play video and sound clips and launch helper applications for known file types.

- **Web browsers support many protocols:** Web browsers support several data transfer protocols, including FTP, Gopher, HTTP, and NNTP.

The FTP Server—Installation and Configuration

If you have a PC or Macintosh on your desk, think for a moment about how you use that computer in a network situation. You may have a computer elsewhere in your building that acts as a *file server*, a computer that holds the files shared in your facility or your department. How do you ask that server to transfer a file from itself to your computer? You may say, "I don't do that"; but you *do*. Whenever you attach to a shared network resource, you're asking that system to provide your computer with shared files. Now, how you actually *ask* for them is very simple: You just connect to a server, which looks like an extra folder on your desktop if you're a Mac user, or an extra drive letter, like X: or E:, if you are a PC user. The intranet world has a facility like that, a facility that lets you attach distant computers to your computer as if that distant computer were a local drive: It is called NFS, the Network File System. But NFS is relatively recent in the TCP/IP world. It's much more common to attach to a host, browse the files that it contains, and selectively transfer them to your local host. You do that with FTP, the File Transfer Protocol.

There are three essentials of FTP: how to start it up, how to navigate around the directories of the FTP server, and how to actually snatch a file from an FTP server. We'll also look at a special kind of FTP called *anonymous* FTP. So let's get started by looking at how the files on an FTP server are organized.

FTP Organization

The first time that you get on an FTP server, you'll probably want to get right off. FTP, like much of the TCP/IP world, was built from the perspective that software's got to be *functional* and not necessarily, well, pretty—or to use an overused phrase, "user-friendly." If you're a PC user, the UNIX file structure will be somewhat familiar, as the DOS file structure was stolen—uh oops, we mean, *borrowed*—from UNIX. Mac users will have a bit more trouble.

Now, we just referred to the UNIX file structure. That's because FTP servers *usually* use UNIX. But some don't, so you may come across FTP servers that don't seem to make any sense. For the purposes of this discussion, we'll assume that the FTP servers here are UNIX, but, beware—you may run into non-UNIX FTP servers. These oddball FTP servers run on a DEC VAX, and probably run the VMS operating system. Some others may run on an IBM mainframe, and may be running either MVS or VM. Very rarely, an FTP server may even run under DOS, OS/2, NT, or some other PC operating system. But let's get back to our look at a UNIX FTP server.

FTP uses a tree-structured directory represented in the UNIX fashion. The top of the directory is called `ourfiles`, and it has two directories below it—*sub*-directories—called `ourfiles/bin`, and `ourfiles/text`, as shown in Figure 11.1. In the UNIX world, `/bin` refers to executable files—files we might call program files in other operating systems, or more specifically, EXE or COM files in the PC world, and load modules in the IBM mainframe world. The text directory contains two directories below it; one is called `contracts` and the other is called `announcements`.

FIGURE 11.1

An example of how files
on an FTP server are
organized

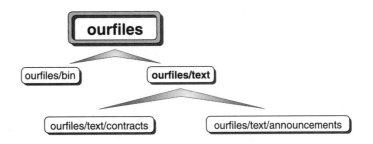

A couple of notes here. PC users may think that things look a bit familiar, but look closely—there *are* a couple of differences. First, notice the subdirectory named announcements. That name is more than eight characters long, which is quite acceptable, even though it isn't at all acceptable in the DOS world. UNIX accepts filenames comprised of hundreds of characters. Second, notice that there are not *backslashes* between the different levels, but, instead, there are *forward* slashes. That's also a UNIX feature. Now, what complicates matters for users of non-UNIX systems is that FTP pretty much assumes that *your* system uses the UNIX file system too. That means that you have to be comfortable with traversing *two* directory structures—the one on the remote FTP server, plus the one on your local hard disk.

File Navigation

You get an FTP command line—we'll demonstrate it in a minute—that expects you to tell it where to get files *from*, and where to send files *to*, using these two commands:

- remote: cd

- local: lcd

That's because there's a tree structure on both the remote system—the one that you're getting the files from—and the local system. Let's look at a few examples to nail down exactly how all this cd-ing works.

Moving in FTP

When you enter an FTP site, you start out at the top of the directory structure. This top is called the *root* of the directory. In our example, the root is called ourfiles. To move down one level, to ourfiles/text, you could type **cd text**. That says to FTP, "Move down one level relative to the current location." Alternatively, you could skip the relative reference and just say, "Absolutely go to ourfiles/text." The way that you do that is by typing **cd /ourfiles/ text**. The fact that the entry *starts* with a slash tells cd that your command is not a relative one, but an absolute one.

Now let's try moving back up a level. At any point, you can back up one level either by typing the command **cdup**, or by typing **cd ..**. The two periods (..) mean one level upward to both DOS and UNIX. Or you can do an absolute reference, as in **cd /ourfiles**.

Now suppose you're all the way at the bottom of this structure. It's a simple three-level directory, and you often see directory structures a good bit more complex than this one. To move back up from ourfiles/text/announcements to ourfiles/text, you can do as before, and either type **cdup** or **cd ..**. Or you could do an absolute reference, as in **cd /ourfiles/text**. To go back *two* levels, you can either issue two separate **cdup** or **cd ..** commands, or use an absolute reference, as in **cd /ourfiles**. To type two **cdup** or **cd ..** commands you type the command, then press Enter, and then type the second command. Do not try to issue two commands on the same line.

An Example of Navigation

Now that you can navigate the twisty passages of FTP directories, let's take a look at how we can use FTP to pull files from the Internet.

We found earlier that we could get some interesting information by searching for Microsoft. One of those sites we found was `terminator.rs.itd .umich.edu (141.211.164.2)`.

Let us FTP to that site and get some files. We type **run ftp terminator .rs.itd.umich.edu (141.211.164.2)**.

This site doesn't know us, so we can't log on with a local name and password. That's where the idea of *anonymous* FTP becomes useful. You see, you can often log onto an FTP site and download data that's been put there specifically for public use. Anonymous FTP is just the same as regular FTP, except that you log in with the name *anonymous*. It responds that a guest login is OK but wants our e-mail address for a password. We type in our e-mail address, and we're in. Now, it might be that there are places on this server that we *cannot* get to because we signed on as anonymous, but that doesn't matter. Next, we can do a dir command and see what's on this directory.

```
Connected to terminator.rs.itd.umich.edu.
220 terminator.rs.itd.umich.edu FTP server (SunOS 4.1) ready.
User (terminator.rs.itd.umich.edu:(none)): anonymous
331 Guest login ok, send ident as password.
Password:
230 Guest login ok, access restrictions apply.
ftp> dir
200 PORT command successful.
150 ASCII data connection for /bin/ls (153.34.190.137,1211) (0 bytes).
total 19
d--x--s--x  2 root      wheel       512 Oct 27  1992        bin
dr-xr-sr-x  2 root      wheel       512 Jul 18  1993        dev
lrwxrwxrwx  1 root      wheel         8 Jul 17  1993 dns -> unix/dns
d--x--s--x  2 root      wheel       512 Oct 27  1992        etc
drwxr-sr-x  5 x500      isode       512 Nov 19  1996        ietf-asid
drwxr-sr-x  2 x500      isode       512 Nov 15  1996        ietf-ids
drwxr-sr-x  2 root      wheel       512 Nov  5  1992        ietf-remmail
drwxrwsr-x 12 root      isode       512 Apr 23 18:08        ldap
drwxr-sr-x  4 20039     staff       512 Aug  2  1995        mac
```

```
drwxrwsr-x  2 root     wheel     512 Apr 16 14:53    pub
drwxr-sr-x  6 root     wheel     512 May 21 1993     shakespeare
drwxrwsr-x  5 root     wheel     512 Nov  2 1996     unix
drwxr-sr-x  2 news     news      512 Dec 17 1992     usenet
drwxr-sr-x  3 root     wheel     512 Nov 30 1995     users
d--x--s--x  3 root     wheel     512 Oct 27 1992     usr
drwxrwsr-x  3 root     staff     512 May  8 15:58    win
drwxr-sr-x  2 5725     wheel     512 May 10 1996     www
drwxr-sr-x  4 20039    staff     512 Apr 27 1995     www-public
drwxrwsr-x  6 x500     isode    1024 May  3 1995     x500
226 ASCII Transfer complete.
1186 bytes received in 0.66 seconds (1.80 Kbytes/sec)
ftp>
```

No. It's not beautiful, but let's see what we can see. Notice all the *r*'s, *x*'s, *w*'s, and *d*'s to the left of each entry? That represents the privilege levels of access to this file. One of the important things is whether or not the left-most letter is *d*—if it is, then that's not a file, it's a directory. Notice that entry shakespeare; it's a directory. Since we're such literary types, let's see what's in it. Type **cd shakespeare** and then **dir**.

```
ftp> cd shakespeare
250 CWD command successful.
ftp> dir
200 PORT command successful.
150 ASCII data connection for /bin/ls (153.34.190.137,1215) (0 bytes).
total 63
-r--r--r--  1 root     wheel       978 Feb 15 1994 README
drwxr-sr-x  2 root     wheel       512 May 21 1993 comedies
-r--r--r--  1 root     wheel     58966 Feb 15 1994 glossary
drwxr-sr-x  2 root     wheel       512 May 21 1993 histories
drwxr-sr-x  2 root     wheel       512 May 21 1993 poetry
drwxr-sr-x  2 root     wheel       512 May 21 1993 tragedies
226 ASCII Transfer complete.
392 bytes received in 0.05 seconds (7.84 Kbytes/sec)
ftp>
```

Notice that, in general, you must be careful about capitalization—if the directory's name is Literature with a capital *L*, then trying to change to a directory whose name is literature with a lowercase *l* will probably fail. Why *probably*? It's another UNIX thing; the UNIX file system is case-sensitive. In contrast, if you found yourself talking to an OS/2-based TCP/IP host, then case would be irrelevant. How do you know what your host runs? Well, it is sometimes announced in the sign-on message, but not always. The best bet is just to assume that case is important.

There are lots of directories to look at: comedies, glossary, histories, poetry, and tragedies. Let's cd to comedies and see what's there.

```
ftp> cd comedies
250 CWD command successful.
ftp> dir
200 PORT command successful.
150 ASCII data connection for /bin/ls (153.34.190.137,1225) (0 bytes).
total 2247
-r--r--r--  1 root      wheel      135369 Mar 24  1992 allswellthatendswell
-r--r--r--  1 root      wheel      125179 Mar 24  1992 asyoulikeit
-r--r--r--  1 root      wheel       89525 Mar 24  1992 comedyoferrors
-r--r--r--  1 root      wheel      165209 Mar 24  1992 cymbeline
-r--r--r--  1 root      wheel      129986 Mar 24  1992 loveslabourslost
-r--r--r--  1 root      wheel      130473 Mar 24  1992 measureformeasure
-r--r--r--  1 root      wheel      122658 Mar 24  1992 merchantofvenice
-r--r--r--  1 root      wheel      131576 Mar 24  1992 merrywivesofwindsor
-r--r--r--  1 root      wheel       96508 Mar 24  1992 midsummersnightsdream
-r--r--r--  1 root      wheel      123413 Mar 24  1992 muchadoaboutnothing
-r--r--r--  1 root      wheel      111604 Mar 24  1992 periclesprinceoftyre
-r--r--r--  1 root      wheel      124237 Mar 24  1992 tamingoftheshrew
-r--r--r--  1 root      wheel       99379 Mar 24  1992 tempest
-r--r--r--  1 root      wheel      158946 Mar 24  1992 troilusandcressida
-r--r--r--  1 root      wheel      116759 Mar 24  1992 twelfthnight
-r--r--r--  1 root      wheel      102007 Mar 24  1992 twogentlemenofverona
-r--r--r--  1 root      wheel      145794 Mar 24  1992 winterstale
226 ASCII Transfer complete.
1231 bytes received in 0.82 seconds (1.50 Kbytes/sec)
ftp>
```

Notice that none of these files have a .zip or .txt.z extension. If they did, they would be compressed. An extension of .zip on a file usually means that it has been compressed using the pkzip algorithm, probably on an MS-DOS system. The UNIX counterpart to that is a file ending simply in .z, like the second file. It can be uncompressed with the gzip program that you can find on many libraries. More specifically, suppose you download file.zip to a PC. If you tried to look at the file, it would be even uglier than the stuff we just showed you—absolute gibberish. That's because the file is compressed and must be uncompressed before it'll become intelligible. It was compressed so that there would be fewer bytes to transfer around the network; after all, this *is* a book, and why clog up the network with millions of bytes when thousands can do the job. You'd transfer this to your PC, and then you'd use an un-zipper program to uncompress the file. But the file that ends off with .z, the one done with gzip, can be unzipped *while transferring*! Suppose you don't have a copy of either pkunzip or gzip and don't want to have to mess around with finding an unzipper. All you need do is to just request the file not as file.txt.z, but instead as file.txt. The FTP program is smart enough to know that it should uncompress the file as it transfers it to your machine! Very cool.

Before we snatch a file, there's one more thing we should point out. Years ago, most files that were transferred were simple plain-text ASCII files. Nowadays, many files are *not* ASCII—even data files created by spreadsheets and word processors contain data other than simple text. Such files are, as you probably know, called *binary* files. FTP must be alerted that it will transfer binary files. You do that by typing **binary** at the ftp> prompt. FTP responds by saying Type set to I. That is FTP's inimitable way of saying that it's now ready to do a binary file transfer, or, as FTP calls it, an *image* file transfer.

Transferring a File

Now let's get a file:

```
ftp> binary
200 Type set to I.
ftp> get allswellthatendswell
200 PORT command successful.
150 Binary data connection for allswellthatendswell
(153.34.190.137,1222) (13536
9 bytes).
```

```
226 Binary Transfer complete.
135369 bytes received in 29.82 seconds (4.54 Kbytes/sec)
ftp>
ftp> bye
221 Goodbye.
```

Notice that once we got the file, the system reported some throughput statistics.

When snagging the file, be patient—it'll take some time to transfer—and there's no cute little bar graphic or anything like that to give you a single clue as to how far the blasted transfer has proceeded. However, there *is* a command that'll give you *some* idea about how the transfer is progressing—*hash* —imagine that. Well, what can we say—it's UNIX. Type **hash**, and from that point on the system will print an octothorpe (#) for each 2K of file transferred. "If the living be enemy to the grief, the excess makes it soon mortal." We got the file on our desktop (our destination directory), and it opened with Word-pad. Great stuff!

FTP versus Telnet

Now let's review what we've seen so far. First, you use the FTP program to log onto a remote system, in a manner similar to Telnetting onto a remote system. In fact, it's so similar, some people have trouble understanding why there's a difference between Telnet and FTP. Telnet is for terminal emulation into another facility's computing power; FTP is for transferring files to and from another facility's computers. Once you FTP to another site, you'll find that the site usually has its files organized into a set of directories arranged in a tree structure. You move FTP's attention from one directory to another with the cd command. You also may have a tree-structured directory on your system; if you wish to tell FTP to transfer to or from a particular directory, then you use the local cd command, or lcd. You use the binary command to tell FTP that you're going to transfer files that aren't simple ASCII. The get command requests that the remote system give you a file, and the put command requests that the remote system *accept* a file from you. And there you have the basics of FTP.

Internetwork Printing

Microsoft TCP/IP Network Printing Support provides the ability to:

- Print to a printer attached to a Windows NT 4 print server from a UNIX host (LPDSVC service).

- Print to printers attached to UNIX hosts from any computer that can connect to a Windows NT computer. The Windows NT computer communicates with the UNIX printer using the LPR and LPQ utilities.

- Print to printers that use a network interface with TCP/IP.

Printer Utilities

Microsoft provides three utilities to allow TCP/IP printing with NT:

- LPD

- LPQ

- LPR

Once you've installed and configured the TCP/IP printer support, you can connect to the printer using Print Manager or the LPR command. LPQ and LPR are client applications that communicate with LPD on the server. The three utilities provide the following functions:

LPD

The LPD (Line Printer Daemon) runs as a service on the Windows NT computer (LPDSVC), and enables any computer with TCP/IP and LPR to send print jobs to the Windows NT computer. See "Installing a TCP/IP-based Printer" below.

The configuration parameters for the TCP/IP Print Server are located under the following Registry key:

```
HKEY_LOCAL_MACHINE\System\CurentControlSet\Services\LPDSVC\
Parameters
```

LPQ

LPQ (Line Printer Queue) allows a user to view the print queue on an LPD server. It displays the state of a remote LPD queue. The command format is this:

    lpq -Sserver -Pprinter -1

-S*server*   Is the name, or IP address, of the host providing the LPD service.

-P*printer*   Is the name of the print queue.

-1   Specifies that a detailed status should be given.

LPR

For command-line situations, or when you're printing from a UNIX host, use the LPR (Line Printer) command line utility. The Line Printer utility allows jobs to be sent to a printer which is serviced by a host running LPD server. To send the print jobs, LPR makes a TCP connection to the LPD service using ports 512 and 1023. The command format looks like:

    lpr -Sserver -PPrinter [-CClass] [-JJobname] [-oOption]
    [-x] [-d] filename

-S*server*   Is the name, or IP address, of the host providing the LPD service.

-P*printer*   Is the name of the print queue.

-C*class*   Is the job classification for use on the banner page.

-J*job*   Is the job name to be printed on the banner page.

-o*Option*   Indicates type of the file (the default is text file; use -ol for binary files such as postscript, etc.).

-x   Is for compatibility with SunOS 4.1.x or prior version.

-d   Is for sending a data file first.

Installing a TCP/IP-Based Printer

To install the TCP/IP-based printer, you do the following:

1. In the Control Panel, double-click on Network. The Network dialog box appears.

2. Click on the Services tab. The Services property sheet appears.

3. Click on Add. The Select Network Services dialog box appears.

4. Click on Microsoft TCP/IP Printing and then click on OK. The Windows NT Setup box appears, prompting you for the full path of the Windows NT distribution files.

5. Type **C:\I386** or wherever your distribution files are located and then click on OK. The appropriate files are copied to your workstation, and then the Network dialog box appears.

6. Click on Close. A Network Settings Change message box appears, indicating that the computer needs to be restarted.

7. Click on Yes.

8. Log on as Administrator.

9. In the Control Panel, double-click on Services. The Services dialog box appears.

10. Select TCP/IP Print Server and then click on Start.

11. Click on Close.

Creating a TCP/IP-Based Printer

1. In the Control Panel, double-click on Printer. The Printers window appears.

2. Double-click on Add Printer. The Add Printer Wizard dialog box appears.

3. Click on My Computer and then click on Next.

4. Click on Add Port. The Printer Ports dialog box appears.

5. Click on LPR Port and then click on New Port. The Add LPR Compatible Printer dialog box appears.

6. In the Name or Address of Server Providing LPD box, type your own IP address.

7. In the Name of Printer or Print Queue on That Server box, type
name_of_printer and then click on OK.

8. Click on Close.

9. Click on Next.

10. Complete the Add Printer Wizard dialog box by entering the Share
name, if necessary.

11. An Insert Disk message box prompts you for a floppy disk.

12. Click on OK. A Windows NT Setup dialog box appears, prompting you
for the location of the Windows NT Server distribution files.

13. Type in the path to the distribution files.

14. An icon should appear with the TCP/IP printer created.

Printing to a TCP/IP-Based Printer by Using Print Manager

1. In the Printers window, double-click on Add Printer. The Add Printer
Wizard dialog box appears.

2. Click on Network Printer Server and then click on Next. The Connect to
Printer dialog box appears.

3. In the Printer box, type the name of your TCP/IP printer. The Add
Printer Wizard prompts you to make this printer the default printer.

4. Click on Yes and then click on Next.

5. Click on Finish. An icon representing the printer will then be created in
the Printers window.

So, how do we keep track of all these heterogeneous computers running
TCP/IP? Great question, and that brings us to our next subject, Simple Network Management Protocol. Read on.

CHAPTER

12

Microsoft SNMP Services

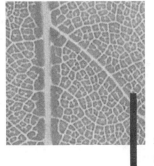

n this chapter, we're going to take a look at Simple Network Management Protocol. Sound simple? Not really. SNMP is actually a pretty complex protocol, but it *is* simple to administrate—that's the beauty of it!

We'll start out by explaining the purpose of SNMP and the different operations performed by an SNMP agent and an SNMP manager. Then we'll define Management Information Base (MIB) and show you how to install and configure the Microsoft SNMP service.

An SNMP Overview

SNMP (Simple Network Management Protocol) is one very important protocol in the TCP/IP suite. It allows you to monitor and manage a network from a single workstation or multiple workstations called SNMP managers. SNMP is actually a family of specifications that provides a means for collecting network management data from the devices residing in a network. It also avails a method for those devices to report any problems they are experiencing to the management station. From an SNMP manager, you can query the network's devices regarding the nature of their functions. Examples of machines you'd want to monitor include:

- Computers running Windows NT

- LAN Manager servers

- Routers and gateways

- Minicomputers or mainframe computers

- Terminal servers

- Wiring hubs

Figure 12.1 shows the network administrator at an SNMP management station making queries to various devices on the internetwork. A router can be queried for the contents of its routing table or for statistics relating to the amount of traffic it's forwarding. A mainframe computer can be surveyed to determine which ports are listing for requests or for what connections have been established with clients. A Windows NT computer can also be monitored and can alert the manager of pertinent events, such as when a particular host is running out of hard disk space. Regardless of the type of device that is queried, the SNMP agent on the device is able to return meaningful, highly useful information to the manager.

FIGURE 12.1

SNMP managers and
SNMP agents

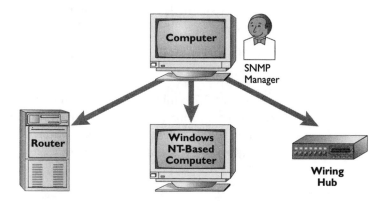

SNMP is defined in RFC 1157.

Management Systems and Agents

SNMP uses a distributed architecture consisting of management systems and agents. It works like this: The manager first submits a request to the agent to either obtain or to set the value of a networking variable within the agent's Management Information Base (MIB). The agent satisfies the request according to the community name accompanying the request. A community name can be compared to a password, and will be discussed more thoroughly later in this chapter.

The SNMP protocol is simple in that only five types of commands are defined within it. They are:

- **GetRequest:** The command used by the manager to request information from an agent.

- **GetNextRequest:** Also employed by the manager, this command is used if the information desired is contained within a table or array. The manager can use this command repeatedly until the complete contents of the array have been acquired.

- **GetResponse:** The queried agent uses this command to satisfy a request made by the manager.

- **SetRequest:** The manager uses this command to change the value of a parameter within the agent's MIB.

- **Trap:** A special command the agent uses to inform the manager of a certain event.

Figure 12.2 outlines the primary function of the management system—requesting information from an agent. A management system is any computer running the SNMP management software. This system can initiate the GetRequest, GetNextRequest, and the SetRequest operations.

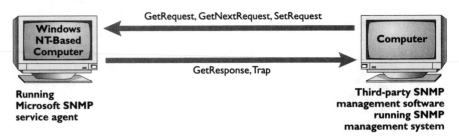

FIGURE 12.2

Management systems and agents

An SNMP agent is any computer running SNMP agent software—most often, a server or router. The chief obligation of an SNMP agent is to perform the tasks initiated by the GetRequest, GetNextRequest, and SetRequest commands, as required by a management system. The Microsoft SNMP service is the SNMP agent software. The only operation initiated by an agent is through the trap command, which alerts management systems to an extraordinary event, such as a password violation.

MIB: The Management Information Base

A MIB describes the objects, or entries, that are to be included in the SNMP agent database. For this reason, SNMP agents are sometimes referred to as MIBs. Objects in a MIB must be defined so that developers of the management station software will know which objects are available, the object names, and their related values. This information is included in a MIB specification.

A MIB records and stores information about the host it is running on. An SNMP manager can request and collect information from an agent's MIB, as well as inspect or alter the objects contained therein. For example, from the SNMP manager, you can examine the number of sessions that have taken place on a certain remote host. The Microsoft SNMP service supports Internet MIB II, LAN Manager MIB II, DHCP MIB, and WINS MIB. Here's a description of each of these tools.

- **Internet MIB II:** A superset of the previous standard, Internet MIB I. It defines 171 objects essential for either fault or configuration analysis. Internet MIB II is defined in RFC 1213.

- **LAN Manager MIB II for Windows NT:** Contains a set of objects specifically designed to support computers running Windows NT. It defines approximately 90 objects including statistical, share, session, user, and logon information. Most LAN Manager MIB II objects have read-only access because of the nonsecure nature of SNMP.

- **DHCP MIB:** Windows NT includes a DHCP MIB that defines objects to monitor DHCP server activity. This MIB (DHCPMIB.dll) is automatically installed when the DHCP server service is installed. It contains approximately 14 objects for monitoring DHCP, such as the number of DHCP discover requests received, the number of declines, and the number of addresses leased out to clients.

- **WINS MIB:** Windows NT includes a WINS MIB that defines objects to monitor WINS server activity. This MIB (WINSMIB.dll) is automatically installed when the WINS server service is installed. It contains approximately 70 objects for monitoring WINS, such as the number of resolution requests successfully processed, the number of resolution requests that failed, and the date and time of the last database replication.

Microsoft's SNMP Service

In order to take advantage of Microsoft's NT SNMP services, you must have an SNMP manager that can monitor and display SNMP alerts. The Microsoft SNMP service provides SNMP agent services to any TCP/IP host that's running the SNMP management software. Microsoft SNMP service can run on Windows NT, as long as it's also running TCP/IP.

There are two methods that the Microsoft SNMP service management software can employ to collect information about devices. One way is to have devices send alerts to an SNMP manager, or to any other manager within the community. Another method is to have the SNMP manager poll devices every few seconds, minutes, or hours.

By adding the public community to the alert list, any management station within the community will receive alerts and be able to make changes to the configuration.

Microsoft's SNMP service can use a HOSTS file, DNS, WINS, or the LMHOSTS file to perform host name to IP address translation, and to identify which hosts it will report information to and receive requests from. It also enables counters for monitoring TCP/IP performance using Performance Monitor.

Planning and Preparing for Implementation

If you plan on using the SNMP service with a third-party manager, you'll need to:

- Record the IP addresses and host names of participating hosts.

- Add host name/IP address mappings to the appropriate name resolution resource.

- Identify the third-party management systems and Microsoft SNMP agents.

Host Names and IP Addresses: When installing the SNMP service on an agent, make sure you have the host names or IP addresses of the hosts to which your system will send SNMP traps, as well as those to which your system will respond regarding SNMP requests.

Host Name Resolution: The SNMP service uses normal Windows NT host name resolution methods to resolve host names to IP addresses. If you use host names, be sure to add all host name/IP address mappings of the participating computers to the appropriate resolution sources (such as the HOSTS file, DNS, WINS, or the LMHOSTS file).

Management Systems and Agents: A management system is any computer running the TCP/IP transport and third-party SNMP manager software. The management system requests information from an agent. To use the Microsoft SNMP service, you need at least one management system.

An SNMP agent is a Windows NT-based computer running the Microsoft SNMP service. The agent provides the management system with requested status information and reports any extraordinary events.

Defining SNMP Communities

Before you install SNMP, you'll need to define an SNMP community. A community is a group to which hosts running the SNMP service belong. A community parameter is simply the name of that group by which SNMP communities are identified. The use of a community name provides some security and context for agents receiving requests and initiating traps, and does the same for management systems and their tasks. An SNMP agent won't respond to a request from a management system outside its configured community, but an agent can be a member of multiple communities at the same time. This allows for communications with SNMP managers from different communities. Figure 12.3 illustrates how a community name is used.

In Figure 12.3, Host A can receive and send messages to Host Manager B because they are both members of the public 1 community. Host C through Host E can receive and send messages to Manager F because all these machines are members of the default public community.

SNMP Installation and Configuration

Okay, now we're going to talk about installing and configuring the SNMP service on a Windows NT computer. If you want to monitor TCP/IP with Performance Monitor, you'll need to install the SNMP service. Also, if you want to monitor a Windows NT-based computer with a third-party application, you'll need to configure the SNMP service.

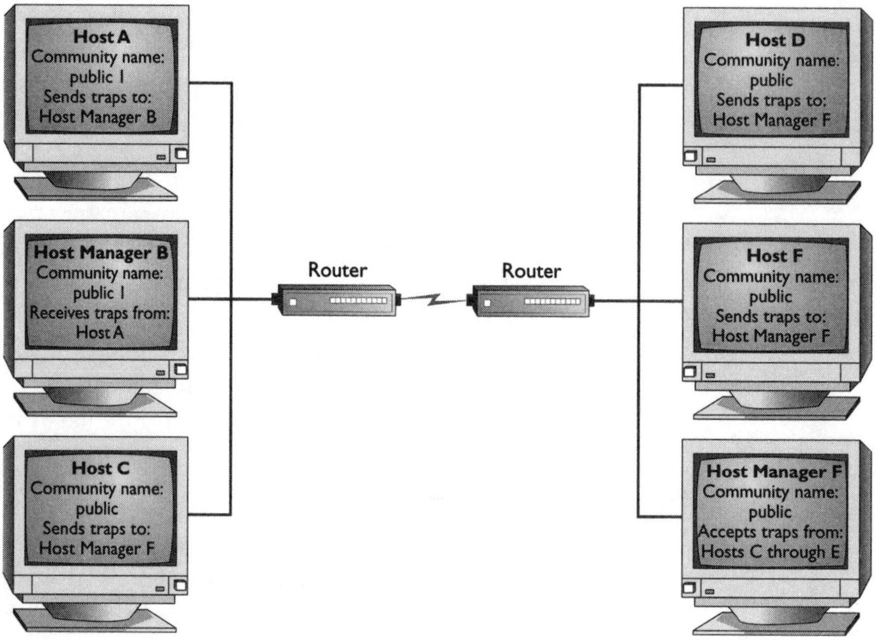

FIGURE 12.3

How an SNMP community is used to group hosts

SNMP Service Security

There is minimal-level security available with SNMP, inherent in the processes of management and agent systems when initiating and receiving requests and traps. However, don't allow yourself to be lulled into a false sense of security! If your SNMP-managed network is connected to the Internet, or any public internetwork, a firewall should be in place to prevent intrusion from outside SNMP management consoles. When installing SNMP, keep in mind the following security configuration options:

- **Send Authentication Trap:** Used if you want the computer to send a trap for a failed authentication. When the SNMP service receives a management request that does not contain or match the community name, the SNMP service can send a trap to the trap destination.

- **Accepted Community Names:** This specifies community names from which the computer will accept requests. A host must belong to a community that appears in this list for the SNMP service to accept requests from that host. Typically, all hosts belong to the community named public.

- **Accept SNMP Packets from Any Host:** By default, this option is checked. Accepts packets from everybody.

- **Only Accept SNMP Packets from These Hosts:** If checked, the computer should only accept packets from hosts that have specific IP or IPX addresses, plus the host name that's in the associated box.

Installing and Configuring the SNMP service

1. From the Control Panel, double-click on Network.

2. From the Network Settings dialog box, click on Add.

3. Click on the Services tab and then click on Add. The Select Network Services dialog box appears.

4. Click on SNMP Service and then click on OK.

5. Type the path to the distribution files.

6. After the appropriate files are copied to the computer, the SNMP Service Configuration dialog box appears. Configure the following parameters:

   - **Send Trap with Community Names:** The community name to which traps are sent. A management system must belong to the designated community to receive traps. The default community name for all hosts is public.

   - **The Trap Destination:** The trap destination consists of names or IP addresses of hosts to which you want the SNMP service to send traps. If you use a host name, make sure it can be resolved so the SNMP service can map it to the IP address.

SNMP Agent Services

A Simple Network Management Protocol agent is a database of information about a device, and/or its environment, which is installed on the device designated for management or monitoring. Data contained in the agent database depends on the specific function of the devices that are to be monitored. The agent in the managed device doesn't volunteer information, because doing so would take away from its primary function. The only exception to this rule is that an agent will send an alarm to the management station if a critical threshold is crossed. Microsoft SNMP agent services give a Windows NT-based computer the ability to provide an SNMP management system with the information on activity that occurs at different layers of the Internet Protocol suite.

Assuming that TCP/IP and SNMP have already been installed, click on SNMP Properties to access a menu, which is broken down into three parts: Agent, Traps, and Security. The SNMP configuration that you'd enter is the same information that you would under Windows NT 3.5x.

Under Windows NT 3.5x, SNMP is added by selecting Add Software and TCP/IP and Related Components rather than by adding it under services.

To configure the SNMP Agent, select the Agent tab on the Microsoft SNMP Properties page. Under Service, select the type of service to report. Select all boxes that indicate network capabilities provided by your NT computer. SNMP must have this information to manage the enabled services. Notice that Applications, Internet, and End-to-End are default services.

The SNMP agent generates trap messages that are then sent to an SNMP management console—the trap destination. Trap destinations are identified by a computer name, IP address, or IPX address of the "host of hosts" on the network to which you want the trap messages sent. The trap destination must be a host that is running an SNMP manager program. To configure the trap destination on a Windows NT 4 computer, use the Traps tab in the Microsoft SNMP Properties page to enter the host name, IP address, or the IPX address of the computer(s) running an SNMP manager program.

Community names provide a rudimentary security scheme for the SNMP service. You can add and delete community names by using the Security tab on the Microsoft SNMP Properties dialog box. You can also filter the type of packets that the computer will accept. You must configure the SNMP service with at least one community name. The default name is public.

Configuring the SNMP Agent

I. In the Microsoft SNMP Properties dialog box, click on the Agent tab.

2. Type in the Contact and Location Information on the Agent page.

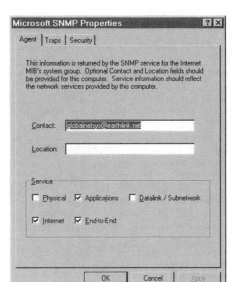

3. Choose the Service types, or accept the defaults.

4. Choose the Traps tab.

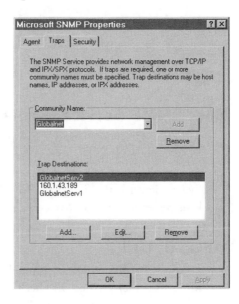

5. Add a new Community Name if needed; Public is the default.

6. Add the Trap Destination host or hosts.

7. Choose the Security tab.

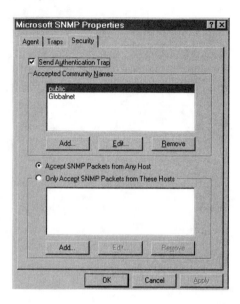

8. Add any new names under Accepted Community Names, then choose Add.

9. Click on OK.

10. Restart the computer.

How to Spot SNMP Service Errors

After SNMP is installed, you can then view SNMP errors from the Event Viewer system log. The Event Viewer will record all events occurring with the system components of SNMP, even failure of the SNMP service starting. The Event Viewer is the first place you should look to identify any possible problems relevant to the SNMP service.

The SNMPUTIL Utility

The SNMPUTIL.exe utility is available only in the Windows NT 4 Resource Kit. This utility verifies whether the SNMP service has been correctly configured to communicate with SNMP management stations. SNMPUTIL makes the same SNMP calls as an SNMP management station, as shown in the following example:

```
snmputil command agent community object_identifier_(OID)
```

The valid commands are:

get   Get the value of the requested object identifier

getnext   Get the value of the next object following the specified object identifier

walk   Step through (walk) the MIB branch specified by the object identifier

If you wanted to determine the number of DHCP server addresses leased by a DHCP server name MAXamillion in the public community, you would issue the following command:

```
snmputil getnext MAXamillion Public .1.3.6.1.4.1.311.1.3.2.1.1.1
```

The command will respond with the OID and counter value for the object ID in question, which is the number of IP leases that are issued.

How SNMP Works

Figure 12.4 illustrates how SNMP works and responds to a third-party management system request:

1. A third-party SNMP management system running on Host 1 requests the number of active sessions from a Microsoft SNMP agent. The SNMP management system uses the host name to send the request. The request is passed by the application to socket (UDP port) 161. The host name is resolved by using the HOSTS file, DNS, WINS, B-node broadcast, or LMHOSTS.

2. An SNMP message that contains the GetRequest command is formed to discover the number of active sessions with the community name of public.

3. The Host 2 Microsoft SNMP agent receives the message and verifies the community name, as well as if the message has been corrupted in any way. If the community name is wrong, or the message got corrupted somewhere along the way, it's discarded. If the message is valid, and the community name is correct, then the host verifies the IP address to make sure the address is authorized to accept messages from the management station.

4. An SNMP message stating that eight sessions are active is then sent back to the SNMP manager.

FIGURE 12.4

How SNMP works

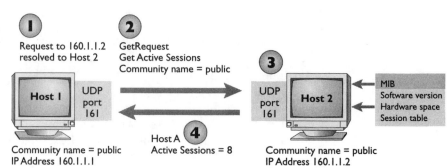

Continuing on to the next chapter, let's take a look at building our own Web site.

CHAPTER

13

Building Your Web Site

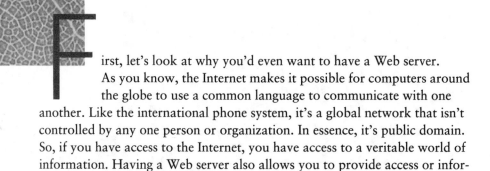

irst, let's look at why you'd even want to have a Web server. As you know, the Internet makes it possible for computers around the globe to use a common language to communicate with one another. Like the international phone system, it's a global network that isn't controlled by any one person or organization. In essence, it's public domain. So, if you have access to the Internet, you have access to a veritable world of information. Having a Web server also allows you to provide access or information to Internet users all over the world.

If you've ever used the Internet (if you haven't—you soon will), you've noticed the dizzying array of information. And you can use that Web server for:

- **Advertising and marketing:** Post a Web site on the Internet containing your corporate profile, job postings, marketing information—even a company newsletter.

- **Convenience and easy consumer access:** Publish a product catalog and take orders right over the Internet.

- **Making contacts and sharing information:** Provide remote users with access to your corporate database.

- **Management:** Monitor your company's Internet services.

In this chapter, we'll go over two ways you can build a Web site with NT: FrontPage 97 and Internet Information Server.

FrontPage

To create an Internet site that other Web surfers can see, you must generate that site in something known as HyperText Markup Language (HTML). Up 'til now, if you wanted to create your own Web site, you had to become an expert at using HTML.

For those of us not donning pocket protectors on a regular basis, Microsoft has happily changed that imposing fact with a very cool product called FrontPage. It allows mere mortals to create fabulous Web sites! Even if you've played with HTML some, and are fairly comfortable with it, Microsoft Front-Page opens up whole new vistas, and affords delicious new freedoms in creating sophisticated Web sites.

So, what do you need to run Microsoft FrontPage anyway? Well, first you need to have access to the Internet via an Internet service provider and possess an Internet browser. Next, you'll obviously need to get your paws on FrontPage. Microsoft Internet Explorer is bundled with the FrontPage 97 Bonus Pack, and you can use Internet Explorer to help you find and sign up with an Internet service provider. Netscape Navigator also works beautifully with FrontPage.

What's in FrontPage 97?

The Microsoft FrontPage 97 Bonus Pack is a suite of five programs (see Figure 13.1):

- Microsoft FrontPage 97

- Microsoft Image Composer

- Microsoft Personal Web Server

- Internet Explorer

- Web Publishing Wizard

FIGURE 13.1

The FrontPage
Bonus Pack

Of these, FrontPage 97, the actual program that lets you create a Web site, is clearly required, and even though Microsoft Image Composer is optional, it's a very powerful graphics package that lets your creative energies fly. With it, you can design all kinds of images that'll greatly enhance your Web site.

Microsoft Personal Web Server allows you to test your Web site on your own computer before you contract with a site provider to place your creation on the Web. It's also handy for editing your site offline. You can't use the Personal Web Server on Windows NT; only on Windows 95. If you try it on NT, you'll be met with a grayed out button, bringing things to a grinding halt.

Internet Explorer comes with the FrontPage 97 bundle, and even if you use Netscape Navigator 3.0 or higher, Internet Explorer has some features that do come in handy for testing your site. The Web Publishing Wizard lets you publish your Web site on a server that doesn't actually support the features that FrontPage 97 allows you to use.

Microsoft FrontPage 97 comes with everything you need to create a Web site. The only thing not provided is an Internet service provider (maybe in the next version) to rent the space for your pages.

Installing FrontPage 97

1. Insert the FrontPage 97 CD into your NT Server.

2. If it doesn't start by itself, choose Start ➤ Run, and then browse to the CD drive and double-click on the Setup icon (see Figure 13.2).

FIGURE 13.2

Beginning the installation process

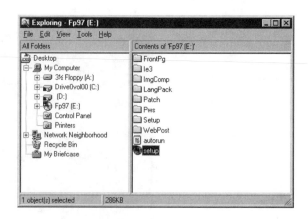

3. Click to select FrontPage 97 installation. If you already have any components installed, a message appears, "Already Installed," next to the buttons.

4. Enter your Name and Company, as shown in Figure 13.3 and click on Next.

FIGURE 13.3

Registering with
FrontPage

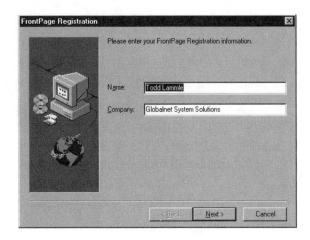

5. Enter your CD key.

6. Click on Next after specifying the directory in which to install FrontPage 97.

7. Then choose Typical or Custom setup, as shown in Figure 13.4.

FIGURE 13.4

Choosing your preferred
Setup type

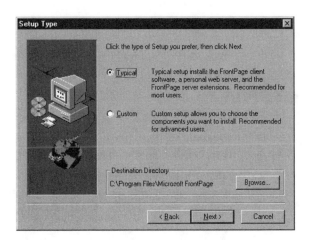

8. Click on Next twice. The files are then copied to your hard drive.

9. Put a password in the Password text box (see Figure 13.5) and re-enter it in the Confirm Password text box. Then choose OK.

F I G U R E   13.5

Use this dialog box to set
your password.

10. Click on Finish and choose to Start FrontPage Explorer Now.

11. FrontPage will start and then try to determine your TCP/IP address and host name. As shown in Figure 13.6, the program warns you that it may take a while.

F I G U R E   13.6

Now may be a good time
for a coffee break.

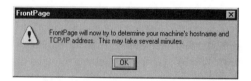

After determining your TCP/IP address and host name, FrontPage is ready to get to work after one more thing—testing TCP/IP.

The TCP/IP Test

FrontPage 97 checks and, if necessary, installs TCP/IP connectivity. Passing the test doesn't actually mean that your system is directly connected to the Internet, but only that connective capability exists. If you're at a stand-alone workstation, but plan on copying your Web page to a server, the TCP/IP protocol on your system simulates connecting with the Internet and lets you work as if you were actually on the Internet itself.

To run the TCP/IP test:

I. Select Start ➤ Run ➤ Browse. Go to the folder where you installed Microsoft FrontPage.

2. Click on the Bin folder.

3. Click on the Tcptest icon.

4. Click on the Start Test button.

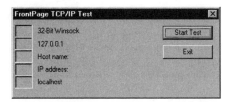

5. When the test acknowledges that your machine is compatible with TCP/IP, it will look like the following box:

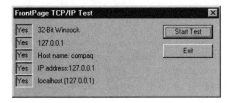

After the test is successful, you're ready to roll.

Creating Your Web Page

One of the things that makes FrontPage powerful is the FrontPage Explorer. It keeps all your connections straight, and when the time comes to upload the Web site to an Internet service provider, it ensures all your files get to their final location in one piece.

To create a new Web site with FrontPage Explorer:

I. Select Start ➤ Programs ➤ Microsoft FrontPage.

2. Click on the Blank FrontPage Web (see Figure 13.7), and then click on OK.

FIGURE 13.7

You have several options for creating a new Web page.

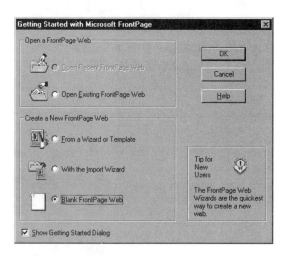

3. Leave the Web Server or File Location at its default (ours is `compaq .cts.edu`, as you can see in Figure 13.8), and then enter a name for your Web site (we've used "TeachGlobal"). The name can be up to 256 characters in length. Click on OK.

FIGURE 13.8

Set your Web page address and name here.

4. In the Name and Password Required dialog box, enter your Name and Password and click on OK.

If you didn't assign a password during the installation process, you can do so now by following the steps here:

1. Select Start ➤ Run ➤ Browse.

2. Launch the program fpsrvwin.exe, found in the folder where FrontPage is installed in the Bin directory.

3. Click on the Security button, as shown in Figure 13.9.

FIGURE 13.9

Assigning a password

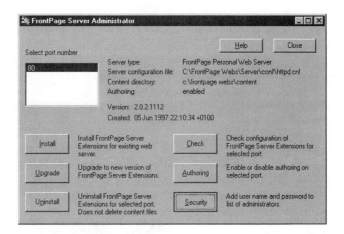

4. Enter your name in the Name box, and type a password in the Password box (see Figure 13.10). Click on OK.

FIGURE 13.10

Enter your name and password here.

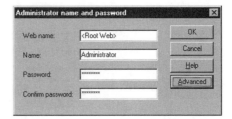

Using FrontPage Explorer to Examine a Web Site

1. Click on the Hyperlink View button in the FrontPage Explorer, shown in Figure 13.11. This window shows links between pages in your Web site, but don't worry if there are none there. Remember, so far we don't have any.

FIGURE 13.11

Hyperlink view

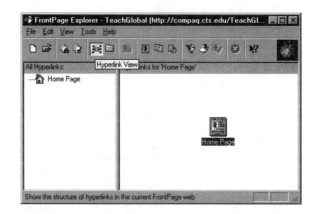

2. Click on the Folder View button to switch to the FrontPage Explorer Folder view shown in Figure 13.12.

FIGURE 13.12

Folder view

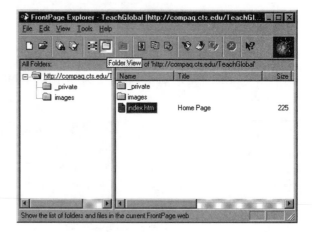

Our new Web site already has two folders. FrontPage automatically created these for us, and stores necessary files as we construct our Web site. Index.htm is our Web site home page, now blank and waiting for us.

HTML files have the filename extension .htm (or .html).

FrontPage asks something of you…when you work on a Web page, you must always open the Web site first in the Explorer.

Your Web Page doesn't have anything in it yet. Change that by opening the blank page from FrontPage Explorer. Just double-click on the file, either in Folder view or in Hyperlink view.

Keeping FrontPage Explorer open at all times ensures the integrity of your Web site.

Adding a Heading with FrontPage Explorer

1. Double-click on the file, either in Folder view or in Hyperlink view.

2. Type in a heading. You can set the style for your heading here, as shown in Figure 13.13, by changing the font and size or adding attributes such as bold or italic text.

FIGURE 13.13

Setting the style for your Web page heading

3. You can also use the built-in style formats. Highlight the text you just typed. Pull down the Change Style list from the Formatting toolbar (see Figure 13.14) in FrontPage Editor, and select Heading 1.

Adding Graphics to Your Web Page

To add graphics into FrontPage Editor, copy them over from the Windows 95/NT Clipboard like you would from any Microsoft Office application. FrontPage even supplies clip art for you. Here's how to add figures from it:

1. Decide where you want the graphic to appear on your page, place your cursor there, and select Insert ➤ Image.

2. Click on the Clip Art tab in the Image dialog box.

3. Pick from the icons in the category list, like in Figure 13.15, and double-click on the clip art you like. The graphic will then be placed on your Web page.

4. You cut-and-paste text by highlighting it, and then doing a right-mouse click that'll give you a menu. From it, choose Copy. Next, go to the Web page, put your cursor where you want the text, then do another right-mouse click. That'll give you another menu from which you choose Paste.

FIGURE 13.15

The Category list

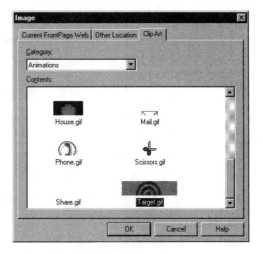

The Ubiquitous Save-Your-Work Thing

FrontPage Web pages are saved with a filename and a title that are used to identify the page in the Web site URL (Uniform Resource Locator). The URL is the address visitors will use to get to your Web site on the World Wide Web. All Web Pages need unique filenames, but one filename is special—the one named index.htm—the page that visitors to your site go to by default when they type in your URL. The index.htm file is your Web site home page.

Web pages also have titles, and these can be longer and more descriptive than page filenames. Filenames must have an .htm filename extension.

Okay. So you've got a new page, and you want to name it. When you do, you'll be prompted to enter both a page title and a page name. Enter the title first—FrontPage, ever helpful, comes up with the closest possible filename for you.

Page salvation in FrontPage Editor:

- We know you probably guessed on this one. That's right—click on the Save button on the toolbar! You won't be prompted to enter a filename or title for your page because that filename (index.htm) was already assigned in FrontPage Explorer where you opened the file. The title "home page" was also already created for you.

- If you put a graphic on a page that's not yet part of the Web site, FrontPage will prompt you to save it as part of the site. FrontPage Explorer is just doing its thing dutifully in the background. Click on OK when it prompts you to save image files.

The Great Unveiling

Remember when we peeked at our site before in FrontPage Explorer? It had only two files, and no links at all between them. Let's see what's there now after the changes we've made.

To view links in FrontPage Explorer:

- Shift to Explorer by clicking on the FrontPage Explorer button in the Explorer toolbar, then click on the yellow Hyperlink View button in the same toolbar. Hyperlink view will then show you the new link between the graphic image and the HTML page.

- If you want to hide graphic files, click on the Links to Images button in the FrontPage Explorer toolbar. Why would you want to *hide* them after you went to all that trouble to create them? Well, sometimes sites get humongous and difficult to administrate. Hiding all those pretty pictures can help ease your administrative pains.

Okay—it's again test time for your site. If you're using Windows 95, you can use the Personal Server; if you're using NT Server, you can't. With the latter, you must install the Internet Information Service (IIS).

Place your FrontPage 97 home page into the wwwroot folder and break the champagne bottle on your monitor. Away you go.

What if you're contracted with a service provider, and you want to edit your page from home, or what if the IIS server holding the home page is at an ISP? How do you remotely edit your Web page?

Editing Your FrontPage 97 Home Page Site Remotely

The minute you copy your Web site over to its new home on the WWW server, you have two copies of it: one on the server, and one on your local hard drive. It's slower to edit your site online than if you were at the server using FrontPage. Worse—you could find yourself ponying up big time if you pay by the hour for Internet access, which can get pretty costly. It's that ubiquitous time/money issue again!

But there's a way around this: Do all your editing using the copy of your site, making all your changes before logging onto the Internet. Then, just recopy your site to your Web site provider. Recopying is an especially wonderful idea if you have input forms linked to other pages—they'll get replaced automatically when you copy over your site!

The other option: Log onto the Internet using your Internet access provider and then reopen your site in FrontPage Explorer. A good tip on keeping your online clock from strangling your wallet is to make a list of what you want to change before you start editing.

To edit your Web site while logged onto the Internet:

1. Log onto the Internet, and then open your browser.

2. Select File ➤ Open FrontPage Web from the FrontPage Explorer menu.

3. Pull down the Web Server list in the Open FrontPage Web dialog box and select the Web on which your site is located.

4. Enter your Name and Password.

5. Click on OK.

Patience. This could take a while.

6. Edit your pages.

7. Save the changes.

Next, we'll take a look at how to build an Internet server with NT so we can place the Web page we just built onto the Internet.

Internet Information Service

The Internet Information Server (IIS) allows you to publish information on the Internet or on an intranet. It transmits information using HyperText Transfer Protocol (HTTP). You can also configure FTP and Gopher services for the server. FTP allows users to transfer files between their site and your site. Gopher services use menus to locate documents and link to other computers and services, but in recent years Gopher has been overtaken by HTTP. In this section, we'll show you how to install and configure your Internet server to take advantage of this bounty of information.

Before Installing Internet Information Server

If your server has other versions of World Wide Web, Gopher, or FTP installed, disable them before you install the IIS. See the documentation provided with each service on how to do that.

You need to be logged onto the server with administrator permissions before you can install the IIS. You also need administrative permissions to configure services with the Internet Service Manager.

Installation

While installing NT, you can install the IIS by following the prompts during installation. If you don't do it then, you can install the IIS in either of two ways. One way is to start the Installation Wizard by clicking on the Install Internet Information Server icon on the desktop after you log into NT. If this icon doesn't exist, you can also start the Wizard by clicking on the Network icon in the Control Panel, clicking on the Services tab, clicking on Add, and selecting Microsoft Internet Information Server 2. Click on OK, and the Installation Wizard will then start. You'll be asked the same questions by the Wizard no matter how you choose to start the installation. This will load IIS version 2 by default. Version 3 is located on the Service Pack 2 CD, or you can pull it down from the Microsoft Web server. In this section, we will upgrade our existing IIS version 2 server to IIS version 3. Then, we'll delete the installation and install IIS version 4. But first, let's install using version 2 from the NT Server CD.

Initially, you'll be asked what drive and folder the files are in. These files can be found in the <platform> directory on your Windows NT Server 4 CD, where <platform> is I386 (for Intel-based computers), Alpha, MIPS, or PPC (PowerPC).

Type in the path to the files if it is different from that shown, and click on OK. You'll be given several options of Internet services to install, as you see in Figure 13.16.

The services shown in this dialog box include the following:

- **Internet Service Manager** allows you, as an administrator, to keep track of Internet use and services, a necessary ingredient in a well-managed system.

- **World Wide Web Service** allows you to maintain a Web site on the World Wide Web.

- **WWW Service Samples** installs sample images, HyperText Markup Language (HTML) files, sound clips, and movie clips for you to view.

- **Internet Service Manager (HTML)** works exactly the same way as the Internet Service Manager, but as an administrator, you can access the Manager from a remote site across the Internet.

FIGURE 13.16

Available Internet
services to install

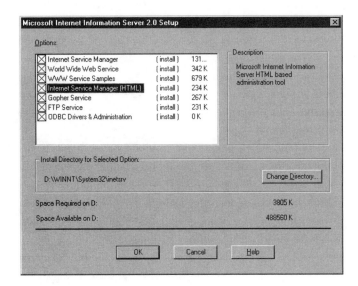

- **Gopher Service** is practically a precursor to the Internet. Gopher service has mostly been taken over by the World Wide Web.

- **FTP Service** is commonly used to allow users to download large files and to give users access to archives.

- **ODBC Drivers and Administration** installs Open Database Connectivity (ODBC) drivers. In order to log onto ODBC files and to enable ODBC access from the WWW Service, you'll need to install these drivers.

If you want to provide access to databases using the Microsoft Internet Information Server, you'll need to configure the ODBC drivers by opening the ODBC applet in the Control Panel. You'll probably receive an error message stating that components are in use. Close all of the applications and services that use ODBC before you continue.

Click on Change Directory if you wish to change their file location. When you have chosen the services you want and approved of their file location, click on OK.

Next, you'll see the dialog box in Figure 13.17. You're asked which folders or directories you'd like to use as the default when publishing information. If you wish to change that default, click on the Browse button to select the directory you want instead, or type in the directory path.

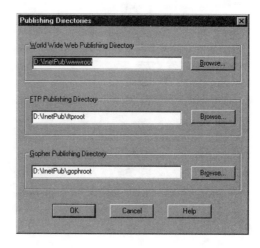

FIGURE 13.17

Publishing Directories
dialog box

If you previously chose to install the ODBC Drivers and Administration, you'll see the dialog box shown in Figure 13.18. In this example, we have only the SQL Server driver available.

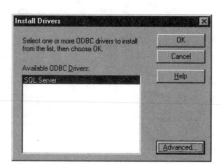

FIGURE 13.18

Installing ODBC drivers

Click on Advanced to see the Advanced Installation Options screen, shown in Figure 13.19.

FIGURE 13.19

Advanced Installation
Options screen

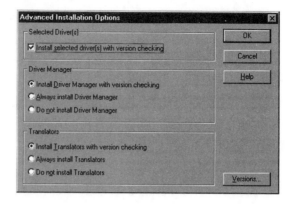

Most users won't have to make changes to this dialog box, but double-check the three choices presented:

- If the Selected Driver(s) box is checked, version checking is turned on. You'll be asked to verify the installation of drivers that have the same or earlier version numbers than drivers that are currently installed. If this box isn't checked, any drivers you select will be installed, and you won't be required to confirm their installation. If this is the first time a driver has been installed, checking this box will have no effect.

- The Driver Manager radio buttons indicate whether the ODBC Driver Manager should be installed. If it is installed, the Driver Manager icon can be found in the Control Panel.

  Install Driver Manager with Version Checking: The ODBC Driver Manager will be installed only if it is the same or newer than the existing driver manager.

  Always Install Driver Manager: The driver manager will always be installed even if it is older than the current version.

  Do Not Install Driver Manager: The driver manager is not installed regardless of what version you are using.

- The Translators radio buttons can be checked to install the translator groups. Note that translators are always installed in a group. These options are the same as the options under Driver Manager.

Click on OK when you're done. The Internet Information Server should now be installed correctly.

Configuring the Internet Information Server

Now that you have the Internet Information Services installed, it's time to configure them. In the Program menu, under the Start button, you'll now see the Microsoft Internet Server (common) folder icon. This folder has four services, all shown as icons:

- **Internet Information Services Setup:** Adds or removes Internet services.

- **Internet Service Manager:** Manages the Internet services you've installed.

- **Key Manager:** Security measures built into NT that you can use to help transfer data securely over the Internet.

- **Product Documentation:** Instructions on how to set up and use these services. These instructions are written in HTML (located in the INETSRV folder on the Windows NT Server 4 CD). When you click on this option, Microsoft Internet Explorer will load the documents as a Web page.

Of these services, we'll be discussing only the Internet Service Manager. It's the one you'll probably be using the most.

Internet Service Manager

To configure and track your Internet Services, open the Internet Service Manager, and you'll see a list of the NT Servers and NT Workstations which have Internet Services attached to them. In Figure 13.20, the server WHITESTAR is running these Internet Services: WWW, Gopher, and FTP.

FIGURE 13.20

Internet Service Manager's list of installed Internet Services

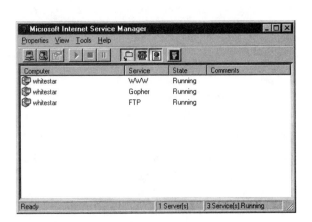

WWW Service Properties

Double-click on the WWW Service to see its properties. Here, you'll be able to maintain the WWW service by changing anonymous user accounts, directories, and log files. The FTP and Gopher services, however, have slightly different properties which we'll discuss later in this chapter.

Service Tab

This page allows you to change connections to the Internet. Figure 13.21 shows the Service tab for the WWW service.

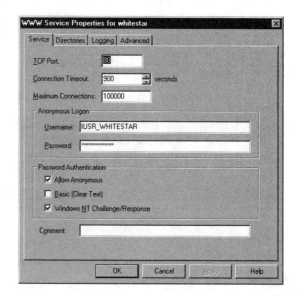

The properties you can change for the WWW service include the following:

- **TCP Port:** Indicates which port the WWW service is using. The default is 80. You'll have to restart the computer if you want to use a different port number.

- **Connection Timeout:** The length of time allowed before closing the connection of an inactive user.

- **Maximum Connections:** The maximum number of computers on the network allowed to use this service at any one time.

- **Anonymous Logon:** Creates the NT user account permissions of all anonymous connections. By default, the user name IUSR_*computername* is created and used by the Internet Information Server. Also by default, this account is given the Log on Locally user right. If you want to grant anonymous user logon access to your server, the account must have this right. The same goes for specific users. If you want to give a specific user access, you must assign that user the right to log on locally. Also, if the IIS is installed on a stand-alone server, IUSR_*computername* will be a local account. Other computers in the domain won't be able to validate user accounts that have been created on the stand-alone server. If you want to access information on other servers in the domain using the IIS service on a stand-alone server, you must change the IUSR_*computername* account to an account with domainwide permissions.

- **Password Authentication:** Initiates the authentication process if you choose not to allow anonymous access or if the remote client requests authentication. At least one of the following options must be selected.

  Allow Anonymous allows access through an anonymous logon user name, IUSR_*computername*, and password. If this box isn't checked, all anonymous user logins will be rejected. When logging in anonymously, users don't actually use this user name and password—they're only used internally within NT. Essentially, it'll appear as if the user name and password have been bypassed. You'd use this option if you didn't want to restrict user access to your Web site.

If the Allow Anonymous option is selected and either the Basic (Clear Text) or Windows NT Challenge/Response option is also selected, users will be prompted to enter a user name and password when trying to access resources located on a Windows NT File System (NTFS) drive that does not allow the ISR_*computername* account.

If only the Allow Anonymous box has been checked and the Basic and Windows NT Challenge/Response boxes have been cleared, all requests to the server are processed as Anonymous. This means that even if the user supplies a valid user name and a password, IIS will use the anonymous user name instead.

Basic (Clear Text) means Basic authentication is encoded, and is often used in combination with Secure Sockets Layer (SSL) to encrypt user names and passwords prior to transmission. Most Internet browsers support this type of authentication. If not used in combination with SSL, Basic authentication sends passwords in unencrypted text. By default, this box isn't checked for security reasons.

Windows NT Challenge/Response means passwords and user names are automatically encrypted. Browsers such as Internet Explorer 2 and above support this type of authentication.

- **Comment:** You may type in a comment that'll be displayed in the Internet Service Manager Report view.

The Anonymous account is assigned a random password and must stay the same in both the User Manager and the Internet Information Server. You can change the password, but you *must* remember to change it in both places, making sure the passwords match. If they don't, no one will have access to your Internet server—not even the administrator. Following that train of thought, make sure the Password Never Expires and the User Cannot Change Password boxes are checked. These boxes are in the user properties dialog box, which can be found by double-clicking the IUSR_*computername* account in the user manager for domains. If they're not checked, the next user who logs onto the server can change the password. Should this occur, it won't match the password on the IIS. And, as we just said, if the passwords don't match, no one will have access to the server—a very bad thing. Also, remember that this account won't allow you to use a blank password.

Directories Tab

Click on the Directories tab in the WWW Services Properties dialog box to maintain directories and set their permissions. Figure 13.22 shows the directory we chose when installing the WWW service.

Clicking on the Enable Default Document box and specifying a document causes a default document to be displayed if a user doesn't specify a particular file. For example, if you type **http://www.mmco.com**, you'll download the TechTeach International home page. The actual filename is default.htm, but since the Enable Default Document box is checked, it's not necessary to type the name of the file.

This is helpful especially if you can't remember the name of the site's home page. If this box isn't checked, and Directory Browsing Allowed is enabled, users will be able to navigate through your directory structure.

A bit of advice. It's a bad idea to enable directory browsing—period. If you want to have users nosing through your directory structure, use FTP instead. It allows users to download files faster and is a little more secure. You can monitor users' use of your site and permit or deny use to specific users—a feature not available in the WWW service.

Directory permissions can be set by highlighting the directory and then clicking on Edit Properties; you'll see the dialog box shown in Figure 13.23. You can make a directory private by clicking on the Virtual Directory radio button and adding the user's name and putting in the user's password.

You can also set permissions for the directory:

- **Read** permission is needed for all of the content directories. If you don't provide Read access permissions, no one will be able to view or download the files located in those directories.

FIGURE 13.23

WWW Directory
Properties dialog box

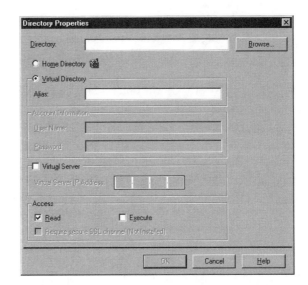

- **Execute** permission is needed for directories containing API applications, scripts, and programs. Make sure any directory given Execute permission is not also marked Read—this will prevent users from viewing interactive executable files.

Back on the Directories tab, click on the Add button, and you'll be able to add more new directories. These additional directories are called *Virtual* directories. If the directory is listed using a Universal Naming Convention (UNC), you can enter a user name and password that has permission to access the directory if you wish to restrict access to the share.

Many Web sites have a public/private feature in that they allow the general public to access portions of their site and allow specific users or "members" to access restricted areas. An example of this type of site would be *e-zines,* online magazines such as *ComputerWorld* that provide users with up-to-date information, news, etc., just as the paper version of the magazine would. Some charge their subscribers a fee to access their Web site and, in return, the subscribers receive a password that gives them access to the restricted areas of the site.

For example, say you have a directory on your Internet server containing some documents that you'd like only a certain group of users to access. You can do this by sharing the directory and assigning a password to the directory; only users who know the password can have access. Now, you have a choice here: You can either assign a universal account and password to the directory, or you can let each user use his or her unique user name. Both options have their advantages and disadvantages. Assigning one user name and account to all users who want to access a directory is less work for the administrator. However, assigning only one user name creates a problem when an unauthorized user discovers the user name and password. On the other hand, assigning individual accounts to each directory saves you the headache of unauthorized access, but it creates another type of headache if you have fifty users that you have to create access rights for (as you'll soon see). One thing to remember, however, is that any account you use will have to be entered into the User Manager for Domains and the IIS.

Adding a single user account is simple enough. All you have to do is provide a Universal Naming Convention. For example, suppose you want to give users restricted access to /wwwroot/samples. You would then share the Samples directory, giving it a UNC named //whitestar/samples. Once you've provided the UNC, the Account Information section of the Directory Permissions dialog box will light up. Here, you'll provide a user name and password. It's that simple. Just make sure you also go to the User Manager for Domains and change the user rights for this account to Log On Locally.

Okay, but what if you want to give individual users access to a given directory? That, my friends, is going to be a lot of work—there's no way around it. Let's say that you have three users, Lisa, Donna, and Paul, who you'd like to have access to a specific restricted directory on the server, but you don't trust them enough to let them share a user name to access that directory. Since the IIS Manager only allows one account to access a directory, how would you go about giving each user their own access rights to the directory?

The answer's easy enough, but it's a bit tedious: Give each user their own directory share. If you have a large number of users, this could definitely take some time. Open Windows NT Explorer and locate the directory you want to share. In the pull-down menu, click on File, then Sharing. If the file isn't shared, give the directory a share name. The name must be unique to the server. If a share already exists, click on New Share and enter a new name. This name won't replace the old one. Instead, the directory will have two share names.

Now that you've named the share, you'll need to restrict access to it. Click on the Permissions button. You'll see the dialog box shown in Figure 13.24. Click on Add and then Show Users to include all user accounts assigned to the domain. Double-click on the user to whom you want to assign access, and the user name will appear at the bottom of the screen. Click on the pull-down list at the bottom of the screen to choose the kind of permission you want this user to have. Also, you'll have to deny everyone else access to this share. Follow this process for each of the users to whom you want to assign access.

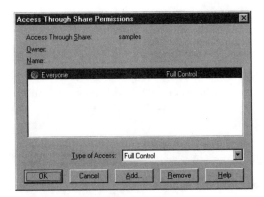

Once you have created a share for each user, you must then add the users' names and shares to the IIS. Go to the WWW Directory tab and click on Add in the IIS Manager (Figure 13.20). Enter the UNC share name for the first user, which in our example was Lisa. We named her share **//whitestar/ Lisasamples.** The Account Information Section will then light up, allowing us to enter her user information. Click on OK, and Lisa will now be able to access the Samples directory with her user ID. The same can be done for each user. Virtual directories will not show up in a directory listing, so users must know a virtual directory's alias and type in its URL address or click on a link on an HTML page to access them. An *alias* is a subdirectory name used to access information in the virtual directory. Essentially, an alias is a one-word token that's used in place of a directory path. If they're not specified by the administrator, alias names are automatically generated by the Internet Service Manager.

This can be better explained with an example. Let's say that we define the following two directories for the WWW service:

```
C:\wwwroot <home directory>
C:\salesdata alias = sales
```

Suppose that C:\wwwroot contains the subdirectory "news" and D:\salesdata contains the subdirectory "july." This means that the following URLs can be requested by a WWW user:

```
http://www.abcd.com
http://www.abcd.com/news/stock.htm
http://www.abcd.com/sales/yearly.htm
http://www.abcd.com/sales/july/top10.htm
```

Logging Tab

You log events by clicking on Enable Logging in the Logging tab, shown in Figure 13.25. You can log to the SQL/ODBC database or log to a file. Fill in the location you want for the log file and tell it when to create a new log file. If you log to an ODBC data source, you must specify the SQL/ODBC Data Source Name (DSN), table, and valid user name and password to the database.

FIGURE 13.25

Logging events on the WWW service

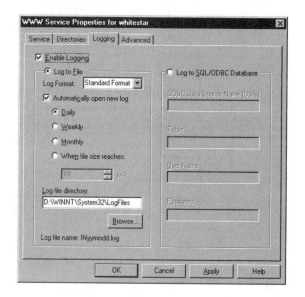

Advanced Tab

Administrators control who has access to WWW services. You can see the choices in Figure 13.26.

Permissions are given to computers, not people, and can be granted or denied to one computer, or to groups of computers. Click on the Granted Access radio button and click on Add if you want to grant access to a computer or group of computers (see Figure 13.27). Fill in the IP Address of the computer, or fill in the Subnet Mask of a group of computers to which you want to grant Internet access. For example, in Figure 13.28, we've indicated that only computers from TechTeach's range of IP addresses will be allowed to access the service.

FIGURE 13.26

Granting and denying
access to the Internet by a
computer's IP address

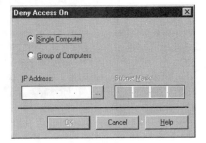

FIGURE 13.27

Adding computers to the
Deny Access list

Likewise, if you click on the Denied Access radio button and click on Add,
you'll get a dialog box similar to the one shown in Figure 13.27. The exception, of
course, is that you'll be denying access to specific computers instead of granting
them access to your server. In Figure 13.29, you'll see that we're granting everyone access except a certain group of Microsoft employees.

Finally, you'll be warned that whatever changes you make to the current
service will also be made to all other services. This means if you deny a specific computer access to your FTP service, you also deny it access to WWW
and Gopher services. Click on Yes, and you're done.

FIGURE 13.28

Granting access only to computers with an IP address in the 199.34.57.0 range

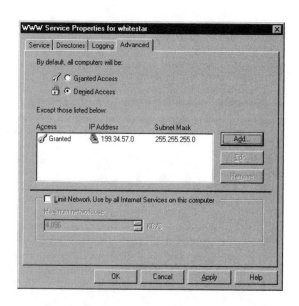

FIGURE 13.29

Denying access to a group of Microsoft computers

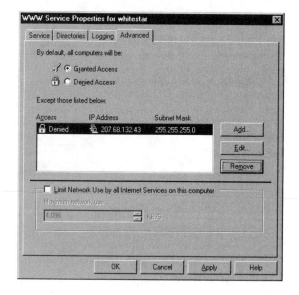

Gopher Service Properties

The Gopher service property options are quite like those of the WWW service. There are some differences, though, which are listed next.

Service Tab

Instead of password authentication, there's a Service Administrator section. This section supplies users with the name and e-mail address of the Gopher service administrator. The TCP default port is set to 70 here, and the Gopher Service Properties dialog box has a slightly different look to it, as shown in Figure 13.30.

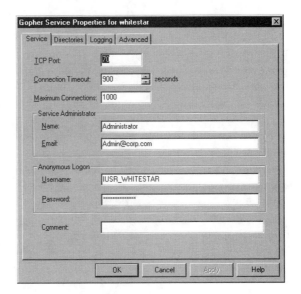

Directories Tab

Similar to the WWW service, you can add, remove, and edit directories in this dialog box. Here, however, you do not have a choice of how the directory is listed, as shown in Figure 13.31.

Also, to add and edit directories in the Gopher service, in the Directory Properties dialog box shown in Figure 13.32, you'll be given the opportunity to add and edit directory paths, but you won't be able to give permissions (Gopher is read-only), nor will you be able to give access to a virtual server.

FIGURE 13.31

Gopher Directories tab

FIGURE 13.32

Adding and editing
directories for the
Gopher service

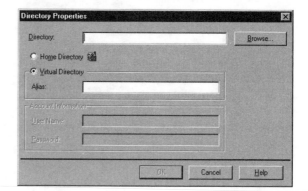

Logging Tab and the Advanced Tab

These options are the same as they are for the WWW service.

FTP Service Properties

The properties of the FTP service are similar to those of the WWW and
Gopher services. However, there are again a few exceptions.

Service Tab

As you'll notice in Figure 13.33, the Service Properties screen is relatively close to those for the WWW and Gopher services.

FIGURE 13.33

FTP Service tab

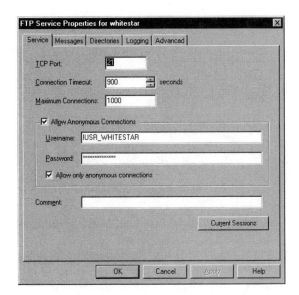

The differences between FTP and those services are as follows:

- The default TCP port for the FTP service is 21.

- In FTP there is no password authentication option. Instead, there's a checkbox to allow anonymous connections. Along those lines, you may also indicate that *only* anonymous connections to your site will be allowed. Allowing only anonymous connections is especially useful if you don't want users to log in with their own user names and passwords because FTP passwords are not encrypted. On the other hand, all users logging in anonymously will be given the same access privileges that are defined by the anonymous account.

- Click on Current Sessions to view the users connected to your server and the time they signed on. The example in Figure 13.34 shows that one user is logged on. This is an anonymous user. Otherwise, you would see the user's user name instead of an e-mail address. Of course, users are not required to use their e-mail addresses. An anonymous password can be anything the user wants it to be.

FIGURE 13.34

FTP User Sessions screen

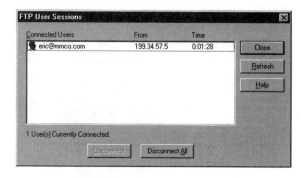

Messages Tab

Unlike the WWW and Gopher services, FTP allows you to provide messages to users when they sign on, when they exit, and when the maximum number of users has been reached. Figure 13.35 shows this dialog box with some sample messages included.

FIGURE 13.35

FTP Messages tab

Directories Tab

Like the WWW and Gopher services, you'll be able to give users access to your directories by indicating which directories are available and what permissions they have. The directory listing box is the same as it is for the WWW and Gopher properties (see Figure 13.36). However, you'll also have the opportunity to decide whether you'd like users to view the directory listing in either the UNIX or MS-DOS style. Because many browsers expect the UNIX format, you should choose that for reasons of compatibility.

FIGURE 13.36

FTP Directories tab

When you want to add or edit a directory, you'll see the dialog box shown in Figure 13.37. In FTP, you won't be able to indicate a virtual server to use with the directory you've chosen like you could in the WWW service.

FIGURE 13.37

Adding and editing
directories for the
FTP service

Creating a Drop Box   You can create a drop box on your server that'll allow users to deposit files in it, but not access them. To create a drop box, you'll need an NTFS partition. Create the drop box by opening Windows NT Explorer and creating a folder that will become the drop box. Right-click on that folder, click on Properties, then Security, and then Permissions. Set the permissions for all users to Write-Only in the Special File Access dialog box. Once you've set the permissions, users will only be able to put files in the directory, but not see, read, or copy any of the files there. Only users with Read permissions, such as administrators, will be able to view the files. This is useful if you want to create an employee suggestion box, for example.

Logging Tab and the Advanced Tab

These tabs allow you to change parameters just as those used in the WWW and Gopher services.

Creating Virtual Servers on the World Wide Web

Typically, each domain (for example, `www.abcd.com`) represents a specific computer, but it's possible to have more than one domain name for a specific computer. For instance, say you wanted to have a corporate Web site and have separate sites for your sales, engineering, and marketing groups. We'll call these `sales.abcd.com`, `engineeering.abcd.com`, and `marketing.abcd.com`. You won't need a separate computer for each domain name. Instead, we'll create *virtual servers* for each domain name, thus keeping each domain on the same computer.

Before you're able to create these virtual servers, you'll need to get an IP address from your Internet service provider for the primary server and for each virtual server you're going to create. For example, the primary Internet server (`www.abcd.com`) may be assigned the first IP address in the Domain Name System (DNS), let's say `53.236.124.166`, and assigned C:\wwwroot as its home directory. You can then assign the second IP address, `53.236.124.167`, to `www.sales.com` and assign a different directory or drive as its home directory. The same holds true for the engineering and marketing groups. When you're finished, it'll appear that there are four separate WWW servers on your single server running the WWW service.

The IP address can be assigned to a single network adapter card or to multiple cards. Use the Network applet in the Control Panel to bind the IP addresses to your card. Once you've assigned an IP address to an adapter card, you'll need to assign a home directory to that address. In the Directory Properties dialog box, shown in Figure 13.37, select the Virtual Directory box and enter the IP address.

You can also restrict virtual directories to one virtual server. When you create a virtual directory, you have to specify which virtual server has access to that directory. If you don't supply an IP address, the directory will be visible to all virtual servers.

IP addresses aren't assigned to the default directories when the Internet Information Server is installed. You may also have to assign IP addresses to the default directories when you add virtual servers.

Once you've installed and configured your server, all you have to do is place the files you want to make available in the wwwroot folder (or ftproot or gopherroot folder, depending on which services you wish to use), and you're finished.

Upgrading to IIS Version 3

We installed and configured the IIS version 2 server, and now let's upgrade to version 3. You can do this two ways. If you have the Microsoft Service Pack 2 CD, then you can install IIS version 3 from this. You can also pull the files down free from the Microsoft Web site. We will install from the CD.

1. First, insert the SP2 CD into your server. Open the CD, and it will automatically open Microsoft Internet Explorer. Scroll down about a half page to find Internet Information Server 3.0 on the left side (see Figure 13.38).

2. Click on Internet Information Server 3.0. This is actually a shortcut to the IIS files.

3. Scroll down almost all the way to the bottom of the page. Click on Install IE 3.01, as shown in Figure 13.39.

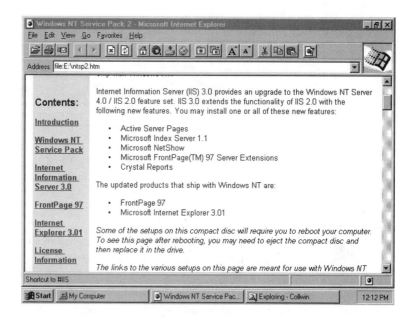

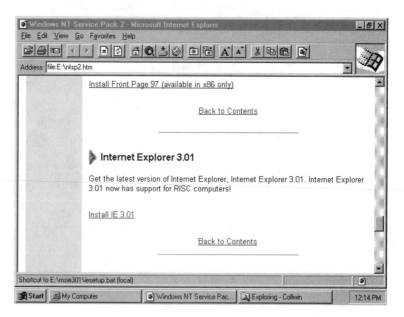

4. At this point, you can save the file to your desktop or anywhere else on your computer, or just open the file, and it will start upgrading your installation of IIS. Let's just open the file.

5. Click on Yes to start the IIS 3 installation (see Figure 13.40). The program will then extract the files needed for the installation.

F I G U R E 13.40

Beginning the installation

6. Click on I Agree on the license agreement form. Your files will continue to be copied and you will be asked to restart your computer.

7. Click on Yes.

Installing IIS Version 4

If you are going to install IIS version 4, you have to delete any previous version of IIS on your machine first. So, basically it's not an upgrade, but a fresh installation. As of the publishing of this book, IIS version 4 is still in beta. Let's take a look at how we can install version 4. But first, make sure you have Service Pack 3 installed and then download the appropriate IIS version 4 files from the Microsoft Web site.

1. Go to the Microsoft Web site and either order the CD for IIS version 4, or download the installation files. On a 28.8 modem, this will take around four hours! The download options are shown in Figure 13.41. If you are on your NT Server, you can download and install at the same time. We will choose Download Only, then click on Next.

2. Choose your Language and CPU/Operating System, as shown in Figure 13.42, then click on Next.

FIGURE 13.41

IIS version 4 download
options

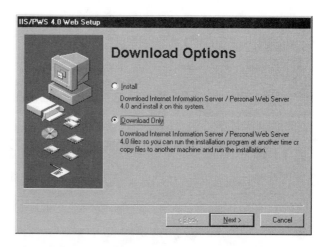

FIGURE 13.42

Language and CPU/
operating type

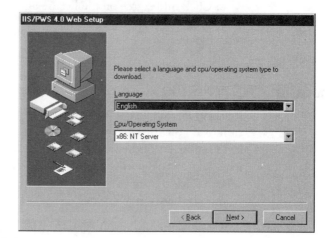

3. Select the installation option you prefer (see Figure 13.43), then click on Next. Remember, if you choose Minimal, then you can't choose a Typical Installation later. If you have a 28.8 modem, you should choose Minimal Installation at this point; but if you want the Full Installation, start the download at night, and it should be done by the time you get to work in the morning!

4. Next fill in the Save in Folder path, shown in Figure 13.44, then click on Next.

F I G U R E   1 3 . 4 3

Installation options

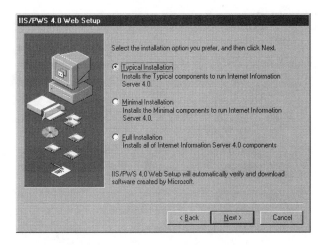

F I G U R E   1 3 . 4 4

Enter the location where
you want your files saved.

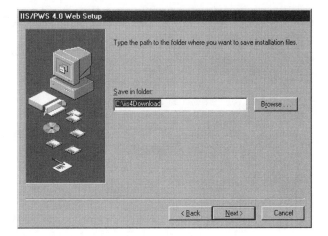

5. The installation program will now go to the Microsoft Web site and
download the necessary files (see Figure 13.45). Choose a site to download the files.

6. When complete, go to the download directory—by default it is
C:\iis4Download—and click on Setup. First make sure you have Ser-
vice Pack 3 installed. You should get a screen like the one shown in
Figure 13.46.

7. Click on Next.

FIGURE 13.45

Downloading files from available Microsoft sites

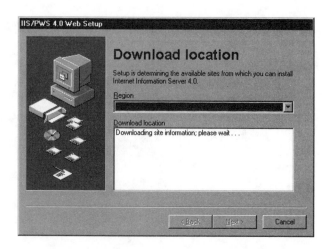

FIGURE 13.46

IIS 4 Setup

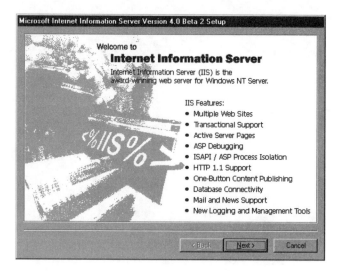

8. Click on Accept on the Microsoft License agreement, then click Next.

9. Choose your preferred installation option. The options are shown in Figure 13.47.

10. We're going to choose Minimum because those are the files we pulled from the Microsoft site.

11. Click on Next to accept the default directories for WWW, FTP, and application files (see Figure 13.48).

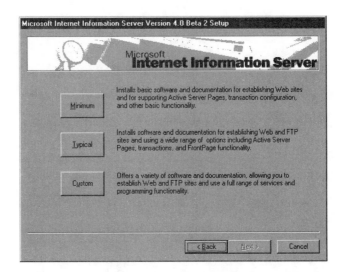

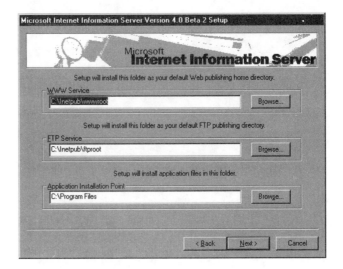

12. Setup will then copy the files; this takes several minutes. When finished, you get a nice "Thank you" from Microsoft. Click on Finish.

13. Restart your computer for the new setting to take effect.

There's more to the Internet than files, Web servers, and home pages, which is why we'll move on to explore the vagaries of electronic mail in the next chapter.

CHAPTER

14

E-Mail on TCP/IP

By themselves, computers are little more than glorified calculators. Hooking them up via networks has been the thing that's really made computers useful, and of course networks are a big part of communications. But even networks aren't of much value unless people use them—and people won't use them without a reason. This brings up electronic mail. E-mail is often the "gateway" application for people—the first network application they use. For some, it's the *only* application they'll ever use. In addition, e-mail is probably the most important thing running on the Internet, and the ins and outs of it will be the focus of this chapter.

Using EMWACS Mail Software to Make Your NT Server a Mail Relay Agent

Most offices have some kind of internal e-mail, such as Microsoft Exchange, Lotus cc:Mail, or the like. But connecting that e-mail to the outside world—that is, the Internet—is an expensive proposition, coming in with price tags around $4,000. That's a shame, as the protocols for Internet mail are well-documented, and there's lots of free code around to support them. In this section, we'll tell you about our favorite—a piece of software from the European Microsoft Windows Academic Centre (EMWACS).

Internet E-Mail Protocols

There are two main Internet e-mail protocols that most of us care about: the Simple Mail Transfer Protocol (SMTP) and the Post Office Protocol (POP3).

SMTP is the Internet e-mail protocol. SMTP grew up at a time when most users on the Internet were running UNIX machines, each with their own IP address. Each UNIX machine ran two mail programs. The first was a program that could package up a mail message and send it to its destination—the most common one of this type being *sendmail*. The second program was a so-called *daemon* (a program that always runs in the background), kind of like a DOS Terminate and Stay Resident (TSR) program and analogous to NT services. The daemon would constantly listen for incoming mail in the form of TCP/IP packets sent from another system running sendmail.

The SMTP/sendmail approach works fine as long as every system on the Internet can run some kind of mail daemon, *and* so long as every system is up and running 24 hours a day, seven days a week. But primitive PC operating systems don't handle daemons well, and most people don't leave their workstations up and running all the time, even if they *are* running an operating system that handles daemons well. Additionally, while many systems may run all of the time, and while they may have an operating system that works well with daemons, they aren't connected to the Internet all of the time. Because of this, it'd be nice to enhance SMTP with some kind of mail storage system, allowing one computer to act as a kind of "post office."

In a scenario where you've got 500 people on your network with varying operating systems and uptimes, you could set up one computer that *is* up 24 hours a day, seven days a week. This computer runs the mail daemon, the program that listens. You'd tell that computer, "Accept mail for everyone in the company, and hold onto it." That's the computer we'll dub the "post office." When a user wants her mail, she simply connects to that post office and pulls down her mail. In the Internet world, we let a client computer, like the one on her desktop, communicate with a post office computer using a protocol called POP3, the Post Office Protocol. Such a program is a small program referred to as a *POP3 client*. Actually, every POP3 client that we know of might be better referred to as a *POP3 Message Receiver/SMTP Message Sender*. That's because the program only uses POP3 to get your mail; when you create a new message, it just sends it to a computer running the SMTP receiver service (the daemon), which then hands it to the SMTP delivery service (sendmail or one of sendmail's cousins).

So, in order for *your* office to send and receive Internet mail, you'll need a computer to act as a post office. The computer uses SMTP to talk to other post offices, and those post offices may choose to communicate with you at any hour of the day, so the computer must be attached to the Internet at all times. So that your users can retrieve their mail, they'll need programs that act as POP3 clients. Finally, that post office computer will need to run a POP3 *server* so that it can respond to mail requests.

EMWACS' Internet Mail Service (IMS) software can take you a good ways toward that goal. It consists of three services that'll run on any NT Server machine:

- **The SMTP receiver service:** This is the listening daemon program. The program that carries this out is called smtprs.exe. When another post office computer gets mail for you, it'll communicate with smtprs.exe. Similarly, if you create a new mail message and tell your mail client to send it out, the mail client will then send the message to smtprs.exe.

- **The SMTP delivery service:** This sends messages to other post offices. The delivery service is called smtpds.exe. Smtpds only has to listen to smtprs. When the receiver service gets a new piece of mail, it gives it to smtpds, the delivery service. If the mail is destined for another post office, smtpds establishes a connection with that other post office, and shoots the mail over there. If the mail is destined for *this* post office, then smtpds just drops the mail into the proper user's mail box.

- **The POP3 server:** This program, called pop3s.exe, responds to requests from POP3 client programs by delivering mail to appropriate clients when requested to do so.

Where can you find a POP3 client? Right in NT or Windows 95—the program attached to the Inbox tool can act as a POP3 client. We'll show you how to set that up later, but first let's get the server software set up. An alternative, if you don't like the Microsoft tool, is to surf on over to `http://www.eudora.com/light.html`, where you'll find Eudora Lite, an excellent mail client written by the Qualcomm people. They write terrific software, and, even better, they have a 32-bit version of their Eudora mail client that they give away absolutely free!

Setting Up Your Mail Server: IMS Limitations

Before you install IMS, you should be aware of some of its limitations. There are a few things you must do to an NT machine before it can serve well as a post office. Because you might find some of the constraints unduly confining, let's take a look at them before you go further.

The Mail Server Must Have a Static IP Address

Each service must be able to find the IP address of the computer that it's running on. You can check this by typing the name of each service, followed by the -ipaddress parameter. For example, once you have IMS installed on an NT machine, you can type **smtprs -ipaddress**, and you should see the IP address and DNS name of that machine.

In our experience, the IMS components can't find a machine's IP address if that machine gets its IP address from DHCP—just being in a DNS table doesn't seem to do the trick. So you've got to run IMS on a machine with a static IP address.

DNS Must Be Able to Find the Mail Server

This ought to be kind of obvious, but we thought we'd mention it anyway. If you send mail to bob@fin.shark.com, and DNS can't find fin.shark.com, then the mail isn't going to get very far. The IMS services actually try to resolve the name of the computer they're sitting on when they first start. If the IMS services *can't* resolve the name, they'll refuse to run.

The Mail Server Only Serves Users in Its Users Group

If the mail server receives mail for a user it doesn't recognize, it'll simply refuse the mail. How, then, does it distinguish the users that it recognizes? They must be in the mail server's Users group, that's how. If the mail server has joined a domain, then that domain's Domain Users group will be sitting in the server's local Users group.

The POP3S Server Doesn't Accept Blank Passwords

There may be a way to do this, but we haven't figured it out. If you try to get your mail, then of course you'll be asked for your username and password. If your password is empty, then POP3S will refuse your connection, and you won't be able to retrieve your mail.

The Software Doesn't Have Performance Monitor Counters

Unlike a lot of NT software, the EMWACS mail software won't install Performance Monitor counters. Yes, this may be a bit nitpicky about a piece of *free* software, but it sure would be nice to use the power of Perfmon with IMS!

How the IMS Software Works

First, you install the three services on an NT Server. Once they're up and running, anyone can send mail to *somename*@*servername*, where *somename* is a valid NT user on that server, and *servername* is the Internet host name of the server. So, for example, if our local server were named altair.mmco.com and our username were allofus, you could send mail to allofus@altair.mmco.com.

Downloading the EMWACS Software

As we write this, the EMWACS folks have progressed to version 0.8*x* of their mail software. Always get the most up-to-date version, because they're always improving on the program. At this writing, you'll find it at `http://emwac .ed.ac.uk/html/internet_toolchest/ims/ims.htm`. Just point your Web browser to that location and you'll see instructions on how to download the software. They also have documentation on the product in HTML format—be sure to get that, because it'll have more detailed installation instructions than you can read here.

Unzipping the EMWACS Software

As we're using an Intel-based server for our mail system, the file we downloaded was named IMSi386.zip. Since it's a zipped file, you'll need PKUNZIP or a similar program to decompress the files.

Create a directory into which you'll unzip the files. (Mark called his C:\ EMWACS.) Copy the IMSi386.zip file there, open up a command line, and type **PKUNZIP -d IMSi386**. That'll unzip the file and create any necessary directories. Do the same with the zip file containing the documentation, which will create a directory called HTML to contain the documentation.

Then, copy these files to the \winnt\system32 directory:

- smtprs.exe (the receiver daemon)

- smtpds.exe (the sendmail delivery agent)

- pop3s.exe (the POP3 server)

- ims.cpl (the Control Panel applet to control the mail server)

- imscmn.dll (a DLL to support the programs)

You can put most of them in different directories, but it's easiest to just stick them in the system32 directory. The ims.cpl file *must* go in \winnt\system32.

Installing the Services

Next, register the services with NT. Open up a command line, change the drive and directory to the \winnt\system32 directory, and type the name of each service, followed by **-install**:

```
smtprs -install
```

```
smtpds -install
```

```
pop3s -install
```

Each module should acknowledge that it has installed correctly. Next, tell NT to automatically start these services whenever your start the computer. Go to the Control Panel and open the Services applet. You'll see three new services named:

- IMS POP3 Server

- IMS SMTP Delivery Agent

- IMS SMTP Receiver

One at a time, click on each service, and then click on the Startup button. Choose Automatic, and the service will start when the computer does. Do this for each of the three services. Because they haven't been started yet, be sure to also click on the Start button for each service.

Set Users to Log On As Batch Jobs

IMS requires that any user who tries to access his mailbox be able to log onto the server running IMS as a *batch job*. Odd as it sounds, it's necessary. Just start up the User Manager and point it at the particular machine that is going to run the IMS services. For example, if you're going to run IMS on a server named MAILSRV, then start up the User Manager or the User Manager for Domains, choose User ➤ Select Domain, then type in **\\MAILSRV** where it asks for a domain. You'll just be editing the Security Accounts Manager (SAM) of the mail server machine, rather than the domain.

Select Policies ➤ User Rights, and check Show Advanced User Rights. Then, find the right *Log on as a batch job*, and add in the Users group from this computer. That users group (MAILSRV\Users, in this example) should contain the Domain Users groups of all of the NT domains that this machine will serve as a mail server.

Remember, you can only add a Domain Users group from another domain if your domain *trusts* the other domain.

If users aren't able to log on as batch jobs, they'll be denied login to the NT mail server from their client software (Inbox, Eudora, or whatever—doesn't matter). Once again, don't forget that the mail server will *refuse* to receive mail from users who aren't in its local Users directory. So you want to set up a mail server M1 in domain RED, but you want it to accept mail for people in domain BLUE as well. First, make sure that RED trusts BLUE, then go to User Manager on server M1 and make sure that the group M1\Users contains both RED\Domain Users and BLUE\Domain Users.

Configuring the Services

Next, you'll see an applet labeled EMWAC IMS in the Control Panel. Double-click on that, and you'll see a screen like in Figure 14.1.

FIGURE 14.1

Configuring directories for IMS mail

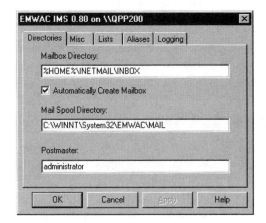

First, tell IMS where to put the mailboxes. Each user gets their own subdirectory in which IMS keeps their mail. If you check the Automatically Create Mailbox checkbox, then IMS will (surprise) create a user's mailbox automatically. That way, IMS only creates a directory when necessary.

IMS lets you specify a couple of ways to organize user mailboxes—with the %home% and %username% variables. If you use %home% in the mailbox name, IMS will substitute the user's home directory, the one specified in the Profiles button on the User Manager. If you use %username% in the mailbox name, then IMS will substitute the user's NT username.

For example, suppose you've got users named Sue and John as accounts on an NT server. Their home directories are on the server at D:\Users*username*. You could put their mailboxes in a directory E:\MAIL by telling IMS to set Mailbox Directory to E:\MAIL\%username%. As mail came in for Sue and John, IMS would end up creating directories E:\MAIL\JOHN and E:\MAIL\SUE. Mail messages would then accumulate in each directory as each user received mail. Note two things: First, E:\MAIL need not be shared and second, neither John nor Sue need have File and Directory permissions on E:\MAIL or on either subdirectory.

Does that sound like it violates NT security? It doesn't. You see, neither John nor Sue ever tries to access E:\MAIL; rather, John and Sue run programs—POP3 mail clients—that communicate in client/server fashion with the POP3S service, which in turn provides them with their mail messages. Now, it *is* a fact that POP3S must have access to that mailbox directory, or as mentioned, nothing will happen.

If you set up the mailbox directories as we've just suggested, then they are very secure from user tampering. If, on the other hand, you don't care whether users can directly access their mailboxes, then use the %home% variable. For example, if you were to tell IMS to put mail in %home%\mail, John's mail would sit in D:\USERS\JOHN\MAIL, and Sue's would sit in D:\USERS\SUE\MAIL. In general it's wise to avoid the %home% variable because, first, it confuses the mail server if a user does not have a home directory, and second, it puts the mail directories under direct user control, which is not always a good idea.

The Mail Spool directory is just a temporary holding directory for the mail server—just use the default. "Postmaster" is the e-mail name of the person who gets the error messages. (It's a good idea, by the way, to log into the mail server with the postmaster's name.)

Next, click on the Misc tab and you'll see Figure 14.2.

FIGURE 14.2

Misc configuration in IMS

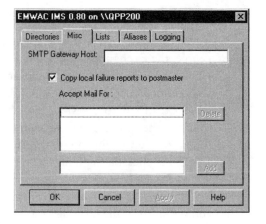

You can use this tab to tell the mail system to accept mail for other Internet domains; however, you *can't* use this to tell it to accept mail for other NT domains. Remember, you do that by putting global groups from other domains into the mail server's local Users group. The only thing we'd suggest you do here is to check *Copy local failure reports to postmaster*. That way, you can keep track of systemic problems. Finally, click on the Logging tab and enable logging for each of the three services.

Once you've got IMS configured as you like it, close the Control Panel applet and start and stop each service so your configuration changes take effect. Or, if you don't want to wait around for the services to stop and start, write a batch file to do it:

```
net stop "IMS POP3 Server"

net start "IMS POP3 Server"

net stop "IMS SMTP Delivery Agent"

net start "IMS SMTP Delivery Agent"

net stop "IMS SMTP Receiver"

net start "IMS SMTP Receiver"
```

By now, you should be ready to set up your mail client.

Configuring the Microsoft "Inbox" Exchange Client for Internet Mail

If you've installed Windows 95 or Windows NT, then you've noticed that Microsoft has included a mail client application labeled Inbox or, to some people, the Exchange Client. This program is actually two programs in one. First, it's a client for someone running Microsoft Mail or Exchange, and second, it can act as a POP3 client. Unfortunately, people who aren't using Exchange or Microsoft Mail, but who need a simple POP3 client, tend to overlook the Inbox. In this section, we'll show you how to configure the Inbox to receive your Internet mail.

Double-click on the Inbox icon for the first time, and you'll see the dialog box in Figure 14.3.

Click on Yes, and you'll be prompted to insert the NT Setup CD (unless you set up from the hard disk). It'll copy a few files and return you to the desktop. Double-click on the Inbox tool again, and you'll see the dialog box in Figure 14.4.

F I G U R E   14.3

Initial Inbox setup dialog

F I G U R E   14.4

Choosing services
to configure

Uncheck Microsoft Mail (unless you *do* use Exchange or Microsoft Mail, of course) and click on Next. You'll see a dialog box like Figure 14.5.

F I G U R E   14.5

Connecting via
the network

Since you're locally connected to your IMS mail server, choose the Network radio button, and then click on Next. You'll see a dialog box like in Figure 14.6.

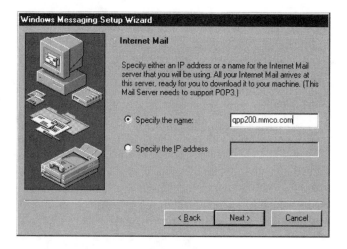

Here you can choose whether to point at the server with its name or its IP address. Specify the machine on which you've just installed IMS. Click on Next, and you'll see the dialog box in Figure 14.7.

This controls whether you receive your messages as they come in, or if you must request them with the Tools ➤ Deliver Now option. Since most people like to control when they retrieve and send messages, choose Off-line. Use whichever option works best—you can change it later if you don't like what you've first selected. Then click on Next, and you'll fill in some information about your mail account, as you see in Figure 14.8.

FIGURE 14.8

Specifying your
mail address

This may seem redundant—you already specified a server, right?—but it's not. Note that Mark didn't enter mark@qpp200.mmco.com, he entered **mark@mmco .com**. He did that because mark@mmco.com is the e-mail address he gives to the outside world, so his network then internally figures out that mark@mmco.com really means mark@qpp200.mmco.com.

How it does this is the business of your DNS server. If you read Chapter 9 on setting up the DNS server, you learned that you can insert records called MX or Mail Exchange records into the DNS server. In the case of Mark's network, he would insert a record that would tell DNS that whenever someone wants to send mail to him at mark@mmco.com, the mail should go to mark@qpp200.mmco .com. The Your Full Name field is used to identify you in the header of a message; you can actually put anything in there. Click on Next, and you'll see Figure 14.9.

The Inbox mail tool will allow you to log onto a POP3 server running on any kind of operating system. Most require that you log in with a username and password; you enter that here. You must enter the username and password that the mail server knows you as. In Mark's case, he's a recognized member of the

FIGURE 14.9

NT security logon
information

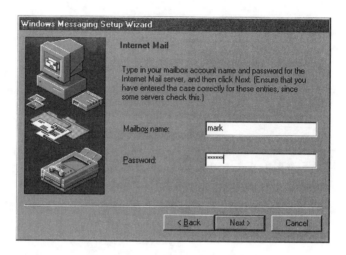

Users group on QPP200 by virtue of the fact that QPP200\Users contains his domain's Domain Users account. That being so, he'd fill in his domain username (Mark), plus his domain password. Click on Next, and you'll have an opportunity to point the Inbox tool to two more files, your personal address book and your personal folders.

We're not going to reproduce the screens here, as they're straightforward ("Please enter the name of the directory... "); what we *do* want to emphasize is that you've got to be careful where you put the address book and folders. By default, the Inbox will sometimes want to put them in \winnt. Instead, we suggest you put them in a personal location; however, be careful about *what* personal area you use. Your NT profile contains an area named \winnt\profiles\ *username*\personal, and many Microsoft products use that as the place to keep your personal information. But if you reinstall NT as a fresh install (rather than an upgrade), then the NT Setup program *deletes* the old personal folders. Our advice: Create a directory that's yours—perhaps a home directory on some server—and put the folders and address book there. That way, if you must reinstall NT and the Inbox tool, you can just point the newly installed Inbox at your folders and address book, and you won't lose any old messages or addresses. (The address book is actually not bad; it lets you store snail mail addresses and phone numbers as well as Internet mail addresses.)

The mail client will then be installed. The initial screen looks like Figure 14.10.

That first "message" is bogus, just an advertisement from Microsoft. To retrieve your mail, click on Tools ➤ Deliver Now, and you'll get your mail.

If you load up the EMWACS mail service, set it up right, and use the built-in Inbox. You can wire your company to the Internet in no time at all—and except for the cost of connecting your network to the Internet, for no cost!

FIGURE 14.10

Initial mail client screen

E-Mail Security Concerns

As the Internet grows, more and more gateways will be built to other e-mail systems. You can't get everywhere, but, in time, you'll be able to reach anyone from the Internet. Now that's a good thing, but as e-mail becomes more important, it's also essential to keep your mind on the fact that e-mail is *not secure*. Your mail packets get bounced all around the Internet, as you know—but think about what that means. Suppose you send a message to someone on the Internet, and our computer is part of the Internet—a piece, as it happens, that sits between you and the person to whom you're sending mail. Mail can sit in intermediate computers like ours, *on the hard disk*, for seconds, minutes, or hours at a time. It's a simple matter to use any number of utility programs to peek into the mail queue on the mail that's "just passing through." *Never* say anything on mail that you wouldn't want as public knowledge. Even if someone doesn't peek at your mail, the fact that someone probably backs up his or her disk regularly means that the message may sit on magnetic media for years in some archive. Imagine—in the middle of the 21st century, we'll see "the unpublished letters of Douglas Adams"—e-mail notes that someone stumbled across while picking through some 70-year-old backups. It'll be the latter-day equivalent of going through some dead celebrity's trash. Anyway, the bottom line is: Don't write anything that you wouldn't want your boss, your spouse, your parents, or your kids to read!

E-mail is one of the most important applications that your business can have, second only to security. So let's take a look at network security in the next chapter.

CHAPTER

15

NT Internet Security

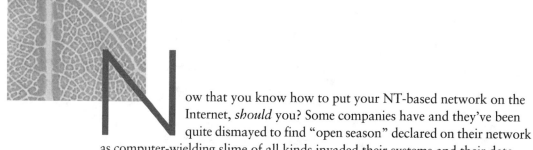

ow that you know how to put your NT-based network on the Internet, *should* you? Some companies have and they've been quite dismayed to find "open season" declared on their network as computer-wielding slime of all kinds invaded their systems and their data.

Putting your local LAN on the Internet *can* leave you open to attacks from criminals, because the Internet wasn't really designed with security in mind. But remember that you're running NT, one of the more security-conscious networks.

Please don't consider this section as guaranteed advice on how to secure your network from outside attack. Instead, follow along with us, and let's see if a little common sense can help you shore up your computers and data.

Finding Security Breaks

Where do the security holes exist in an NT network? Here are some of the main problems we see, whether on an Internet or not.

Internal Users Can Easily Get a List of User IDs

If you've taken a look at the NT Workstation or Server books, you've probably learned how to configure a set of home directories. If you haven't, here's a summary: First, you create a share called Users on an NTFS volume, giving the Everyone group or, better, the Domain Users group, Full Control. Then, you set the top-level directory permissions to Read and Execute, and assign Domain Users no file permissions at all. Users need Read and Execute to navigate from the top-level directory to their individual home directories. After that, you set the file and directory permissions for each directory to Full Control for each particular user.

The problem is, there's no way to keep a user from moving up to the top-level directory and seeing the names of all of the users' home directories. Result: Now that person has a list of all of the users' IDs, making hacking a bit easier.

Additionally, any user on an NT workstation can type **net user\domain** and get a list of users in the workstation's domain. Again, these are mainly things you're concerned about for internal users, but inside hacking is probably more prevalent than outside hacking.

Internal Users Can Easily Crash Shared Volumes

Since there are no disk quotas, any user with Write access to a volume can, either accidentally or purposefully, write as much data to a shared volume as the volume can hold. The result is that now there's no space left for other users. Worse yet, if that's the volume that held the page file, then the page file can't grow in size, which might crash NT altogether.

Passwords Can Be Sniffed When Changed

In general, NT has a nifty system for exchanging password information that's encrypted and essentially uncrackable. But when you change your password, your workstation must send the new password in clear text over the network. If someone happened to be running a program like Network Monitor at that moment, they'd be able to capture that new password.

Microsoft File and Print Services Will Operate across the Internet

There's no surprise here—heck, it's a feature, and we don't mean that facetiously. But it's also a security hole if you don't look closely into it.

First of all, what is it that you want to secure? We'll assume it's your data. Because you don't want an outside intruder to be able to destroy data on your servers, or lock you out of your own network, let's consider this question: How could someone get access to your data?

For the moment, we'll assume you're not running any Internet services like FTP, Gopher, or Web servers—we'll get to them in a minute—but for now, let's consider a network consisting of standard file servers.

Attacks could come in the following forms:

- Someone with Read access to your files could steal company information.

- Someone with Write access to your files could modify or delete them.

- Someone with Write access could also use your file servers to store their own personal data—data they may not want to keep on their own computers, perhaps because the data is unlawful to have—like someone else's credit card numbers.

- Someone with Write access could cripple your servers by filling up their free space with nonsense files, crashing the servers.

- Presumably someone could crash your mail servers by sending thousands of automatically generated pieces of mail to them. Enough mail messages will fill the hard disks of those servers as well.

- Access to your print servers could, again, let intruders fill up the print servers' hard disks with spooled files, as well as cause your printers to run out of paper.

There are, however, several types of actions you can take to detect and/or deter an outside attack...

Detecting Outside Attacks

NT comes with some built-in tools you can use to make detecting attacks easier:

- Audit failed logons.

- Use the Performance Monitor to alert you when logon failures exceed some reasonable value.

- Periodically log network activity levels. If all of a sudden your network gets really busy at 3 A.M. for no good reason, then look closely into exactly *what's* going on at 3 A.M.!

Deterring Attacks

The main steps to take to deter attacks include the following:

- Don't use obvious passwords.

- Don't enable the Guest account.

- Rename the built-in Administrator account.

- Don't let the built-in Administrator account access the servers over the network.

- Lock out users after a certain number of failed attempts.

- Make passwords expire after a certain length of time.

- Install a firewall to filter out UDP ports 136 and 137.

- Put the Web, FTP, and Gopher servers on a separate machine in its own domain, with no trust links to other domains.

- Don't put any services on your DNS servers except DNS.

It seems that only by directly accessing your file servers through the normal net use interface, via an NFS interface or through an FTP service, would someone be able to read or write data on your computers over the Internet. We'll assume that you're not going to run NFS, that you'll put the FTP server where compromising it won't matter, and that you'll focus on the file server interface.

In a nutshell, here's the scenario that you should worry about. Suppose we know you've got a server named S01 whose IP address is 253.12.12.9, and that it has a share on it named Secret. We could just create an LMHOSTS file with one line in it, like so:

```
253.12.12.9 S01
```

Now we can type **net use X: \\s01\secret**, and our Internet-connected PC sends a request to 253.12.12.9 for access to the share. Assuming the Guest account isn't enabled on S01, then S01 will first ask our PC, "Who are you?" We'll see that as a request for a user name and password. When we respond with a valid user name and password from the server's domain, we're in. Actually, this is a way to access your network's resources from across the Internet when on a client site—two seconds' work with an LMHOSTS file and a net use, and you're accessing your home directory from thousands of miles away.

To do that, you need to know:

- A valid user name on the network

- The password for that account

- The IP address of a server on the domain

- The name of a share on the domain

All right, suppose you want to hack some company with the name `bigfirm` `.com`. Where do you start? Step one is to find out what its range of IP addresses is. That's easy. Just Telnet to `internic.net` and type **whois bigfirm** **.com**, and you'll get the network number and person responsible for that network. You'll also get the IP address of their DNS name servers. The other way to find this information is to type:

```
nslookup
set type=all
bigfirm.com
```

Bigfirm will dump the names and addresses of their DNS servers and their mail servers. Because there has to be a secondary DNS server to make the InterNIC happy, there will be at least two name servers. Now, if Bigfirm is thinking, the way most of us do, "It doesn't take much CPU power to run a DNS server—let's put some shared directories there, too," then Joe Slimeball Hacker thinks, "Cool! Fresh meat."

You see, you've got no choice but to publish two of your IP addresses, the addresses of your DNS server and its backup. *So don't put anything else on it.* You know those 25MHz 486s that you can't figure out what to do with? Use them for your DNS servers.

Now suppose you're smart, and there's nothing else on the DNS servers. Well, Joe S. Hacker would have to fish a bit, but that's not hard because whois told him your range of IP addresses. Yes, he's a slimeball, but he's a *thorough* slimeball! Since this is what that hacker lives to do, he's willing to try all of your IP addresses to find out which ones have servers. It's a simple matter to create an LMHOSTS file that includes a NetBIOS name for every possible IP address. For example, if J.S.H. knows you have Class C network `200.200.200.0`, then he can create an LMHOSTS file with NetBIOS named N1, which equals `200.200.200.1`, N2 equals `200.200.200.2`, and so on. Then he need only do a `net view \\`*servername* for each name from N1 through N254. The IP addresses that have a computer attached to them running the server service will be the ones that challenge him for a name and password—the ones that *don't* won't respond at all.

What can you do? Well, you could decide not to worry about it, since the bad guys can't get in without a user name and password. But if you won't sleep nights until you plug this hole, just go to the servers in question and disable the Browser service.

The next thing hackers will look for is a user account name or two. How can they get this? Well, we don't think you can do a net user remotely without contacting the domain controller. This means someone would have to have a domain ID and password to get net user to work from the outside—whew, that's one less thing to worry about!

But you're not out of the woods yet—there *is* a way to find at least some user names. When a user logs onto an NT machine, it registers not only its own machine name on the network, but the user's name as well. It does that so alerts with that name on them can get to the proper user. For example, suppose you've asked the Performance Monitor to alert you in your user name of JILL02 if a server gets low on free space. How does the network know where you are?

It's quite simple. When you log on, the Messenger Service—assuming that it's running—registers your user name as one of the NetBIOS names attached to your workstation. Assuming you're logged onto a server whose IP address is 200.200.200.200, anyone doing an nbtstat -A 200.200.200.200 would not only see the computer's name, they'd see your name as well.

So, supposing that someone named *paulad* was logged in at the 200.200 .200.200 machine (that's physically logged in, not connected over the network), a look at the nbtstat output would show the hacker that there's a user named paulad who's logged on.

So now the hacker's got a user name, and probably the user name of an administrative account, since paulad is logged onto a server; very good news for Joe S. Hacker. What can you do about that? Disable the Messenger service, and the name never gets registered. And, by the way, speaking of nbtstat, if you run an nbtstat -A, and the name MSBROWSE shows up, you've found a Master browser. There's a good chance that a Master browser is a domain controller, right? So maybe it's a good idea to set MaintainServerList=No for the domain controllers. Let the other servers handle the Master browser part—you'll remove a clue that a hacker could use. Unfortunately, however, all domain controllers have other names registered to them that pretty much identify them as domain controllers.

Now that J.S.H. has got a user name, he needs a password. Now *that's* a problem. Even if we could physically attach our computer to your network, we wouldn't get a password with a network sniffer. Why? Because NT uses a challenge/response approach to password verification. When you try to log onto an NT domain, the domain controller sends your workstation a random number that your workstation then applies to your password using some kind of *hashing* function—a mathematical function that produces a number when supplied with two inputs. The result is what gets sent over the network, not the password. (As said earlier, there is one exception to this rule; when you change your password, the new password *does* go over the network to the server, but that's pretty rare.)

So, where does our hacker get the password? He can do one of two things. First, taking what he knows about the user, he can try to guess a password. Second, he can run a program that tries to log on repeatedly, using every word in the dictionary as passwords. This is sometimes known as a *dictionary attack*.

The defense against this should be obvious. First, don't use easy-to-guess passwords. Use more than one word with a character between it, like *fungus#polygon*. Second, don't make it easy for people to try a lot of random passwords: Lock them out after five failed tries.

That leads us to a caution about the Administrator account. If you don't have the Resource Kit, you can't lock it out. The Windows NT 4 Resource Kit now contains a utility for locking out the Administrator account. It's called Passprop.exe. When enabled, the Administrator account can only be used to log on at the domain controllers, not remotely or over the network.

If you don't have the new Resource Kit, then no matter how many times you try a faulty password, the Administrator account doesn't lock. So if you don't do something about it, all the slimeballs on the Internet can spend all of their free time trying to figure out your Administrator password. What can you do about that?

There are two possibilities. First, rename the account. Don't leave it as *Administrator*. Second, limit its powers. You cannot delete the Administrator account, nor can you disable it, but you can remove its right to access the server over the network. By removing this right, you force someone with the Administrator password to physically sit down at the server in order to control that server. Unfortunately, that won't be easy, because the ability to log onto a server locally is granted to the Administrators group, and the Administrator account is a member of that group. You aren't allowed to remove the Administrator account from the Administrators group, so all you can do is to remove the entire Administrators group's right. Then, just grant the individual administrative accounts the Log On over the Network right. (You'll also have to remove the Everyone group and add user accounts back in one at a time—unfortunately, the Administrator is built into the Domain Users group and can't be removed.)

Now, these measures—disabling Guest, renaming Administrator, removing Administrator's right to log on over the network, locking out repeated penetration attempts, setting Performance Monitor to alert you to excessive failed logon attempts, using well-chosen passwords—may be sufficient, and you've no doubt noticed that they're all options that don't cost a dime. But if you want greater security, then look into a firewall. The firewall doesn't have to do much, but it's got one really important job: to filter out two ports on UDP. UDP is the sister protocol to TCP; just as there is a TCP/IP, there is also a UDP/IP.

Remember, TCP is connection-oriented, whereas UDP is not connection-oriented; it just drops messages on the network like messages in a bottle, hoping that they'll get where they're supposed to go. Whenever you execute a Microsoft networking command, such as net use or net view, you're running an application that sends commands to a server using UDP and UDP port numbers 136 and 137. *Ports* are software interfaces that are used to identify particular servers; for example, when you send mail from your desktop, you usually use TCP port number 25. When you receive mail from your desktop, you usually do it on TCP port 110. Web browsers listen on TCP port 80, in another example.

Firewalls are powerful and sometimes complex devices. Once you install them, they have a million setup options and you're likely to wonder if you've caught all the ones you need. Running NetBIOS over IP services happens on UDP ports 136 and 137; tell your firewall to filter those, and it's impossible for someone to access normal file server services.

Application Security Holes

One way that Internet hackers have gotten into Internet domains is through bugs in common UNIX Internet programs. Those things happen in NT, as well, which leads us to this final piece of advice: Put the Internet services, such as FTP, Gopher, Web servers, Finger servers, and the like, on a machine all by themselves. Make sure the machine is in a domain all by itself without any trust relationships.

Is this because we know of any security holes in NT implementations of common Internet programs? Not at all. There *was* one reported in Internet Information Server version 3.51, but we haven't heard of any security problems with the latest version. No, this advice is just common sense—put simply, we don't know that they *can't* be compromised, so we counsel caution.

Many security consultants seem to be approaching Internet security in the same way that they handled virus consulting 10 years ago: They're shouting, "The sky is falling!" and spinning frightening worst-case scenarios in the hopes of drawing droves of frantic customers to them. In the end, however, just a few common-sense steps protected most of us from viruses. With a bit of knowledge, we can also move out of the "bogeyman" stage of Internet security and into the "rational planning" stage.

CHAPTER

16

Microsoft Proxy Server

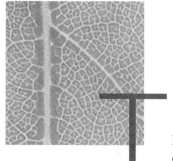

The Internet's unparalleled effectiveness as an information sharing/communication tool has shifted access to it from a simple benefit to an absolute requirement for the business user of today. But Internet access can be a complex thing, further complicated by inherent security bugaboos—and protecting your company's internal network from marauding intruders is only step one. Internet access begets managing that access, and all that propagating network traffic automatically becomes your next challenge.

We've found that many of our clients are not on the Net already because they simply don't want all their employees surfing the Web in pursuit of personal stuff and interests on company time. They just don't want to allow complete Internet access to everyone. A second worry is that companies want Internet access, but they don't want to make a whole bunch of time-consuming, potentially expensive changes to their existing network architectures. These are legitimate concerns, and in this chapter, we'll create an environment in which to evaluate the features of Microsoft Proxy Server, and analyze exactly what it can and cannot do. We'll also cover its installation, management, performance, and that all-important security factor.

What *Is* a Proxy Server, Anyway?

Well, consulting ol' Webster, we find *proxy* defined as: "To do anything by the agency of another." So we might deduce that a proxy server is one that directs clients to a server that will act as an agent, or *proxy*, for those clients to the Internet.

Microsoft Proxy Server is an easy, secure way to bring Internet access to every desktop in an organization. It installs easily, and don't let the phrase "every desktop" scare you either. It places Internet access control where it belongs—in the hands of the network administrator.

Proxy Server also supports all popular Internet protocols including:

- WWW (HTTP)

- FTP

- IPX/SPX

- TCP/IP

- Real Audio

- VDOLive (streaming video)

- IRC (real-time chat)

- Mail

- News

One of our favorite features is how Microsoft Proxy Server proactively caches frequently accessed documents to ensure the availability of refreshed data. This alone can help save precious bandwidth, improve response time, and reduce network congestion!

Another very cool feature is how easily an administrator can grant or deny inbound and outbound connections by user, service, port, or IP domain. Also, specific sites can be blocked—like, perhaps, xxx-pics.com. This little feature could prove to keep a corporation out of lots of trouble!

Security

And now for that ubiquitous security thing... Microsoft Proxy Server was designed with firewall-class security. How about that! Many organizations will run their proxy servers in direct contact with the Internet alongside such devices as packet-filtering routers and firewalls. Microsoft Proxy Server has a built-in Network Address Translation (NAT) feature, which lets you run an illegal (or, of course, legal) TCP/IP address scheme on your internal network and run a valid Internet address to the Internet. The InterNIC set up an invalid IP address scheme for all three classes of networks. In a Class A network, 10.0.0.0 is reserved and cannot be used. However, if you use a NAT, you can run the 10.0.0.0 address internally to get an extra level of security. In a Class B network, the invalid address is 172.16-32.0.0, and in a Class C network that address is 192.168.0.0. As an example, at one of our clients in Walnut Creek, California, we set up an NT Server with two NIC cards (see Figure 16.1).

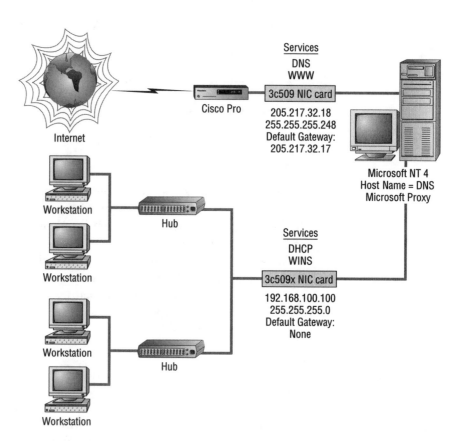

As the figure shows, the customer is running DHCP and WINS on one side of the server with an address of 192.168.100.100, and their valid IP address on the Internet side. The user only had to pay their ISP for a couple of valid IP addresses, enough to run the router interface and the server NIC card, and we ran their DNS and WWW server on that interface. The client only has a handful of users, so a Class C address is sufficient here. Typically, you would use 10.0.0.0, as it gives you the most flexibility.

The proxy server by default only allows outgoing IP traffic through the server. But since the user is using an invalid IP address, even if someone could get through the proxy server, their request would be denied. Through its IP address aggregation features, Microsoft Proxy Server ensures that the internal network's topology and addressing are kept cloaked in mystery and never revealed to the outside network.

According to Microsoft, their proxy server has been rigorously tested by Coopers & Lybrand's Information Technology Security Services, and they claim that the proxy server is resistant to attacks such as IP Spoofing, Satan, and ISS.

The Web Proxy server (which we'll talk about in a minute) supports both HTTP Basic authentication, which transmits passwords in clear text, and NT C2 encrypted authentication. The WinSock Proxy client (which we'll talk about in two minutes) provides support for NT C2 encrypted authentication.

By using the built-in filtering, administrators can select a list of sites which are exclusively permitted or denied to users behind the proxy server. You can also set detailed user and group permission lists per protocol in both the Web Proxy and WinSock Proxy components. The server generates extensive logs that can be processed by text parsers or database queries, providing a detailed audit trail. These logs can grow to Sequoia proportions—very large indeed—and begin to monopolize your hard drive, so it's a good idea to clear out the forest now and then, or archive them.

The Web Proxy also supports Secure Sockets Layer (SSL) tunneling to provide an encrypted path between the client and remote server. You can install an NT Server running Microsoft Proxy, and then place the proxy server between the main corporate LAN and a secure private LAN. In doing so, administrators can control user access between network segments.

Management

Microsoft Proxy Server is often used by small to medium-sized businesses (just like in our example above) as the primary gateway onto the Internet. In these environments, having a Sun box running a proxy service may well be too costly, in terms of hardware, software, and administration. Here's a short list of features for Microsoft Proxy Server management:

- A full graphical setup program gets the user from CD to working proxy server in the blink of an eye. After that, the proxy server can be managed from any Windows NT system on the network by using the Internet Service Manager interface.

- User accounts do not have to be recreated, nor do users have to log onto the proxy server. You can, however, authenticate users to limit access to the Internet. This is done by assigning permitted users a logon and password to the proxy server. Everyone else will be denied.

- Using the included Auto-Dial tool, Microsoft Proxy Server provides exceptional support for networks that use dial-up links (for example, a 28.8 modem or ISDN lines) for access to the Internet.

- In contrast to the "direct connect" method of tying desktops to the Internet, the Microsoft Proxy Server provides a single point of management for the entire organization's Internet connectivity.

- Proxy Server generates a suite of Windows NT Performance Counters for monitoring the state of any proxy server on the network.

- Proxy Server also generates event log messages which can be viewed by the administrator across the LAN.

- You can examine the current status of any Microsoft Proxy Server on the network using an SNMP console such as HP OpenView.

Web Proxy

The Web Proxy component of Microsoft Proxy Server supports the industry standard CERN proxy protocol.

The CERN proxy protocol requires that client programs be specifically configured to use the proxy server to access the Internet via a modified version of the HTTP protocol that's widely supported in popular browsers. The Web Proxy service supports all popular Web browsers including:

- Microsoft Internet Explorer 3.0

- Netscape Navigator 3.0

- PointCast Network

And it supports all platforms including:

- Windows NT Server

- Windows NT Workstation

- Windows 95

- Windows for Workgroups/Windows 3.1

- UNIX

- Macintosh

It also supports the following protocols:

- HTTP

- FTP

- Gopher

- SSL (HTTPS and SNEWS)

WinSock Proxy

The WinSock Proxy component does things a bit differently than Web Proxy. It goes above and beyond by providing expansive, transparent capacities way past the HTTP, FTP, Gopher, and SSL protocol suites and into the wild blue yonder of many wonderful non-Web protocols like streaming audio and video. We mentioned the word transparent for good reason—the WinSock Proxy functions *transparently*. Unlike the Web Proxy, which demands explicit client awareness of the proxy, the WinSock Proxy doesn't require any modification to the client program's protocol. Here's a list of some WinSock Proxy features:

- No modifications to client applications are needed, so it therefore works with existing clients. On the other hand, CERN-style and SOCKS-style proxies demand exact versions of the individual client application, specially made for a certain kind of proxy server.

- From the WinSock Proxy server, you can enable or disable any client/server protocol implemented with the industry standard WinSock 1.1 API. WinSock Proxy pops out of the box preconfigured with a whole melange of popular protocols like NetShow, RealAudio, and IRC; plus, you can easily configure it with new protocol suites as they are standardized (like LDAP), using a very cool graphical tool.

- WinSock supports connectionless/UDP protocols, which other proxies don't. As an example, SOCKS v4-based proxies only work with connection-oriented transports, and so they turn up their noses and stubbornly refuse to support popular new protocols like streaming audio and video. A true performer, WinSock Proxy also renders logging of all transactions, full access control, and encrypted authentication.

Caching

To help control the explosive growth of the Internet and the World Wide Web, the Web community is really counting on Web proxies. Microsoft Proxy Server can significantly reduce your company's total bandwidth consumption by caching frequently used documents on disk. This translates into big-time connectivity savings! How? Well, by keeping handy local copies of popular Internet stuff around, and having cache hit rates of up to 50 percent, the Web Proxy thwarts that need to upgrade and expand your Internet connection bandwidth. Also, because those cached objects are retrieved at LAN speeds, clients enjoy increased throughput, plus reduced latency—yes!

One more thing—and this is a very, very cool thing... Like a thoughtful buddy, Microsoft Proxy Server zestfully goes out and nabs stuff off the Internet even *before* a user requests it! It does this by analyzing a user's particular usage trends. It matches those trends with any new stuff the user might find interesting, based on what they've habitually gone after in the past. As if that weren't enough, active caching even takes into account the load on the server at the time it makes an individual's object pre-fetch decision—it's considerate too! It metrically gears its active-caching activity to cycles of low server utilization, like at night, and prepares the cache for high-traffic intervals occurring later.

Microsoft Proxy Server fully supports the multivendor ISAPI Filter specification that enables third parties to write value-enhancing add-ons to the proxy server. A list of current third-party add-ons is available from `http://www.microsoft.com/proxy/partners.htm`.

The Web Proxy service of Microsoft Proxy Server stores cached Internet objects on one or more of the server's drives. The particular drives used for this purpose are selected during installation. For best cache performance, we strongly recommend that all drives having space allocated to the cache be configured as NTFS drives.

If your current server disk volume is formatted to use FAT partitions, you can convert these partitions to NTFS using the Convert program included with Windows NT Server (before or after installing Microsoft Proxy Server).

Setting Up the Network Adapters

It's important to verify that the network adapter cards are installed and configured properly before you install Microsoft Proxy Server. To create a secure configuration, the Microsoft Proxy Server computer must have at least one network adapter connected to the private network, plus one network adapter, modem, or ISDN adapter to connect to the Internet.

Configuring Additional Network Adapter Cards

1. Open the Control Panel.

2. Double-click on the Network icon, then click on Adapters to display that property sheet.

3. Add the additional network adapter card by clicking on the Add button in the Adapters property sheet.

4. Select your card from the list or click on Have Disk to install from a disk.

5. Click on OK.

Configuring the External Network Adapter Card

Keep the following considerations in mind when setting up the network adapter card that will be connected to the Internet:

1. Set protocol bindings appropriately for the external adapter card. You do this by using the Bindings property sheet in the Network application of the Control Panel. Disable bindings for SMB Server, NWLink IPX/SPX Compatible Transport, WINS Client (TCP/IP), and the NetBEUI protocol. For the WINS Client listing, disable bindings for all interfaces (Server, Workstation, and NetBIOS interfaces). The only binding to be enabled for the external network adapter card should be TCP/IP Protocol.

2. Verify that TCP/IP properties are configured properly for the external adapter card. This can be done from the Protocols property sheet in the Network application of the Control Panel. For external TCP/IP connection to the Internet, you should check with your ISP to obtain correct information for TCP/IP settings. In particular, you'll need to know the IP address, subnet mask, default gateway, Domain Name System (DNS) domain name, and IP addresses for DNS servers to be used in DNS name searches.

3. Perform initial communications testing for the external network adapter card. Use Ping.exe (or similar utilities), provided with Windows NT and Windows 95, on another internal IP client computer to verify that the server external adapter card is set correctly. You'll need to use another computer located on the external segment when using ping or other echo-reply type testing.

Configuring the Internal Network Adapter Card

Follow these steps to configure the network adapter card that will be used to connect Microsoft Proxy Server internally to your private network:

1. From the Control Panel, click on the Network icon and select the Bindings property sheet. Set protocol bindings appropriately for each network adapter card.

2. Disable any bindings that are not needed or currently used on your internal network, such as NetBEUI Protocol or WINS Client (TCP/IP). You must enable bindings for either NWLink IPX/SPX Compatible Transport or TCP/IP Protocol on this adapter card.

3. Verify that NWLink IPX/SPX Compatible Transport and/or TCP/IP Protocol are installed and their properties configured properly. From the Control Panel, click on the Network icon, and select Protocols. Check the following:

Make sure to enter the same network number for Internal Network Number that is used by other Novell-based servers and clients on your network. In most cases, you can use Auto Frame Type Detection to have Windows NT automatically detect the correct frame type that is in use on your internal network. In some cases, you may need to enter the frame type manually by using Manual Frame Type Detection. If you manually enter a frame type, be sure it's the same frame type supported by other Novell-based servers and clients on your network.

4. If your internal network uses RIP routing, you can also choose to enable RIP routing on the Routing tab as well. Remember from our discussion in Chapter 4 that RIP routing can add a considerable amount of traffic to your network—enable this only where it's needed for devices to communicate on your network.

5. Don't use the *Obtain an IP address from a DHCP server* option for obtaining an IP address for use on the internal network. Always assign a permanent reserved IP address for the Microsoft Proxy Server.

WARNING Do not enter an address for Default Gateway for the internal network adapter. If you do, the internal network will not be able to get to the Internet!

Perform Initial Communications Testing for Both Server Network Adapter Cards

Use Ping.exe (or similar utilities), provided with Windows NT and Windows 95, on another internal IP client computer to verify that the server internal adapter card is set correctly. Also, if you are using IPX/SPX exclusively on your internal network, there's an IPX-based utility that does pinging.

Words of Wisdom for Setting Up Two Adapters

When setting up two network adapter cards for gateway operation, install one card at a time into the server and configure that card, then remove that card, and install the second card and configure it. Next, install the first card back into the server. This helps to stop any of the possible conflicts explained below:

- In most cases, device conflicts are possible where hardware settings are preconfigured for memory base I/O addresses or IRQ levels on each of the adapter cards. Check that the base I/O and IRQ settings are set differently for each card, and use settings that don't conflict with other devices that are currently installed on your system.

- Make note of the configured settings used for each network adapter card as the card is installed and update these notes if changes are made while you are installing. Keeping notes can help reduce the amount of time required to troubleshoot any hardware device conflicts later.

- Verify that both adapter cards are installed and configured correctly by using the Adapters property sheet in the Network application of Control Panel. Check for each adapter's unique I/O base address and IRQ values.

When we installed two 3COM cards in the NT Server we were using as the proxy server, the customer had two 3c509 cards. We found it confusing to keep track of which adapter we were configuring. Windows NT identifies each adapter added to the system with a leading number, such as [1] for the first adapter installed and [2] for the second adapter installed. Refer to these numbers when attempting to verify or change settings for a specific hardware adapter.

Setup Considerations When Using a Single Adapter

In some cases, the Microsoft Proxy Server can be used with a single network adapter on a private network. In this type of installation, no gateway services for Internet access are configured, and the Microsoft Proxy Server is used primarily to provide a document-caching service for local network users.

For configuring a Microsoft Proxy Server for a single network adapter connection to the internal network, you can use IP and DNS settings that are appropriate for servers and clients on your local TCP/IP network. There aren't any special considerations for TCP/IP network settings in this type of installation.

You can choose to implement Microsoft Proxy Server on a server that has only one network adapter card. This configuration can be used primarily for providing limited proxy service in the following ways:

- Caching service for internal Web Proxy clients

- An IP application-level gateway to support internal IPX clients that use WinSock Proxy service

The Local Address Table

When you actually install Microsoft Proxy Server, you'll be asked to fill in the Local Address Table Configuration dialog box. The stuff you enter is used to create a Local Address Table (LAT). Microsoft Proxy Server uses that LAT to define your private network. Both the Web Proxy and WinSock Proxy services use it actively when they process client requests. With this in mind, you can imagine the resulting chaos if there are any discrepancies between addresses recorded in the LAT and addresses used on your network! Monitoring and correcting any inconsistencies as they occur is tantamount to smooth sailing because the LAT is so fundamental to a healthy, happy proxy service. If things get tangled and dark, you can modify or even replace the whole LAT tamale stored on your server.

More about That LAT

The Microsoft Proxy Server's Setup program helps you author a list of the IP addresses that make up your network during installation. The stuff you enter is used to form the LAT, which in turn defines your network, and any external IP addresses are strictly excluded from it.

After you've done your thing, the Setup program proceeds to install the LAT on your server. It'll be in a file named Msplat.txt, and its default location is C:\Msp\Clients. If, for some reason, you decide to install Microsoft Proxy Server somewhere else on your server, the Msplat.txt file will be relocated accordingly. Microsoft Proxy Server's Setup program doesn't stop there—it'll also install a client setup program in that directory.

When you set up the Microsoft Proxy Server, it configures the client's subdirectory on the server called Mspclnt. Make sure and designate this directory as a network share. Clients can then connect to this share via \\Servername\ Mspclnt, and then by running the client setup program (setup.exe). This configures the client computer as a client of the WinSock Proxy service, and also configures the client computer's Internet browser as a client of the Web Proxy service. (The exact client configuration depends on configuration choices you make during Microsoft Proxy Server setup.)

When the client is set up, the LAT file (Msplat.txt) is copied to the client. Then, to keep client LAT files current, the Msplat.txt file is automatically checked and updated, if needed, from the server. Whenever a client attempts to establish a connection to an IP address using a Windows Sockets application, the LAT is used to determine whether the IP address is on the local network or the external network. If the address is internal, the connection's made directly; if it's an external address, the connection's made remotely through the WinSock Proxy service on Microsoft Proxy Server.

When Is the LAT Defined?

The Local Address Table Configuration dialog box can first be configured when installing the Microsoft Proxy Server. But what if you need to add addresses after the initial installation? Your answer lies in following these next steps to add addresses to the LAT:

1. Click on the Construct Table button in the Local Address Table Configuration dialog box. This generates the list of IP address pairs from internal routing tables used by Windows NT Server. (You'll see this during the installation on the next page.)

2. Use the edit controls in the Local Address Table Configuration dialog box to manually enter pairs of IP addresses.

You can also use a combination of both techniques (generate a list of IP address pairs, then use the edit controls to manually add and remove addresses).

When you're installing Microsoft Proxy Server, it's wise to click on the Construct Table button in the Local Address Table Configuration dialog box. This will generate a list of IP address pairs from internal routing tables used by Windows NT Server. However, sometimes it won't find subnets on your internal network, or could include addresses external to your private network. It's important that you review the generated list of IP addresses. Use the edit controls to add any needed IP address pairs until all addresses of your internal network are defined. Always remove any IP address pairs that define external (Internet) addresses.

> If you find that a subnet of your private network is omitted when constructing the Local Address Table configuration, you will need to add the IP address pairs as described above. Make sure to review the server network configuration to ensure that you have removed any IP addresses to external networks.

Installing Microsoft Proxy Server

Finally, we're going to actually install the Microsoft Proxy Server. Get to your NT 4 Server. Make sure you have IIS installed, and at least Service Pack 2. Now, get comfy and plop the CD into the server.

1. Log on using a user account that has administrative privileges on the server.

2. From the root directory of the Microsoft Proxy Server CD, run Setup. The Welcome dialog box appears, as shown in Figure 16.2.

FIGURE 16.2

Microsoft Proxy Server welcomes you.

3. Click on Continue. The CD Key Number dialog box appears, as shown in Figure 16.3.

FIGURE 16.3

Enter your product
ID here.

4. To record the product identification number (displayed on the Certificate of Authenticity provided with the product), type that number in the CD Key box, click on OK, and then click on OK in the Confirmation dialog box that appears. The program searches to make sure IIS is installed, and if it finds all the necessary files, the Change Folder dialog box appears (see Figure 16.4).

FIGURE 16.4

Deciding where to place
Proxy Server

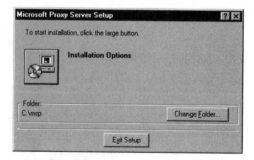

5. To change the folder into which Microsoft Proxy Server is installed, click on Change Folder and complete the dialog box that appears. To accept the default folder, click on the Installation Option button to reach the Installation Options dialog box shown in Figure 16.5.

F I G U R E 16.5

Select the items
you want to install.

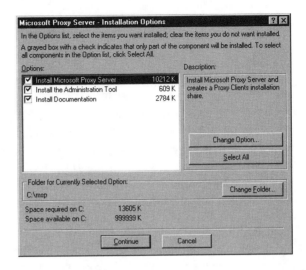

6. To determine which Microsoft Proxy Server components to install, select
or clear the checkbox for each option. This dialog box contains checkboxes for installing Proxy Server, the Administration Tool, and Documentation. By default, all components are selected. When the installation
options are set appropriately, click on Continue.

If you don't have an NT Service Pack loaded, the installation will abort right
here. If this happens to you, install the Service Pack and reinstall Proxy Server. If
the Service Pack was already installed, the Microsoft Proxy Server Cache Drives
dialog box appears (see Figure 16.6). The server's local drives are listed.

F I G U R E 16.6

Assigning a cache drive

7. To assign a disk to store cached data, select the drive from the list, type a number under Maximum Size (MB), and click on Set. Repeat as necessary to assign additional drives to store cached data.

When configuring the cache drives, you must, at a minimum, allocate at least one drive and 5MB for caching. However, the recommended minimum allocation is higher. We recommend that you allocate at least 100MB plus 0.5MB for each Web Proxy service client. Be sure to round up to the nearest full megabyte. For example, if a server will be servicing 79 Web Proxy service clients, you should allocate 140MB or more to the cache. For each server, the optimal cache allocation varies depending on load and configuration, but in general, increasing the disk space allocation benefits the cache.

Allocate drive space to the cache in increments of 5MB. If you assign a number to the cache that can't be evenly divided by five, the allocation is rounded down to the next lowest 5MB increment. For example, if you assign 194MB to the C drive, 190MB will be allocated from that drive to the cache. We strongly recommend that you use only NTFS volumes for caching.

8. Click on OK when you finish assigning cache drives. The Local Address Table Configuration dialog box appears, as shown in Figure 16.7. Use this dialog box to define all the internal IP addresses of your network, and to exclude all external IP addresses.

F I G U R E 16.7

Setting your network IP addresses

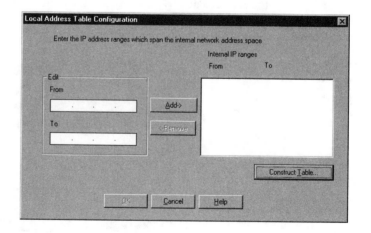

9. To create a table of your internal network's IP addresses, click on the Construct Table button. The Construct Local Address Table dialog box appears (see Figure 16.8).

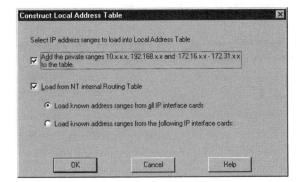

10. You can add to the LAT three ranges of IP addresses defined by IANA as private address ranges, which can be used in a private IP network not connected to the Internet. To do so, select the Add the Private Ranges checkbox.

11. To choose the network adapter cards on the server whose IP addresses are included in the LAT, select Load from NT Internal Routing Table, and complete its options:

   ■ If you don't know which of the server's network adapter cards are connected to the private network, select *Load known address ranges from all IP interface cards.*

   ■ If you know which of the server's network adapter cards are connected to the private (internal) network and which are connected to the Internet, select *Load known address ranges from the following IP interface cards.* This will load only those IP addresses associated with the server's internally connected cards. Then, in the list of network adapter cards, select the checkbox for each of the internally connected cards, and clear the checkbox for each of the externally connected cards.

12. When you've completed the Construct Local Address Table dialog box, click on OK. The Local Address Table Configuration dialog box now returns. A list of IP address pairs is displayed in the Internal IP Ranges box.

13. Verify that the entries in the Internal IP Ranges box correctly identify your internal network. Add any needed IP address pairs until all addresses of your internal network are defined. Again, remove any IP address pairs that define external (Internet) addresses.

   ■ To add a range of IP addresses to the list, go to the Edit area and type a pair of addresses in the From and To boxes. Then click on the Add button.

   ■ To add a single IP address to the list, go to the Edit area and type the same address in both the From and To boxes. Then click on the Add button.

   ■ To remove an IP address or address pair from the list, select it from the Internal IP Ranges box, and then click on the Remove button.

14. When the LAT configuration is properly set, click on OK. The Client Installation/Configuration dialog box appears (see Figure 16.9). Use this dialog box to enter information that's used by the client setup program, which Microsoft Proxy Server Setup installs into the Mspclnt share.

FIGURE 16.9

Setting configuration options for Setup

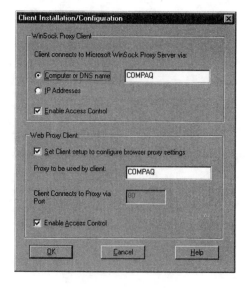

15. Use the choices under WinSock Proxy Client to specify how the client setup program will configure WinSock Proxy clients that install from this server.

- Select either Computer or DNS Name or IP Addresses. If you select Computer or DNS Name, verify that the name is correct. If necessary, type in the appropriate name.

- When the Enable Access Control checkbox is selected, WinSock Proxy service security is enabled, and only those clients that have been assigned permissions are able to use the WinSock Proxy service on this server. If you clear this checkbox, all internal clients will be able to use the WinSock Proxy service on this server. By default, this checkbox is selected.

16. Use the choices under Web Proxy Client to specify how the client setup program configures Web Proxy clients that install from this server.

- Select *Set Client setup to configure browser proxy settings* to have the client setup program configure client browsers as a Web Proxy client (if the browser is Netscape Navigator or Microsoft Internet Explorer). If you select this option, verify that the name shown in the Proxy to be Used by Client box is correct. Again, if necessary, type in the correct name. Also, the Client Connects to Proxy Via Port value will display the port number that Web Proxy clients will be configured to use. The value in this box cannot be changed here. It's the TCP port number that's set for Internet Information Server, and is changed using Internet Service Manager to administer the WWW service.

- When the Enable Access Control checkbox is selected, Web Proxy service security is enabled. When this checkbox is cleared, the Web Proxy service won't attempt to validate connections from clients. By default, this checkbox is selected.

17. When the Client Installation/Configuration dialog box is complete, click on OK.

If all goes well, your files should be copied at this time, and you'll receive a confirmation that Proxy Server was set up correctly.

Using Internet Service Manager

Internet Service Manager is an administrative tool provided by IIS. Internet Service Manager can be used to administer properties for two services provided by Microsoft Proxy Server: the Web Proxy and WinSock Proxy services.

For administering access to Web Proxy and WinSock Proxy services, we recommend that you add users to groups, and then assign permissions to those groups. By using group assignments, you can simplify the administrative tasks needed to grant or revoke user permissions for Microsoft Proxy Server.

To configure Microsoft Proxy Server services with Internet Service Manager:

1. Select Start ➤ Programs ➤ Microsoft Internet Server (Common) ➤ Internet Service Manager.

The Microsoft Internet Service Manager window is displayed, as shown in Figure 16.10. All installed Internet services for the current server are listed.

FIGURE 16.10

The Microsoft Internet
Service Manager

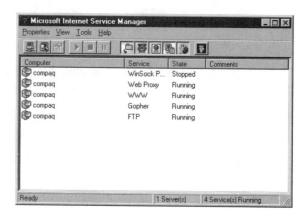

2. If you'll be managing a remote server, connect to that server by going to the Properties menu. Click on Connect to Server and complete the Connect to Server dialog box that appears. To connect to all Microsoft Proxy Servers on your network, go to the Properties menu and click on Find All Servers.

The WinSock Proxy service on other server computers is not detected when Find All Servers is used. To connect to WinSock Proxy service for different computers, use Connect to Server and specify the server name for connection.

3. To administer a server's Internet service, double-click on the computer name next to the service name. To administer a server's Web Proxy service, double-click on the computer name next to that service. To administer a server's WinSock Proxy service, double-click on the computer name next to that service. The Service Properties window for the selected service appears. Figure 16.11 shows the Web Proxy Service Properties window for a Compaq computer.

FIGURE 16.11

Setting service properties for a specific server

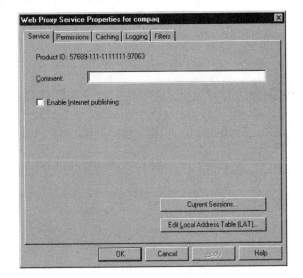

Setting Up a Modem or ISDN Adapter

With Microsoft Proxy Server, you can use the Windows NT Remote Access Service (RAS) dial-out client to connect to an ISP. RAS dial-out requires the use of a modem 28.8Kbps or higher, or an ISDN adapter.

Setting Up RAS

RAS can be installed during the initial Windows NT Server installation, or any time afterward. Log on as an administrator, and make sure you have the TCP/IP protocol installed before installing RAS.

To install the RAS client with Microsoft Proxy Server:

1. Select Control Panel ➤ Network, click on the Services tab, and click on Add.

2. From the Network Service box, select Remote Access Service, and then click on OK.

3. Follow the on-screen instructions to complete the installation of Remote Access Service.

   - Select Dial Out Only for Port Usage to configure RAS for a dial-out-only connection to an ISP. Port usage can be set by clicking on Configure in the Remote Access Service Setup dialog box.

   - Network protocol settings should include TCP/IP only (the IPX/SPX and NetBEUI checkboxes should be cleared). Network protocols can be set by clicking on Network in the Remote Access Service Setup dialog box.

Configuring RAS Options with Microsoft Proxy Server

To configure dial-up support for Microsoft Proxy Server, first verify that RAS has been installed and configured properly. Once RAS is installed, you must configure port usage for dial-out only.

To set or verify a RAS client for dial-up support:

1. Choose Start ➤ Settings ➤ Control Panel and double-click on the Network icon. The Network Properties dialog box appears.

2. Click on the Services tab, then select Remote Access Service.

3. Click on Properties. The Remote Access Setup dialog box appears. If necessary, select a port from the list. If only a single port has been set up for RAS use, this port will be selected by default, as shown in Figure 16.12.

FIGURE 16.12

Selecting a port in
the Remote Access
Setup dialog box

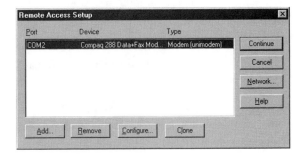

4. Click on Configure. The Configure Port Usage dialog box appears (see Figure 16.13).

FIGURE 16.13

Configuring port usage

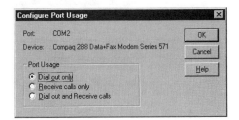

5. From the Port Usage options, select Dial Out Only, then click on OK.

6. From Remote Access Setup, click on Network. The Network Configuration dialog box appears (see Figure 16.14).

FIGURE 16.14

Configuring your
network for TCP/IP

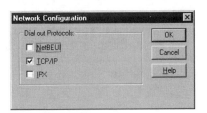

7. Select TCP/IP from the list of dial-out protocols, then click on OK.

8. From Remote Access Setup, click on Continue.

9. Click on Close from the Network Properties dialog box, then select Yes when prompted to restart the computer.

Once the RAS client is installed, you have to reconfigure Remote Access Autodial Manager and Remote Access Connection Manager services to use Microsoft Proxy Auto Dial so you can manage dial-up support.

To reconfigure Remote Access Service for dial-up support:

1. Choose Start ➤ Settings ➤ Control Panel and double-click on the Services icon. The Services dialog box appears, as shown in Figure 16.15.

FIGURE 16.15

The Services dialog box

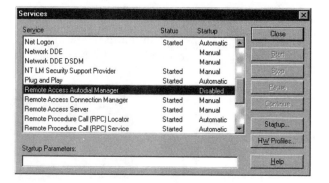

2. Select Remote Access Autodial Manager from the listed services and click on Startup. The Service dialog box appears (see Figure 16.16).

3. Click on Disabled from the Startup Type area, then click on OK. The Services dialog box returns.

4. Select Remote Access Connection Manager from the listed services and click on Startup. The Service dialog box appears again.

5. Click on Automatic from the Startup Type area, then click on OK to return to the Services dialog box.

6. Click on Close.

Creating RAS Phone Book Entries

Once a RAS client has been configured, an initial dialing entry must be created by using the Dial-Up Networking program. This entry will be used to dial your ISP's phone number. Before creating a dialing entry, first check with your ISP for any specific connection settings that you'll need to use when creating your dialing entry.

To create a default RAS phone book entry for dial-up support:

1. Choose Start ➤ Programs ➤ Accessories, then click on Dial-Up Networking.

2. If the phone book is empty, click on OK to add a new entry.

3. Enter a name for the new phone book entry (see Figure 16.17), then click on Next.

4. In the Server dialog box shown in Figure 16.18, click on I Am Calling the Internet, then click on Next.

F I G U R E   16.17

Type your new phone
book entry here.

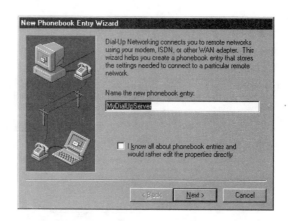

F I G U R E   16.18

Use this box to describe
your server connection.

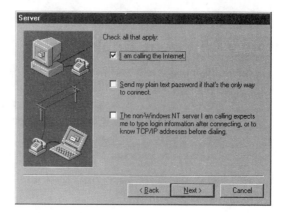

5. Select the modem you will use, then click on Next.

6. In the Phone Number dialog box (see Figure 16.19), enter the phone number used to call your ISP. Click on Next.

7. Click on Finish. The Dial-up Networking dialog box appears, as shown in Figure 16.20.

8. Select the new phone book entry to dial from the drop-down list box.

9. Click on More, then click on Logon Preferences. The Logon Preferences dialog box appears (see Figure 16.21).

FIGURE 16.19

Tell your dial-up server
what number to call.

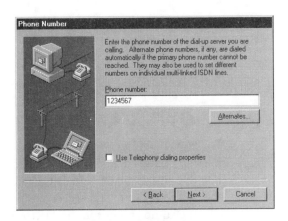

FIGURE 16.20

The Dial-Up Networking
dialog box

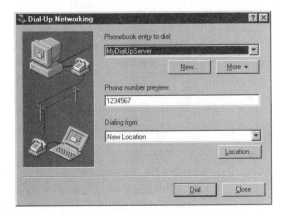

FIGURE 16.21

Setting your logon
preferences

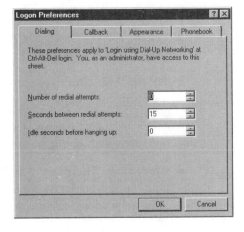

10. From the Dialing tab, click on the up arrow next to Idle Seconds before Hanging Up to change the default value from 0 to 1. This will ensure that RAS always disconnects after each dialing attempt.

11. Click on OK, then click on Close.

Using Microsoft Proxy Auto Dial

For now, most Internet connections are dial-up connections. This could quite possibly change in the future as more ISDN, Cable-Modem, and Frame-Relay lines become available and as prices continue to come down to somewhere in this galaxy. For now, however, support for dial-up is still a very important thing. Dial-up support in the Microsoft Proxy Server for connecting to an ISP is managed by using the Microsoft Proxy Auto Dial utility, Adialcfg.exe.

To open Microsoft Proxy Auto Dial:

1. From the server's desktop, click on Start ➤ Programs ➤ Microsoft Proxy Server.

2. Select Auto Dial Configuration. The Microsoft Proxy Auto Dial dialog box will appear.

When a RAS client is installed and configured on the server computer, Dial-Up Networking can be used to create RAS phone book entries for service dialing with Microsoft Proxy Server. Microsoft Proxy Auto Dial can use RAS phone book entries to perform on-demand dial-up connections as a RAS client. We'll configure both the RAS client and the phone book entries in a minute.

For dial-up support, connections are made by Microsoft Proxy Server when the following service demands occur:

■ **For the Web Proxy service:** A dial-up connection is used when a requested object can't be located and returned by the Web Proxy caching service.

■ **For the WinSock Proxy service:** All client requests are processed by using a dial-up connection.

You can also use the Auto Dial tool to configure the following options for any configured RAS phone book entry:

■ **Credentials:** These can include additional logon information used when connecting, such as user name, password, and domain name credentials required for logging onto your ISP.

■ **Dialing hours:** Although service dialing is only performed on demand, dialing hours can be set to enable or disable dialing during selected hours of the day, or for selected days of the week.

Let's take a minute to look into setting credentials and dialing hours.

Setting Credentials

You can use the Credentials property sheet of the Microsoft Proxy Auto Dial dialog box if your ISP requires additional user and password information to be entered when a dial-up connection is made. This information can be stored for use by Microsoft Proxy Auto Dial and used each time when dialing a specific phone book entry.

To set credentials to be used when dialing a RAS phone book entry:

1. Open Microsoft Proxy Auto Dial as described above and select the Credentials property sheet.

FIGURE 16.22

Setting credentials

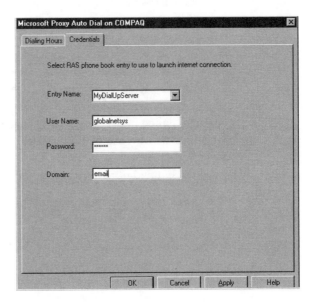

2. Click on the arrow to display the Entry Name list box. Select the name of the RAS phone book entry to be used when dialing with Microsoft Proxy Server.

3. Under User Name, specify the user name to be used when logging onto a service provider's dial-in server.

4. Under Password, specify a user password (if one is required) to be used when logging on.

5. Under Domain, specify a domain if the dial-in server requires that one be provided when logging on. (This parameter is not usually required and can be left blank in most cases.)

6. Click on Apply, then OK. Credentials entered will be used each time Microsoft Proxy Server initiates a dial-up connection by using this RAS phone book entry.

Setting Dialing Hours

You can use the Dialing Hours property sheet to specify selected hours or days during the week when service dialing is to be allowed. When dialing hours are selected, Microsoft Proxy Server will allow on-demand dialing to occur. When dialing hours are cleared, service dialing will not occur.

This little control freak feature can be used to prevent service dial-up connections from being made during certain selected hours of the day, or for selected days of the week. In some cases, limiting dialing to certain specified hours can be useful where Internet access is billed by connection time, or where toll charges are applied each time an ISP's access number is dialed.

When dialing hours are set for a specific phone book entry, this information stored by Microsoft Proxy Auto Dial and used each time when dialing the entry.

To set dialing hours for use when dialing a RAS phone book entry:

1. Open Microsoft Proxy Auto Dial as described above and select the Credentials property sheet.

2. Click on the arrow to display the Entry Name list box. Select the name of the RAS phone book entry to be used when dialing with Microsoft Proxy Server.

3. Click on the Dialing Hours property sheet (see Figure 16.23).

4. To disable service dialing during specified hours of the day, or for specified days of the week, take your mouse and click on the hour(s). By default, service dialing is set to be enabled for all hours and isn't restricted.

FIGURE 16.23

Select specific dialing
hours here.

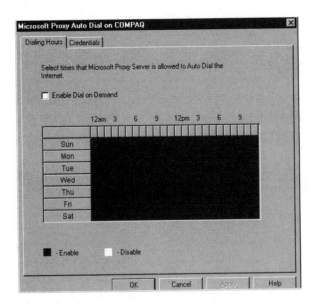

5. When dialing hours have been set or modified, click on Apply, then OK. The dialing hours entered will be used each time Microsoft Proxy Server initiates a dial-up connection by using this RAS phone book entry.

Restarting Services after a Dial-Up Connection

When Microsoft Proxy Auto Dial is used to establish a dial-up connection to an ISP, the WWW, Web Proxy, and WinSock Proxy services must be restarted when Microsoft Proxy Auto Dial is being used for the first time. Also, when any time settings are cleared, services must be restarted for new parameters to take effect. You can stop and restart all services (WWW, Web Proxy, and WinSock Proxy) by using Internet Service Manager.

After the Microsoft Proxy Auto Dial has been used at least once, changes to Auto Dial settings will then be used by Web Proxy and WinSock Proxy services for subsequent dial-out connections without having to stop and start each service.

Just for fun, if you're really bored, you can stop and start the WWW, Web Proxy, and WinSock Proxy services from the command prompt:

```
net stop w3svc
net stop wspsrv
net start w3svc
net start wspsrv
```

It isn't necessary to issue a separate command to stop and start the Web Proxy service. Stopping and starting the WWW service also stops and starts the Web Proxy service.

Web Proxy Clients

Run the client setup program by going to the share on the server \\Servername\ Mspclnt. It will then install the proxy client onto the computer. Typically, this will configure the Internet browser on the workstation.

If the browser proxy settings configured by the client setup program are not appropriate for a particular client, you'll have to reconfigure that client's Web browser by using the Web browser's own configuration interface after installing the client software. Also, if a client's Web browser isn't Microsoft Internet Explorer or Netscape Navigator, or if client setup doesn't successfully configure a client's Web browser to use the Web Proxy service, then you must use the Web browser's own configuration interface to specify the name of the appropriate Microsoft Proxy Server and the protocol port number. (It's usually 80.)

You can configure Internet Explorer by using the Internet application in the Control Panel.

WinSock Proxy Clients

The WinSock Proxy client components are installed by running the client setup program, as described above. The client setup program doesn't configure individual Windows Sockets applications. Instead, the client computer is configured to use the WinSock Proxy service on a server. All Windows Sockets applications on that computer access the Internet through the WinSock Proxy service on Microsoft Proxy Server.

The server must be configured to permit access for the required protocol on the required outbound and inbound ports before a Windows Sockets application can access the Internet through Microsoft Proxy Server.

In a local network running multiple Microsoft Proxy Server gateways, install an equal number of WinSock Proxy clients from each gateway to balance Internet traffic across all the gateways.

WinSock Proxy Client Considerations

The following are some considerations for WinSock Proxy client computers:

- **Don't set Windows Sockets client applications to use Microsoft Proxy Server.** Even if the configuration parameters for the application allow it, *do not* set a Windows Sockets application on a computer configured as a WinSock Proxy client to use Microsoft Proxy Server.

- **Don't install Microsoft Exchange Server on WinSock Proxy clients.** Microsoft Exchange client software and WinSock Proxy client software can be installed on the same computer. However, do not install Microsoft Exchange server software and WinSock Proxy client software on the same computer.

- **What if the client is upgraded?** If the computer running the WinSock Proxy client is upgraded, the client installation will have to be reinstalled.

But Now I Can't Dial Out!

After a computer has the WinSock Proxy client software installed, it can use the Windows Sockets applications to access Internet sites through Microsoft Proxy Server. However, the client will be unable to use Windows Sockets applications to access any Internet sites through a dial-up connection to a private ISP. For example, a user might have a computer at home that's sometimes used to connect to the corporate network and other times to a private ISP. You can turn the WinSock Proxy client on and off by using the Client application in the Control Panel.

To turn the WinSock Proxy client on or off:

1. From the client computer, open the Control Panel and double-click the WSP Client icon. The Microsoft WinSock Proxy Client dialog box appears.

2. Select or clear the Enable WinSock Proxy Client checkbox.

   - To turn on the WinSock Proxy client software and use Windows Sockets applications with Microsoft Proxy Server, select the Enable WinSock Proxy Client checkbox.

   - To turn off the WinSock Proxy client software and use Windows Sockets applications with a private ISP, clear the Enable WinSock Proxy Client checkbox.

3. Click on OK, then reboot the computer.

Wow, we've just gone through 16 chapters of great TCP/IP information! Only, one more to go and it's important—troubleshooting.

CHAPTER

17

Shooting Trouble

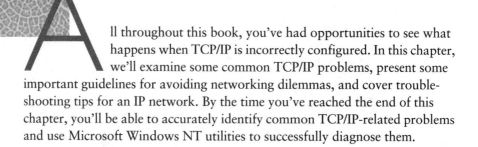

Il throughout this book, you've had opportunities to see what happens when TCP/IP is incorrectly configured. In this chapter, we'll examine some common TCP/IP problems, present some important guidelines for avoiding networking dilemmas, and cover trouble-shooting tips for an IP network. By the time you've reached the end of this chapter, you'll be able to accurately identify common TCP/IP-related problems and use Microsoft Windows NT utilities to successfully diagnose them.

Getting to the Source

Although it may certainly seem, during a major network outage, that you've found and are experiencing an entirely new, never-before-encountered network problem, 99 percent of the computer puzzles you'll experience on the job won't be new ones at all. It's highly likely your hand up isn't unique, but rather common, with a proven, successful method to lead you happily toward its solution. In the networking industry, contacts are your best friends, so the old adage of never burning your bridges at work strongly applies. The network world is a small world after all, and you just never know when you might need the insights of a former colleague!

When an outage occurs on a large or small network, time-honored problem-solving strategies like staying calm, thinking logically, and the good ol' process of elimination also apply. Lots of network problems can be grouped into categories. It's important to understand these different categories, and then work deductively through them until the culprit's exposed. Many Microsoft TCP/IP-related problems can be grouped into the following categories:

Source Category	Typical Associated Problems
Configuration	If your network configuration is incorrect, it can result in one or more services not starting when you bring up your NT Workstation or Server.

Source Category	Typical Associated Problems
IP addressing	The host can hang up when trying to communicate with other hosts. This could be caused by the existence of an improper subnet address or duplicate IP address. Windows NT will give you a pop-up message if there are duplicate IP addresses on your network.
Subnet addressing	Related to the above. If your host has an improper subnet address assigned to it, it may not be able to talk to other local or remote hosts.
Resolution	You can ping a host with an IP address, or connect to a network drive using a host's IP address, but you cannot establish a connection using only its host name.

The source of the problem implicates the problem itself. Identifying the source narrows down the field of possible causes and expedites finding a solution. For example, if you ping to "Host Bob," and receive an error stating host unknown, you can then ping Host Bob from the host's IP address, 160.1.56.89. If the ping is successful, a resolution problem is the culprit, and you can begin troubleshooting the resolution methods used on your network. If the ping was unsuccessful, you can start troubleshooting Host Bob for connectivity issues.

Tools for Diagnosis

TCP/IP has been around for quite a while, so there are a whole bunch of tools around to help you in troubleshooting problems related to it. Some of these tools can be used to locate the source, while others can be employed to track errors. Microsoft Windows NT includes plenty of utilities that can prove very helpful when attacking a TCP/IP network-related problem.

The following TCP/IP tools are included with Microsoft NT:

Tool	Purpose
ping	Verifies connections between hosts by sending ICMP echo packets to the specified IP address.

Tool	Purpose
ARP	Gathers hardware addresses of local hosts and your default gateway. You can view the ARP cache and check for invalid or duplicate entries.
netstat	Checks your current connections and protocol-related statistics of your TCP/IP host.
nbtstat	Reports statistics and connections for NetBIOS over TCP/IP.
ipconfig	Displays TCP/IP configuration settings for a host. This utility is particularly useful when the host obtains address information dynamically from DHCP, or a host name from WINS.
tracert	A route reporting utility that sends ICMP echo requests to an IP address, and reports ICMP errors that are returned. Tracert produces a report that lists all of the routers crossed in the process.
route	Used to view or modify the local routing table.
SNMP	Used to remotely manage network devices by collecting, analyzing, and reporting data about the performance of network components.
Event Log	Tracks errors and certain noteworthy events.
Performance Monitor	A versatile tool that can be used to analyze performance and detect bottlenecks. Remember, Microsoft SNMP must be enabled on a host in order to monitor TCP/IP counters.
Registry Editor	The fault-tolerant database in which configuration data is stored for Windows NT. REGEDIT32 is the editor that allows you to browse and edit the configuration of the host.
Network Monitor	Captures incoming and outgoing packets to analyze a problem.
nslookup	Displays information from DNS name servers.

General Guidelines to Follow

When faced with a troubleshooting dilemma, it's a good idea to keep some simple guidelines in mind to help you stay focused. In a difficult, high-pressure situation, these guidelines can prevent you from duplicating your efforts. Often, in a "network down" predicament, people panic and just start recklessly resetting routers, rebooting servers, and so on. After these attempts, when the network still doesn't function, they call on someone else, who then enters the situation, and begins resetting routers, and rebooting servers—taking up critical time with redundant approaches, and getting everyone nowhere fast! It's so important to approach these often complicated quandaries in a sensible, logical manner—with a plan—so if you do get stumped, you can turn the problem over to someone and equip them with organized knowledge of exactly what you've already done. Also important is to document the error and solution path for other colleagues who may come across that very problem again later. Figure 17.1 shows the different layers of the DoD reference model and the different protocols related to each layer. A firm understanding of the different layers and the protocols that are specified at each layer will help you intelligently troubleshoot network problems—and make you sound smart in meetings, too!

FIGURE 17.1

Protocols at each layer of the Internet Protocol suite

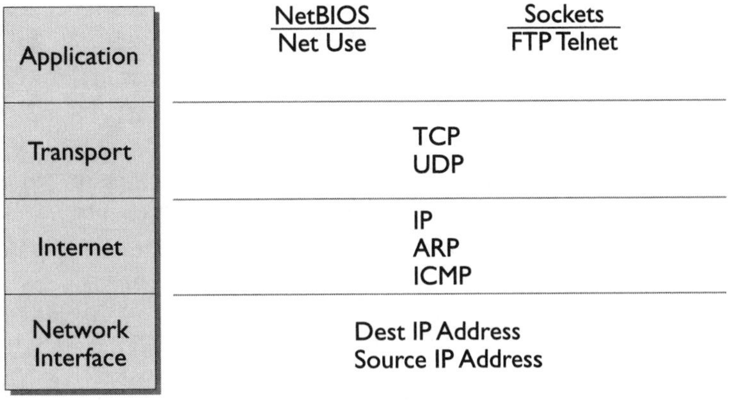

		NetBIOS	Sockets
Application		Net Use	FTP Telnet
Transport		\multicolumn{2}{c|}{TCP UDP}	
Internet		\multicolumn{2}{c|}{IP ARP ICMP}	
Network Interface		\multicolumn{2}{c|}{Dest IP Address Source IP Address}	

Using Figure 17.1 as a troubleshooting guide, let's say that a user calls, complaining that they can't log onto the NT domain. Begin by analyzing the bottom layer of the DoD model, working up through the model to the Application layer until a likely problem source is established. You must determine that the protocols at each layer of the TCP/IP suite can communicate with those operating at the layers above and below.

- First, try to ping the device in question. If you can ping the host, then you have verified IP communication between the Network Interface layer and the Internet layer. Why? Because ping uses ARP (Address Resolution Protocol) to resolve the IP address to a hardware address. If pinging worked, then the resolution was successful, meaning the culprit isn't in the lower layers.

- Next, try to either Telnet or net use to the host. If you can establish a session, you have successfully verified TCP/IP communication from the Network Interface layer through the Application layer. At this point you will have to go to the host in question to find out what the user is typing in. The problem can sometimes be something as simple as a domain name being spelled incorrectly.

- If you are unable to resolve the problem, try using a network analyzer like Network General's Sniffer or Microsoft Network Monitor to help you discover the problem.

Verifying IP Communications

Pinging a host is a very popular way of troubleshooting problems. It can be a great place to start—sometimes leading you straight to the problem. If you can ping a host on a remote network, you have verified connectivity through routers, gateways, bridges, and possibly other network devices. That's a pretty good test. Your first weapon when trouble strikes is to try to ping the host. If pinging the host by its host name doesn't work, then try pinging with the host's IP address. If the ping is successful when using just the IP address, then you have a resolution problem.

Here are some general guidelines to keep in mind when pinging a host:

- First, ping the local host address of 127.0.0.1. This will tell you if the host can see itself on the network, and that TCP/IP is loaded correctly.

- Next, ping your IP address to check the correct configuration. If this doesn't work, select Control Panel ➤ Network and check for IP address, subnet, and default gateway entry errors.

- If you're successful pinging your own IP address, ping the default gateway next. If this doesn't work, check your configuration again, and then check to make sure the router is up and working.

- Next, ping the IP address of a remote host located on the other side of the router to verify that the router and WAN are working correctly. If this doesn't work, make sure that IP routing is enabled on all router interfaces. (Typically this is on by default, but someone could have accidentally disabled it.) Also, make sure the remote host is up and functioning.

If all is successful and all problems seem to be fixed, throw caution to the wind and try pinging the host by its host name. If things still aren't working, it's time to troubleshoot your resolution methods, like HOSTS file, WINS, LMHOSTS, and DNS. Refer to previous chapters if you get stuck.

Verifying TCP/IP Session Communications

After you ping your network to death and fix the problem, or find that all is well, the next step is to establish a session with the remote host. You can use a few different methods to verify communication between the Network Interface layer and the Application layer.

- To connect to a host using its NetBIOS name, make a connection using the net use or net view command. An example would be `net use G: \\Alpine\share`. If this isn't successful, make sure you're using the correct NetBIOS name, or that the host even has a NetBIOS name. Also, make sure the destination host is in your LMHOSTS file (entered correctly), if the destination host is located on a remote network.

- If you're still having problems connecting with the NetBIOS name, it's time to check Scope IDs. Each host can be given an extension on their NetBIOS name to keep hosts from seeing each other on the network. Check to make sure that the Scope ID is the same as yours.

- To connect to a host that is not NetBIOS-based, use the Telnet or FTP utility to make a connection. If by chance this was unsuccessful, make sure the remote host has TCP/IP running, and that it also has a Telnet or FTP daemon running. Additionally, make sure you have the correct permission on the remote host to enable you to perform Telnet or FTP. If you're still unsuccessful, check your HOSTS file to make sure the entry for the remote host is correct.

So now you can successfully troubleshoot your NT TCP/IP network. We hope this book has helped you understand NT TCP/IP, and that you'll continue to use it as a reference in the future. And as Microsoft delivers new products, we'll be sure to keep this series up to date.

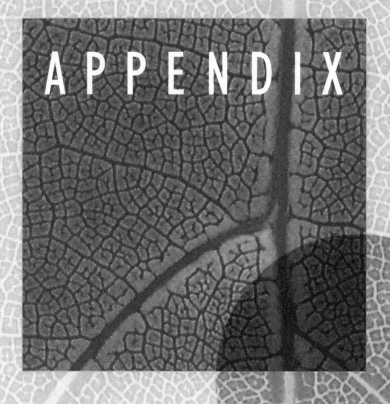

APPENDIX

A

Terminology and NetBIOS Names

Terminology

There are various means of name-to-IP-address mapping for name resolution.

B-Node   Broadcast nodes communicate using a mix of UDP datagrams (both broadcast and directed) and TCP connections. They interoperate with one another within a broadcast area but cannot interoperate across routers in a routed network. B-nodes generate high-broadcast traffic. Each node on the LAN must examine every broadcast datagram.

P-Node   Point-to-point nodes communicate using only directed UDP datagrams and TCP sessions. They relay on NetBIOS name servers, local or remote. If the name server is down, the P-node cannot communicate with any other system, even those on the same local network.

M-Node   Mixed nodes are P-nodes which have been given certain B-node characteristics. M-nodes use broadcast first (to optimize performance, assuming that most resources reside on the local broadcast medium) for name registration and resolution. If this is unsuccessful, point-to-point communication with the name server is used. M-nodes generate high-broadcast traffic, but can cross routers and continue to operate normally if the name server is down.

H-Node   Hybrid nodes (currently in RFC draft form) are also a combination of B-node and P-node functionality. H-node uses point-to-point communication first. If the NetBIOS name server cannot be located, it switches to broadcast. H-node continues to poll for the name server and returns to point-to-point communication when one becomes available.

NetBIOS Names

Microsoft networking components, such as Windows NT Workstation and Windows NT Server services, allow the first 15 characters of a NetBIOS name to be specified by the user or administrator, but reserve the sixteenth character of the NetBIOS name (00-FF hex) to indicate a resource type. Following are some examples of NetBIOS names used by Microsoft components:

Unique Names

\\computer_name[00h]   Registered by the Workstation Service on the WINS client.

\\computer_name[03h]   Registered by the Messenger Service on the WINS client.

\\computer_name[06h]   Registered by the Remote Access Service (RAS), when started on a RAS server.

\\computer_name[1Fh]   Registered by the Network Dynamic Data Exchange (NetDDE) services—will only appear if the NetDDE services are started on the computer. By default under Windows NT 3.51, the NetDDE services are not automatically started.

\\computer_name[20h]   Registered by the Server Service on the WINS client.

\\computer_name[21h]   Registered by the RAS Client Service, when started on a RAS client.

\\computer_name[BEh]   Registered by the Network Monitoring Agent Service—will only appear if the service is started on the computer. If the computer name is not a full 15 characters, the name will be padded with plus (+) symbols.

\\computer_name[BFh]   Registered by the Network Monitoring Utility (included with Microsoft Systems Management Server). If the computer name is not a full 15 characters, the name will be padded with plus (+) symbols.

\\username[03h]   User names for the currently logged on users are registered in the WINS database. The username is registered by the server component so that the user can receive any net send commands sent to their username. If more than one user is logged on with the same username, only the first computer at which a user logged on with the username will register the name.

\\domain_name[1Bh]   Registered by the Windows NT Server primary domain controller (PDC) that is running as the Domain Master browser and is used to allow remote browsing of domains. When a WINS server is queried for this name, a WINS server returns the IP address of the computer that registered this name.

\\domain_name[1Dh]   Registered only by the Master browser, of which there can only be one for each subnet. This name is used by the backup browsers to communicate with the Master browser to retrieve the list of available servers from the Master browser.

WINS servers always return a positive registration response for domain _name[1D], even though the WINS server does not "register" this name in its database. Therefore, when a WINS server is queried for the domain_name[1D], the WINS server returns a negative response, which will cause the client to broadcast to resolve the name.

Group Names

\\domain_name[00h]   Registered by the Workstation Service so that it can receive browser broadcasts from LAN Manager-based computers.

\\domain_name[1Ch]   Registered for use by the domain controllers within the domain and can contain up to 25 IP addresses. One IP address will be that of the primary domain controller (PDC) and the other 24 will be the IP addresses of backup domain controllers (BDCs).

\\domain_name[1Eh]   Registered for browsing purposes and is used by the browsers to elect a Master browser (this is how a statically mapped group name will register itself). When a WINS server receives a name query for a name ending with [1E], the WINS server will always return the network broadcast address for the requesting client's local network.

\\--_MSBROWSE_[01h]   Registered by the Master browser for each subnet. When a WINS server receives a name query for this name, the WINS server will always return the network broadcast address for the requesting client's local network.

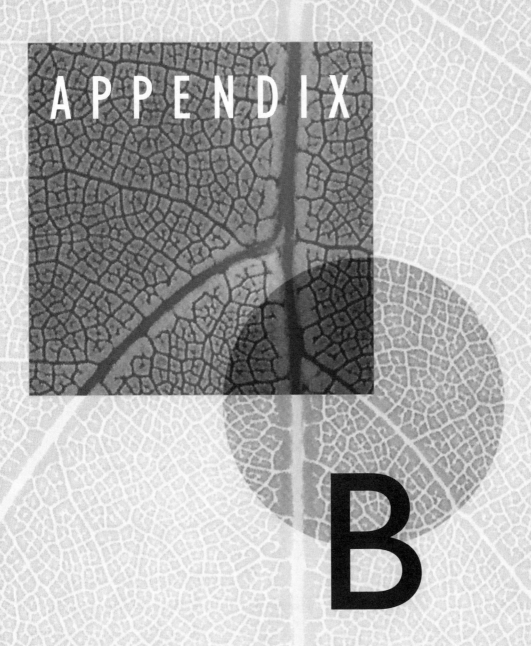

APPENDIX

B

NetBT Configuration Parameters

Introduction

All of the NetBT (NetBIOS over TCP) parameters are Registry values located under one of two different subkeys of `HKEY_LOCAL_MACHINE\System\CurrentControlSet\Services`:

- `Netbt\Parameters`

- `Netbt\Adapters\<Adapter Name>`, in which `<Adapter Name>` refers the subkey for a network adapter that NetBT is bound to, such as Lance01.

Values under the latter key(s) are specific to each adapter. If the system is configured via DHCP, then a change in parameters will take effect if the command `ipconfig /renew` is issued in a command shell. Otherwise, a reboot of the system is required for a change in any of these parameters to take effect.

Standard Parameters Configurable from the Registry Editor

The following parameters are installed with default values by the network Control Panel during the installation of the TCP/IP components. They may be modified using the Registry Editor (regedt32.exe).

BcastNameQueryCount

Key: Netbt\Parameters
Value Type: REG_DWORD - Count
Valid Range: 1 to 0xFFFF
Default: 3
Description: This value determines the number of times NetBT broadcasts a query for a given name without receiving a response.

BcastQueryTimeout

Key: Netbt\Parameters
Value Type: REG_DWORD - Time in milliseconds
Valid Range: 100 to 0xFFFFFFFF
Default: 0x2ee (750 decimal)
Description: This value determines the time interval between successive broadcast name queries for the same name.

CacheTimeout

Key: Netbt\Parameters
Value Type: REG_DWORD - Time in milliseconds
Valid Range: 60000 to 0xFFFFFFFF
Default: 0x927c0 (600,000 milliseconds = 10 minutes)
Description: This value determines the time interval that names are cached in the remote name table.

NameServerPort

Key: Netbt\Parameters
Value Type: REG_DWORD - UDP port number
Valid Range: 0 - 0xFFFF
Default: 0x89
Description: This parameter determines the destination port number to which NetBT will send name service related packets, such as name queries and name registrations, to WINS. Microsoft WINS listens on port 0x89. NetBIOS name servers from other vendors may listen on different ports.

NameSrvQueryCount

Key: Netbt\Parameters
Value Type: REG_DWORD - Count
Valid Range: 0 - 0xFFFF
Default: 3
Description: This value determines the number of times NetBT sends a query to a WINS server for a given name without receiving a response.

NameSrvQueryTimeout

Key: Netbt\Parameters
Value Type: REG_DWORD - Time in milliseconds
Valid Range: 100 - 0xFFFFFFFF
Default: 1,500 (1.5 seconds)
Description: This value determines the time interval between successive name queries to WINS for a given name.

SessionKeepAlive

Key: Netbt\Parameters
Value Type: REG_DWORD - Time in milliseconds
Valid Range: 60,000 - 0xFFFFFFFF
Default: 3,600,000 (1 hour)
Description: This value determines the time interval between keepalive transmissions on a session. Setting the value to 0xFFFFFFFF disables keepalives.

Size/Small/Medium/Large

Key: Netbt\Parameters
Value Type: REG_DWORD
Valid Range: 1, 2, 3 (Small, Medium, Large)
Default: 1 (Small)
Description: This value determines the size of the name tables used to store local and remote names. In general, Small is adequate. If the system is acting as a proxy name server, then the value is automatically set to Large to increase the size of the name cache hash table. Hash table buckets are sized as follows:

Large: 256   Medium: 128   Small: 16

Optional Parameters Configurable from the Registry Editor

These parameters normally do not exist in the Registry. They may be created to modify the default behavior of the NetBT protocol driver.

BroadcastAddress

Key: Netbt\Parameters
Value Type: REG_DWORD - Four byte, little-endian encoded IP address
Valid Range: 0 - 0xFFFFFFFF
Default: The ones-broadcast address for each network.
Description: This parameter can be used to force NetBT to use a specific address for all broadcast name related packets. By default, NetBT uses the ones-broadcast address appropriate for each net (that is, for a network of 11.101.0.0 with a subnet mask of 255.255.0.0, the subnet broadcast address would be 11.101.255.255). This parameter would be set, for example, if the network uses the zeros-broadcast address (set using the UseZeroBroadcast TCP/IP parameter). The appropriate subnet broadcast address would then be 11.101.0.0 in the example above. This parameter would then be set to 0x0b650000. Note that this parameter is global and will be used on all subnets that NetBT is bound to.

EnableProxyRegCheck

Key: Netbt\Parameters
Value Type: REG_DWORD - Boolean
Valid Range: 0 or 1 (False or True)
Default: 0 (False)
Description: If this parameter is set to 1 (True), then the proxy name server will send a negative response to a broadcast name registration if the name is already registered with WINS or is in the proxy's local name cache with a different IP address. The hazard of enabling this feature is that it prevents a system from changing its IP address as long as WINS has a mapping for the name. For this reason, it is disabled by default.

InitialRefreshTimeout

Key: Netbt\Parameters
Value Type: REG_DWORD - Time in milliseconds
Valid Range: 960000 - 0xFFFFFFFF
Default: 960,000 (16 minutes)
Description: This parameter specifies the initial refresh timeout used by NetBT during name registration. NetBT tries to contact the WINS servers at one-eighth of this time interval when it is first registering names. When it receives a successful registration response, that response will contain the new refresh interval to use.

LmhostsTimeout

Key: Netbt\Parameters
Value Type: REG_DWORD - Time in milliseconds
Valid Range: 1000 - 0xFFFFFFFF
Default: 6,000 (6 seconds)
Description: This parameter specifies the timeout value for LMHOSTS and DNS name queries. The timer has a granularity of the timeout value, so the actual timeout could be as much as twice the value.

MaxDgramBuffering

Key: Netbt\Parameters
Value Type: REG_DWORD - Count of bytes
Valid Range: 0 - 0xFFFFFFFF
Default: 0x20000 (128Kb)
Description: This parameter specifies the maximum amount of memory that NetBT will dynamically allocate for all outstanding datagram sends. Once this limit is reached, further sends will fail due to insufficient resources.

NodeType

Key: Netbt\Parameters
Value Type: REG_DWORD - Number
Valid Range: 1, 2, 4, 8 (B-node, P-node, M-node, H-node)
Default: 1 or 8 based on the WINS server configuration
Description: This parameter determines what methods NetBT will use to register and resolve names. A B-node system uses broadcasts. A P-node system uses only point-to-point name queries to a name server (WINS). An M-node system broadcasts first, then queries the name server. An H-node system queries the name server first, then broadcasts. Resolution via LMHOSTS and/or DNS, if enabled, will follow these methods. If this key is present, it will override the DhcpNodeType key. If neither key is present, then the system defaults to B-node if there are no WINS servers configured for the network. The system defaults to H-node if there is at least one WINS server configured.

RandomAdapter

Key: Netbt\Parameters
Value Type: REG_DWORD - Boolean
Valid Range: 0 or 1 (False or True)
Default: 0 (False)
Description: This parameter applies to a multihomed host only. If it is set to 1 (True), then NetBT will randomly choose the IP address to put in a name query response from all of its bound interfaces. Usually, the response contains the address of the interface that the query arrived on. This feature would be used by a server with two interfaces on the same network for load balancing.

RefreshOpCode

Key: Netbt\Parameters
Value Type: REG_DWORD - Number
Valid Range: 8, 9
Default: 8
Description: This parameter forces NetBT to use a specific opcode in name refresh packets. The specification for the NetBT protocol is somewhat ambiguous in this area. Although the default of 8 used by Microsoft implementations appears to be the intended value, some other implementations, such as those by Ungermann-Bass, use the value 9. Two implementations must use the same opcode to interoperate.

SingleResponse

Key: Netbt\Parameters
Value Type: REG_DWORD - Boolean
Valid Range: 0 or 1 (False or True)
Default: 0 (False)
Description: This parameter applies to a multihomed host only. If this parameter is set to 1 (True), then NetBT will only supply an IP address from one of its bound interfaces in name query responses. By default, the addresses of all bound interfaces are included.

WinsDownTimeout

Key: Netbt\Parameters
Value Type: REG_DWORD - Time in milliseconds
Valid Range: 1000 - 0xFFFFFFFF
Default: 15,000 (15 seconds)
Description: This parameter determines the amount of time NetBT will wait before again trying to use WINS after it fails to contact any WINS server. This feature primarily allows computers that are temporarily disconnected from the network, such as laptops, to proceed through BOOT processing without waiting to timeout out each WINS name registration or query individually.

Parameters Configurable from the Network Control Panel Applet

The following parameters can be set via the NCPA. There should be no need to configure them directly.

EnableDns

Key: Netbt\Parameters
Value Type: REG_DWORD - Boolean
Valid Range: 0 or 1 (False or True)
Default: 0 (False)
Description: If this value is set to 1 (True), then NetBT will query the DNS for names that cannot be resolved by WINS, broadcast, or the LMHOSTS file.

EnableLmhosts

Key: Netbt\Parameters
Value Type: REG_DWORD - Boolean
Valid Range: 0 or 1 (False or True)
Default: 1 (True)
Description: If this value is set to 1 (True), then NetBT will search the LMHOSTS file, if it exists, for names that cannot be resolved by WINS or broadcast. By default, there is no LMHOSTS file database directory (specified by Tcpip\Parameters\DatabasePath), so no action will be taken. This value is written by the Advanced TCP/IP configuration dialog of the NCPA.

EnableProxy

Key: Netbt\Parameters
Value Type: REG_DWORD - Boolean
Valid Range: 0 or 1 (False or True)
Default: 0 (False)
Description: If this value is set to 1 (True), then the system will act as a proxy name server for the networks to which NetBT is bound. A proxy name server answers broadcast queries for names that it has resolved through WINS. A proxy name server allows a network of B-node implementations to connect to servers on other subnets that are registered with WINS.

NameServer

Key: Netbt\Adapters\<Adapter Name>
Value Type: REG_SZ - Dotted decimal IP address (i.e., 11.101.1.200)
Valid Range: Any valid IP address
Default: Blank (no address)
Description: This parameter specifies the IP address of the primary WINS server. If this parameter contains a valid value, it overrides the DHCP parameter of the same name.

NameServerBackup

Key: Netbt\Adapters\<Adapter Name>
Value Type: REG_SZ - Dotted decimal IP address (i.e., 11.101.1.200)
Valid Range: Any valid IP address
Default: Blank (no address)
Description: This parameter specifies the IP address of the backup WINS server. If this parameter contains a valid value, it overrides the DHCP parameter of the same name.

ScopeId

Key: Netbt\Parameters
Value Type: REG_SZ - Character string
Valid Range: Any valid DNS domain name consisting of two dot-separated parts, or an asterisk (*).
Default: None
Description: This parameter specifies the NetBIOS name scope for the node. This value must not begin with a period. If this parameter contains a valid value, it will override the DHCP parameter of the same name. A blank value (empty string) will be ignored. Setting this parameter to the value "*" indicates a null scope and will override the DHCP parameter.

Nonconfigurable Parameters

The following parameters are created and used internally by the NetBT components. They should never be modified using the Registry Editor. They are listed here for reference only.

DhcpNameServer

Key: Netbt\Adapters\<Adapter Name>
Value Type: REG_SZ - Dotted decimal IP address (i.e., 11.101.1.200)
Valid Range: Any valid IP address
Default: None
Description: This parameter specifies the IP address of the primary WINS server. It is written by the DHCP client service, if enabled. A valid NameServer value will override this parameter.

DhcpNameServerBackup

Key: Netbt\Adapters\<Adapter Name>
Value Type: REG_SZ - Dotted decimal IP address (i.e., 11.101.1.200)
Valid Range: Any valid IP address
Default: None
Description: This parameter specifies the IP address of the backup WINS server. It is written by the DHCP client service, if enabled. A valid Backup-NameServer value will override this parameter.

DhcpNodeType

Key: Netbt\Parameters
Value Type: REG_DWORD - Number
Valid Range: 1 - 8
Default: 1
Description: This parameter specifies the NetBT node type. It is written by the DHCP client service, if enabled. A valid NodeType value will override this parameter. See the entry for NodeType for a complete description.

DhcpScopeId

Key: Netbt\Parameters
Value Type: REG_SZ - Character string
Valid Range: A dot-separated name string such as `microsoft.com`
Default: None
Description: This parameter specifies the NetBIOS name scope for the node. It is written by the DHCP client service, if enabled. This value must *not* begin with a period. See the entry for ScopeId for more information.

NbProvider

Key: Netbt\Parameters
Value Type: REG_SZ - Character string
Valid Range: _tcp
Default: _tcp
Description: This parameter is used internally by the RPC component. The default value should not be changed.

TransportBindName

Key: Netbt\Parameters
Value Type: REG_SZ - Character string
Valid Range: N/A
Default: \Device\
Description: This parameter is used internally during product development. The default value should not be changed.

APPENDIX

C

Glossary

Abstract Syntax Representation, Revision #1 (ASN.1) A description of a data structure that is independent of machine-oriented structures and encodings.

Address In TCP/IP, an IP address is a 32-bit numeric identifier assigned to a node. The address has two parts, one for the network identifier and the other for the node identifier. All nodes on the same network must share the network address and have a unique node address. For networks connected to the Internet, network addresses are assigned by the Internet Activities Board (IAB).

Addresses also include IPX addresses—the internal network number and external network number—and the MAC (Media Access Control) address assigned to each network card or device.

Advanced Research Projects Agency Network (ARPANET) A packet-switched network developed in the early 1970s. The "father" of today's Internet. ARPANET was decommissioned in June 1990.

Agents In the client/server model, the part of the system that performs information preparation and exchange on behalf of a client or server application.

American National Standards Institute (ANSI) A nonprofit organization responsible for the ASCII (American Standard Code for Information Interchange) code set, as well as numerous other voluntary standards.

Application Layer The layer of the OSI model that interfaces with user mode applications by providing high-level network services based upon lower-level network layers. Network file systems like named pipes are an example of Application layer software. See *Named Pipes, Open System Interconnection*.

Application Program Interface (API) A set of routines that an application program uses to request and carry out lower-layer services performed by the operating system.

Archie A program that helps Internet users find files. Participating Internet host computers download a listing of their files to Archie servers, which index these files. Users can then search this index and transfer these files using FTP. Archie functions as an archive search utility, hence its name.

ARP (Address Resolution Protocol) IP address to hardware address translation protocol.

Asynchronous Data Transmission   A type of communication that sends data using flow control rather than a clock to synchronize data between the source and destination.

Autonomous System   Internet TCP/IP terminology for a collection of gateways (routers) that fall under one administrative entity and cooperate using common Interior Gateway Protocol (IGP).

Bandwidth   In network communications, the amount of data that can be sent across a wire in a given time. Each communication that passes along the wire decreases the amount of available bandwidth.

Batch Program   An ASCII file that contains one or more Windows NT commands. A batch program's filename typically has a .bat or .cmd extension. When you type the filename at the command prompt, the commands are processed sequentially.

Binary   The numbering system used in computer memory and in digital communication. All characters are represented as a series of 1s and 0s. For example, the letter *A* might be represented as 01000001.

Binding   A process that establishes the initial communication channel between the protocol driver and the network adapter card driver.

Bits   In binary data, each unit of data is a bit. Each bit is represented by either 0 or 1, and is stored in memory as an ON or OFF state.

Boot Partition   The volume, formatted for either an NTFS, FAT, or HPFS file system, that contains the Windows NT operating system's files. Windows NT automatically creates the correct configuration and checks this information whenever you start your system.

Bridge   A device that connects two segments of a network and sends data to one or the other based on a set of criteria.

Browser   A computer on a Microsoft network that maintains a list of computers and services available on the network.

Browsing   The process of requesting the list of computers and services on a network from a browser.

Buffers A reserved portion of memory in which data is temporarily held pending an opportunity to complete its transfer to or from a storage device or another location in memory.

Carrier Sense, Multiple Access with Collision Detect (CSMA/CD)
Different devices on a network may try to communicate at any one time, so access methods need to be established. Using the CSMA/CD access method, a device first checks that the cable is free from other carriers and then transmits, while continuing to monitor the presence of another carrier. If a collision is detected, the device stops transmitting and tries later. In a CSMA network with collision detection, all stations have the ability to sense traffic on the network.

Checksum A number that is calculated based on the values of a block of data. Checksums are used in communication to ensure that the correct data was received.

Circuit Switching A type of communication system that establishes a connection, or circuit, between the two devices before communicating and does not disconnect until all data is sent.

Client Any device that attaches to the network server. A workstation is the most common type of client. Clients run client software to provide network access. A piece of software which accesses data on a server can also be called a client.

Client/Server Network A server-centric network in which some network resources are stored on a file server, while processing power is distributed among workstations and the file server.

Coaxial Cable One of the types of cable used in network wiring. Typical coax types include RG-58 and RG-62. The 10base2 system of Ethernet networking uses coaxial cable. Coaxial cable is usually shielded. The Thicknet system uses a thicker coaxial cable.

Communication Protocol For computers engaged in telecommunications, the protocol (i.e., the settings and standards) must be the same for both devices when receiving and transmitting information. A communications program can be used to ensure that the baud rate, duplex, parity, data bits, and stop bits are correctly set.

Connectionless   The model of interconnection in which communication takes place without first establishing a connection. Sometimes called datagram. Examples: LANs, Internet IP, and OSI, CLNP, UDP, ordinary postcards.

Connection-Oriented   The model of interconnection in which communication precedes through three well-defined phases: connection establishment, data transfer, connection releases. Examples: X.25, Internet TCP and OSI TP4, registered letters.

Consultative Committee on International Telegraphy and Telephony (CCITT)   A committee, sponsored by the United Nations, that defines network standards, including X.400 and X.500. This committee has been recently renamed to International Telecommunications Union/Telecommunications Standardization Sector (ITU/TSS).

Control Panel   Windows family utility containing management tools.

CSNET (Computer+Science Network)   A large computer network, mostly in the U.S. but with international connections. CSNET sites include universities, research labs, and some commercial companies. Now merged with BITNET to form CREN.

Cyclic Redundancy Checksum (CRC)   A redundancy check in which the check key is generated by a cyclic algorithm. Also, a system checking or error checking performed at both the sending and receiving station after a block check character has been accumulated.

Daemon Program   A utility program that runs on a TCP/IP server. Daemon programs run in the background, performing services such as file transfers, printing, calculations, searching for information, and many other tasks. This is similar to a TSR program in DOS. Daemons are fully supported by UNIX, however.

DARPA (Defense Advanced Research Projects Agency)   The U.S. government agency that funded the ARPANET.

Data Frames   Logical, structured packets in which data can be placed. The Data Link layer packages raw bits from the Physical layer into data frames. The exact format of the frame used by the network depends on the topology.

Data Link Layer   The OSI layer that is responsible for data transfer across a single physical connection, or series of bridged connections, between two network entities.

Data Packet   A unit of data being sent over a network. A packet includes a header, addressing information, and the data itself. A packet is treated as a single unit as it is sent from device to device.

Data Transfer Rate   The data transfer rate determines how fast a drive or other peripheral can transfer data with its controller. The data transfer rate is a key measurement in drive performance.

Datagram   A packet of information and associated delivery information, such as the destination address, that is routed through a packet-switching network.

Dedicated Line   A transmission medium that is used exclusively between two locations. Dedicated lines are also known as leased lines or private lines.

Default Gateway   IP uses the default gateway address when it cannot find the destination host on the local subnet. This is usually the router interface.

Device Driver   A piece of software that allows a workstation or server to communicate with a hardware device. For example, disk drivers are used to control disk drives, and network drivers are used to communicate with network boards.

DHCP (Dynamic Host Configuration Protocol)   A method of automatically assigning IP addresses to client computers on a network.

DoD Networking Model   A four-layer conceptual model describing how communications should take place between computer systems. The four layers are Process/Application, Host-to-Host, Internet, and Network Access. DoD is the acronym for Department of Defense, the government agency that provided the original funding for the development of the TCP/IP protocol suite.

Domain   A logical grouping for file servers within a network, managed as an integrated whole.

Domain Controller   Primary server within a domain and primary storage point for domain-wide security information.

Domain Names   The name by which a domain is known to the network.

DNS (Domain Name System)   The distributed name/address mechanism used in the Internet.

Dumb Terminal   A workstation consisting of keyboard and monitor, used to put data into the computer or receive information from the computer. Dumb terminals were originally developed to be connected to computers running a multi-user operating system so that users could communicate directly with them. All processing is done at and by the computer, not the dumb terminal. In contrast, a smart terminal contains processing circuits which can receive data from the host computer and later carry out independent processing operations.

EGP (Exterior Gateway Protocol)   A reachability routing protocol used by gateways in a two-level Internet. EGP is used in the Internet core system.

Error Control   An arrangement that combines error detection and error correction.

Error Correction   A method used to correct erroneous data produced during data transmission, transfer, or storage.

Ethernet   The most popular Data Link layer standard for local area networking. Ethernet implements the carrier sense multiple access with collision detection (CSMA/CD) method of arbitrating multiple computer access to the same network. This standard supports the use of Ethernet over any type of media including wireless broadcast. Standard Ethernet operates as 10Mbps. Fast Ethernet operates at 100Mbps. See *Data Link Layer*.

FDDI (Fiber Distributed Data Interface)   A network specification that transmits information packets using light produced by a laser or light-emitting diode (LED). FDDI uses fiber-optic cable and equipment to transmit data packets. It has a data rate of up to 100Mbps and allows very long cable distances.

File Transfer Protocol (FTP)   A TCP/IP protocol that permits the transferring of files between computer systems. Because FTP has been implemented on numerous types of computer systems, file transfers can be done between different computer systems (e.g., a personal computer and a minicomputer).

Frame   A data structure that network hardware devices use to transmit data between computers. Frames consist of the addresses of the sending and receiving computers, size information, and a checksum. Frames are envelopes around packets of data that allow them to be addressed to specific computers on a shared media network. See *Ethernet, FDDI, Token Ring*.

Full-Duplex   A method of transmitting information over an asynchronous communications channel, in which signals may be sent in both directions simultaneously. This technique makes the best use of line time but substantially increases the amount of logic required in the primary and secondary stations.

Gateway   In e-mail systems, a system used to send and receive e-mail from a different e-mail system, such as a mainframe or the Internet. Gateways are supported by Message Handling Services (MHS).

Gopher   An Internet tool that organizes topics into a menu system that users can employ to find information. Gopher also transparently connects users with the Internet server on which the information resides.

GOSIP (Government OSI Profile)   A U.S Government procurement specification for OSI (Open Systems Interconnection) protocols.

Half-Duplex   A method of transmitting information over a communication channel, in which signals may be sent in both directions, but only one way at a time. This is sometimes referred to as local echo.

Handshaking   In network communication, a process used to verify that a connection has been established correctly. Devices send signals back and forth to establish parameters for communication.

Hardware Address   See *Media Access Control (MAC) Address.*

Hop   In routing, a server or router that is counted in a hop count.

Hop Count   The number of routers a message must pass through to reach its destination. A hop count is used to determine the most efficient network route.

Host   An addressable computer system on a TCP/IP network. Examples would include endpoint systems such as workstations, servers, minicomputers, mainframes, and immediate systems such as routers. A host is typically a system that offers resources to network nodes.

Host Name   A TCP/IP command that returns the local workstation's host name used for authentication by TCP/IP utilities. This value is the workstation's computer name by default, but it can be changed by using the Network icon in Control Panel.

Host Table   The HOSTS or LMHOSTS file that contains lists of known IP addresses.

Host-to-Host Layer   The DoD model layer that references to the Transport layer of the OSI model.

Hub   An Ethernet Data Link layer device that connects point-to-point Physical layer links, such as twisted pair or fiber-optic cables, into a single shared media network. See *Data Link Layer, Ethernet.*

IAB (Internet Activities Board)   The technical body that oversees the development of the Internet suite of protocols (commonly referred to as TCP/IP). It has two task forces (the IRTF and the IETF), each charged with investigating a particular area.

ICMP (Internet Control Message Protocol)   A protocol at the Internet layer of the DoD model that sends messages between routers and other devices, letting them know of congested routes.

IEEE (Institute of Electrical and Electronics Engineers)   A professional ANSI-accredited body of scientists and engineers based in the United States. IEEE promotes standardization, and consults to the American National Standards Institute on matters relating to electrical and electronic development. The IEEE 802 Standards Committee is the leading official standard organization for LANs.

IETF (Internet Engineering Task Force)   One of the task forces of the IAB. The IETF is responsible for solving short-term engineering needs of the Internet. It has over 40 Working Groups.

IESG (Internet Engineering Steering Group)   The executive committee of the IETF.

IGP (Interior Gateway Protocol)   The protocol used to exchange routing information between collaborating routers in the Internet. RIP and OSPF are examples of IGPs.

Integrated Services Digital Network (ISDN)   A new network standard that allows high-speed communication over ordinary category 3 or 5 copper cabling. It may someday replace conventional phone systems with high-speed, digital lines.

International Standards Organizations (ISO) A worldwide federation of national standards bodies whose objective is to promote the development of standardization and related activities in over 90 countries, with a view to facilitating international exchange of goods and services.

Internet A global network made up of a large number of individual networks interconnected through the use of TCP/IP protocols. The individual networks comprising the Internet are from colleges, universities, businesses, research organizations, government agencies, individuals, and other bodies. The governing body of this global network is the Internet Activities Board (IAB). When the term *Internet* is used with an upper-case *I*, it refers to the global network, but with a lower-case *i*, it simply means a group of interconnected networks.

Internet Address A 32-bit value displayed in numbers that specifies a particular network and a particular node on that network.

Internet Layer The layer in the DoD model that relates to the Network layer of the OSI model.

Internet Protocol (IP) The Network layer protocol upon which the Internet is based. IP provides a simple connectionless packet exchange. Other protocols such as UDP or TCP use IP to perform their connection-oriented or guaranteed delivery services. See *TCP/IP, Internet*.

Internetwork Packet eXchange (IPX) The Network and Transport layer protocol developed by Novell for its NetWare product. IPX is a routable, connectionless protocol similar to TCP/IP but much easier to manage and with lower communication overhead. See *Internet Protocol*.

Internetworking The process of connecting multiple local area networks to form a wide area network (WAN). Internetworking between different types of networks is handled by a *router*.

IP Address A four-byte number that uniquely identifies a computer on an IP internetwork. InterNIC assigns the first bytes of Internet IP addresses and administers them in hierarchies. Huge organizations like the government or top-level Internet service providers (ISPs) have Class A addresses, large organizations and most ISPs have Class B addresses, and small companies have Class C addresses. In a Class A address, InterNIC assigns the first byte, and the owning organization assigns the remaining three bytes. In a Class B address, InterNIC or the higher level ISP assigns the first two bytes, and the organization assigns the remaining two bytes. In a Class C address, InterNIC or the higher level ISP assigns the first three bytes, and the organization assigns the remaining byte. Organizations not attached to the Internet can assign IP addresses as they please. See *Internet Protocol, Internet.*

IPTUNNEL   A software driver that permits the encapsulation of IPX packets inside of IP packets for transmission over an IP network. This allows NetWare servers to communicate through links that support only TCP/IP, such as UNIX machines.

IPX External Network Number   A number that is used to represent an entire network. All servers on the network must use the same external network number.

IPX Internal Network Number   A number that uniquely identifies a server to the network. Each server must have a different internal network number.

IRTF (Internet Research Task Force)   One of the task forces of the IAB. The group responsible for research and development of the Internet protocol suite.

Local Area Network (LAN)   A network that is restricted to a local area—a single building, group of buildings, or even a single room. A LAN often has only one server, but can have many if desired.

Local Procedure Call (LPC)   A mechanism that loops remote procedure calls without the presence of a network so that the client and server portion of an application can reside on the same machine. Local procedure calls look like remote procedure calls (RPCs) to the client and server sides of a distributed application.

Mailslots   A connectionless messaging IPC mechanism that Windows NT uses for browse request and logon authentication.

Management Information Base (MIB)   The entire set of objects that any service or protocol uses in SNMP. Because different network-management services are used for different types of devices or for different network-management protocols, each service has its own set of objects.

Map   To translate one value into another.

Master Browser   The computer on a network that maintains a list of computers and services available on the network and distributes the list to other browsers. The Master browser may also promote potential browsers to be browsers. See *Browser, Browsing, Potential Browser.*

Media Access Control (MAC) Address   Hardware address burned into the Network Interface cards. Six bytes long, three given to the manufacturer from the IEEE, and three bytes designated by the manufacturer.

Message Switching   A type of network communication that sends an entire message, or block of data, rather than a simple packet.

Metropolitan Area Network (MAN)   A network spanning a single city or metropolitan area. A MAN is larger than local area networks (LANs), which are normally restricted to a single building or neighboring buildings, but smaller than wide area networks (WANs), which can span the entire globe. The term *MAN* is rarely used outside of Novell education.

MILNET (MILitary NETwork)   Originally part of the ARPANET, MILNET was partitioned in 1984 to make it possible for military installations to have reliable network service, while the ARPANET continued to be used for research.

Modem   A device used to convert the digital signals produced by a computer into the analog signals required by analog telephone lines, and vice-versa. This process of conversion allows computers to communicate across telephone lines.

Multihomed Host   A computer connected to more than one physical data link. The data links may or may not be attached to the same network.

Multilink   A capability of RAS to combine multiple data streams into one network connection for the purpose of using more than one modem or ISDN channel in a single connection. This feature is new to Windows NT 4.

Named Pipes   An interprocess communication mechanism that is implemented as a file system service, allowing programs to be modified to run on it without using a proprietary application programming interface. Named pipes were developed to support more robust client/server communications than those allowed by the simpler NetBIOS.

NetBEUI (Network Basic Input/Output System Extended User Interface)   The primary local area network transport protocol in Windows NT. A simple Network layer transport developed to support NetBIOS installations. NetBEUI is not routable, and so it is not appropriate for larger networks. NetBEUI is the fastest transport protocol available for Windows NT.

NetBIOS   A client/server interprocess communication service developed by IBM in the early 1980s. NetBIOS presents a relatively primitive mechanism for communication in client/server applications, but its widespread acceptance and availability across most operating systems makes it a logical choice for simple network applications. Many Windows NT network IPC mechanisms are implemented over NetBIOS.

NetBIOS over TCP/IP (NetBT)   A network service that implements the NetBIOS IPC over the TCP/IP protocol stack. See *NetBEUI, TCP/IP*.

Network Address   A unique address that identifies each node, or device, on the network. The network address is generally hard-coded into the network card on both the workstation and server. Some network cards allow you to change this address, but there is seldom a reason to do so.

Network Information Center (NIC)   Originally there was only one, located at SRI International and tasked to serve the ARPANET (and later DDN) community. Today, there are many NICs operated by local, regional, and national networks all over the world. Such centers provide user assistance, document service, training, and much more.

Network Interface Card (NIC)   Physical devices that connect computers and other network equipment to the transmission medium used. When installed in a computer's expansion bus slot, a NIC allows the computer to become a workstation on the network.

Network Layer   The layer of the OSI model that creates a communication path between two computers via routed packets. Transport protocols implement both the Network layer and the Transport layer of the OSI stack. IP is a Network layer service.

Network Operating System (NOS)   The software that runs on a file server and offers file, print, and other services to client workstations. Windows NT Server 4 is a NOS. Other examples include NetWare, Banyan VINES, and IBM LAN Server.

NFS (Network File System)   A distributed file system developed by Sun Microsystems which allows a set of computers to cooperatively access each other's files in a transparent manner.

Node In TCP/IP, an IP addressable computer system, such as workstations, servers, minicomputers, mainframes, and routers. In IPX networks, the term is usually applied to nonserver devices: workstations and printers.

Octet A set of eight bits or one byte.

Open System Interconnection (OSI) A model defined by the ISO to conceptually organize the process of communication between computers in terms of seven layers, called protocol stacks. The seven layers of the OSI model help you to understand how communication across various protocols takes place.

OSPF (Open Shortest Path First) A proposed standard, IGP for the Internet.

Packet The basic division of data sent over a network. Each packet contains a set amount of data along with a header, containing information about the type of packet and the network address to which it is being sent. The size and format of packets depends on the protocol and frame types used.

Packet Switching A type of data transmission in which data is divided into packets, each of which has a destination address. Each packet is then routed across a network in an optimal fashion. An addressed packet may travel a different route than packets related to it. Packet sequence numbers are used at the destination node to reassemble related packets.

Packets A unit of information transmitted as a whole from one device to another on a network.

Peer-to-Peer Communication A networked computer that both shares resources with other computers and accesses the shared resources of other computers.

Peer-to-Peer Network A local area network in which network resources are shared among workstations, without a file server.

Physical Layer The cables, connectors, and connection ports of a network. These are the passive physical components required to create a network.

Ping (Packet Internet Groper) A packet used to test reachability of destinations by sending them an ICMP echo request and waiting for a reply. The term is used as a verb: "Ping host A to see if it is up."

Polling   The process by which a computer periodically asks each terminal or device on a LAN if it has a message to send, and then allows each to send data in turn. On a multipoint connection or a point-to-point connection, polling is the process whereby data stations are invited one at a time to transmit.

Potential Browser   A computer on a network that may maintain a list of other computers and services on the network if requested to do so by a Master browser.

PPP (Point-to-Point Protocol)   This protocol allows the sending of IP packets on a dial-up (serial) connection. Supports compression and IP address negotiation.

Presentation Layer   That layer of the OSI model that converts and translates (if necessary) information between the Session and Application layers.

Primary Domain Controller (PDC)   The domain server that contains the master copy of the security, computer, and user accounts databases and that can authenticate workstations. The primary domain controller can replicate its databases to one or more backup domain controllers and is usually also the Master browser for the domain.

Process/Application Layer   The upper layer in the DoD model that refers to the Application, Presentation, and Session layers of the OSI model.

Protocol Suite   A collection of protocols that are associated with and that implement a particular communication model (such as the DoD networking model or the OSI reference model).

Public Switched Telephone Network (PSTN)   A global network of interconnected digital and analog communication links originally designed to support voice communication between any two points in the world. It was quickly adapted to handle digital data traffic when the computer revolution occurred. In addition to its traditional voice support role, the PSTN now functions as the Physical layer of the Internet by providing dial-up and leased lines for private, exclusive use.

RARP   The TCP/IP protocol that allows a computer with a Physical layer address (such as an Ethernet address) but not an IP address to request a numeric IP address from another computer on the network.

Registry   Windows NT combined configuration database.

Request for Comments (RFCs)   The set of standards defining the Internet protocols as determined by the Internet Engineering Task Force and available in the public domain on the Internet. RFCs define the functions and services provided by each of the many Internet protocols. Compliance with the RFCs guarantees cross-vendor compatibility.

RIP   Routing Information Protocol. A distance-vector routing protocol used on many TCP/IP internetworks and IPX networks. The distance vector algorithm uses a "fewest-hops" routing calculation method.

Router   (A) A device that connects two dissimilar networks, and allows packets to be transmitted and received between them. (B) A connection between two networks that specifies message paths and may perform other functions, such as data compression.

Serial   A method of communication that transfers data across a medium one bit at a time, usually adding stop, start, and check bits to ensure quality transfer.

SLIP (Serial Line Internet Protocol)   A protocol that permits the sending of IP packets on a dial-up (serial) connection. Does not by itself support compression or IP address negotiation.

Session Layer   The layer of the OSI model dedicated to maintaining a bidirectional communication connection between two computers. The Session layer uses the services of the Transport layer to provide this service.

Simple Network Management Protocol (SNMP)   A management protocol used on many networks, particularly TCP/IP. It defines the type, format, and retrieval of node management information.

Simplex   Data transmission in one direction only.

SMTP (Simple Mail Transport Protocol)   The Internet electronic mail protocol. Defined in RFC 821, with associated message format description in RFC 822.

Start Bit   A bit that is sent as part of a serial communication stream to signal the beginning of a byte or packet.

Stop Bit   A bit that is sent as part of a serial communication stream to signal the end of a byte or packet.

Subnet Mask   Under TCP/IP, 32-bit values that allow the recipient of IP packets to distinguish the network ID portion of the IP address from the host ID.

Switched Line   A communications link for which the physical path may vary with each usage, such as the public telephone network.

Synchronous   Pertaining to two or more processes that depend upon the occurrence of a specific event, such as a common timing signal.

TCP (Transport Layer Protocol)   Implements guaranteed packet delivery using the Internet Protocol (IP).

TCP/IP (Transmission Control Protocol/Internet Protocol)   Generally used as shorthand for the phrase "TCP/IP protocol suite."

Telnet   A TCP/IP terminal emulation protocol that permits a node, called the Telnet client, to log into a remote node, called the Telnet server. The client simply acts as a dumb terminal, displaying output from the server. The processing is done at the server.

Terminal Emulation   The process of emulating a terminal, or allowing a PC to act as a terminal for a mainframe or UNIX system.

Token-Passing   See *Token Ring*.

Token Ring   The second most popular Data Link layer standard for local area networking. Token Ring implements the token passing method of arbitrating multiple-computer access to the same network. Token Ring operates at either 4 or 16Mbps. FDDI is similar to Token Ring and operates at 100Mbps. See *Data Link Layer*.

Transport Layer   The OSI model layer responsible for the guaranteed serial delivery of packets between two computers over an internetwork. TCP is the Transport layer protocol for the TCP/IP transport protocol.

Transport Protocol   A service that delivers discrete packets of information between any two computers in a network. Higher level connection-oriented services are built upon transport protocols.

UDP (User Datagram Protocol)   A nonguaranteed network packet protocol implemented on IP that is far faster than TCP because it doesn't have flow-control overhead. UDP can be implemented as a reliable transport when some higher level protocol (such as NetBIOS) exists to make sure that required data will eventually be retransmitted in local area environments.

Universal Naming Convention (UNC)   A multivendor, multiplatform convention for identifying shared resources on a network.

UNIX   A multitasking operating system, created by AT&T's Bell Labs, that is used on a wide variety of computers including Internet servers.

UseNet   A massive distributed database of news feeds and special interest groups maintained on the Internet and accessible through most Web browsers.

Wide Area Network (WAN)   A network that extends across multiple locations. Each location typically has a local area network (LAN), and the LANs are connected together in a WAN. Typically used for enterprise networking.

Windows Internet Name Service (WINS)   A network service for Microsoft networks that provides Windows computers with Internet numbers for specified NetBIOS names, facilitating browsing and intercommunication over TCP/IP networks.

World Wide Web (WWW)   A term used for the collection of computers on the Internet running HTTP (HyperText Transfer Protocol) servers. The WWW allows for text and graphics to have hyperlinks, which connect users to other servers. Using a Web *browser* such as Netscape or Mosaic, a user can cross-link from one server to another at the click of a button.

Index

Note to the Reader: Throughout this index **bold** page numbers indicate primary discussions of a topic. *Italic* page numbers indicate illustrations.

logons failed
    auditing, 416–417
    locking out after, 420
logs
    for DHCP, 187
    for proxy servers, 428
    for security, 416
    for WINS databases, 229
    for WWW services, 380, *380*
loopback addresses, 101–102
    in IP addressing, **63**
    in testing, 129
LPCs (local procedure calls), 493
LPD (Line Printer Daemon) utility, 39, **334**
LPQ (Line Printer Queue) utility, **335**
LPR (Line Printer) utility, **335**
ls command, 271
LSPs (link-state packets), 90–92

M

M-nodes for NetBIOS names, 163, 167–168, **210–212**, 468
MAC (media access control) address, 50
    with BootP, 179
    defined, 494
    with DHCP, 179–180
    in DoD Internet layer, 44
    in DoD Network Access layer, 46
mail clients, 154. *See also* e-mail; Internet Mail Service (IMS)
Mail Exchange (MX) records
    in DNS, 257, **268–269**, *269*, 277
    with Internet Mail Service, 409
mail routers, 154–155
Mail Spool directory, 405
mailboxes for Internet Mail Service, 404
mailslots, 493
MaintainServerList parameter, 300, 419
management
    proxy servers for, **427–428**
    in RRAS, 132
    in SNMP, **341–343**, *342*, 345
Management Information Base (MIB)
    defined, 493
    in SNMP, **343**
MANs (metropolitan area networks), 494
Manual Frame Type Detection option, 433
mapping, 493
Mappings ➤ Backup Database command, 221
Mappings ➤ Restore Database command, 221
Mappings ➤ Restore Local Database command, 222
Mappings ➤ Show Database command, 230
Mappings ➤ Static Mappings command, 219
maps in NIS servers, 150
marketing, Web sites for, 354

masked bits, 74
masks, subnet, 70–74, *71–73*
    for CICR, 78
    defined, 499
    in IP addressing, 64
    in WWW service access, 380
Master browsers, 297
    announcements by, **301–302**
    defined, 493
    elections for, **297–299**
    NBT names for, 214–215
    routers with, 302
master name servers, 251–252
MaxDgramBuffering parameter, 476
maximum connections for WWW services, 373
maximum hop counts, 89
MaxRecsAtATime parameter, 235
MBone network, 94
media access control (MAC) address, 50
    with BootP, 179
    defined, 494
    with DHCP, 179–180
    in DoD Internet layer, 44
    in DoD Network Access layer, 46
memory base I/O addresses for network adapter cards, 434
memory for link-state protocol, 91
message switching, 494
Messages tab, 386, *386*
Messenger services
    NBT names for, 213–214
    in security, 419
metropolitan area networks (MANs), 494
MIB (Management Information Base)
    defined, 493
    in SNMP, **343**
Microsoft-CHAP protocol, 112
Microsoft DNS, **246–247**
Microsoft Exchange dialog box, 406, *407*
Microsoft Internet Information Server 2.0 Setup dialog box, 368–369, *369*
Microsoft Internet Information Server 4.0 Beta 2 Setup dialog box, 393–395, *394–395*
Microsoft Proxy Auto Dial, **452–456**, *453, 455*
Microsoft Proxy Auto Dial dialog box, 452
Microsoft Proxy Server
    Auto Dial for, **452–456**, *453, 455*
    for caching, **430–431**, 440
    installing, **437–443**, *437–442*
    Local Address Tables for, **435–437**
    for management, **427–428**
    managing, **444–445**, *444–445*
    network adapters for, **431–435**
    RAS for, **446–452**, *447–451*
    for security, **425–427**, *426*

N